ARTISANS AND POLITICS IN EARLY NINETEENTH-CENTURY LONDON

ARTISANS AND POLITICS IN EARLY NINETEENTH-CENTURY LONDON

John Gast and his Times

I. J. PROTHERO

Senior Lecturer in History, University of Manchester

DAWSON

First published in 1979

© I. J. Prothero 1979

Wm Dawson & Son Ltd, Cannon House
Folkestone, Kent, England

British Library Cataloguing in Publication Data

Prothero, I. J.
Artisans and politics in early nineteenth-century
London.
1. Ship-building workers — England — London —
   Political activity — History
2. Artisans — England — London — Political activity
   — Case studies
3. Gast, John
4. Trade-unions — Great Britain — Biography
I. Title
322'.2   HD8039.S512G7
ISBN 0–7129–0826–9

Film set in 10/12 point Times
Printed and bound in Great Britain
by W & J Mackay Limited, Chatham

To Leena

CONTENTS

ACKNOWLEDGEMENTS

I am very grateful to Mr E. P. Thompson, Mrs Dorothy Thompson and Dr G. Stedman Jones for reading this book in draft and making many valuable comments. The faults that remain are entirely my own. My general debt to Mr Thompson's *The Making of the English Working Class* (1963) will be obvious. I wish to thank for their assistance the librarians and staff at the British Library (departments of printed books, newspapers, manuscripts and State Papers); Public Record Office; Goldsmiths' and Map Libraries, University of London; Library of Political Science, London School of Economics; City of London Guildhall Library; University of Manchester John Rylands Library; Manchester Central Reference Library; Co-operative Union Library, Manchester; Bibliothèque Nationale, Paris; Archives Nationales, Paris; Bristol City Library; Bristol Archives Office; Kent County Archives Office, Maidstone. The University of Manchester granted me two terms' leave of absence which helped me carry out work on this book. For many years I have profited from being in the very stimulating atmosphere of the modern history section there, especially through discussions with Dr B. S. Manning and Mr J. J. Breuilly. I have learned a lot from the latter's studies of nineteenth-century German artisans. The final stages of the research for the book were facilitated by a grant from the Twenty-Seven Foundation. Towards the end of the book are some comments on French artisans' movements based on research that I have begun with the help of a grant from the Social Science Research Council. I am grateful to my mother for doing much of the typing work and to Mr R. M. Seal for very sympathetic and helpful editing. Above all, I must express my gratitude to my wife for bearing so much of the suffering that work on this book has entailed.

ABBREVIATIONS

In text, index and notes:

BAPCK	British Association for Promoting Co-operative Knowledge
CNA	Central National Association
CTU	Grand National Consolidated Trades' Union
(E)LDA	(East) London Democratic Association
FSOC	Friendly Society of Operative House Carpenters and Joiners (= General Union of Carpenters)
LCS	London Corresponding Society
MPU	Metropolitan Political Union
NPU	National Political Union
NUWC	National Union of the Working Classes
RRA	Radical Reform Association
WLLA	West London Lancasterian Association
WMA	Working Men's Association

In notes only:

AN	Archives Nationales
Artizans' Chronicle	*Journeyman, and Artizans' London and Provincial Chronicle*
BL	British Library
GL	Goldsmiths' Library
HO	Home Office Papers, Public Record Office
IW	*Independent Whig*
LD	*London Dispatch*
MM	*Mechanics' Magazine*
NS	*Northern Star*
Penny Papers	*Penny Papers for the People, by the Poor Man's Guardian*
Place Coll.	Place Collection, British Library Reading Room

PMG	*Poor Man's Guardian*
PRO	Public Record Office
SC 1825	*Select Committee on Combination Laws,* Parl. Papers, 1825, IV
TFP	*Trades' Free Press*
TN	*Trades' Newspaper*
TS	Treasury Solicitors' Papers, Public Record Office
Webb Coll.	Webb Collection of Trade Union Manuscripts, London School of Economics
WFP	*Weekly Free Press*
WMF	*Working Man's Friend*
WPG	*Cleave's Weekly Police Gazette*

In all quotations the original spelling, punctuation and capitalisation have been retained. In the text the writing of street names has usually been modernised.

Place of publication is London unless otherwise stated.

INTRODUCTION

This study focuses on working-class movements in London in the first four decades of the nineteenth century. These were momentous years when Britain experienced its industrial revolution and the rise of labour movements. Under profit-making entrepreneurs industrial capital took control of and expanded production, above all in textiles. By the end of the 1820s the cotton industry had been revolutionised, with a succession of labour-saving machines in its various branches, purpose-built factories, job specialisation, the creation of an unprecedented demand at home and abroad, and an enormous expansion of the industry as a whole. The old woollen industry, now increasingly centred in the West Riding, saw similar changes, though later and more slowly. There was a tremendous expansion of coal and iron production to meet demand; the metal-working and engineering industries developed. Industrial towns grew with staggering speed.

As the most important and advanced industrial nation in Europe, Britain was scrutinised from all parts of the Continent as an illustration of possible future developments there, a novel society characterised not only by new methods but also by the destruction of old crafts and social hierarchies and the transformation of market towns into slums. It also seemed to be typified by working-class revolt. There was both intensification and change in popular protest. Older forms, notably food-riots, died out, to be replaced by wage-disputes. Workers' organisations developed, new in form, extent and power. Popular literacy was achieved and new ideas appeared—of economic analysis, of conflicting interests, of working-class solidarity. Some workmen seemed even to be adopting Owenite socialist ideas of abolishing private property and the employing class. Most strikingly, there arose extensive political protest and agitations to establish political democracy, culminating in the great Chartist movement of 1838–50, a movement unprecedented in its levels of sustained commitment and national organisation, and unparalleled anywhere else in Europe.

All these developments in working-class activity were fully exemplified in London, and so a study of this, the largest urban centre of all, is easily justified. But London was not revolutionised, it was not a city of factories or thousand-man workshops, its industry remained small-scale in organisation and traditional in technology. A study of London workers' movements is therefore a study not of factory-workers or miners, but of workmen in the old, unmechanised handicraft trades—the artisans. This in no way diminishes its importance, quite the reverse. For few people then worked in factories. Even in 1850 England was not yet an industrialised country but one still undergoing the early stages of industrialisation, changes basically confined to industries in the textile sector, notably cotton. Factory workers were far outnumbered by skilled artisans. Factory employment was certainly growing, and at an accelerating rate, but this did not usually entail the *replacement* by factory labour of more traditional forms—handicraft, small workshop, domestic. Industrialisation created new skills and also helped old ones to develop further, for hand and steam technologies were concurrent and mutually dependent phases in nineteenth-century capitalist growth. Demographic and economic expansion vastly enlarged the demand for clothing, building, furniture and the products of a mass of other trades, and increased the supply of labour for them. Such industries experienced a tremendous expansion which mainly took the form of a multiplication of small units of production. There was a great increase in the numbers of artisans.[1]

Nor should we assume that the 'modern' workers were more prominent in labour activity. The pattern on the Continent was indeed the exact reverse.[2] All those who study movements in England during this period must be indelibly influenced by Mr Thompson's outstanding book on the 'making of the English working class'. What this term means is not merely the growth in the number of wage-earners, both absolutely and relatively, or the growth of institutions confined to such people. There was also the rise of activity, confined to working men, which transcended the boundaries of their various occupations. The growth of such activity was accompanied by feelings of solidarity and common interests, often expressed in a class terminology. But such developments were certainly not uniform and were mainly confined to certain groups of workers, notably artisans, domestic outworkers (handloom weavers, framework-knitters and nailmakers) and some factory-workers, such as cotton mule-spinners.[3] But factory-workers, of whom only a quarter anyway were adult males, figure very little in Mr Thompson's account.

It now seems generally recognised that artisans were the backbone of the first worker's movements everywhere. 'Few historians today would contest the thesis that conscious militance in the early industrial revolution was to be found largely among artisans.'[4] 'The working class was born in the workshop, not the factory. It is one of the cherished dogmas of social history that artisans, their status and jobs threatened by economic change, fathered the labour movement.'[5] In Europe during the nineteenth century, 'artisans became politically active and tended to espouse democratic and socialist doctrines. This was an epoch-making change, one which actually encompasses much of what historians mean when they speak of the "rise of the working class".'[6] Nineteenth-century European artisans are now at last receiving proper attention,[7] and this study is intended as a contribution to the process.

In England some groups of factory-workers, notably cotton mule-spinners, were very different from their continental counterparts. But here too the subject of artisans and politics is of equal importance.

> The 'artisans' were the natural leaders of ideology and organization among the labouring poor, the pioneers of Radicalism (and later the early, Owenite, versions of Socialism), of discussion and popular higher education—through Mechanics' Institutes, Halls of Science, and a variety of clubs, societies and free-thinking printers and publishers—the nucleus of trade unions, Jacobin, Chartist or any other progressive movements . . . in the cities little groups of handloom weavers, printers, tailors, and perhaps a few small businessmen and shopkeepers provided political continuity of leadership on the left until the decline of Chartism, if not beyond.[8]

None of this is to minimise the importance of the development of industrial capitalism, which affected many more people than those employed in factories. But it is to emphasise the importance of other groups of workers and their protests. 'As industrialisation proceeded, its short-term effect was to create, not an increasingly united class of proletarians, but an increasingly desperate and disunited mass of small producers and semi-proletarians.'[9] But the 'middle sort of people' had for centuries been the main element in popular movements, and the artisans, who had formed a part of them, had long been the least deferential and most organised of all working men. We must therefore agree with Mr Thompson that 'too much emphasis upon the newness of the cotton-mills can lead to an underestimation of the continuity of political and cultural traditions in the making of working-class communities.'[10] Moreover the same author does not even see industrialisation as the overriding dominant factor in the process he analyses. As well as stressing the continuity of popular attitudes and changes making for an increase in popular protest *before* industrialisation, he picks out three great influences in this period—the industrial revolution, the enormous increase in population, and the political context—and sees the last as equal to any other.[11] The definitions of the 'language of class' were as much political as economic,[12] and his book is as much about political consciousness as anything else. Indeed it is basically about the sources of Chartism.

It is for these reasons that the present book on movements in the greatest artisan centre in the world adopts its chosen form. It seeks to avoid an artificial compartmentalisation of different activities, for political, trade union, co-operative and educational movements overlapped. It lays emphasis on enduring traditions and social ideals. It stresses the importance of demographic expansion. It emphasises the political context. It covers what seem the formative years in leading artisans into new outlooks and forms of activity. The process culminated in Chartism. But despite the new levels of agitation that Chartism often marked, the crucial changes, as Thompson implies, had been earlier. And so, apart from considerations of length and the fact that I have written elsewhere on subject,[13] this book attempts no account of London Chartism proper.

Their continued numerical and social importance does not make artisans at all a static object of study. On the contrary, they were experiencing great changes and were themselves changing. This is reflected in the very ambiguity of the term 'artisan', a term used much more widely by historians than by men at the time. In the nineteenth century it clearly no longer means the independent medieval craftsman. To some historians, artisans are handworkers in old, unmechanised trades, those trades with an 'artisanal' industrial structure. To others the term means a skilled worker, sometimes even including those in new trades like engineering. This is not the same definition, as not all of those in the former category, such as tailors, were really skilled workers. The term itself was not a very common one; far more common words were 'journeyman' and 'mechanic'. The former signified members of one of the specialised and usually old trades who had learned it through apprenticeship and were wage-earners. They and the masters together formed the 'tradesmen' in the old meaning of the term. The distinction between those with and those without a trade was crucial, and the distinction between journeyman and labourer was traditionally as important as that between journeyman and master, and often more so. Journeyman is a more useful term than artisan, but the latter is the usual term employed by historians, and it also includes the working master. There were small masters involved in several organisations, such as benefit and co-operative societies, and in political movements especially, and, as we shall see, developments in several trades were to degrade the position of both journeymen and masters and the distinction between them. The term 'artisan' is best understood as meaning a member of 'the artisan trades', the old, specialist, unrevolutionised handworking trades, which required a certain amount of skill, but within wide limits, and had a definite status connotation. 'Mechanic' is a more restricted term, meaning the skilled artisans, the better-off journeymen who belonged to trade societies.

A thorough study of some of the trades highlights the inadequacy of many established approaches to artisans. They are seen as 'backward-looking', a categorisation which contains a great deal of ıth but does not do justice to their actions. They are said to be ısically 'reformist' or moderate because of their nearness to the employers and lower middle class, yet these elements were ly those among which the greatest amount of bitterness and sm was found, groups that did not support the development al capitalism, while journeymen were often more hostile to than to larger employers.[14] The skilled artisans are said after entury to have developed a greater distinctiveness from the skilled workers and to have become a 'labour aristocracy', but they were always aware of this distinction. Skilled men, with powerful sense of occupation and status, and with well-developed customs and traditions of organisation, many experienced a 'crisis of expansion'.[15] In their efforts to combat the surplus of labour and attendant changes associated with capitalism, changes that could threaten their whole way of life, they were led into new fields of action. They were certainly not *intrinsically* any less militant, radical, anti-capitalist or class-conscious than any other workers. *Level* of proletarianisation is in itself no explanation of their action, for even in the case of some highly skilled, highly-paid and privileged trades, certain developments could lead them into very radical activities. Above all, although the skilled artisans were a definable social group with shared social ideals, it is quite wrong to regard them uniformly. Their experiences varied so much that they followed very divergent paths. Instead of remaining at the level of treating 'the artisans' collectively, we must analyse the differing experiences of some of the trades. Occupational differentiation is essential.

In general, the largest trades receive most attention in the following pages (see Appendix). But they did not participate equally in the movements studied here. Broadly, there were two main types of trades which, because they were unable to maintain their position through action confined within their own industry, participated in activity beyond the confines of their own industry, in 'supra-trade activity', whether wider unionism, co-operation, political action or whatever. First there were those which met very basic needs of the population, needed little capital, were not so highly skilled, underwent a great increase in demand and in their numbers, and experienced the growth of mercantile capitalism. These included tailors, shoemakers, cabinet-makers and carpenters, who became constant elements in all forms of supra-trade activity, and so figure largely in this study. Secondly, there were trades which experienced, often temporarily, certain more specific problems (such as serious competition from elsewhere, or a new machine) and so also took part in supra-trade activity, but often only temporarily while the problem remained acute. One very good example was provided by the Thames shipwrights, on whom there is an unusual amount of information and who also figure very largely in this study.

The shipwrights of the Port of London were an especially important group of men, given the size of the great port and the fact that Britain was at war from 1793 to 1815. They were an extremely proud and skilled body, classic examples of the skilled artisan, and were at times very strongly organised. They worked in an unusually capitalised industry, and indeed for several centuries shipwrights in Europe's great naval arsenals had been unusual for their high degree of trade union activity, even if of an informal, *ad hoc* kind. Moreover, the three greatest strikes in London in this period were those of the shipwrights in 1802 and 1825, and of the tailors in 1834. The 1825 strike was also a crucial element in the struggles of that year concerning trade union legislation. For a while, though not proletarianised, the Thames shipwrights took a leading role in inter-trade union activities, as in 1812–14, 1818 and, especially, the 1820s—a crucially important decade which has been badly neglected by historians and figures fully here. Suffering as they did from both provincial and overseas competition, and very dependent on their situation in the capital and on a demand for expensive products of high quality, the shipwrights demonstrated features characteristic of many of the London trades and so repay closer attention. If we are to understand the nature of workers' movements in these years, it is as important to study shipwrights as cotton-spinners.

The leader of the shipwrights, from about 1800 until his death in 1837, was John Gast. He is the central figure in this book, the focus of my study of London artisans. This is partly because of his undoubted importance. It was the Webbs who were the first to recognise that 'John Gast, a shipwright of Deptford, was evidently one of the ablest Trade Unionists of his time.'[16] They stressed his leading role in the strikes of 1802 and 1825, his position among the London trades generally, especially in the agitation over the Combination Laws, his pioneering activity as early as 1818 in favour of a general union of all existing trade unions, and his predominant role in setting up the world's first trade union journal, the *Trades' Newspaper*. The judgement has received general acceptance and was echoed by Mr E. P. Thompson: 'He was, with Gravener Henson and John Doherty, one of the three truly impressive trade union leaders who emerged in these early years.'[17] But he has received much less attention than the other two. Mr Thompson also stressed the importance of the *Trades' Newspaper*, both as a source for trade union history and in expressing trade union opposition to the orthodox economic theories of the day. Other historians have noted in passing, but only in passing, Gast's involvement in such things as mechanics' institutions, the National Union of the Working Classes, and the London Working Men's Association which drew up the famous 'People's Charter'.

It was during my research on the London trades in the 1820s in connection with a B.A. History dissertation at Manchester University, that I became convinced of Gast's central role. I later discovered his involvement in a number of other important activities, such as among the benefit societies, in the co-operative movement, and anti-Christian propaganda. It seemed clear that he was an outstanding figure in every way who deserved far more attention than he had received. When I pushed my researches further back I also discovered that he played a prominent part in the radical group that planned the Cato Street Conspiracy and in the Queen Caroline affair. Gast was, in fact, involved in an important way in every single one of the movements dealt with in this book. Pre-Chartist London has been called 'the London of Francis Place'. It should, with much greater accuracy, be known as 'the London of John Gast'. But a close examination of Gast is justified not only by his pre-eminence. Equally important is the fact that he, as a 'typical' artisan, was

concerned with those problems, voiced those attitudes and advocated those remedies that were characteristic of artisans generally.
A study of Gast becomes a way of studying the London artisans.

There may be attractions in a biographical approach, as a correc-
tive to excessive generalisation. But this study is not a biography,
and has nothing on Gast's private or family life. A full biography
would in any case be impossible. He was born in 1772, but hardly
anything can be discovered about him before 1802, and very little
before 1818. His activity can be followed fairly continuously from
1818 to 1834, the years of his greatest importance. Thereafter his
work outside his own trade was very spasmodic, and his death in
1837 was virtually unnoticed. There are, of course, no private Gast
papers, though the papers of Francis Place do contain five precious
letters from him. These early workers' leaders hardly ever preserved their papers, which makes particularly galling Gast's remark
in 1825: 'I always minute everything I do, and I can go back for
thirty years and say where I was.'[18]

This book, then, is primarily a study of London artisans, not of
Gast. It treats him as an artisan figure, a focus for a general study.
This is possible, even unavoidable, because he was the outstanding
artisans' leader and spokesman. It is axiomatic that we cannot
understand such a figure without examining the situation of his
trade. It is a particularly useful approach to take a member of a very
aristocratic, unproletarianised trade, who was yet involved in these
wider movements. It is also a very rewarding way of studying artisan
political activity, for my approach is emphatically not that of first
classifying political outlooks in intellectual terms and subsequently
seeking social explanations or labels for them. To understand the
political involvement of artisans, we must first begin with their
position, outlook, ideals and experience.

The book is organised as follows. The first five chapters deal with
different aspects of artisan activity up to 1818, the year when Gast
became a public figure, and with the formative influences on him
and his fellow-artisans. They examine the outlook, experience and
political attitudes of artisans generally, as well as dealing briefly
with Gast's early life and the Thames shipwrights. These analyses
form the groundwork for the book and establish the basic artisan
features from which the events of the rest of the book can be
'deduced'. The remainder of the book is broadly chronological,
dealing with the radical politics of the post-war period, the multi-
form artisan activities of the 1820s ending with co-operation, and
the developments of the 1830s which led up to Chartism.

Part One
ARTISANS IN
WAR AND PEACE

1
THE MAN FROM DEPTFORD

On Sunday 30 August 1818 Dr James Watson left his dwelling at
Surrey Street, off the Strand, and set off for the nearby White Lion,
a dingy pub in the equally dingy Wych Street. In these discouraging
surroundings about thirty or forty would gather in the large room
upstairs for the weekly meeting of the radical revolutionaries of
London.

Desperation and fury marked their reaction to the plight of
England. The long wars launched against republicanism had ended
in 1815 with the removal from France of a ruler whom the French
themselves had wanted, the cruel banishment of 'the brave
Napoleon' and the installation in his place of the hateful, bigoted
Bourbons who fomented a 'White Terror' and massacres of French
Protestants. The results of the wars had been the destruction of the
ancient republics of Venice and Genoa, the imposition of unwanted
rulers on Norwegians, Poles, Belgians and Neopolitans, and the
establishment of the monstrous Tsar's dominance in Europe. Under
his leadership all the chief rulers had now combined in a league to
resist liberty anywhere, and Britain was a party to this 'Holy
Alliance' through her despicable foreign secretary, Castlereagh.
This was the man who got on so well with continental despots and
who introduced repressive legislation into the Commons, knowing
he could call on Russian or Austrian troops if needed. But while the
benefits had gone elsewhere, the British people had paid, in life and
vast taxation, to support the wars against liberty, and still, after
three years of peace, taxation, corruption and oppression were as
bad as ever.

Thomas Preston the lame cobbler would be at the meeting with
his close Spitalfields cronies, indulging in private conversations on
his latest plan to capture the Tower, rob a bank, or 'destroy the
system in two hours'. But Preston would say little at the actual

meeting, and the chief speakers would be Watson himself, Edward Blandford, a poverty-stricken hairdresser whose children supported him through employment on the stage, and William Washington, the tall, dark Lancastrian who had been prosecuted in 1812 for Luddism. These three all knew it would have to come to fighting in the end, for their rulers would never allow radical reform to come about legally or give up their privileges without a fight. But they had little patience with Preston's fantasies and knew it was madness to provoke the authorities before they were themselves mobilised. 'The Doctor' had his work cut out opposing irresponsible declamations and documents on revolution and the confiscation of land. 'The reformers have completely Bishop'd their business they all want to be leader, all to be great men'.[1] Instead he worked for legal action to build up a strong, popular movement. The Seditious Meetings Act of March 1817 had placed very stringent restrictions on the right of public meeting. But it had now expired and Watson wanted to hold big public meetings. The gathering he was going to that evening would be preceded by one in the parlour downstairs of a select committee of twelve. This was trying to arrange a public meeting as soon as they could raise seven pounds to cover costs, an achievement which at present seemed unlikely. The main speaker would have to be Henry Hunt, the only 'draw' who would have anything to do with them. They had just so enthusiastically supported him in June when he stood for Westminster in the general election, the first man ever to have stood on a programme of universal suffrage, annual parliaments and secret ballot.

Watson was hopeful of carrying his approach because of the absence of Preston's great friend, Arthur Thistlewood. Thistlewood always carried a swordstick with him and was on the look-out for the 'few determined men' who were all that was needed. But he had challenged the Home Secretary, Lord Sidmouth, to a duel and so was now serving a year's sentence in prison. Here he complained about his treatment, brooded on the Roman virtue of tyrannicide, and told his son to read Gibbon's *Decline and Fall*, for Britain, under her corrupt tyrannical monarchical system, was heading for the disaster which tyrants had brought to Rome; she needed the restoration of republican virtue by a new Brutus or Cassius.[2]

The disagreements within this group reflected a feeling of despair. In the distressed winter of 1816–17 they had had real hopes of destroying the system, and had held huge mass meetings at Spa Fields in November and December 1816. Through these, at the second of which a rising was attempted, Watson, Thistlewood and

Preston had achieved national fame. But disagreements, arrests, repression and economic recovery had ended that position, a second conspiracy in 1817 had been a fiasco, and the press no longer paid any attention to them. They knew that the authorities were keeping an eye on them, and over the next few months whenever they started to meet at a public house, its landlord would be threatened with the loss of his licence and they would have to move on: 'the Dr. said that they had been going about from public house to public house for a twelvemonth & nothing has been done'.³

But their radical friends in the north seemed to be achieving much more, and might profit from the current wave of strikes in Lancashire. Even now there were two cotton-spinners in town urging some united action that promised to be the new departure Watson wanted.

Two men at the White Lion meeting were of special importance, though Watson did not know why. John Williamson, the very tall silk-weaver and ex-sailor from Spitalfields, was well known for his prowess in throwing dirt at Castlereagh and, in the late Westminster election, stones at the Tory candidate. He was one of Preston's close group, and in the 1817 conspiracy had been Thistlewood's 'aid-de-camp'. At that time he had lost his nerve and secretly revealed the plot to the police, and now he regularly gave reports, once or twice a week, on the activities of the group to the Crown solicitor, Lichfield, who wrote down and sent the report of 'C' to the Home Office. Also present that night was James Hanley, a Spitalfields tradesman, who had given information at the time of Spa Fields and since then, as 'A', gave occasional reports to a magistrate who forwarded them to the Home Secretary. Hanley and Williamson were sending reports independent of each other yet confirming their accuracy.⁴

On 30 August the unusually large number of fifty attended, including a new figure. 'C's' report ran as follows:

> A gentleman from Deptford whose name examt. does not know, attended and spoke pressing Dr. Watson not to give too long a notice of the time of the Public Meeting in Palace Yard for fear it should be prevented & said that he had something to lay before the public at the Meeting which was of great consequence & would risk his life to make it known.

'A' reported thus:

> A stranger of respectable appearance addressed the company with considerable ability he stated himself to be the friend of Mr Hunt and the company on the motion of Watson invited him to lend his assistance at the Public meeting. This person I find is a shipwright of Deptford and

attended at the White Lion last Friday in that capacity where deputies from different Trades met for the purpose of forming a Union as mentioned in my last letter.[5]

Thus Gast stepped on to the public scene. He was rapidly to become a leader of the group. The days of the huge Spa Fields meetings had gone, for they came out of the specific circumstances of the terrible distress of 1816 and the large number of discharged seamen. These conditions no longer prevailed, and Gast was seen by Watson as possibly providing the contacts with artisans which now seemed the best hope of a mass organisation. The involvement of artisans in radical politics, their growing organisation and assertiveness—these were to be such important features of post-war London. But it was more under the leadership of Gast than of Watson that it occurred. And in 1818 Gast was now forty-six, his outlook already formed. To understand it we need to understand the context of the three aspects that Hanley picked out—the shipwright, the participant in inter-trade activity and the radical.

John Gast was born in 1772 and grew up in Bristol. His father, Robert, was in 1786 a 'seller of milk', and John had at least two brothers, William becoming a venetian-blind-maker but dying in 1820, while the other was in London in 1830. In 1786 John was apprenticed to Richard Toombs, one of the largest shipbuilders in Bristol.[6] Thus he entered one of the oldest and most honourable trades in the land.

In 1793 he finished his apprenticeship, and for the rest of his life he remained 'a working shipwright', proud to be one of those manual workers whose skill and labour supported British society. As a member of a highly skilled industry in a great city that looked out to a wider world, he was no typical member of the working population. It was as a skilled artisan, or 'mechanic', that he proclaimed his identity.

Shipbuilding was an old industry and an important one.[7] Nearly half of the British ships in Gast's time were small vessels of fifty tons and under, mostly used in fishing, and they were built by any competent carpenter in sheltered waters in coastal towns all round the coast. But since the late seventeenth century there had been an enormous expansion of trade in bulk cargoes, with British shipping doubling between 1748 and 1788, and redoubling by 1815. The need for the larger ships was met by professional men in the ports who had permanent slipways for building and employed craftsmen—ship-carpenters or shipwrights. But these shipbuilders were small men whose equipment was scanty and primitive, whose yards were often merely pieces of firm land, who needed little capital and indeed often had to obtain wood from timber-merchants on credit and pay the wages of their men by mortgaging the ship under construction.

The industry was not only small-scale, it was very traditional. Master-builders despised theoreticians and innovators and relied on the tremendous skill of their shipwrights. Building was a craft operation in a small-scale handicraft industry, relying on skill in using basic simple tools. It was one of the most demanding of all the old, unmechanised crafts, combining a very high degree of skill on a variety of tasks (for a shipwright had to be acquainted with nearly all parts of the work of building a ship) with a great deal of physical effort, as Mayhew knew:

> The work of the ship-builder is very hard, and demands not merely the customary skill and quickness of the handicraftsman, but great manual strength; they must carry heavy beams or woodwork from the work-shops to the ship, or else they must convey ponderous timbers complete to the workshop for affixing in the ship, and with these they must ascend and descend the ladder.[8]

Many tasks were arduous, accidents were common, and the work was exposed to the elements. Few men over sixty could do ship-wrights' work, and most of those over fifty could not do a full day's work. In addition to practical skills shipwrights also needed the ability to do mechanical drawing, and the rudiments of writing and arithmetic. As well as building they did much repairing (which wooden ships constantly needed), and larger ships might take a shipwright with them for repairs needed on the voyage.

Despite the increased demand for shipping, the shipbuilding industry was hampered by a shortage of its raw materials. White oak for frame timber and planking, and pine and fir for masts and spars had to be imported in large quantities, which raised costs. But British policy rested on a strong navy, and thus needed a strong mercantile marine to maintain a reserve of trained seamen on which to draw in wartime. It also required a healthy shipbuilding industry which, with its large number of shipyards and trained shipwrights, could provide trained workmen for the naval yards and indeed itself build warships. Therefore only ships built in Britain or the colonies were admitted to the British registry, and the higher costs were offset by giving British shipowners the protection of a trading monopoly through the Navigation Acts. Gast thus grew up in an industry that stood in a special relation to the government, dependent on its protection.

In 1793 he came out of his time and became a journeyman, and so joined a group of men who regarded themselves as superior in skill and status to most other artisans, and were convinced of their special value to a maritime nation whose navy was the basis of its power. They were better paid than most artisans, a situation maintained by the fact that they were organised, though never to the extent of the powerful Liverpool shipwrights. Gast joined the society of shipwrights at Bristol, which was certainly in part a benefit society, with regular subscriptions, relief in sickness, and grants to widows of deceased members. But it only admitted men who had served a regular apprenticeship, and probably tried to regulate some of the conditions of work and even prevent the employment of 'strangers', men from outside Bristol.[9]

But by 1793 Britain had entered a new era. An end had come to the 'golden age' of the early eighteenth century, when slow population growth and increasing agricultural productivity had meant a rising standard of living; now a period of rapid demographic expansion had begun. Those momentous changes of the early industrial revolution were under weigh. In 1793 began the long wars with revolutionary France. The outbreak of war brought economic hardship in Bristol, as elsewhere. The year 1794 was a bad one for the shipbuilding industry and there was a serious shipwrights' strike in Bristol. Bad harvests made 1795 a year of frightful distress. In these bad times, Gast left Bristol and later, in 1826, hinted at his reasons: 'Bristol is now, as it has been for years, notorious for overbearing and despotic masters, which made me leave it between thirty and forty years ago, and shake off the dust from my feet against them, as I went down Totterdown-hill.'[10]

The close connection between shipbuilding and government is further underlined by Gast's arrival in January 1797 at Portsmouth dockyard, the greatest naval arsenal in the world.[11] The change in scale from Bristol was enormous, for a ship of over 350 tons at Bristol was large, while an average ship of the line was 2,000 tons, and the yard employed three thousand men. The naval dockyards needed large resources and made enormous demands for labour and supplies of coal, metals, tars and ropes, and were in some respects the largest industry in the country.

The King's visit in 1795 had emphasised the importance of Portsmouth in wartime.[12] The great pressure of work led to an increase in the number of workmen and the presence of several gangs from other royal yards, and shipwrights were in a strong bargaining position. There were a number of disputes before Gast arrived, and the gangs from other yards were restless and anxious to return home. Then a new crisis blew up. As in other English and French yards, the men worked in companies, each headed by an inferior officer, the quarterman. Gast entered the fifteen-strong company of William Allen. Another quarterman, George Boddy, had a quarrel with a man in his company, and came to blows, and the shipwrights insisted that Boddy be expelled from the yard.[13] A meeting was held of a representative from each of the shipwrights' companies, at which Gast took the leading part. He was chosen by his company, though he was only 26 and but newly arrived. He was reluctant to go.

> I said my objection was this: 'I am a very young man, I know nothing of the affair; I am unacquainted with it.' But however, the company imposed upon me the necessity of attending on their behalf. I totally objected to it; I said, 'No, I will not attend unless you will admit of some person who is an older person in the company than myself.' A person of the name of Dukes went with me to this said meeting that was held respecting Mr Boddy . . . The chairman called upon Mr Allen's company. I objected to rise. Mr Dukes got up and addressed the chairman; says he, 'There is a person that we have appointed here by the name of Gast; he has not been long with us, but he is better able to explain to you the nature of our complaint than what I am myself.' The general call was for me to state it. I got up, and I stated the case to them, rather different from the general mode of stating which they had been accustomed to. The result was, they absolutely removed the chairman from the chair, and appointed me as chairman for that evening.[14]

Gast then took over the leadership of the negotiations.

A memorial was drawn up in language characteristic of the protest documents of the time in its assertion of rights and dignity as men—'knowing likewise our worth & as men Cannot put up with the Tyriney of our inferior Officers'—and taken to Saxton, the Commissioner of the yard, by a deputation composed of Gast and two others. Since the men would not accept Boddy's reinstatement, he was discharged.

The Navy Board was now free to turn again to the restive Deptford and Woolwich companies, and allowed them to return home without being replaced. The Plymouth shipwrights thereupon petitioned to return, and were all allowed to. The Board repeated an earlier instruction to take on more men but, on the officers' reply that there was no hope of doing so, then decided to reduce the labour force still further by taking on no new men and even discharging all shipwrights who had entered that year. And so in May

Gast was one of those dismissed.[15] For the rest of his life he was convinced that this order was a deliberate device to get rid of him because of his part in the Boddy affair. There is no evidence at all that this was so, but Gast's feeling of victimisation was intensified by his difficulties in getting paid.

> I had an interview with Sir Charles Saxton and the builder upon the same subject. I asked them for what I was discharged; none could answer me immediately. 'Is there any fault with my work?' 'No, your quarter-man has given you an excellent character; you are a very good workman; you are a very steady man.' On pressing to know what I was discharged for, Sir Charles Saxton, I shall ever recollect it, says, 'Young man, you know too much for a shipwright.' I said, 'This is one of the most singular cases I ever recollect, that a man should be discharged for knowing too much.'[16]

So Gast left Portsmouth, having learned at first hand the importance of shipwrights to the nation and how much could be achieved by united action, and also with a feeling of victimisation. He now came to the Thames, where he remained for the rest of his life.

Almost thirty years later Gast seemed to reflect on his own move to London.

> The country places are still labouring under great ignorance and oppression; wages are too low to allow workmen any chance of education, and if nature should endow one or more with a better knowledge of his own value than others, and he has courage to assert it, the masters catch the alarm—'we must discharge him, or he'll contaminate the rest.' Driven from his own place, he makes for London as his only city of refuge. Hence arises the great influx from all parts of the country; and as long as this state of ignorance and poverty prevails in the country, the same spirit of persecution will exist, and so long will the trades in London have to provide for their persecuted brethen.[17]

Up to 1814 he mainly worked in one of the largest shipbuilding yards in the country, John Dudman's at Deptford. Most of his work was on warships, which underlined his conviction of the importance and value of his trade: 'I am a working shipwright and one who has contributed towards erecting those best bulwarks of the nation,—her wooden walls,—which is the principal safeguard of our country.'[18] For many years he was apparently in charge of most of the yard's work and confidently expected to become foreman. He also became a Dissenting preacher in Deptford, and in 1810 took over a public house, the King of Prussia in Union Street.[19]

The move to London was a crucial one for him. For here this member of an old, traditional and conservative craft was to become a man of national importance. By 1802 he was leader of the Thames shipwrights. By 1819 he was not only 'well known in Deptford' but was on the list in the Home Office of 'leading reformers', a list which also included Arthur Thistlewood. To the Lord Mayor of London he was in 1821 'Gast of notorious memory', and to *The Times* he became in 1825 'Gast, the destroyer of the Thames shipping trade'. In 1834 a new arrival from America, Dr Black, in search of influential working men, was advised to contact Gast.

Gast was adequate to the role of leader of working men. His was one of the most highly skilled of all the old crafts, and he was a particularly good shipwright. He was able to take responsibility, as in Dudman's yard. Like most members of the old crafts Gast was literate, but more than this, he was one of that number of workmen who ornament the labour history of this time, men who by tremendous persistence, self-discipline and sacrifice availed themselves of the growing educational and cultural opportunities to acquire highly impressive levels of education, breadth of knowledge, facility of expression and political awareness. In addition to the Bible he could quote Locke, Pope or Virgil. He stood out from his fellow workmen. His administrative ability and efficiency are shown by the number of positions he held among the Thames shipwrights. His writings, though often misspelt, were extremely fluent, and characterised by a breadth of vocabulary and expression, and a clarity of thought and argument. His range of activities was equally outstanding: 'for the last three or four weeks', he wrote in 1827, 'I have not had one hour free from some engagement or the other; in fact not time to read the Public Papers'.[20] He was, wrote Francis Place, who was very hard to impress, very intelligent, 'a steady, reliable man'.[21] He was the classic respectable artisan, and his respectable appearance was several times commented upon. When in 1818 he entered the world of underground politics, he naturally figured frequently in the reports of Home Office informers, but whereas the rest were referred to by their surnames merely as 'Watson', 'Blandford' or 'Thistlewood', he was often 'Mr Gast'. Ever after his days as Dissenting preacher, he was an outstanding public speaker. When he made his first public political speech, in 1818, the reporter of the *Morning Chronicle*, to whom he was completely unknown, was very impressed. Supposing him to be a shipbuilding employer, he reported:

Mr GREST addressed the meeting, and in the course of his speech evinced a variety of information and a force of thinking which presented to our mind the strongest evidence of the progress of knowledge among the middle ranks of society. This gentleman, who is, we understand, a ship-builder of Deptford, manifested such a degree of intelligence upon political topics, as we have seldom witnessed among established and professional statesmen.[22]

Had he known that Gast was in fact a journeyman, he would have been astounded.

It was as spokesman for traditional groups of workers that Gast found his metier. For although the years of his lifetime, 1772–1837, were years of industrial revolution, London industry itself did not on the whole undergo much technological change. London remained 'the Athens of the artisan'. The fluidity of the boundary between artisans and lower middle-class is demonstrated by Gast's own family. His father was a milk-seller, his brother had his own venetian-blind-making business, and John nearly became a foreman and for a time ran a public house in Deptford. There was often no great gap between journeyman and small master or shopkeeper, tradesman, self-employed engraver, printer, apothecary, teacher, journalist, surgeon or Dissenting clergyman.[23] Gast entered this world when he came to London, and was later to work with the surgeon Watson, the journeyman apothecary Griffin, the printer Hetherington, journeymen who had become masters like Warden (saddler) and Styles (carpenter), or became shopkeepers like Lovett (cabinet-maker), Neesom (tailor) and Goldspink (carpenter).

But these people were experiencing great pressures, and the very absence of uniformity in their experience aroused great bitterness. One may well speculate whether, had Gast not failed as a publican in 1812 and his employer's business not failed in 1813 and so destroyed Gast's expectations of becoming foreman, his whole career might have been different. But certainly there was no necessary link between level of proletarianisation and degree of militancy and class terminology as an expression of discontent, as Gast and his fellow shipwrights clearly showed.

Gast thus became spokesman for the skilled artisans. As the following chapters show, these had old, persistent and well-defined attitudes and consciousness of social status. They had developed a number of journeyman's associations, often very strong, fulfilling a variety of functions directly related to their situation and aspirations. The long wars with France, bringing rising prices and demand for labour, led to repeated and successful efforts to secure wage rises. These often involved conflicts with employers, the greatest being the shipwrights' strike of 1802. The high-point for wages was 1812, by which time journeymen's trade societies had become greatly strengthened and there was a clear consciousness that wages were directly affected by the men's combined power against the masters, or at least the 'foul' wage-cutting ones. But during the war years there also were developments that boded ill for the skilled artisans—a great expansion of the number of workmen, dilution of the skilled workforce, and the growth in some industries of capitalist enterprises seeking to cheapen the labour force. The artisans' apprenticeship campaign of 1810–14, in which shipwrights played a leading part, illustrated many enduring features of the artisan mentality, and also an awareness of the changes taking place and the growing solidarity between the trades. The last years of the wars and, especially, the first years of peace were mainly ones of depression and suffering, and the trade societies, after the developments of the war years, were now on the defensive and often bitter, none more so than the shipwrights. These were among the trades that turned to the remedy of general union, while many artisans also turned to political action. This latter often included political radicalism, in which the artisan concept of 'labour' was an important ingredient. This tendency, exemplified most clearly in Gast, the various groups of radicals allied to Henry Hunt sought to harness.

2
THE LONDON ARTISAN

Respectable Mechanics

When Gast came to the Thames he settled at Deptford, in Kent. The stretch of the river opposite Deptford was the lowest part of the Port of London, which reached up to London Bridge. The Port might have 1,400 vessels in it at any one time, including colliers, to the number of 300, and coasting vessels. But the largest merchant ships, over 500 tons, only used the deep Deptford stretch, and here was one of the three anchorages of the great ships of the East India Company, the other two being at Blackwall and Northfleet. The Port was the basis of London's economy.

London had early on been the dominant port for overseas trade. But in the eighteenth century, the colonial trade had tended to shift to the western seaports, and the Baltic and Norwegian to those in the north-east, both areas moreover serving industrialising areas in the north and Midlands, while coal and corn exports led to dramatic increases in the East Anglian and coal ports. Though London shipping and trade grew rapidly in the late eighteenth century, this was not relatively but only as part of the general rise. But this still left it as the outstanding port. In 1800 it had 1,810 vessels in foreign trade (totalling 504,000 tons), to Liverpool's 796 (141,000), Newcastle's 632 (140,000), Sunderland's 506 (75,000) and Hull's 611 (69,000). In the coastal trade it had 856 vessels totalling 65,000 tons. Altogether it had more registered shipping than its nearest rivals combined. But the growth of shipping had not been accompanied by great changes in the harbour, docks, quays, piers or warehouses, and the result was a lack of mooring accommodation, congestion and great delays, with a large number of boats and barges used to land cargoes and passengers and even to guide smacks alongside the wharfs. Not until after Gast arrived were new docks begun further down the river—the great West India Docks were finished in 1802 and the London Docks by 1805, to be followed by the East India, Commercial and Surrey Docks.[1]

The size of the port had been responsible for the growth of a seafaring, boatbuilding and shipbuilding community east of the City, in Stepney, Ratcliffe, Shadwell, Blackwall, Rotherhithe and Bermondsey, and there was now a rapidly growing centre of industry and population on the north side of the river past the Isle of Dogs. But the dockside area included not only firms connected with shipbuilding and repairing, but many others supplying shipping needs and dependent on the great port for supplies of coal and raw materials. These included coopers, cork manufacturers, brassfounders and braziers. Many of them were also highly capitalised consumption industries supplying the great urban population—brewers (the greatest of all London firms), distillers, sugar-refiners and soap-manufacturers, while imported hides and the great wholesale livestock markets supplied the great tanning and currying centre in Bermondsey. The areas south of the river—Rotherhithe, Bermondsey, Deptford and Greenwich—were now big town parishes, with large populations and minimal government, a rowdy and lawless region.[2]

Although the port was the basis of London's economy, further up the Thames were the centres of government, administration, law and society. The proportion of London's population engaged in distribution, administration and education grew. Yet London also remained a large and important industrial centre.[3] Some industry catered for the west end, the area of the Court, nobility, high fashion and conspicuous luxury consumption. Other industry catered for the mass consumption of the huge metropolis. London industry therefore showed a great variety, from those dependent on the port to a wide range of luxury trades (coachmakers, saddlers, upholsterers, milliners, peruke-makers, hatters, goldsmiths, silversmiths, jewellers, silk-manufacturers) and to those catering for the mass consumption of clothes, shoes, furniture and so on. Many industries had different sections catering for the different markets. But these industries had certain common characteristics. They were old, well-established and traditional (and were also found in many other European capitals); they were unmechanised, impressive not for technological change but for high standards of skill and their wide range, numbering over 150 trades in 1815; and though the capitalism of the dockside industries was also found among makers of vinegar, colours, blue, varnish, glue, printers' ink, tobacco and snuff, London industry was on the whole small-scale, with over 30,000 separate businesses in 1815, and often concentrated, such as the dockside industries, the old silk-weaving industry of Spitalfields, the coachmakers of Long Acre, the hatters of Southwark and the clock and watchmakers of Clerkenwell. In fact every trade that had capitalist business at the top had also small working masters at the bottom. This included shipbuilding, for in addition to the twenty-two main shipyards, there were many small men along the shores and the Surrey Canal, often without any premises at all, making a total of about fifty firms doing repairs.

The dominant forms of industrial organisation were small workshops under a master who had very little capital, employed a very small number of journeymen and himself worked alongside them, and domestic, where orders were taken from customers, shopkeepers or trading masters by workmen who were either self-employed little masters or journeymen who did the work at their own home or in a room specially hired individually or by a few clubbing together. Often domestic workers were helped by their wives, who for example bound or closed shoes or picked the coarse hairs out of the stuff used by hatters, and by their children. Or they might hire assistants for these tasks and pay them out of their own earnings. But journeymen in non-domestic trades, like coopering and calico-printing, also employed assistants.

The industry was very traditional. It was traditional in its techniques. It was characterised by irregular work and lack of industrial discipline, for those who worked at home could, to a large extent, choose their own hours of work, and in the workshops journeymen could often go in and out as they wished, and many of them did not work on Mondays. Since they often did not have a single employer they spent a lot of time going to masters in turn in search of work, and often found none available. Many of the trades were seasonal; the hatters had full work in spring and summer, but the next three months were the slack time; tailors had twice as much work in April–June as in August–October; brushmakers were often idle in the three months after Christmas; coopers were busy in the second half of the year because of harvest-times, the Baltic thaw and trade winds; building workers were often inactive in the winter; the fellmongers were very busy after the great Michaelmas slaughtering of sheep and lambs.[4] For the shipwrights, the brisk period was from September, after the great East and West Indian fleets came in for refitting, until January, and during this period building work usually stopped. With the departure of the fleets, the slack season lasted through March and April, and the main work was building. The trades were traditional in pace of work, customs, and status hierarchies between and within trades according to tradition, skill, degree of independence or need for a decent external appearance (upholsteres had to have a new coat every six months).[5] Levels of reward tended to correspond to this hierarchy.

These were characteristics of the bulk of London industry and even Gast and his fellow shipwrights, exceptional though they were in working in a capitalised industry with fixed hours, were like other London artisans in owning their tools, in their degree of independence at work, frequent changing of employers (for many men did not have a regular employer but preferred to move from yard to yard as work appeared), freedom to take time off (especially half or whole days to take the family on the traditional Saturday excursion), traditional techniques, irregular work (employment fluctuated greatly according to the state of tides or trade or war demand, and men were often brought into a yard for half a day's work or even less) and seasonal fluctuations. In each tailoring shop the men had a 'captain' who ran much of the business; the shipwrights had their equivalent in their gang-leader, for they worked in gangs or companies, from four to thirty in number, according to the work, but usually about ten or twelve. These companies were self-formed, and some might persist for years while others came together for a specific job. They had an elected 'leading hand', often the oldest member, and it was he who, in the name of the company, made an agreement or contract with the builder or foreman to do a certain job.[6]

London was a city of huge contrasts and extremes of wealth.[7] Ancient and vast, with a mass of mysterious streets, courts and alleys, it was characterised by anonymity, casual contact and lack of social intercourse; there were even great variations in wealth between families sharing the same room. There was a mass of destitute poor, unskilled labourers, casual workers of all sorts and streetsellers, suffering from undernourishment, bad housing, overcrowding, dirt, bad drainage, bad water, adulteration of food and drink, disease and the elements. Observers noted the vagrant children, hideous exploitation of juvenile labour, insecurity of life, youthful 'blackguards' at their notorious clubs and brothels, widespread drunkenness, wives hanging around public houses hoping for a little of the husband's wage before he drank it all, violence, and the crime which pervaded London life.

But from the mass of 'the poor' were distinguished those who were above subsistence level and who, because they earned more than covered their everyday needs, could save towards other items and activities. This living above subsistence level and ability to save was a crucial material and psychological dividing-line. Those above it could be free from pressing fear of want, could afford to take time off from work, and could indulge in a variety of leisure occupations and expenses.

Many of the skilled artisans, or 'mechanics', were above this line because of their higher and more regular income, which was due to customary levels of reward in their trade, demand for their workmanship, and relative rarity of the skill they possessed, a skill acquired not easily but through a full 'servitude' of seven years and then years of work in different firms and, often, different towns. In this position they had much more in common with small employers, shopkeepers and dealers (which many journeymen might become) and professional men than with the mass of 'the poor'.

With its great size and large demand for high-quality goods, one of the distinctive features of London society was the large number and relatively high proportion of these mechanics (see Appendix). These were very conscious of being distinguished from the poor by their 'respectability'. This concept is difficult to define, but it must not be assumed to be equivalent to Victorian ideals of respectability or a mere assimilation of the famous 'middle class values'. Its basic component was the ability to maintain oneself by one's labour without recourse to such things as charity; most of the poor were unable to do this. Respectability also implied other things that followed from this situation—treatment with dignity and respect, relative freedom over hours of work, freedom from the need to work on Sundays and Mondays, self-respect, pride and a general 'independence'. It did not necessarily entail some of the Victorian values, such as abhorrence of drunkenness. It is true that the old Puritan virtues of hard and regular work, thrift and sobriety could be reinforced insofar as they helped achieve and maintain this position; respectability did include decent appearance and cleanliness; and in the course of time further attributes developed, such as education for oneself and one's children. But these were not the products of artisan aping of the middle class; they were developments that certainly did widen social divisions among the working population, but they were as much an internal process among artisans as among other sections of the old 'middle sort', of which the skilled artisans were a part. Nor should these aspects of respectability be exaggerated. Its chief elements lay not in behaviour but in a position of independence and in a status derived from possession of a skill and membership of a respectable occupation such as an honourable trade of value to the community. One of the chief aspects of this independence was freedom from charity; many preferred to send their children to schools charging low fees instead of to free ones, and one of the chief forms of charity was poor relief. 'Attempt not to destroy the ideal of the skilled workman by sundry offers for the the care of his children. The man wants work. His ideal is a home with the man as wage-earner. The approach of the philanthropist is mockery to this.' It was a bitter experience for proud shipwrights to apply to the parish in 1814, men hitherto 'maintaining their families in an honourable way, and who were above applying for relief to any body'.[8] When, later on, appalling misery came to Spitalfields silk-weavers, some starved to death in private rather than go to the parish.[9]

It was not only artisans who possessed these attributes, but the respectable artisans regarded their ability to maintain themselves in a decent situation by their labour as their right or, as it was often put, their 'property'. This traditional right derived from the proudly-held skill so often acquired painfully and with sacrifices, but they often also believed it to be theirs legally. In theory this was the case, as a large number of past enactments outlawed certain practices, shoddy work and machines that threatened skills, recognised and regulated apprenticeship, and fixed prices and wages at fair levels. Knowledge of these statutes, some of which dated from Tudor times, was surprisingly tenacious.[10]

But we must not exaggerate the prosperity or security of these artisans. Many fell into the ranks of the destitute, and respectability was often more aspiration or ideal than reality. Many of the reasons for failure were personal ones, but there were several general and ever-present threats to a respectable artisan's position. Sickness and epidemic were never far away, and there were occupational diseases—sedentary work led to fistula among shoemakers, tailors and weavers; compositors suffered from pulmonary diseases; type-founders and house-painters breathed noxious fumes. The danger of accident was very real, especially as so many of the unmechanised trades involved great physical effort, as in the hot and hard work of the coopers. Sickness or accident could end earnings and plunge an artisan into destitution and poor relief. Old age was another threat that so often brought dependence and pauperisation. Working time was often lost through going from master to master looking for work, and under-employment was a constant feature of this type of economy. Periods of economic depression, including seasonal fluctuations, were another threat. And there were always the dangers of too many men after the same work and a consequent shortage of employment, and of competition from people ready to work more cheaply and so lower wages. All these things—accident, sickness and old age; loss of time; underemployment; periodic unemployment; a labour surplus—might, though no fault of his own, ruin a skilled man willing to work hard. To meet these threats the artisans supported four basic institutions—friendly benefit society, house of call, tramping and apprenticeship.

Artisan Institutions

Friendly societies and box clubs had flourished among artisans since the seventeenth century as efforts to guard against calamities arising out of accident, sickness and old age, to meet the age-old desire to have a decent funeral, and to avoid the stigma attached to poor relief.[11] In return for regular subscriptions, usually monthly, they gave sickness and accident benefit, but only if this was not the members' fault—often none was given if the cause was fighting, gaming, drunkenness or venereal disease. They also, often for an additional subscription, gave a sum on a member's death to his family or friends to cover funeral expenses. They were usually very small, and often by their regulations limited in size. Their government was democratic, with regular monthly or fortnightly meeting-nights under an elected chairman, and a committee either elected or serving in rotation. They met at a public house. There was no real alternative, for small societies could not afford the rent and taxes of a large house, and householders were reluctant to let a room for such a gathering, and there was no real legal security in buying anything through trustees. Yet a publican would give the use of a room free, knowing he would thereby gain custom, and the publican was often a member or official of the society. In rotation, each person had to act as the steward, who had charge of paying relief and had to visit sick members (which meant losing working time). The office was unpaid and there was a fine, often heavy, for refusing to serve. To check disorder at meetings there were fines for drunkenness and for political or religious arguments. The funds and papers were kept in a strong box, which had three different locks, the keys to which were held by different people.

But the societies were only really available to respectable men most likely to be able to support themselves, and not to the mass of the poor. The Bristol Union of Carpenters, formed in 1768, did not admit anyone who earned less than 10s. 6d. a week. It was usual not to admit anyone over forty, or any from particularly noxious trades like painting or type-founding.[12] The societies only benefited a member who kept up regular payments; if these had lapsed (because of unemployment, for instance) before old age or death, all claims to benefit were lost. There were even fines for falling into arrears, which made things even more difficult. Because of the duties of the officials, many preferred not to serve but to pay a fine. This meant that only the poorest members served, and these could least afford the loss of earnings through attending to their duty (though these duties were not very onerous, and visits to the sick might be fitted into dinner-time). The system of fines thus increased the difficulties of the poorest members.

But even better-off members who kept up their payments regularly might see the effort wasted if the society broke up, and this happened very frequently. Dishonesty among holders of funds was a common reason. Some societies were merely social or sharing-out clubs, or they invested their funds in lottery tickets. The high funeral grants were a drain on funds, and to outsiders seemed a terrible waste, made worse by the obligation on members to give up working time to attend the funeral. The almost universal feature of meetings at public houses meant that some of the subscriptions were spent on drink, sometimes as much as a third; this, after all, was why the publican let them use his house. Friendly societies were often regarded as a cause of drunkenness, though many of those who attended the meetings were single men who lodged in public houses (for accommodation in a private house that included fire, candle-light and a place to sit and talk in would be much dearer) and so would spend the evening drinking anyway. But many societies were started by landlords to attract business, and the financial soundness of the society did not worry them much. Often the clerk or secretary received a salary in proportion to the number of members. Both clerk and publican (who might be one and the same) were therefore interested in a large membership and might favour high benefits to attract members, even though this would soon lead to bankruptcy. When this tendency was checked by limiting the size of the society, this might leave it too small to have adequate funds. Funeral grants were therefore often financed by a special levy when a member died, but if several members died close together, there might be an exodus to avoid the levies. Young men preferred to join new societies that did not have old members, so that several societies became composed only of older men. But apart from all this, collapse often resulted from an ill-calculated ratio of contributions to benefit payments; the requisite actuarial skill was at that time lacking anywhere, for it was very difficult to calculate the likelihood of deaths and injuries. Whatever the reasons, when a society failed the contributions of a lifetime were lost.

Yet we should not minimise the function or appeal of these institutions. They did provide some protection, though in the main only for those above subsistence level, against some of the hazards of life. They were found everywhere because they offered a hope of maintaining respectability and avoiding charity, for the benefits were regarded not as charity but as a right.

The problem of underemployment and waste of time looking for work was reduced by houses of call in many trades. These were, again, public houses, where members looking for work registered their names, and where masters applied when they needed men; men were then sent to them in the order in which their names stood in the book, so that those who had been waiting longest received priority.[13]

Given the irregular nature of employment, especially when there were seasonal fluctuations, unemployment benefit was not usually really practicable, especially as it would need large organisation and funds. But several trades did develop tramping networks with provincial towns, whereby tramps went to a succession of towns in a set order, presented a membership certificate or 'blank' at the local house of call, and either obtained work or received maintenance before moving on to the next town.[14] By enabling men to move from an area where demand was slack to one where it was brisk, the system was an important means of providing relief, and indeed was the only properly developed form of unemployment relief. But it was clearly also based on the tradition of wandering journeymen, so prevalent also on the Continent. It was often assumed that young men would wander before they married, and the French *compagnonnages* had an organised Tour de France which was regarded as the final stage in an artisan's instruction and, like tramping, catered for unmarried men. But in some trades, like shoemaking, wives did tramp with husbands.[15]

Finally, artisans had always faced threats to their position from underworking masters who sought to employ youthful, unskilled, cheaper labour and were thereby a menace to the livelihood and reputation of the workmen as a whole; from masters who had not been brought up to the trade and were therefore often ignorant of the complexities of its customs, procedures, pace and quality of work, many of which were difficult to comprehend, and so tended to introduce new, often more rational methods, techniques and 'innovations'; from masters seeking to expand their businesses rapidly, often at the expense of their colleagues, and seeking to cheapen labour costs. Such masters and their cheap, unskilled labour were best guarded against by insisting on proper apprecticeship procedures.

Apprenticeship basically meant that a lad was attached to a master or journeyman and through helping and working alongside him gradually mastered the different aspects of the work.[16] It was the usual, traditional way of starting in an industry or trade, for there were few alternatives, and it was this suitability for technical training that ensured its survival in many trades for much of the nineteenth century. But strong traditions and a number of past enactments gave the practice something of the character of a system. Above all, by the 1563 Statute of Artificers, no-one could exercise a trade in England or Wales unless he had first served a seven years' apprenticeship under a legal indenture which defined the mutual obligations of master and apprentice. By various other enactments, the parish authorities were charged with putting the sons and daughters of destitute poor to work. And in many trades guild regulations or custom defined a ratio of apprentices to adult workers. The variety in types of apprenticeship is not surprising in view of the varying purposes of the enactments (the 1563 Act seeking to check industry and promote agriculture), the different outlooks of the old guilds and companies (some seeking to control the number of apprentices and the quality of their training, others merely selfishly concerned to restrict the number of masters and indifferent to any exploitation of youthful labour) and of parish officers (many of whom were glad to have pauper children taken off their hands by anyone). As the means of entry into a skilled trade, apprenticeship usually required an entrance fee or premium, which was often high (though this was often waived in the case of a son of a member of the trade, and there were some endowments to apprentice poor children). Such apprentices were often already of the same social stratum as the master, and some such trades became virtually hereditary monopolies, like the millwrights, but this form of apprenticeship could provide real education in the 'mysteries' of the craft. In other cases, boys were apprenticed 'for labour', taken merely to suit the master, usually as a form of cheap labour. Such apprentices were often merely non-adult workers. Parish apprentices were bound compulsorily to a master who took them for the fee paid by the parish and exploited them, making this sort of apprenticeship a system of child-slavery involving years of misery, drudgery and oppression.

The 1563 Act was never enforced systematically, and was continually broken by employers. Apprenticeship remained most usual in the old corporate towns, where it was often essential for entering a trade and for gaining the freedom of the town. Bristol was one of these, with 23 old incorporated companies in 1719, but these gradually faded out during the century. One of the last attempts to enforce the Act, in 1772, failed. But apprenticeship remained usual there, and was registered on official printed forms, as in Gast's case.[17]

At best, apprenticeship might provide a patriarchal regimen that inculcated discipline and sobriety. But this aspect became steadily less important with the growth of outdoor apprenticeship in which the lad did not live in the master's house and was not fed and clothed by him. This arrangement avoided disputes over food, beds and Sunday-work, but the boy had instead to be paid some wage. Outdoor apprenticeship grew in the course of the eighteenth century, and seems to have been more general in the provinces than in London. Often there was an informal agreement or contract instead of legal indenture, but in Bristol a modification was printed on the back of the document.

Gast's apprenticeship seems clearly to have been of the better sort, giving admission to an ancient and skilled craft, and he may well have been thereby rising socially. Such a large employer as Toombs was unlikely to take him merely for the premium, though the motive of cheap labour is possible, as in the eleven years 1777–87 Toombs took 45 apprentices (as well as binding his two sons to himself).[18] One disadvantage of apprenticeship was that many masters turned out not to have the substance to guarantee maintenance and employment for as long a period as seven years, and it may have been business difficulties that led Toombs in 1792 to change his premises and transfer nearly all his apprentices, including Gast, to a much smaller builder, William Hosey.[19]

Apprenticeship, then, was weakening as a system in a period of economic and technological change. A rigid system was impossible when an industry or business was expanding rapidly. But it remained the usual way of giving a lad a start because there was little alternative, it was a cheap way of learning a trade, and many masters felt it was in their best interests to train well so that the boy's labour was more productive. It survived also through force of tradition, a number of obsolescent statutes and corporate rights, and because journeymen saw it as their best defence against a flood of cheap labour and underworking masters. For it restricted the supply of labour and put them in a strong position.

Thus it was that the combination of relatively high earnings, irregularity of work and a number of problems led the skilled artisans to develop these four basic institutions. And since these overlapped, we can see them as the four basic elements of the 'trade society', though not all such societies had all four components—the shipwrights had no tramping. Many benefit societies, especially in London, were confined to members of a single trade, as among shipwrights and caulkers. The meeting-house was often also a house of call and rendezvous for men on tramp. Benefit societies that, like the shipwrights' and caulkers', confined membership to 'legal' men, who had served a full seven-year apprenticeship, were thus enforcing apprenticeship. There were several shipwrights' benefit societies on the Thames in the 1790s, but one stood out in importance, the Friendly Society of Shipwrights, formed in 1794 and usually called the St Helena Benefit Society, or the 'Blues'. Only legal shipwrights could join. It carried out trade union activities and grew to include most of the shipwrights on the river. Indeed it seems to have insisted that all working shipwrights belong either to it, the Britannia Society or affiliated societies. The caulkers' society even forbade each member to take more than one apprentice during his lifetime, apart from a son; it allowed foreman caulkers to take two apprentices but forbade their being used instead of journeymen.[20] Many trade societies fixed the ratio of journeymen to apprentices, to check the labour supply.

Yet this functional analysis of trade societies has by no means exhausted their characteristics. We must, first, not take too institutional a view of trades or too bureaucratic a definition of 'membership'. Too often trade union studies focus narrowly on the institutional structure, especially leadership, to the exclusion of the much more important substructure of workshop practice. Yet here was an infinite number of usages and practices that were generally known and adhered to, and were therefore enforced within the shop without any recourse to a supra-workshop organisation. There were traditional privileges, like the right to bring a son as apprentice, the compositors' entitlement to pay for 'fat' and wrappers as pages even though they did not have a full page of print, or the tailors' right to double pay during court mourning (when the wearing of black meant a sharp fall in work). There were traditional holidays, like the shipwrights' for nutting. There were traditional 'stints' or amount of work done in a day, with disapproval of both slacking and excessive zeal. There was the examination of a new arrival's indentures to check he was a legal man. All this and much more was enforced at shop level by common adherence and consensus, even coercive consensus. Apprenticeship played at vital role in preserving these traditions, for in working alongside older men the lad absorbed the lore, pace of work and customs of the trade, which was one reason why the men supported it. There were important rituals of the workshop, some very practical like the calling of a shop meeting by ringing a bell to bring a matter forward. There were formal admissions of new workmen or lads just out of their time, with their obligation to pay their 'footing' or 'maiden garnish', that is drink for their mates. The initiations were often brutal and coarse; shipwrights' apprentices paid a footing of two guineas, the penalty for non-payment being flogging with a hand-saw. When a workman was to be married, there were special ceremonies, often coarse and obscene.[21] In the nineteenth century some artisans, who had widened their education and outlook by sacrifices and detachment from some of these time- and money-consuming practices, were to react against many of these customs and the 'rigorous and unmanly persecution' of those who resisted them. These men included Francis Place, Gast himself, and William Lovett who, having constantly had to provide drink for his mates in cabinet-making workshops, became a bitter opponent of trade union drinking customs.[22] But the general affection for these customs isolated such men.

> Most well regulated shops are governed internally by a particular code of laws, for the maintenance of justice and good order among the men, and also for the prevention of such persons exercising their employment who have no just claim to it—a jealousy which equity allows; for I consider every artizan and operator who has been in bondage for seven years, and who frequently for that time endures complete privation of his liberty, chiefly in order that he may afterwards enjoy a superior right to a trade, is as much entitled to stand forward for his prerogative, and to use every means in his power for the support of the same, as the monarch has to the throne. It is well known among mechanics, that there are men who have but an indifferent knowledge of the practical part of a business, and who will offer their services to the master-tradesmen at reduced wages, to obtain employment till they become more perfect in the art, often to the great injury of the regular operator.

Now, as there are no constitutional laws to prevent such encroachments on their rights, they have established shop-laws among themselves, which they attend to with all the deference that could be shown to
any legislative enactment.

When a mechanic who is a stranger in a shop is first engaged, his
fellow-workmen endeavour to ascertain whether he has a proper claim
to the business he professes. If there is any doubt, an objection is made
to his footing, till it is satisfactorily explained; and if he fails to do so, he is
then considered as an invader of their rights, and immediately (to use
their own phrase) they send him to *Coventry* . . . He is likewise never
spoken to by his shopmates, but obliged to experience practical jokes
and vexatious insults, which generally terminate by the man being
obliged to leave the shop . . .

It [a trial] is generally proceeded in after the following manner:— The
oldest workman in the establishment presides as the judge, and for this
purpose he is provided with a full-bottomed wig, when, with all the
earnestness and gravity imaginable, he fills his important office. A jury is
empanelled from among the men. After the plaintiff and defendant have
selected their counsel (for there is usually a Demosthenes and a Cicero
to be found even among Cyclops), they proceed after the form of a
King's-Bench trial, and decide agreeably to the verdict, which is generally for a trifling fine as damages . . . I must not omit to remark, that
there is a principle acted upon in many shops, which is most praisewor-
thy wherever it exists. It is that of appropriating the money received for
fines, &c. towards a fund, for the purpose of assisting any fellow-
workman, who may have the misfortune to meet with any accident while
in the practice of his employment.[23]

Given the high mobility of the journeymen, this consensus and
solidarity extended beyond the workshop to the trade in general in
the area. Pride and interest in their work, the fact that they could
often talk during work that did not entail the 'thunder of machines',
the spare time consequent on irregularity of work, the freedom
during work, all reinforced the social bonds between members of
the trade that were continued in leisure time. But whereas in France
this still had some religious focus, in Britain it centred wholly on that
great secular institution, the public house, source of drink, food,
lodging, employment, entertainment and company. Here, in the
public house to which members of a particular trade resorted, was
strengthened the occupational community and the particularism so
concerned with the honour and reputation of the trade, and here
were reproduced workshop practices and concerns. Men loved the
regular lodge meetings, conviviality, rituals, ceremonies, banners,
celebrations (like St Crispin's day among shoemakers), annual procession and dinner. 'Membership' consisted of admission to this
honourable social group or community, and need be no more formal than going to the meeting-place and participating in joint

activity. Being a member of this group was a badge of one's 'respectability'. 'As the skilled workman's life is his trade he must see to it that the Trade is kept respectable.'[24] This included making a good show in public activities, and keeping members off the parish. Many trade societies, like the tailors', forbade their members to receive poor relief. The shipwrights' union formed in 1824 sought to support its aged. 'We conceived it was disgracing our trade that so large a body of men should not be able to keep their own poor, that they should ever go to the parish workhouses.'[25]

The establishment of benefit societies was making this membership more formal, as there had to be clear entitlement and regular subscriptions, while the expansion of tramping during the wars necessitated a definition of membership. But these institutions were based on widespread informal actions of support and passing the hat round, and could still remain fairly indeterminate and *ad hoc*. The caulkers had a sixpenny levy when a member broke a limb, while the disablement and widows' benefits paid by the shipwrights' St Helena Society were not fixed in amount but were 'at discretion'. Despite the rules of the brushmakers' society, all decisions were really made by referendum.[26]

A trade society thus performed certain functions vital to the artisans' position, and expressed the customs and emotions focused on the trade. This is to stress its traditional features, which could include that inferiority of young to old that was so much more marked a feature, ultimately a disruptive one, in the *compagnonnages*. At some tailors' houses of call there were two or even three books; more senior members had their names on the first book and always received priority in gaining work over those on the second.[27] The Benevolent Society of Coachmakers, formed in 1816, had, like some *compagnonnages*, three categories of membership—citizens, subjects and people.[28]

Many of these features characterised the old guilds, and in some senses the journeymen's trade societies were their indirect descendants. They fulfilled many similar functions. The guilds also had tried to control recruitment, with kinship an important qualification, to maintain a formal system of apprenticeship, regulate the amount and kind of work, insure members' tools, help meet funeral expenses and maintain widows. They had emphasised ceremonial. As the old guilds and companies had declined, with disputes between large and small employers and victory to the former, the latter had often tried to organise on their own and even form separate companies. They also tended to ally with the journeymen, especially as they were sometimes themselves forced down to their level.[29] One of the chief issues of contention was apprenticeship, with larger masters, in their wish to expand, seeking to exceed the ratio of apprentices and employ unbound boys to secure a larger and cheaper labour force. In these and in other ways, some journeymen's organisations arose on the old models. On the Thames, the journeymen sawyers had in 1670 tried to escape from the Shipwrights' Company and set up a new company.[30] In 1799 the Thames caulkers, reacting against the employment of non-indentured caulkers in the royal yards, actually tried to incorporate their trade as a company.[31] The issue of apprenticeship was in fact one which the journeymen made their own.[32]

But whether or not they were actually directly connected or adopted their forms, the journeymen's trade societies shared the ideals of the guilds. There was the basic assumption that the possession of a skill of value to the community was a man's property, and that regulation was necessary to ensure that all who had learned it could maintain the respectable position that was their due. Stability and security were prime aims, and within this framework there could be 'fair' competition. It could be legitimate for men to secure greater rewards if they were more skilful or worked harder, and it was assumed that older people would not earn as much, though they had still earned the right to a decent standard of living. (In 1802 the shipwrights explained 'that they thought the old men ought not to be discarded on account of their years—for having exhausted their strength in the service of the Builders, they had a right to expect some little indulgence when old'.)[33] But such competition must never be so excessive as to threaten the respectability of others. Thus many societies sought to limit working hours lest some deprive others of work, and would not allow any member to boast about his skill, while the caulkers' society forbade anyone to take work from another.[34] Naturally then, trade societies performed many of the functions of the old guilds, being arbiters of quality and fair practice, and controlling recruitment, hiring and dismissal.[35] They could thereby be very strong indeed. The hatters controlled employment through strict apprenticeship, houses of call and tramping. The tailors by 1812 had about twenty-five houses of call which had a monopoly of the best workmen needed by respectable firms. But this power was not necessarily at all resented by the masters. It was not only that many of them had been journeymen and supported such societies during that time, or that many were still very near the journeymen economically and socially. The societies' insistence on

apprenticeship guaranteed a certain level of skill among the workmen, while the houses of call were a very great convenience in that
several men of assured ability could be thence obtained very quickly
even for half a day's work. The brushmakers gave a certificate of
skill to members, the hatters fined a member who robbed a master
and entered the fact on his blank, while if a journeyman tailor was
complained of three times by masters, he was expelled from the
house of call.[36] Above all, most masters wanted a stable system
where a certain level of reward was guaranteed, and not a competitive free-for-all of price-cutting and too many people struggling for
orders in which a few prospered and the rest failed. Journeymen and
most masters were therefore usually natural allies against the few
'unscrupulous' and 'foul' masters who, in their efforts to expand and
cut costs, threatened this stability, and against 'dishonourable' and
'illegal' workmen who worked at lower prices. The aim of the trade
society was essentially to protect the trade as a whole against those
interlopers, masters and men, who threatened stability. It was not
founded on an assumption of conflicting interests between masters
and men.

This being the case, a widespread strike was a rarity. Disputes
usually involved one or a few masters and men, and were more
likely to be over apprenticeship, customary practices, treatment or
hiring than over pay. The transgressors were disapproved of by
masters and men, and were dealt with by proscription and boycott.
There were big strikes in the eighteenth century, but they were
usually among such groups as clothiers, weavers, coalheavers,
sailors or miners, who belonged to occupations where a large
number of men were concentrated and could easily act together
coercively without any real need for organisation.[37] The strike is a
very widespread phenomenon, but has usually been spontaneous.
Conversely the artisan trades, being more diffuse, needed much
greater organisation to effect common action, and this happened.
But, this organisation once achieved, a variety of courses was open
to them apart from mass direct, and often violent, action. One
course was political, whether local or national, for the trades saw
themselves as an interest whose needs should be heeded and, like
other bodies, would frequently petition Parliament for redress, as in
the Thames shipwrights' campaigns against America- or India-built
ships. Trades had recourse to the law. Clauses in the 1563 Act not
only dealt with apprenticeship but also empowered magistrates to
fix wages. Appeals to Quarter Sessions for wage rises were made in
London by tailors in 1800, carpenters in 1803 and shoemakers and

tin-plate workers in 1804, the first three successfully.[38] In 1812 the shoemakers took some employers to court over a wage dispute.[39] There had also been several acts regulating wages and conditions in specific trades, such as for tailors in 1767 and the famous Spital-fields Act of 1773, further extended in 1792 and 1811, which provided for the fixing by statutory bodies of wages in the London silk-weaving industry. It was because of these models and the fundamental belief in regulation that Gast in 1802 expressed the hope that Parliament would pass a bill 'for the better regulating our trade':

> The interference of Parliament, has in many instances been deemed necessary; the better to terminate disputes, between artificers and their employers; and the laws promulgated, by which the price, as well as the time of labor, has been ascertained; so that no disputes thereon can ever exist, without an immediate and efficacious remedy to terminate them.[40]

This should not lead us into loose talk about 'State intervention'. There was no real conception of positive action by the State or of new governmental bodies' being set up. The aim was redress through *the law*, whether to defend the rights and property of artificers, over such things as apprenticeship, just as it should defend all other forms of property, or to give established practices and procedures the force of the law to guard, like all laws, against the malpractices of a few. Under the Spitalfields Acts, the authorities did not themselves work out the prices (no-one outside the trade could hope to master its complexities); these prices were agreed by a joint meeting of masters and men, and then merely ratified by the authorities so that they were legally enforceable. Legal sanction thus upheld what the great majority wanted, against the actions of a few. This was Gast's ideal. Law would impartially guarantee fair play, and regulation by corporate bodies and law courts left no positive role for the State. Towards institutions of the State the attitude of artisans was negative and suspicious. When in 1793 George Rose secured an act allowing friendly societies to register and so gain some legal protection of funds, many were so suspicious of interference that they immediately dissolved, and by 1800 only about half the London societies had registered.[41] This negative attitude was heightened by the illegality of conspiracy and combination, which could encompass many of the practices of jour-neymen's societies. For this reason, many trade societies took the ostensible form of a benefit society and even, like the St Helena Society, registered under the 1793 Act. In 1814 Francis Place poured scorn on Colquhoun's statement that friendly societies were not used to finance strikes, for he well knew that some were begun with no other aim.[42] This involved risks, for a disgruntled member might complain to a magistrate that the funds were being used for illegal purposes, which would enable the magistrate to seize all the misapplied funds. But this was avoided, when a strike was decided on, by officially dissolving the society and ostensibly paying everyone a share of the funds, though in reality only opponents of the strike were paid and the rest went into a strike fund. This, of course, helps explain some of the high mortality among benefit societies. Trade societies therefore nearly always had the formal organisation of a benefit society with membership confined to legal men of a single trade.

This was the situation of such men as Gast. They sought respectability, the ability to support themselves and their families by labour. This ability depended on personal factors—skill, hard work, sobriety or thrift. But it also depended on institutions to guard against sickness, injury and the perils of old age, to help find work, and to prevent excessive rivalry for work. These institutions centred on the trade, focusing emotional allegiance and commitment, expressing the members' pride in a skill of value to the community, and defending their property or right of exclusively and peaceably practising their craft, a right grounded on the value of the craft and the sacrifices and effort involved in its acquisition, through servitude (often involving a premium) and years of application. This defence was seen in very traditional and conservative forms, involving the preservation of the existing system and of customary practices, relationships, privileges and levels of reward.

The Wars

Yet these men were to experience great pressures in the war period, mainly in the form of rising prices and expansion of the labour force. From about 1760 the rising cost of living had brought an increase in strikes in London, and the food-riot proper had long since disappeared there,[43] but it was wartime that brought unprecedented inflation and made wages the chief concern of the trade societies. The artisans' basic attitude was unchanged—wages should be just and fair, sufficient for them to live in the customary style. It was custom and status differentials, not supply and demand, which they though should determine wage rates, and they had no real conception of *improving* their standards of living through higher wages. But with prices rising so persistently, only repeated wage increases could maintain their standard of living. And they were able to gain rises because of the demand for labour. The seasonal character of many of the trades meant that every year there was a period when labour was in short supply and it was then, April and May among the tailors, from June to August among the coopers, after Michaelmas among the fellmongers, that the men could make successful wage demands. The masters were usually unlikely to counter this by reductions in the slack periods, as they needed good labour relations and certainty of obtaining skilled labour (especially when there were strong apprenticeship regulations and tramp relief). But on top of this situation, the French wars brought extensive government orders and a general increase in the demand for labour, and it was this that enabled the men to gain successive rises. This combination of persistent and apparently inevitable rising prices and the greater demand for labour resulted in a steady series of wage rises up to a peak in 1811–12.[44]

But the repeated demands for rises led to growing resistance, and the result was often much stronger organisation. The outstanding example was among the tailors, who in the 1790s developed the strongest union of all the London trades, with a secret and near-military structure that took the masters thirty years to break down.[45] They obtained rises in 1795, 1801, 1807, 1810 and 1813, and it was a measure of their exceptional strength that they had the funds and organisation to pay unemployment relief to members, which made them almost unique. The men's shoemakers also developed a strong organisation, and corresponded with societies all over the country, though in 1804 they split into eastern and western divisions. The ladies' shoemakers were also well organised, with fourteen divisions in London by 1812. But it was a general pattern that led to a strengthening of trade society organisation, much greater emphasis on wages, consolidation of bargaining positions, and even the establishment of regular wage bargaining machinery among carpenters, brushmakers, basketmakers, compositors and pressmen, silk-weavers and tin-plate workers, some of which produced printed wage scales.

The wartime period was thus characterised in London by unprecedented inflation, unprecedented wage demands and an unprecedented number of strikes. This clearly marked a new stage in the history of the London trade societies, who emerged from the wars far more strongly organised than when they had begun. Furthermore, whilst in so many cases small masters and journeymen were natural allies against large masters, this was not necessarily the case when the issue was wage rises. Small masters could not afford wage rises as easily as could the larger employers who anyway needed a much more regular supply of labour. In their desire to avoid any interruption to work and to get a monopoly of the best men, the latter might more readily concede wage demands and agree to a closed shop. Around 1802 the smaller and middling shoemakers promoted a bill to prevent the journeymens' combination, and in 1810–11 the smaller master tailors tried to break their journeymen's houses of call and petitioned Parliament for a bill to suppress the union, an attempt defeated by the larger employers led by Francis Place.[46]

By 1814 there was in London as elsewhere, a new trade union consciousness, and wages were clearly seen as directly connected with the organised power of the men. In some trades where there was a small number of masters who could easily take concerted action, trade unions were weak, as among type-founders and saddlers, or non-existent, as among watchmakers, and wages were therefore miserably low. In 1812 a stockinger from Nottingham was told:

> What would our Trade be, if we did not combine together? perhaps as poor as you are, at this day! Look at other Trades! They all Combine, (the Spitalfields weavers excepted, and what a Miserable Condition are they in). See the Tailors, Shoemakers, Bookbinders, Gold beaters, Printers, Bricklayers, Coatmakers, Hatters, Curriers, Masons, Whitesmiths, none of these trades Receive less than 30s/- a week, and from that to *five* guineas this is all done by Combination, without it their Trades would be as bad as yours . . .[47]

The new trade union strength and consciousness extended to strong links between trade societies. The tramping federations meant contacts between London and many parts of the country. And in London there were informal links between the trades, the most important form being help for a trade in difficulties, usually financial difficulties due to industrial disputes. In 1802, as Gast rather misleadingly puts it, the shipwrights on strike found that 'accounts of our proceedings had spread throughout the Kingdom; and many offers of assistance were made to us by unknown hands'.[48] Between 1807 and 1811 the bookbinders helped the wireworkers, lockfounders, cutlers, papermakers, goldbeaters, pipemakers, corkcutters and brushmakers.[49] Between 1810 and 1812 the goldbeaters gave or lent a total of over £200 to brushmakers, friziers, silversmiths, pipemakers, braziers, bookbinders, curriers, bit and spurmakers, scalemakers, leather-grounders, tin-plate workers, ropemakers, saddlers and millwrights, and received sums from scalebeam makers and musical instrument makers.[50]

The capacity for concerted action in town and country had been demonstrated when in 1799 a millwright's strike led to a parliamentary bill sponsored by their masters to ban combinations in their trade. Under government influence this became a general act outlawing all combinations. It was rushed through the Commons, the trades were unaware of it, and only the London calico-printers awoke to the danger.[51] In 1800 these called for petitions for the repeal of the act, and in June petitions were indeed presented from the trades of Manchester, London, Liverpool, Bristol, Plymouth, Bath, Lancaster, Leeds, Derby, Nottingham and Newcastle.[52] Their simultaneous presentation and virtual identity of content were clear signs of some co-ordinated campaign. The result was that a non-government measure was hastily passed which met some of the criticisms but retained the basic outlawing of combination. But though there were some prosecutions under this act (and no doubt there were several of which no records survive) and the London trades were well aware of it and often took great pains not to transgress it, it could not check the development of trade unionism but merely embittered industrial relations and confirmed hostility to the governing apparatus. Though they evaded it, the trade societies never forgot it.

The other chief development in the wartime period arose out of the huge growth of London's population and from continued economic expansion and growing demand. On the whole industrial expansion to meet this demand took the form of a multiplication of the small units of production, with a consequent large expansion of the labour force. In this situation it became more difficult to implement the ideal of most masters and men, of regulation, uniformity, stability and security within the trade, and it proved impossible for the trade societies to control this large labour force or manage its recruitment through regulated apprenticeship. Thus industrial expansion and even prosperity masked dilution and the use of unskilled and cheap labour. More and more the skilled artisan societies found themselves confined to a sector of their industry, the higher-quality bespoke side. There was therefore a growing distinction between skilled journeymen working in shops making to order, and the ever-growing proportion engaged in mass production, in which cheapness was more important than quality. But even in higher-class establishments, there were efforts to meet the demand by increasing labour intensity and by subdividing labour in the interests of efficiency. Both were resisted. One form of the former, as among shipwrights, was the growth of piece-work instead of day-work, and though if the trade were strongly organised this made little difference, as the men regulated their labour effort so that it was the same, they seem in general to have preferred day-work.

The growing demand also resulted in some larger businesses, especially those receiving government contracts for clothing, boots and shoes, ordnance, victualling and building. The wartime period thus also saw further development of capitalism, with the traditional connection with the state, though this was a minority phenomenon and the labour it employed was usually domestic. The chief examples were among shoemakers and tailors.

The skilled tailors did not have a formal system of apprenticeship, but remained exclusive and prevented an influx of unskilled men by their 'Log', the stint of work each man had to do in a day.[53] This entailed very fast work, and less skilled men like country immigrants simply could not keep up. This exclusiveness had its dangers as a number of those excluded from the workshops worked elsewhere at lower rates of pay and had done so for many years. Whereas the superior 'flints' did day-work, these 'dungs' did piece-work, which opened the way to harder work and cheaper labour. The great wartime demand for labour meant that this was not a serious problem, and the dungs even had some organisation of their own. But towards the end of the wars some of the larger firms working on government contracts began to employ female labour. And by 1815 a growing section of the industry was in the hands of 'show-shops' and 'slop shops' producing inferior and, in the latter case, ready-made articles for the mass market.

The boot and shoemaking trade was divided into a number of branches, but all were domestic. Whereas in 1806 there was a tailors' strike against work being put out (for this impeded uniformity and opened the way to cheaper labour), it was said that shoemakers would strike if forced to work on employers' premises.[54] The shoemaking employer had the leather cut by a clicker and then gave it to the journeyman. The uppers were first closed by a closer (in the case of men's shoes) or binder (in the case of ladies'), who were both usually women. The shoemaker then joined the sole to these uppers, and in the case of a boot there was then further work for the closer. Shoemakers who were single often joined together in small groups to hire a room and employ a few women. Married men usually had their wives as closers or binders. As in tailoring there was a rapid expansion in the number of small

businesses and also a number of large employers stimulated by
government contracts. About 1809 the latter switched to cutting
out the leather and sending it to Northampton to be made at little
more than half the London price, and this development of provincial competition in men's shoemaking, though certainly not new,
was to become very important. In London the wholesale, ready-
to-wear side of the industry grew, with large central warehouses
supplying London, the provinces and overseas markets, and using
country labour or giving orders to small London working
'garret-masters' at low rates. These small masters worked themselves, alongside their wives and their children and often boys pro-
cured from the parish. These last, when they grew up, added to the
labour pool.

At the same time there were some changes in the building industry, where the small craftsman firm also predominated. The practice
was for one master, say a master carpenter, to make himself
responsible for a job and then subcontract specialist parts to master
bricklayers, plumbers, painters, glaziers and stonemasons. But during the wars government contracts, mainly for building barracks,
were restricted to six big contractors, and this and the great amount
of building in London of large office and warehouse blocks and
especially estates of dwellings produced new 'master builders' who
saw to all branches of the work and had a large, permanent labour
force.[55]

These economic changes, mainly the expansion of industries and
the labour supply and the development of capitalism, were threats
to the traditional industrial structure, introduced a mass of strangers
into the trades and brought changes in the interests of rationalisa-
tion and cheapness that affronted men who believed in quality, the
value of skill and the right to a respectable reward. As Gast pointed
out, the problems were to a large extent masked in the wartime
expansion and demand for labour.

> When the War took place with France against liberty; its advocates, by
> means of a fictitious Capital, gave a powerful impulse to trade, the
> Workman experienced a greater call for labourers, and as a natural
> effect his means were increased, and the Country to him was in a
> flourishing condition, for all that were willing to work need not be long
> out.—and in general good wages were paid.[56]

But the problems were not, of course, unnoticed. By 1813 there was
a strong inter-trade campaign in favour of legal enforcement of
apprenticeship, a campaign which clearly illustrates the individual
strength of the London trades, their links with one another and with

the country, the growing pressures on them, and their belief in regulation.

Shipwrights

But 'apprenticeship was most peculiarly attended to among shipwrights',[57] a trade that illustrated many of the general features here outlined and the trade that had had in 1802 the biggest of all the wartime strikes. Like many other London trades, London shipbuilding in Gast's lifetime was characterised by high quality and high costs.[58] 'All whom I saw, no matter from what part of the country, spoke of London-built ships, in the good yards, as being the best in the world.'[59] While small ships of a few score tons were built everywhere, including on the Thames, by the end of the eighteenth century the building of the larger, bulk-cargo ships shifted decisively to the north-east. What London kept was her share of building the very largest merchant ships of all, West and, especially, East Indiamen, where quality was more important. Also, a large proportion of the work in the Thames yards was 'old work' (repairs), for wooden ships usually needed repairs after every sizeable voyage, and London's importance as a port meant that there was a lot of this work. The higher costs were less of a deterrent here, especially as shipowners often had no real alternative.

The Thames was distinctive in having the largest merchant shipyards of all. Of its total of 36 building-slips, 27 were in the five biggest yards, including Dudman's at Deptford Creek where Gast worked. These yards were very dependent on the East India Company. Whereas most merchantmen were under 300 tons, the Company used vessels of 800 and 1,200 tons, very solidly built ships that needed special skill and workmanship in their construction.[60] Nearly all of them were built on the Thames, which the Company could easily afford.

The other main element of Thames work was wartime naval building, for the six royal dockyards were never able to meet the navy's building needs in time of war. The great East Indiamen were solidly built and armed, so were like small ships of the line. It was therefore very useful to the navy that there were the large Thames yards which had the slips, organisation, capital and labour force to build ships of the line themselves, cost again being less important than quality. The famous Blackwall Yard was bigger than the royal yards at Deptford and Woolwich and employed 600 men, and the other big yards were little smaller. During the wars that began in

1793 the transport ships and most of the smaller warships were built in the outports by small men who risked all in building a single ship, whilst the ships of the line, of which the navy usually had about a hundred active, were built in the royal yards and Thames private yards.

The big Thames yards were thus essential to the navy, but were also very dependent on it and the East India Company, and so strikingly illustrate the connections between early capitalism and the state. The Pittite Robert Wigram, who in 1812 became a partner in Blackwall Yard, exemplified these connections to the extent of gaining a baronetcy in 1805 and the presence of the Prince Regent and the Duke of Clarence at his son's christening.[61] These builders were at the head of a big industry. The yards together employed some 1,200–2,000 shipwrights and 1,200–1,300 others (caulkers, sawyers, joiners, smiths and some labourers). On the riverside were also a mass of businesses dependent on shipbuilding—mastmakers, blockmakers, sailmakers, ropemakers, anchor-smiths and makers of metal fittings; furthermore, the industry also supported timber merchants and those employed in felling and transporting timber from Kent, Sussex, Essex, Hampshire and places further afield which new canals now made accessible.

To all these industries the Revolutionary wars which began in 1793 brought prosperity. In the mid-1790s the East India Company also had many large ships built. All in all the Thames built, from 1793 to 1802, 73 ships for the navy (= 67,000 tons), 69 East Indiamen (= c. 70,000) and 316 other merchant ships (= 27,000). The figures for 1788–93, some of which were boom years, had been 11 (18,000), 12 (c. 13,000) and 223 (26,000).[62] All this work benefited the shipyards and related businesses. It was an age of prosperity and high earnings, when every journeyman sailmaker travelled about the docks in his own dog-cart, when shipbuilders encouraged piece-work and earnings rose (caulkers were said to earn 16s. to 18s. in a day), and the great shortage of labour led builders to offer premiums to attract men from elsewhere.[63]

But in March 1802 came the brief Peace of Amiens, and peace always meant a slackening in shipbuilding, wholesale discharges of workmen from royal dockyards, and distress in the Thames yards, with less work and more men after it. In this case, although nineteen East Indiamen were being finished, a fall in freights also meant there were few new merchant orders. In May the Thames builders therefore began to reduce wages back to the peacetime level (in the shipwrights' case from 5s. 3d. a day to 3s. 6d.). This provoked strikes by sawyers, caulkers and shipwrights, of which the last was the most important.[64] Pressure from the builders and the Company eventually led the Admirality to side with the employers and allow men to go from the King's yards to work for the builders. This provoked severe violence, and police and troops had to be sent. The shipwrights' strike was settled on 23 August, but some disputes were not ended until 21 September.

The shipwrights, two thousand of them, had been solid, and their dispute was a 'controversy, which, for the length of time it was agitated, and the rancour, spleen and malice, with which it was carried on, perhaps has not been equalled in the last century'.[65] Their success in gaining a day-rate of 5s., overtime at the same rate, and no victimisation, contrasts with the failures of the caulkers and sawyers. 'How so large a body of men as we are, could possibly resist the combinations of by far the greater part of our employers, assisted by various departments of Government, civil, military and naval; is a mystery, that none but ourselves can develope.'

But in many ways the 1802 strike was academic, for war began again in May 1803 and the naval situation was desperate. During the emergency period before Trafalgar tremendous efforts went into patching up ships for use, and the navy was particularly dependent on the Thames merchant yards. Again labour was in great demand with extra work at special rates. After Trafalgar this frantic work slowed, and a general stagnation in shipping from 1804 to 1807 further reduced demand. But a large fleet was still needed to check any further invasion attempts, and a great number of small ships was needed for the blockade. From 1805 to 1815 the navy built nearly 400 new ships, including over fifty ships of the line.[66]

Until 1811, then, there was plenty of work for shipwrights, earnings were high, and there were no disputes about pay. This well-being is probably reflected in the number of new registered friendly societies among shipyard workers. But the great fluctuations in foreign trade and in naval and East India demand meant that work was not steady, and there was never the prosperity after 1805 that there had been before. There were several caulkers' strikes in individual yards, and only the threat of a general strike gained them a rise around 1809. The expansion of work had also brought with it the dangers of dilution of skilled labour. Already in 1799 the royal dockyards had used some non-indentured caulkers, and in the emergency before Trafalgar they used non-indentured shipwrights. Moreover, though most of the merchant builders were regularly bred shipwrights and only employed such men, there were now five or six firms doing repair work where the masters had not been shipwrights (they were usually sea captains) and employed illegal men.[67]

At the end of 1810 the naval building programme was curtailed; 31 new ships were built in 1810, but only 14 in 1811, and over 50 were broken or sold. The war of 1812 with America led to a resumption of building, but these were smaller vessels like frigates, of which 40 were built in 1812 and 1813. There was also a decline in merchant building after the 1810 boom.[68] This situation worsened when in 1814 peace became probable. Not only would this mean a cessation of naval work and discharges of shipwrights from the royal yards, but the likelihood that about seven-eighths of the ships in the transport service would be sold made merchants very loth to order the building of any new merchant vessels. Moreover, there were in 1813, 518,000 tons of prize ships in the general trade, which reduced demand for building. This all left the Thames more than ever dependent on the East India Company but here, despite an increase of work in 1810–12, a new threat had emerged. Since 1794 the Company had had a number of ships built in India. These became a threat to Thames shipbuilding when in 1795 they were admitted to the British registry. They were built much more cheaply because of lower labour and timber costs, and they were built of teak. 'Till the new principle of East India-built ships was known in England, we did not think anything superior to British heart of oak; and if our ships were kept in repair, they would last for ever.'[69] But teak proved very durable and strong. It was in fact the best timber in the world for ship frames and, especially, planking, and teak ships lasted much longer than oak. Even the navy had begun to have teak warships built in India. From 1802 to 1814 the Company had 31 ships built at London and 38 in India. The Thames was losing repair-work as well as building, as teak ships needed less repairs, and these were usually performed in India.

By 1814, with the prospect of losing naval and Company work, the Thames shipbuilding industry was facing ruin. But the ship-wrights had been experiencing uncertainty since 1811, and their response took three forms. The first was an attempt led by Gast and some others in 1811 to organise a shipwrights' trade union,[70] prob-ably with the aim of standardising piece-work rates, for the uncer-tainty over prices had long caused contention and the aim was a recurrent one. But Gast's attempt failed and his achievement in 1811 was to found the shipwrights' Hearts of Oak Society to erect almshouses for aged and disabled shipwrights.[71]

The second response concerned India-built ships. In 1812 the builders held several meetings on the problem, and Gast was always present, for on this issue masters and men were agreed (as they were also agreed in supporting the continuation of the Company's charter). There were suggestions that builders and men should refuse to do work on such ships,[72] but in this depressed period such collective action seems not to have been achieved and they turned to political action. In 1813 and again in 1814 a number of petitions came from builders, shipwrights, ropemakers and allied workmen urging the Commons no longer to allow India-built ships to be admitted to the British registry and so gain the privileges of the Navigation Acts. But the campaign ended in total defeat in 1814 with the passage of a government bill permanently extending to India-built ships all the benefits and privileges of British ships for the East Indian trade.[73]

The proposed new union of 1811 was probably also an attempt to enforce apprenticeship control, for the shipwrights were worried over non-indentured workmen and masters who had not served an apprenticeship to the trade, while some builders were taking large numbers of apprentices in proportion to the journeymen. The third response of the shipwrights was therefore to take a leading part in the general artisan campaign over apprenticeship.

3
THE APPRENTICESHIP CAMPAIGN

The age-old concern over apprenticeship had long been heightened by opposition among journeymen and many small masters to the larger employers who were expanding their businesses and labour force and found apprenticeship regulations hampered this, and who cut costs by taking numbers of boys and cheap labour, thereby widening the labour supply. Just as in Yorkshire men appealed to Tudor enactments prohibiting gig mills and restricting the number of looms, so on this issue artisans appealed to the statute of Queen Elizabeth of glorious memory. In 1813 the London ladies' shoemakers successfully prosecuted a master for employing an illegal man.[1] In the country there was litigation and agitation to restore apprenticeship control among calico-printers (1803–4), woollen-weavers (1802–6), Scotch cotton-weavers (1808) and Macclesfield silk-weavers (1811).[2] In London industrial expansion provoked efforts among some of the London Companies which still had some connection with their trade to preserve some stability and regulation and prevent a competitive anarchy, among shipwrights, basketmakers, ironfounders and, above all, clockmakers.[3] All of these tried to restore proper apprenticeships.

Between December 1809 and the end of 1812, nineteen cases were brought by journeymen against individual masters, sometimes because they had not themselves served a seven-year apprenticeship but usually for employing men who had not. Thirteen different trades were involved, and the chronological concentration and the fact that in every case the same attorney, a William Chippendale, was used, are clear signs that this was a co-ordinated campaign.[4]

The results were discouraging. The courts were clearly reluctant to convict, and twelve of the cases resulted in acquittals. In four of the cases won, the penalty was a mere 40s., which was the fine for one month's offence, whereas most of the offences had been carried out over a much longer period. Actions brought by informers were subject to a limit of a twelve months' penalty, with half of the fine going to the Crown, and informers, though they had to pay the costs of the defendant if the prosecution failed, were not awarded costs if they won. As it cost about £40 to bring a case, and the costs for unsuccessful actions were nearly £30, a long campaign of litigation was financially crippling. It was therefore obviously not possible to enforce apprenticeship through the 1563 Act, and so in May 1812 the London trades took the remarkable step of forming a delegate committee 'to devise such Measures as may secure to the regular-bred Artisan in future the exclusive Enjoyment of the Trade he has been brought up to', 'which we consider is our exclusive privilege of following, inasmuch as it is purchased by large premiums, and other incidental expenses, incurred by our friends, and seven years ser-vitude on our part'.[5] The means was to be a parliamentary act to amend the act of Elizabeth so as to make it an effective means of enforcing apprenticeship. There was no intention of preventing any existing workers or employers from continuing to be so, but it was intended to guard against the unlimited influx of workmen by insisting that in future no-one could become employer or journey-man unless he had served a proper apprenticeship. The London artisans agreed on a national campaign of masters and men, on a London committee to organise this, receive subscriptions of 1s. 3d. per man and consider suggestions on the proposed legislation, and on the formation in each town of a committee of two delegates from each trade.

In London the Artisans' General Committee (or United Arti-sans' Committee) met every week and grew steadily. They took counsel as to whether it was legal for trades to depute delegates to a general body to petition Parliament and whether the subscriptions infringed the Covention or Combination Acts. The reply was that it was perfectly legal if the aim was really only to petition Parliament but that any attempt to prevent either masters from employing men who had not served an apprenticeship or regular journeymen from working in such places would be conspiracy at Common Law and infringement of the acts of 1799 and 1800.

Advertisements were inserted in the papers, and letters were sent to the provinces calling on the trades in each town in England and Wales to appoint a committee of two representatives from each trade to correspond with London. In Bristol, at least, this was done and a 'Bristol Department' was formed in February 1813,[6] and the same was no doubt true of Liverpool and elsewhere. The campaign was now under weigh. Sixty-two London trades contributed to the committee (though not to the extent of 1*s*. 3*d*. per man) and over 70 places in the country subscribed, which is evidence of a large degree of inter-trade understanding and organisation. A petition was drawn up and signed, it was claimed, by 32,735 masters and men, over half of whom were outside London, praying 'That leave may be given to bring in a Bill to explain and amend, and render more effectual for the purposes aforesaid the said Statute, in such manner and under such regulations as to the House shall seem meet'.[7]

Their parliamentary spokesman was George Rose, the old friend of Pitt and a leading Tory specialist on financial matters. Though 'old George Rose' was notorious as a sinecurist, he was also interested in the artisans. He had secured in 1793 the first act on friendly societies, in 1808 he introduced a bill on behalf of the Manchester cotton-weavers, he was active in 1810 on behalf of the Spitalfields weavers, and in 1812 was a party to secret negotiations with Gravener Henson concerning Luddism and a bill to regulate the hosiery industry.[8] In April 1813 he presented the apprenticeship petition, and in May secured a select committee under his chairmanship. This met eight times in May, heard counsel for the petition and then evidence, nearly all of which was from journeymen and masters from various trades in support of the petition. How long the delegates had prepared for this committee is not known, but evidence came mainly from Londoners, especially from dockside industries, and otherwise only from Liverpool, Bristol and Plymouth, a fact which points to the leading role of the shipwrights. Nearly all the witnesses contented themselves with giving examples of masters who had not served regular apprenticeships or who employed illegal men, but some tried to show that apprenticeship was vital to keep up the high standard of British manufactures. Chippendale explained how the existing act was inadequate. It was a limited case thus presented, on the whole merely showing that the existing act was being increasingly evaded and that it was difficult to bring prosecutions under it, so that it needed to be changed. Little real attempt was made actually to justify apprenticeship, presumably because the benefits were deemed self-evident.

A sub-committee of the delegates several times pressed Rose to introduce the bill they wanted, have it read once and printed, and then let it stand over until the next session. Rose was quite willing to do so if they wished, but advised delay, as he saw nothing to lose by it. In June the General Committee therefore agreed to postpone the bill until the following session, but to print the heads of the intended bill with reasons for them, and give a copy to every MP. Early in the next session Rose would move for leave to bring in a bill, and in the meantime a campaign should be mounted. Every city and town was to draw up a separate petition, signed by masters, journeymen and apprentices in favour of a bill. Deputations of electors were to lobby their MPs. A further subscription was to be raised to finance this and to overawe any opposition, as there was always the danger that opponents might get the committee of the whole House to hear counsel for both sides, a very expensive business.

The campaign was impressive. Eight more London trades and more country adherents joined in, so that by August 1813 altogether £448 had come from London and £538 from 76 places in the country (£103 from Liverpool). Between Parliament's reassembling in November and its rising on 20 December, 22 petitions were presented with a claimed total of 62,825 signatures. It reassembled in March 1814 and between then and 6 May, 18 more petitions for a bill arrived. But for some reason no bill was introduced.

This activity of artisans in London and the country must be set in context. In London the years 1809–10 saw not only a new height in trade union strength but an acceleration in the number of strikes. In the country there were agitations among frame-work knitters against cheap labour, 'cut-ups' and 'colting' (the manufacture of inferior articles and the use of unskilled, especially juvenile, labour), among cotton- and woollen-weavers, and among Yorkshire croppers. All these groups were interested in apprenticeship. They also all took part in Luddism, which in many ways expressed the old economic attitudes and belief in protective legislation, and exemplified a high level of trade union organisation. The apprenticeship campaign was therefore in a national context of growing trade unionism, the problems arising out of rapid economic and population expansion and of production for export, and of a clash between paternalistic, protective economic ideas and the political economy of Laissez-faire. The campaign was an important element in the 'watershed' of 1811–13 and in it, as in Luddism, were attitudes and practices that looked back and forward.[9]

The artisans had long had an awareness of themselves as an 'order'. But the campaign marked a new level of solidarity (though it had been preceded by the 1800 campaign to repeal the Combination Act). The London committee saw itself as more than a short-lived body with limited functions, for 'also it will be the means of keeping up the Spirit of Mechanics, by having an Opportunity of meeting Monthly, for the Attainment of an Object which is strictly legal'.[10] In other words, it was a way of promoting unity yet evading the combination laws. Moreover this unity may have extended to the foundation of a newspaper. For we know that in 1812 a Sunday paper was started in London called the *Beacon*. No copies of it survive, but in 1826 Francis Place referred to it:

> A few years ago an attempt was made to establish a weekly newspaper called the *Beacon* to advocate the cause of the working people, but it failed. The causes were several: 1st. The apathy of the people it was intended to serve. 2d. The want of confidence, as well among workmen themselves, as with respect to others, which the partial, and consequently unjust law against combinations had produced. 3d. Want of knowledge in the conductors. No general principles were advocated—no information of consequence was contained in its columns. 4th. The narrow view it took of circumstances, and the prejudices it fostered, confined it wholly to the working people, who were at that time too ill informed to see the utility of such a vehicle. It advocated seven years' apprenticeships; it was opposed to free trade in all its bearings; and it supported all sorts of trade monopolies; it talked of the working people as the wisest of all classes in the nation; and it wished to make their prejudices and their ignorance the only rules of political economy and government. Such a paper did not deserve the support of any man or body of men, and the consequence was its speedy dissolution.[11]

Its ideas were clearly at variance with Place's but do seem a true reflection of artisan attitudes. The description suggests the new level of artisan solidarity, while the mention of apprenticeship suggests a connection with the campaign.

The campaign clearly shows the mingling of old and new, both in itself and the opposition it met. The London artisans clearly prized apprenticeship for two main reasons. One was its role in preserving the dignity and status of their craft by ensuring a high standard of skill and the exclusion of inferior workmen. 'We must remember that this was a time when there was little schooling, and neither Mechanics' Institutes nor Technical Colleges, and that almost the entire skill or "mystery" of the trade was conveyed by precept and example in the workshop, by the journeyman to his apprentice. The artisans regarded this "mystery" as their *property*, and asserted their unquestionable right to "the quiet and exclusive use and enjoyment of their . . . arts and trades".'[12] But it also restricted entry into the trade and so prevented excessive competition for work and strengthened the bargaining power of the men. Behind all the appeals to 'the wisdom of our ancestors', cloudy assertions that apprenticeship inculcated regular, orderly, moral and sober habits among the

young, and even statements that apprenticeship checked combinations among both masters and men, these were the main considerations.

The 'watershed' character of the campaign is illustrated also in
the debate it provoked. To many, apprenticeship seemed a device
whereby a small number of workmen kept a privileged monopoly of
their trade, to the exclusion of many other men and poor women. It
therefore seemed difficult to defend in justice, and the men reinforced this interpretation by their own arguments in terms of property rights.

The growing belief in free competition and lack of economic
regulation fostered a disapproval of apprenticeship, as any legal
limitations on the size of the labour force, apprenticeship or kinds of
work would check industrial expansion and efficient division of
labour. Such beliefs were not confined to the larger manufacturers
but were becoming the dominant intellectual current. Early in the
century Parliament swept away all protective legislation for the
woollen industry and always rejected proposals for protection and
legally fixed minimum wages in other trades. Even more to the
point, in 1813 they repealed the wage-fixing clauses in the 1563
Act. The situation here was exactly analogous to that of apprenticeship. For the cotton-weavers, having failed in their attempts at
special legislation to regulate their trade, had in 1812 resorted to
the wage-fixing clauses of the 1563 Act and petitioned the magistrates to fix wages at the Quarter Sessions in Easter 1813. Faced
with this revival of an obsolete enactment, the weavers' opponents
moved to secure the repeal of the offending clauses. The apprenticeship clauses were therefore doomed. No less a person than the
Prime Minister, Lord Liverpool, explained:

> The wisest principle of proceeding, with respect to commerce and man-
> ufactures, was that laid down by a foreign Potentate, 'Laissez
> faire'—This principle was particularly necessary to be kept in view with
> respect to the machinery and mechanical inventions of this country,
> which more than any other cause, had raised this kingdom to its high
> rank among the commercial nations of the world.[13]

This belief the artisans rejected:

> the unlimited or promiscuous introduction of various descriptions of
> persons, without apprenticeships, into the manufactures, occasions a
> surplus of manufacturing poor, and an unnecessary competition, ruin-
> ous to the commercial capital and industry of the nation; because the
> overflow of goods causes ALL the productions of the manufactories to
> fall in price, and be sold to foreigners for less money than they cost in
> making.[14]

In asserting this they were opposing the further argument that British manufacturers were now producing for export instead of the home market alone and so checks to expansion, like apprenticeship, must be removed. A more mobile labour force was needed, and since fluctuations in foreign trade were unavoidable they would produce vast unemployment if men were prevented by rigid apprenticeship laws from changing their occupations. For the rest of Gast's lifetime artisans would oppose this emphasis on the foreign market.

But some of the most important sources of opposition to apprenticeship were in connection with combination. The years up to 1812, after all, marked a peak in trade union strength and activity in London and the country. As nearly always happened in such cases, employers were alarmed and there were attempts to gain fresh, more stringent legislation against combinations. The master tailors' attempt in 1810 and 1811 was one example. In 1810 the strength of trade unions in the Manchester area aroused the magistrates there to the fact that they were meeting in the form of friendly societies whose rules had been passed at Quarter Sessions without inspection and 'they in many cases contained clauses directly binding the members to combinations in respect of trade'. After consultations with Spencer Perceval they drew up a bill in 1811, and revised it in 1812 in consultation with the magistrates of Sheffield, Huddersfield, Bolton, Macclesfield and Stockport.[15]

The apprenticeship campaign thus occurred in a context of growing hostility to combinations. In 1813 some of the London engineering employers wrote to the government:

> Your Memorialists have long deplored the Combinations that have been systematically organized and carried on for several years among the Major part of the Journeymen not only in your Memorialists Trade but in most of the manufacturing employments pursued in the metropolitan part of the empire . . . Your Memorialists were anxious to believe that the existing Laws of the Realm would have been adequate to repress these Evils but they are sorry to declare after long and painful experience that these Laws are artfully and efficaciously evaded and defeated by and under the mask of Benefit Societies Institutions which have created cherished and given effect to the most dangerous Combinations among the several Journey men of our district . . . Immense numbers of Journeymen embodied under the legal protection of Benefit Societies congregate together under the specious pretexts of discussing and forming plans and regulations for governing these Societies and which give to them on all occasions the advantage of conferring and forming any resolutions on any point either connected with their particular or general employments. Meetings for promoting these combinations are called with facility and under the existing Laws they are held with perfect

safety to those who attend them they are conducted with a secrecy and a dexterity that place the Master Manufacturers at a defiance . . . Their mischievous influence and overwhelming power is greatly augmented by a system of delegation. A convention of delegates has been sitting in the Heart of the Metropolis for some months composed of two persons from every Trade and profession carried on in the Metropolis and its Neighbourhood. That convention was called together solely to Consider of the best means of applying to the Legislator to enlarge the powers and to extend the Operation of the statute of the 5th. of Elizabeth yet your Memorialists have have well grounded reasons for believing that various other Objects have come under the Consideration of this Convention. Its Meetings have been protracted and discussions have been instituted and have given to the Journeymen of this Metropolis the means of Identifying their several interests ascertaining their strength and Consolidating their power [with a view to uniting] the whole Journeymen of the Metropolis who will form an irresistable phalanx and greatly superior to the united energies of the Masters.[16]

Apprenticeship was thus vitally connected with the strength of combinations. In May 1813 the Bermondsey master fellmongers petitioned against the proposals to strengthen the apprenticeship clauses. Their motives were made quite clear. At the turn of the century they had been forced to give in to a series of wage demands by their men, always strategically made at the autumn brisk period, because they were unable to find replacement labour. They had therefore subsequently started taking men and training them themselves for only three, four or five years as alternative labour to the society men, and they now wanted the total repeal of the apprenticeship clauses to break the back of combinations.[17] In this they were not alone:

> Journeymen being thus enabled to exclude others from employment, are better enabled to carry into execution their combinations, which, it is obvious, from the great number of modern statutes upon the subject, have of late become very injurious to the community. By these means their wages are kept up to an enormously high price; . . . Repeal that statute, and all combinations will cease; wages will rise or fall in proportion to the real demand for labour, and mechanics and manufacturers will be induced, by the competition incident to the freedom of employment, to work with much more care and industry, and to become much better members of society than they are now found to be.[18]

The issues were thus made quite clear, but the situation was complicated by other factors. Workmen who had never served an apprenticeship feared that the proposed bill would prevent them from continuing their work, though in fact it was only to apply to future recruitment, and two petitions expressed this fear. In many corporate towns a regular apprenticeship was the main qualification for the freedom of the borough, and so corporation politics tended to favour apprenticeship, while some MPs, perhaps ignorant of industrial conditions, favoured apprenticeship on moral grounds alone, for its supposed role in disciplining young men and inculcating sober habits.

It was a group of London engineering employers who took the lead against apprenticeship. They were experiencing serious problems in that their new industry was expanding rapidly and in desperate need of labour, and they opposed any restrictions as to whom they could employ. They employed a great variety of workmen—millwrights, joiners, turners, smiths and founders—and so opposed any checks on mobility from organisation and demarcation among trades. They were particularly irked by the three exclusive societies of millwrights, very highly skilled men who could do all branches of engineering work, construct an entire machine, and work in metal or wood. But changes in technique, especially the power-driven lathe, planer and sliding rest, meant this skill was less necessary, and the employers wanted sub-division of labour instead of the millwrights' all-round skill.[19] They wanted to end apprenticeship so as to break combinations and high day-rates, and two of them, Bramah and Galloway, had personally suffered prosecutions for employing illegal men. This group decided to press for the repeal of the apprenticeship clauses, and not only sent the memorial quoted above but found a sympathetic MP in Serjeant Onslow, who had been chairman of Surrey Quarter Sessions during a successful carpenters' prosecution over the 1563 clauses. Onslow had in May 1813 opposed the journeymens' petition, and in July gave notice that he would take up the question.

In October a group of employers set up a committee to organise a campaign, on 5 November Onslow gave notice of a motion on 30 November for the repeal of the apprenticeship clauses, and on 11 November a meeting of master manufacturers was held at the Crown and Anchor to support him. But only forty attended, mainly engineers and other employers who had suffered prosecutions. And opposition was expressed by delegates from the Clockmakers' Company, which was the chief company trying to restore control over its trade. This failure led Onslow to postpone his motion until 22 February, while the Clockmakers' Company and the United Artisans' Committee canvassed the City of London Companies and secured a favourable response from the Recorder, City Remembrancer and Common Council.

The Associated Manufacturers then circularised MPs and provincial manufacturers, and their secretary, John Richter, with his friend Francis Place, conducted a newspaper campaign. They presumably also composed the able pamphlet issued in February.[20] These two were assiduous and experienced workers, but they seem to have had little help from the rest and committee meetings were thinly attended. Luckily for them Parliament did not meet until 1 March and Onslow's motion was set for 27 April. This delay meant that the lawyers Brougham and Romilly, two of the greatest orators in the House, who had both promised their support, would be back from circuit. But the committee totally failed to arouse public support and only a handful of petitions were ever presented in support of Onslow's bill.

In great contrast was the emotion and activity on the other side. A public meeting was held on 14 January, every MP, as well as Lord Liverpool, was canvassed, and a petition campaign was organised. As Romilly recorded:

> There has been a great clamour raised against the Bill. Associations have been formed to resist it, in different towns, by the apprenticed journeymen, who are anxious to retain their monopoly. Numerous petitions against the Bill have been presented, signed by a great many thousand persons . . . I have myself been eagerly canvassed against it by a very large body of artisans and manufacturers in Bristol who voted for me at the last election, and by a London association.[21]

In fact on 27 April Onslow's bill to repeal the apprenticeship clauses passed its first reading, and between 10 May and 6 June 27 petitions were presented against it, from many parts of the country, including a Bristol 'journeymen's Petition' signed by 5,811.[22] And a book appeared, very likely commissioned by the artisans.[23]

But despite this extensive opposition and the feeble support for the bill, things went badly. The vested interests, including the City of London, were placated by alterations to the bill. And the artisans' efforts to arouse general public interest failed because attention focused abroad on the invasion of France, the fall of Napoleon and the peace settlements, while at home interest focused on the Corn Bill. Onslow's bill attracted little interest in the Commons, though there were some debates, in one of which Romilly made a decisive contribution. It finally passed on the understanding that there would be a further bill next session, and without a single division.

Petitions came steadily to the Lords until the committee stage, but these were from London alone, as there was not time to organise provincial ones, despite a request for delay to allow this to be done.

There was no serious debate in the Lords, and the bill finally passed on 18 July.

What part Gast played in all this is unclear, as the names of the leaders of the campaign are not known. But the shipwrights were particularly committed to apprenticeship and they certainly played a leading part in the agitation. They were one of the chief financial contributors, and the evidence to Rose's committee in 1813 came mainly from the dockside trades—shipwrights, ship and anchor-smiths, caulkers, mast and blockmakers, tanners, coopers and fell-mongers. The shipwrights were the only trade specifically mentioned in the resolutions at the January meeting.[24] And they sent a petition against Onslow's bill. Since Gast was at this time a prominent man in his trade, we can probably assume he was involved in the apprenticeship agitation.

4
THE END OF THE WARS

The shipwrights had failed to form a union, establish a price-book, secure legislative enforcement of apprenticeship or achieve the exclusion of India-built ships. Their anxiety was further increased by the fact that the navy itself was not only having fewer ships built but seemed no longer so committed to a healthy British shipbuilding industry. For with the timber crisis after 1804 it had abandoned its conservatism over the kinds of timber used in warships, and had had a number of vessels built in India and Bermuda. The last years of war and, especially, the first years of peace, were bad ones for Gast personally, the shipwrights, and the London trades generally.

By 1814 many Thames shipyards had been without work for some time. In April, with the departure of the East and West India fleets, there was hardly anything to do. In the whole of the 23 main yards there were only one ship being built and 26 receiving repairs, giving total employment to merely 308 shipwrights, 66 blacksmiths, 81 caulkers, 80 sawyers, 32 joiners and 111 labourers.[1] The royal yards were, of course, no refuge now. A number of witnesses testified to the general and unprecedented distress among the workmen, far worse than in 1802 or 1783. 'They are in a deplorable state, I dread to go to them, it looks like Sunday instead of week-days.'[2] Some were near starving, many went to the outports, and by April many were even applying for parish relief, something which, as proud, honourable, skilled men, they had always refused to do before, except some who were old and ill.

Gast suffered with the rest, but he had special disappointments. A leading man in Dudman's yard, he had for many years run much of its business and had every expection of becoming foreman. But things went wrong for Dudman, he virtually ceased business at the end of 1812, and in the autumn of 1813 sold his yard.[3] This cruel blow to Gast's hopes was made worse by the fact that, presumably because of Dudman's failure, he went broke and had to give up his public house, the King of Prussia. These must have been bad and sad years for him, the climax coming in December 1814 when he was imprisoned for fortune-telling.[4]

With the peace in 1814 many transport ships, gun-brigs and sloops-of-war were sold by the navy which, added to the lack of naval and East India Company orders, all depressed building. The resultant unemployment was increased by large discharges of workmen from the public service, and though more of these were house-carpenters, sawyers and labourers than shipwrights (who were the most important men, especially if war returned), the distress along the Thames is undoubted. The need for a proper union, recognised in 1811, was underlined when, with the end of the war, the masters again tried to reduce wages. Only the men's firmness prevented this, but their proposal to standardise piece-rates was rejected. Soon after, the St Helena Society collapsed. An unfriendly commentator saw the situation thus:

> The war, which threw out of employ so many thousands of families in Birmingham, Manchester, and other great manufacturing towns, created an increased demand for every species of labour connected with the dock-yards, whether public or private; the return of peace has reversed this state of things, and the shipwright is now the temporary sufferer.[5]

But the distress was *not* temporary, for the great wartime increase in shipping capacity was well in excess of peacetime needs, as other nations were becoming carriers again. Despite the rapid post-war increase in the total of foreign trade, this over-capacity meant a fall in freights, depreciation of shipping property and a long post-war depression in British shipping and therefore shipbuilding until 1835.[6] As Gast saw it in 1822:

> When this Bill [admitting India-built ships to the British registry] passed, the operative Shipwrights were left in a forlorn condition, and were from that time much in want of employ up to the Peace; but, when that took place, and nations took to be carriers for themselves, their distress became more manifest, and was increased doublefold, because their main city of refuge was broke up, and transferred to Asia.[7]

We may now understand the attitude of Gast and his fellow shipwrights in 1818. They were a highly skilled body of men who regarded themselves as superior to most artisans and entitled to a respectable position in life. The war years had underlined their conviction of their importance to the nation, for their role in the war effort was indisputable. It therefore seemed totally unjust that their ability to work and live in the accustomed way was threatened by changes over which they had no control—competition from out-ports where men could easily live on wages lower than those which in London secured a man a decent position in life, competition from foreign yards where wood was cheaper and labour cheaper because taxes were lower. The Thames shipwrights believed thay had a *right* to work and live in a certain way, and that this right was ignored in a situation where merchants were waiting 'till the price of labour and materials and everything finds its level'. The shipbuilding industry was very dependent on government policy, and the Thames yards stood in a special relation to the government. It was therefore particularly unjust that the government, who again and again had made demands which had been met but which had further increased the Thames' dependence and brought more workmen to London, should, now that they were no longer so vital, be prepared to treat them so callously in the rapid discharges and over Indian ships. The latter seemed particularly unfair because the pressure of naval work had itself at times prevented work being done for the Company and induced it to place orders in India. The shipwrights wanted recognition and protection, but, as Gast wrote, with 'not a Ship to build or repair—workhouses became crowded, and the only consolation from Government was, times would mend—this was only a "transition from War to Peace".'[8]

The distress of the shipwrights was not an isolated case among the artisans. The total defeat of the apprenticeship campaign was accompanied by further disappointments. In 1810 the boom broke, and credit crisis, depression and heavy unemployment made 1811 one of the worst years of the war. Recovery began again in 1812 but there was still a lot of suffering, and though the last years of the war were boom years, food prices had begun to rise rapidly in 1809 to reach an all-time peak in 1813, so that 1812 and 1813 saw heavy erosion of real wages. In 1814 the boom collapsed, and 1815 and 1816 were marked by growing depression, unemployment and wage cuts. Moreover food prices also rose in 1816, making this another very bad year indeed.[9] Many industries in London and the provinces were hit by the end of war contracts, and London, like other ports, also had the usual mass of men discharged from the army and, especially, the navy.

Several London trades experienced wage cuts, especially in 1816, including hatters, compositors, carpenters and coopers.[10] On the whole these were without a contest, though the carpenters put up a bitter fight. But they emphasised the importance of trade union organisation, and it was the strength of the London trades and the seasonal character of their work that prevented the catastrophic wage falls that took place in the provinces. But at the end of the wars the seriousness of the influx of labour into London industry was made plain. There was widespread unemployment among cabinet-makers and destitution among watchmakers. In tailoring and shoemaking the society-men were facing increasing competition from the cheaper labour of the small working masters and those they hired. The great warehouses were able to buy up stocks of shoes or clothes cheaply during depressed periods and release them at brisk times, and thus reduce the advantages to the men from seasonal fluctuations. Because they placed big orders they could force competitive price-cutting on the miserable little masters who therefore worked longer hours and employed more cheap labour to compensate, and so intensified the general competition for work and cheapening of labour.

The basic problem in tailoring and shoemaking was thus a glut of labour. This was equally the case in the Spitalfields silk industry.[11] This was a complex industry with a confusingly high degree of specialisation and constant changes to meet changes in fashion. But there were three main branches of weaving—broad, narrow and engine—and the silk dyers were another important section. Each of these had some societies and houses of call. The industry had been depressed at the end of the eighteenth century, but the expansion of 1798–1800 was a turning point, and the years up to 1816 were generally prosperous for the trade. The number of looms was estimated to have grown by over 2,000 in the years 1800–16, to make a total in the latter year of 13,000 or 14,000 looms and about 45,000 wage-earners. But, as in other trades, much of this expansion consisted of the taking of a large number of apprentices who, when they finished their time, competed for work with the men, and of the employment of women on tasks formerly confined to men. These developments, together with an influx of strangers and, in 1816, of men demobilised from army and navy, meant that in this industry too the labour market was overstocked, unemployment and competition for work grew, and earnings fell. The year 1816 was disastrous, and the sufferings in Spitalfields were far worse than elsewhere, with a number of relief efforts and soup kitchens to prevent actual starvation. Though the number of workers in the trade did continue to grow after 1816, this merely meant a deterioration in the condition of all. At the same time there had developed large employers who held large stocks of materials and, because they often needed work done very quickly, were glad of the existence of a reserve pool of labour, while the post-war depression enabled them to cut rates.

These were the most striking examples of problems common to many London trades—surplus labour, development of new capitalist firms, and competition from cheaper provincial labour. Foreign competition was also already a threat to shipbuilding and soon others were to suffer from it, but already it was clear that export firms were the leaders in attempts to cut labour costs. The larger shoe manufacturers who used Northampton labour were mainly producing for export, and the growing proportion of industrial production destined for export had bulked large in the attacks on apprenticeship.

The London artisans recognised all this, of course, Gast as well as any:

> Since the Peace trade and Commerce have fallen off, and additional population have been thrown into the market of Labour; foreigners meet Englishmen in the field of competition, and heavy taxation forces down the price of Labour, to enable the Tradesman and the manufacturer to meet the foreign markets, all sorts of schemes is had recourse to, to cheapen the Articles for exportation, and the working man as been the greatest sufferer.[12]

In the course of the notorious 'standard of living controversy', it has been suggested that real wages may have fallen during the wars but that thereafter, though money wages fell, food prices fell more quickly so that real wages rose. It is worth noting that Gast's analysis was the reverse. His experience was, of course, confined to some of the skilled London trades, but this may qualify any assumption that this group at least undoubtedly improved its living standards after the war. It has also been said that 'whereas it is generally assumed that living standards declined during the price-rises of the war years (and this is certainly true of the labourers, weavers and wholly unorganised workers), nevertheless the war stimulated many industries and (except during the Orders in Council) made for fuller employment'.[13] We may add that there is evidence that in many London trades earnings declined in the post-war period and much of the 1820s. The situation might then seem to be that during the war many skilled artisans profited while the rest suffered, and that after it the situation was reversed, the fall in prices benefiting the poorer rather than the mechanics experiencing a loss of work. But we cannot even be sure that it was only the mechanics who gained during the war, given the withdrawal of so much of the labour force into the military and considering the difficulty encountered in finding labour for the construction of the new London docks. Thus a recent study suggests that during the war there was no clear movement either way in real wages.[14] But its argument in favour of a rise in real wages after the war does not hold good for the skilled artisans, as it rests on setting a fall in prices against day-rate wages. In many industries piece-work was general, and day-rates take no account of unemployment. We know that after the war the day-rates of shipwrights and tailors remained the same, and those of shoemakers were cut a little; on this line of argument they all became better off. But in all three cases there is unambiguous evidence of a decline in *earnings*, due to unemployment. The calculations of real wages are only valid if the incidence of unemployment stayed constant. But there is evidence that it did worsen, and indeed this is to be expected given the end of the war demand and the demobilisation of 400,000 men (three-quarters of them returned to civilian life when the depression was most severe, between mid-1815 and the end of 1816). After 1815 population growth does seem to have a Malthusian tendency.[15] 'Why should we suppose, in a period of very rapid population-growth, that the proportion of employed and skilled to casual and unemployed workers should move in favour of the former?'[16] In many artisan trades, whatever the situation for the population generally, the development was towards a 'surplus of labour'.

What were the reactions of the London trades? Some were obvious enough—trade union action over wage rates and hours—but this could do little about unemployment, though limiting hours could spread work. Generally the trades clung to apprenticeship and tried to maintain control of recruitment in the better firms at least. But since 1814 this could not be done through the law courts, only through trade union bargaining power. Control of recruitment was a general policy, on the whole successful among shipwrights or hatters, less so among others, but in most cases it tended to leave the skilled artisans clinging on to the control in the better-class sectors of the industry while those they excluded swelled the ever-growing cheaper, dishonourable sector. Trade union enforcement of apprenticeship and high wages thus did not solve the problem of competition with cheaper workers in London and the country. Though apprenticeship was an important concern in the marked trade union consciousness of these years, it also emphasised how this consciousness was still exclusive and concerned with the interests only of the respectable section of the working population.

Apprenticeship was a traditional policy, but in their efforts to maintain their respectable position the artisans could be led into new fields. For in the unfavourable post-war situation, individual societies were finding this defence difficult, and some were led to support supra-trade activity. The chief form of this was inter-trade solidarity. This was not a big step, for it was basically a strengthening of existing practices, and there had been ideas of a permanent delegate body during the apprenticeship campaign. The ideas revived in 1818. The economic recovery of 1817–18 provoked attempts in the latter year to raise wages, not to attain a new standard of living but to undo the 1816 reductions.[17] This continuing conciousness of weakness produced at the end of 1818, under Gast's leadership, the 'Philanthropic Hercules', an attempt to unite the London trades in a general body. Each member trade would have representatives on the general committee, but each would also have its own committee and hold its own funds unless they were required by the central committee.[18] It was thus mainly a formalisation of existing practices. And it truly represented the attitudes of the London artisans. It quite clearly expressed their conviction both of their value to society and the superior reward that was due to skill. It appealed to 'the Working Mechanic', and its aim was to secure a proper reward for 'superior talent and industry' and 'that decent and respectable appearance in society as becomes valuable members'. But equally it reflected the sense that these were being eroded through 'repeated reductions in the fair and proper value of our exertions and talents' due to tyrannical masters and workmen ready to accept lower pay. The result was 'to reduce the Mechanic down to the capacity of a menial servant' so that 'the sun of your independence and respectability has long past the zenith of its splendours'. Mechanics must act to restore their self-respect; they were urged to 'put a proper value on yourselves as MEN and Mechanics', 'consider yourselves members of society', 'unite in the mutual support of your reputation and respectability', 'to regain and support our rank and reputation in society as men'. The aim was thus conservative, the 'just, legal, and customary price for his labour', to maintain the traditional position in society. Custom was to guide wage demands, for 'a book of prices belonging to such trade shall be given in to the committee for the purpose of their guidance', 'but should such trade have no book of prices, the committee shall summon four of the oldest men, or such proficient persons, members of the society who can give every information to elucidate the dispute'. It was, as Place put it, 'John Gast's Scheme to keep up Wages'. Its aim was to preserve the superiority of mechanics to other working men, and it called on them to leave 'the indolent, the careless, and the lukewarm part of your profession'; 'every person or persons desirous of becoming a member must come voluntary, and on his or their own part, and from a just sense of his or their respectability, and who is not a companion of the low and vulgar part of the community'. But changed circumstances made it essential to 'watch over your own interests with attention and vigilance', and adopt new practices; 'for the express purpose of maintaining the rank, as valuable Mechanics, we feel the necessity of Union among all Mechanics', 'therefore we call upon all Trades, desirous of becoming free and respectable, to send their Deputy with proper instructions, to consolidate the GENERAL UNION'.

But in difficult conditions all forms of industrial action might seem inadequate, and the trades were led to consider other forms of action, of which the most obvious was political. The London trades had shown in 1800 and 1813–14 that they were fully conversant with techniques of political campaigning. One of the functions that trade societies shared with the old guilds was that of acting as a pressure group to represent their trade as one of the 'interests' which all agreed it was the aim of the constitution to represent. The mechanics even saw themselves as all belonging to an order or estate of vital importance to the community. And some of the threats that respectable artisans saw to their respectability were very directly concerned with politics. One was taxation, which could cause distress for a journeyman and bankruptcy for a master. Another was currency fluctuations, for an artisan who made the same type of articles using the same techniques and taking the same amount of time, saw his product as having an intrinsic value, and was very conscious of the injustice of fluctuations in the monetary price of the product. The great debates over the currency system at the end of the wars heightened his interest. Taxation and paper money might cause indebtedness, which the debtor laws made much worse by imprisonment. In 1814 Gast's brother William was in prison in Bristol for debt,[19] and in 1816 and 1817 the London debtors' gaols were very full.

In the distress of 1816 many individual trades petitioned Parliament for relief. And in London towards the end of that year a 'committee of trades' was formed with this aim. Four men brought the petition to Sidmouth in January 1817.[20] But all these campaigns, whether by individual trades or joint ones over apprenticeship or distress, ended in failure.

Participation in politics is not the same as seeking political reforms but it was not surprising that this activity and lack of success fostered a bitterness against the rulers and the political system, a receptiveness to the widespread ideas that political power lay with a corrupt few who feathered their own nests at the expense of the nation whose real interests were sacrificed. That vitally important interest, the mechanics, was neglected, and even oppressed by unjust taxation and legislation like the Combination Act which the Philanthropic Hercules denounced. Some, like Gast, felt this interest would not be properly considered unless it were properly represented. The carpenters met at their house of call, the Argylle Arms, and called for Political Reform.[21] The chairman of the 'distressed mechanics', Thomas, was a Jacobin (and police informer), and another leading figure was the Jacobin Thomas Preston, who was building up a following among the desperate Spitalfields weavers. Preston was secretary to the committee which organised the first massive Spa Fields meeting of 15 November, to which placards invited distressed manufacturers, mariners, artisans and others to come to petition the Prince Regent and Parliament for relief.[22] They asserted their *right* to relief from the rich. Preston's associates were the more important James Watson and Arthur Thistlewood, and this group found a great response amidst the bitterness of unemployed artisans, discharged sailors, indebted small masters and the inhabitants of debtors' gaols. The huge crowds at Spa Fields exceeded all expectations. But of these groups the artisans had not only a clearer perception of their specific identity and interests, but they also had the greatest organisation and communication network. By the end of the wars it was to the artisans that the Jacobins looked as the potentially revolutionary class. 'Oh said Thistlewood we must have the Mechanics, and not do as they did in Col. Despard's times.'[23] Thistlewood was later to demonstrate the accuracy of this observation most emphatically. But the adhesion of Gast in 1818 was to intensify their hopes, and emphasised the artisan element in radical activity.

Part Two
POST-WAR
RADICAL POLITICS

PROLOGUE

The Spa Fields meetings of 15 November and 2 December 1816 were of sensational importance. They inaugurated a period of popular radical agitation that lasted, with many fluctuations, until 1821. They drew public attention to the Spenceans, a group hitherto virtually unknown, and made the national reputation of Henry Hunt. Hunt and some of the Spenceans were the central figures in London ultra-radicalism for several years, and it was with them that Gast associated. The Spa Fields meetings also drew condemnation from the established groups of reformers in London who feared that the crowd was escaping their control and felt that the reckless actions the meetings provoked, especially the attempted insurrection on 2 December, would ruin the very real chances of dislodging the government and securing reforms, and would give the ministers a justification for repression. This belief seemed vindicated when in the spring of 1817 the government secured the power of imprisonment without trial and legislation placing very stringent restrictions on the right of public meeting. The Spa Fields meetings therefore divided 'moderate reformers' from the radicals.

Radicalism was not, of course, confined to London, for post-war distress, worst in 1816, created discontent all over the country. Pre-eminently this discontent took a political form and, given the political situation, there was an unprecedented upsurge in political radicalism. For the political situation was unsettled, the government was weak in Parliament and unpopular in the country, and plebeian political agitation was encouraged by preceding propertied campaigns against Corn Laws and Property Tax. These, and the failure of specific campaigns, led, under the direction of veteran Jacobins, to the growth of plebeian radicalism in the winter of 1816 to 1817. But artisan radicalism was not at all a new thing, and its main features had been firmly established. Circumstances now led to its widespread expression, and the extent of the agitation and apparent political polarisation of the country gave this radicalism depth and intensity.

Radical artisans rarely acted alone, and the world of the reformers was characterised by constantly shifting alignments, alliances and rifts. There were established groups of reformers in London, veterans of opposition to successive administrations for ten years and more. They had two foci. One was Westminster, where a group under Samuel Brookes managed meetings, demonstrations and the elections to Parliament of the demagogic Sir Francis Burdett. The other was the City of London, a self-governing republic jealous of its privileges. Reformers' strength lay in the Courts of Common Hall, which all liverymen could attend, and the democratically-elected Common Council. The most active reformer was Robert Waithman, the most prestigious Matthew Wood, who became Lord Mayor in 1815 and was re-elected in 1816.

These reformers were very active in the post-war period. But from 1816 a number of radicals arose in London alienated, for a variety of reasons, from the established reformers. They drew strength from provincial radicals, for the radicalism of the weaving and framework-knitting villages was a tougher affair than the radicalism of urban artisans. It drew on very strong communal solidarity to have a much stronger character, and it was encouraged to be more vehement by the very obvious weakness of the authorities. For these could never hope to control the outlying communities and were often completely in the dark as to what was happening. And so radicals like Hunt, Thomas Wooler and Dr James Watson gained importance and also built up a London following in their opposition to the 'moderate' Westminster and City reformers.

This ultra-radicalism was engaged in conscious confrontation with the political authorities. Its methods, the platform and the press, were a development of techniques developed in the later eighteenth century by groups of reformers and Dissenters. But although 'public opinion' was agreed by all as having a legitimate function in the constitution, it was seen by traditionalists as a checking force, to pronounce opinions on matters raised by Parliament itself, which remained free to notice or ignore the expressions of public opinion. Moreover, the press in the eighteenth century had had a socially restricted readership, and county and other legitimate meetings were called by proper authorities like lord lieutenant, sheriff or mayor. Yet the radicals were now seeking to raise issues on their own initiative and force them on the attention of Parliament; this 'dictation' was seen as unconstitutional. The press now reached a much wider and more humble readership. And public meetings were called by individuals and groups quite independently of properly-constituted authorities. Someone 'irresponsible' like Hunt could, by attending a meeting, bring a town to a standstill; this power was seen as quite illegitimate. And so to loyalists the mere holding of the great 'Peterloo' meeting was 'insurrectionary'. On their side, radicals saw the political structure as so hopelessly corrupt and interlocked that they despaired of achieving reform through legal channels. The most usual means envisaged was a democratically elected National Convention.[1] Their strategy was to enlighten and unite the people in order to build up an irresistible mass campaign but they were always expecting violent repression from the authorities, which they felt justified in resisting. The often ill-informed government, recognising this threat, sometimes to an exaggerated extent (especially in 1817), sought to repress it.

Post-war radicalism had two peaks. The first was 1816–17, with a number of Hampden Clubs, especially in the Midlands, West Riding, and South Lancashire and Cheshire, in touch with one another and with Major Cartwright and Thomas Cleary in London. These two guided the securing of signatures to petitions for Reform, and called the Convention of delegates at the Crown and Anchor in London in January 1817 to organise the presentation of these petitions to the House of Commons. The second peak was in 1819, especially with the wave in the summer of very successful public meetings, culminating in the greatest of all, at Manchester, on 16 August. In both cases, the government countered with repression: in 1817 Habeas Corpus was suspended, leading radicals were imprisoned and public meetings were restricted, and in 1819 'Peterloo', the brutal disposal of the Manchester meeting, was followed by the Six Acts. In both years the repression, coinciding with economic recovery, led to a slump in radical activity. On the one hand, most radicals retreated to educational and cultural activity and 'front' organisations like funds for political prisoners, and on the other, small groups engaged in plans for co-ordinated insurrection. These produced episodes like the Derbyshire Insurrection of 1817 and the Cato Street Conspiracy of 1820, but such efforts were always deranged by spies, real and imagined.

The Six Acts at the end of 1819 were an attempt to return to the eighteenth century by restricting the readership of the press and by only allowing public meetings approved by proper authorities. But this attempt was nullified by the well-nigh incredible Queen

Caroline affair. This, again, was not the creation of radicals, but they certainly exploited it. And although the aim of the agitation might seem insignificant, its political importance was great. Among other things, a large number of artisan trades took part in open radical political activity, and towards the end the radicals and artisans were making all the running and achieved the most successful popular demonstrations of the whole post-war period. In the course of this campaign Gast achieved a level of co-ordination between artisan trades which lasted right through the 1820s.

5
GAST THE RADICAL

Gast's radicalism sprang from the artisan experience and assumptions, and from an assimilation of radical arguments. It became fully articulated in 1818 when he had experienced the post-war depression both generally and in particular in Thames shipbuilding, deserted as it was by the government, and when he became fully involved in London ultra-radicalism. He saw the artisans suffering from wage reductions, unemployment and infringements of their rights. In their distress they needed and deserved relief and protection from government, but this they were not receiving. The mechanics and labouring people also suffered more than any others from the burden of taxation. Here he was expressing the age-old popular resistance to taxes, especially against indirect taxes. British taxes and excises fell mainly on articles of consumption and thus pressed on the poor. Taxes thus, as radicals argued, redistributed wealth, from the poor to the rich (who profited from the State). But, true to his concentration on the artisans, Gast not only stressed that the taxes fell on consumption and that more powerful people merely made up for any losses through taxation at the expense of working people, they also had bad economic effects. They raised the cost of living and therefore the price of British products so that their sale abroad was impaired, and they reduced spending power at home and therefore the home market for British products. The effects of taxation were thus much worse than the actual amount paid in taxes. This is a reminder that we should not automatically write off condemnation of taxation (or the currency system) as an outmoded 'old analysis' that ignored a new economic analysis. Gast's political ideas were always closely related to his economic views.

The mechanics thus suffered from taxation, economic depression and a lack of protection. Whereas other interests received political recognition, mechanics did not. But in fact employers also suffered from the economic effects of taxation, and the fact that this enormous taxation was due to the 'mad-brained war' emphasised how the interests of the nation as a whole were being sacrificed by the corrupt few. So Gast supported Reform, which would reduce corruption and taxation and secure a fairer consideration of the interests of the people at large.

There was in fact no unity among the London reformers, and they could very often only agree on opposing something. A variety of outlooks, influences and traditions were expressed by Sir Francis Burdett, authentic spokesman of eighteenth-century gentry radicalism and of upper-class moral disdain, resentment and intransigeance over favouritism and corruption, and demagogic popular hero; by City of London reformers led by Wood and Waithman; by the Westminster leaders, favourers of liberal reforms and political organisation; and by smaller groups around people like the veteran Major Cartwright. But however much radicals disagreed over arguments, aims, ideals, approach, alliances and tactics, they did have common ground in some broadly shared analysis of the political structure and the nature of the political power held by local and national elites. As they saw it, the undermining of the 1688 system, with its triennial parliaments and exclusion of placemen from Parliament, had enabled a small number of peers and other powerful individuals to monopolise political power. They controlled many constituencies, especially the small boroughs, and so decided the majority of the membership of the House of Commons. They formed governments and tied MPs to them through government and service posts and pensions, so that the Commons further lost their independence. This corrupt oligarchy was the 'boroughmongers', the 'borough faction', whom the nation was unable to control but whom it maintained through taxes. Because there was no check to their power, corruption, debts and taxes grew apace, and the country was debased, robbed and deprived of its rights through unconstitutional innovations. Ministers engaged in the sale of seats, the departments of state were riddled with abuses, and promotions in the armed services dependent on nepotism, favouritism and money. Corruption and abuses were piling up, and few MPs made efforts to check them. Honourable exceptions, like Samuel Whitbread, Lord Folkestone and Colonel Wardle merely threw the general corruption into relief. The system was repressive as well as corrupt, in the use of the very vague law of libel against criticism, the imprisonment of reformers, Pitt's repression of the mid-1790s and a new wave of prosecutions in 1809. Radicals denied the sovereignty of Parliament, for political power was conditional on the safeguarding of people's rights. They affirmed the right of 'resistance' and even the right of the nation to overthrow tyranny. The system resulted in high taxation to meet the costs of prodigal expenditure, the mass of sinecures and the interest on the National Debt. But this debt, which enriched financiers, was not really a national one as it was incurred by the oligarchy in its efforts to put down liberty all over the world. For Britain was to blame for the outbreak of war with France in 1793, which caused the authoritarian perversion of the French Revolution and the Terror, and for the resumption of war in 1803 and again in 1815 to deprive the French people of the ruler they wished for and to restore the contemptible Bourbons who brought with them the White Terror. The peace settlement had many injustices, especially the fate of Poland, and left the odious Tsar dominant in Europe and free to threaten the Mediterranean or India. The wars had been unnecessary, unjust and mismanaged. The remedies for all this varied, but usually involved the destruction of the borough faction by restoring both the separation of powers and the independence of the House of Commons through excluding placemen, shortening the length of parliaments, ending corruption in elections, disfranchising the small boroughs and, often, widening the franchise.

In their tavern clubs, debating groups, coffee houses and discussions of newspapers at work or leisure, radical artisans adopted most of this analysis of the structure of power, the terminology and the techniques of campaigning. These had been developed by other social groups, but this does not mean that artisan radicalism was uncritical, derivative or detached from their basic attitudes, even though for many artisans the changes needed to reform the system did not have to include the vote for themselves. The basically anti-State character of radicalism struck a very responsive chord, for, as we have seen, their attitude to the State was a very negative and suspicious one, and they were strongly against attempts to interfere in such things as benefit societies.[1] The radical concentration on taxation was equally acceptable, as was the radical view of political relationships as primary. Political influence was the way to wealth rather than *vice versa*. The rulers were rich because they were powerful. This was a realistic analysis, when so many of their employers were men of small means, and capitalism had always been linked to the State, the Thames shipbuilders being a good example. Reform could therefore take the negative form of a removal of sources of political power—corruption, privileged chartered companies, Bank of England, or standing army.

A letter of Gast's in the *Independent Whig* is presumably a sign that he read what was then the chief radical newspaper.[2] 'The *Independent Whig* is now the most popular paper in London.'[3] This authentically represented the 'true Whiggism' of the 1770s and 1780s. It condemned the breaches of the 1688 constitution and encroachments on individual liberties, opposed slavery, and supported legal reform, full rights for the Irish, and parliamentary Reform. But it did not support universal suffrage, agreeing with reformers in the City, Westminster and Middlesex in support of Burdett's proposal for giving the vote to all householders paying poor rates and assessed taxes.

In 1812 Gast backed the Bristol candidacy of Sir Samuel Romilly because of his opposition to corruption, taxation and slavery. His attitude must have been typical of many radical artisans. Yet Romilly, though a supporter of parliamentary Reform, disapproved of Burdett's plan as going too far. Gast explained his support for Romilly.

> It appeared to him that Sir Samuel Romilly was not only entitled to support of the opulent, but, perhaps in a more peculiar degree, to the support of the poor and working classes of the freemen, inasmuch as he had always been the advocate of humanity, the friend of his country, and, as he conceived, the true friend of the working classes.—While the system of the present Ministers was extending pauperism all over the land, he thought the honest and able exertions of such men as Sir Samuel could alone check so destructive a system. He himself had left Bristol at a very early age, to seek a residence where he could be free from oppression, and where he could better encourage the generous feelings which he thought became a free-born Englishman.[4]

It is a fairly negative radicalism, but one which has a clear conception of the order to which Gast belonged.

The Bristol elections of 1812 were very stormy ones.[5] Since 1790 the two parties had shared the representation, even to the extent of Whigs' not interfering in the re-election of Tories in by-elections. But in 1812 two rival Whig candidates stood, Edward Protheroe and Romilly, and so for the first time since the 1780s a contest was promised.

The Whig split was mainly over slavery but Romilly's candidacy also revealed the divisions within the Whig party generally, for his liberal views and support for reform, including parliamentary Reform, were well known. His views made him popular, and when he visited Bristol in April he had a great reception, many trade societies joining the procession with their banners. The carpenters' society even started a fund to relieve any members who were dismissed from employment when they voted for Romilly.[6]

Whenever there was a Bristol election, the election agents made their supporters freemen in droves, and arranged for the transport of non-resident freemen to vote. In 1774, 2,100 freemen had been created and 400 freemen brought from London.[7] And so Romilly's supporters set about organising London support. The organiser in Deptford was John Gast, at his public house.[8] He also spoke at a London meeting of Romilly's supporters.

> This speech, delivered with considerable animation by a man stating himself to be a mere working mechanic, excited very considerable applause.

The Bristol election was complicated by the candidacy, on the slogan of independence, of Henry Hunt, who had a beer-brewing business in Bristol. His introduction to Reform ideas had been in 1800, when he became a friend of the reformer Henry Clifford, who opened his eyes to malpractices in the legal profession and corruption generally, and of the City radical Samuel Waddington. Hunt became a member of the Tooke–Burdett set and a Foxite, and as such supported Burdett's candidacy in the Middlesex elections. But he exhibited classic disillusion with the Foxites in office in 1806, as did Burdett and Cobbett, and became the foe of Whig duplicity and a fervent supporter of independent politics. In the 1807 election he not only supported Burdett for Westminster, but also called for independence in his native Wiltshire, where he was a freeholder, and at the Bristol hustings he tried to propose a third candidate. He became leader of a Burdettite group in Bristol:

> We have identified ourselves with Sir Francis Burdett, the independent, honest Representative for the City of Westminster, the man who is the best friend of the Constitution, the whole Constitution, and nothing but the Constitution of England.[9]

He now in 1812 announced his candidacy in opposition to 'those Clubs that have for so many years bought and sold you like Cattle in a market', to all MPs who had voted against Burdett's proposed reply to the speech from the throne in January 1812 (which included Romilly), to the war, and to the Corporation and their current manoeuvres over the common lands.

He could hope to gain support from supporters of independence (in 1812 an institution of 'Bristol Independence' was formed to relieve anyone who lost his job for the way he voted) and from reformers. He could also hope to profit from the discontent among the middling classes more than could Romilly, whom they blamed for the Arrest Bill and the alteration to the bankruptcy law. The possibilities of popular support had been shown in 1810 when a crowd attacked the Recorder, Vicary Gibbs the Attorney General, and walls were chalked with 'No Gibbs' and 'Burdett for ever!'[10] There was also a strong popular dislike of strangers, and so Hunt could benefit from the Protheroe party's cries of 'No London Lawyer' and 'No Frenchified Whig' (Romilly being of Huguenot descent).

A complication ensued in June when the Tory MP resigned, which meant a by-election merely to fill the vacancy until the general election only a few months away. The Whigs did not interfere as it was the Tory seat, but in accordance with his pledge Hunt stood, to the intense annoyance of the Tories. Moreover, since it was Hunt, the Tories could not use bribery so openly, and sent a letter to their parish committees:

> Gentlemen,
>   As our opponents would be glad to take advantage of any inadvertent Act of Mr. Davis's Friends. The Committee of Management think it absolutely necessary to caution the Committees of the several Parishes not to do any Act which can in any shape be deemed contrary to the Statutes against Bribery & Treating—They therefore request that you will not give any Voter even a glass of Beer or the smallest Trifle or Promise whatever in order to influence his Vote.[11]

Hunt kept the poll open to the end, costing the Tories £1,000 a day. But he gained few votes, most of his support coming from the working population, who marched in huge crowds to the cry 'Hunt and Peace' behind a loaf of bread on a pole and a Cap of Liberty, cheered his stentorian harangues, assailed anyone wearing blue with a volley of mud, stones and dead cats, and attacked the White Lion (headquarters of the Loyal and Constitutional Club) and Council House. Troops were called to restore order.

The Bristol general election began on 6 October, and was as violent as expected. Between 29 September and 28 October, 1,689 new freedoms were taken up, including 616 for Romilly (Gast among them), 568 for Davis (the Tory) and 403 for Protheroe.[12] Soon after the poll began Davis and Protheroe, the two political sections of the West India interest, allied, and so Romilly decided defeat was certain and withdrew, though Hunt again kept the poll going as long as possible. The voting reflected a clear division of political opinion into reformers and anti-reformers.[13]

One of the London freemen who voted was Gast, and he voted for both Romilly and Hunt. He had presumably been brought solely to vote for Romilly. According to Hunt, 'almost all the London voters did this, although they were urged to vote for Romilly alone'.[14]

Hunt was probably referring specifically to Gast, for he drew up a petition to the House of Commons to set aside the election result because of corruption, bribery, intimidation, illegal presence of miltary force and treating. A select committee was set up though the result was confirmed. Signatures to the petition were organised in Bristol and London, in the latter place by two men, a Westminster reformer and Gast.[15] In 1812 Gast therefore seems to have transferred political allegiance from Whig to radical, and he remained a Huntite for the next twenty years.

It may have been this association with Hunt, to which he referred in 1818, that drew Gast into support for universal suffrage, but this seems unlikely. The cutting down of government, corruption and taxation did not in itself necessitate giving the vote to all men, but it is hardly surprising that many artisans who supported political reform felt they should themselves have the vote, especially as in many places they already did, like Gast in 1812. Moreover, the more the political nation was widened the more an artisan who had entered it could feel that the vote was an essential recognition of his status and worth in society, and the more artisans felt their needs were being ignored the more did they feel that their 'interest' should be directly represented in Parliament. Universal suffrage (for there was no other system that would give all artisans the vote, though criminals and paupers could be excluded) required no particular expertise, for its main function would be negative, to check tyranny and corruption, prevent the aggrandisement of the State and keep politics a simple business, and artisans could surely analyse their own needs better than anyone else. Popular democracy was all the more desirable because it was familiar; artisan organisations, notably benefit societies, were democratic in government. And so 'universal' (manhood) suffrage was a common aspect of artisan radicalism.

It was Paine who established the language of plebeian radicalism through Gast's lifetime into the Chartist period and beyond. He expressed the basic elements of artisan radicalism—government was parasitic and should be drastically shorn by abolishing nearly all of its institutions; taxes were a form of robbery of the useful part of the nation to the profit of the useless and so should be abolished and replaced by an income tax which above £23,000 a year should be 100%; the sovereignty of the people and the corruption of the system meant that reform should come about not through existing institutions but through a democratic national convention of the people. And Paine also put forward specific proposals that were directly related to what we have seen as some of the artisans' chief concerns: he wanted the ending of taxes on consumption and he advocated old age pensions, funeral grants, and publicly financed lodging houses and workhouses in London for immigrant workmen.

Painite radicalism was kept alive in London throughout the war years by such people as John Gale Jones, a surgeon of very great eloquence who had in the 1790s been one of the chief members and touring speakers of the London Corresponding Society. Throughout the war years he was the chief figure in the popular debating societies where he and other 'shirtless Cicero's' as poverty-stricken as himself maintained some continuity in popular republicanism, despite magisterial harassment.[16] He was steadily shunned by the Westminster reformers. This, and his poverty, no doubt helped his consistent adherence to the Painite republicanism and commitment to mass agitation that he had displayed in the 1790s.

In 1817 this Painite republicanism was given much greater currency in *Sherwin's Political Register*, and the man who eventually took it over, Richard Carlile, the most unswerving and determined publisher of them all, republished a series of Paine's works. Gast's deism and radicalism were later to make him a supporter of Carlile.

But already by 1818, at least, he supported the full radical programme to remove the plentiful abuses (including the Corn Laws), waste and selfish aristocratic misgovernment, to end tyranny, and to restore the exclusive rights of every British subject, the rights of the Constitution. Like other radicals he justified universal suffrage on the grounds of natural rights, and reasoning that all who paid taxes or could fight in army and navy should have representation. Like them, he argued that the prevalent political corruption meant that Reform could never come through Parliament itself. It could only come through action out of doors, by a united nation, and this unity could only be achieved if the Reform were to benefit all, namely universal suffrage; only then would the nation insist on its full and just rights. 'Moderate reform' would therefore not do, and had no more chance of acceptance in Parliament anyway; it was a delusion, a 'mere insinuation and pretence'. He therefore distrusted the Burdettites as not going far enough. 'The intention of Gast I believe is . . . to Form a Political Party to outrival that of Sr. Francis Burdett in Point of Popularity.'[17] Yet radical reform did not mean outrage or slavery but 'the promotion of liberty and the general extension of liberal enlightened principles throughout every corner of the world'.[18] The lower orders had as much ability as the higher, and ran their own affairs and benefit societies better than ministers did public affairs. Gast's acceptance of Paine's ideas included the replacement of all taxes by an income tax.

Journeymen artisans had been the chief element in the radical London Corresponding Society of the 1790s, but they did not form the entire membership. As in earlier and later movements, there were small masters, shopkeepers, printers and booksellers, engravers and professional men (medical men, schoolmasters, Dissenting clergy), as well as porters, coalheavers, labourers, soldiers and sailors. Paine's radicalism was directed at all these, not working men alone. But the artisans were the most important element, and the Corresponding Society was marked in its organisation and government by the forms of their societies. Thus its first rule, 'That the number of our Members be unlimited', was a common rule in benefit societies.[19] With repression and decline, the organisations of the artisans made them of relatively greater importance, and there may have been specific attempts by Jacobins to infiltrate them.[20] But, as we have seen, the artisans also saw themselves as a separate order with specific interests, and political activity was but one among several alternatives. Shopkeepers and professional men were more prone to a purely political radicalism. Thus, although by the end of the wars popular radicalism, fed by high prices, high taxation, indebtedness, war weariness and then unemployment was an established fact in London, it was never confined to working men alone.

Radicals saw those holding power as distinct in interest from the rest of the nation, on which they were parasitic. The nation could therefore function quite well without them. The notion of parasitic implied a concept of usefulness, and for centuries there had been country gentlemen who regarded themselves as useful and indispensable members of society, in contrast to parasitic courtiers, civil servants or lawyers. But in the case of the artisans, we have seen how the concept of labour, and useful, valuable labour at that, was an essential element in their self-definition. It distinguished them from the poor below, but it also distinguished them from those above, and the traditional definition of a gentleman was that he did not have to work for his living. To artisans who felt a pride in their order and worth, this distinction easily became a moral one, and labour became a criterion of value and social criticism. Everyone *should* work; anyone who did not maintain himself by the sweat of his brow, whether poor or rich, was battening on the rest of society. Thus artisan radicalism could easily extend to opposition to the ruling class in general, to the 'idle', whether landowners, holders of office, financiers, or privileged merchants, even to the extent of regarding them as totally expendable. In this the artisans classed themselves with small masters, shopkeepers and professional men, who all lived by useful labour, and so showed themselves true heirs of the seventeenth-century 'industrious sort of people', the yeomen, artisans and small and middling trades, the men of some economic independence, neither propertyless nor privileged, who had adopted Puritanism. And their Puritanism had expressed their ideals in asserting the dignity and worth of labour, that none had the right to live unless they worked, and that it was useful labour that justified property.[21] By 1800 most of the religious Puritanism had gone, but the social ideals were much the same. 'Men were entitled to wealth, but only if they could be *seen* to be hard at work.'[22] Even the entrepreneurial capitalist could be seen as productive, for those who did not work and were rich were mainly landowners and men who gained wealth through the spoils of public office or political connections. But most capitalists, such as in shipbuilding, building or tailoring, not only owed their position to governmental orders but were basically middlemen, so might be regarded also as expendable.

Artisan radicals made labour the chief touchstone of full political rights. But, as we have seen, they often saw this in terms of 'property', and thus gave their demands a conservative form by defining their labour as property which gave them a claim to political citizenship, for the purpose of government was to protect life, liberty and property. And the criterion of labour of course did not necessitate any modification of their sense of superiority to the mass of the poor. In the 1640s radicals who stressed the importance of labour to political representation were willing to exclude paupers and others who did not labour. The concept of 'the people' excluded the very poor.[23] In 1818 the woolsorter John Wade, in his periodical, the *Gorgon*, which was aimed at the trade societies, divided the population into, on one hand, the productive classes (husbandmen, mechanics, labourers, employers, professional men, etc.) and, on the other, corruption (nobles, churchmen, legal officials, civil servants) and nondescripts (paupers and State creditors).[24] In the same year one of the members of Thomas Evans' group of Spenceans divided the nation into five classes—mechanics; working people and labourers; merchants; boroughmongers and great lords; and kings and princes—of which the first was the most important and most useful to society.[25]

Gast was deeply conscious of the interest of the mechanics as a body and their need for direct representation. For though their interests were usually ignored, they deserved the greatest consideration as they created the wealth of the country. In 1802 he had expressed this conviction of the superiority of labour:

> The produce of his labor, to the mechanic, is surely as much an estate of inheritance in him, as the right of ownership over a large tract of land, is to its lordly proprietor; however uninterruptedly it may have decended from father to son, for many generations.—There was a time, when such ownership of land did not exist: and its exclusive proprietorship, depends wholly upon custom, sanctioned by the positive law of the country;—but there never was a time, when, strictly speaking, any man, or description of men, had a right or property in, or to the personal labor, skill, or industry, of the other parts of the community, however they may, at times, have assumed it.—Thus we see, that the labor of the mechanic, stands upon a firmer basis, with respect to the originality of its right, than the right to landed property: in fact, That of the mechanic is physical, and consequently coeval with his existence: the other, at best, is but legal;—and the superiority of the former over the latter, few persons will have the temerity to dispute.[26]

In 1802 Gast had thus contrasted the rights of labour with those of landownership, for landowners were the best and chief example of rich people who did not labour. Radicals were also very concerned about the 'waste lands' of England, areas that were capable of agricultural productivity but which were not so used, mainly because of the policy of their owners. To many people, the fact of hunger alongside uncultivated waste lands upheld a criticism of landowners who were not fulfilling their duty to the community. This interest increased during the French wars, when the need for more food became urgent and there were criticisms of landowners who did not meet their patriotic duty to increase productivity. But many also saw a solution to pauperism in settling some of the destitute on such lands, in small-holdings where they could become self-supporting and regain self-respect. This was especially true among those who saw the basic cause of urban pauperism in the forcing of people off the land and their consequent migration to the towns. The recreation of a peasantry would reverse this process and restore a healthier social system. Many 'Tory' philanthropists supported such schemes, even though they implied a rejection of capitalist agriculture; but these views were also held by many radicals and often implied a criticism of existing property rights.

In this context of criticism of the existing landed system, radicals often had recourse to the famous 'Norman theory', according to which the aristocracy were descendants of the brigands and freebooters who had come over with William the Bastard in 1066 and forcibly seized the lands of England. The possessions and power of the landed aristocracy were therefore not legitimate, being based ultimately on conquest, a conquest that had destroyed the free society, wards and moots of Anglo-Saxon England.

Such ideas help explain support for Spenceanism. After the death of Thomas Spence in 1814, the leadership of the forty-strong group of Spencean 'low tradesmen' was taken over by Thomas Evans, who had been the last secretary of the Corresponding Society. In 1815–16 he wrote a series of articles in the *Independent Whig*, the paper Gast seems to have read. Evans was a typical ultra-radical in his political analysis, and like many others went back to Anglo-Saxon days for his model. He also opposed the war—England should really have fought in alliance with France against Russia, the stronghold of 'feudalism'. He followed Paine's republicanism and his arguments that the Bank of England caused distress through paper money and excess issue, which forced prices up.[27] In this last he was near the view of many artisans, including Gast, as he was also in his rejection of foreign trade and exports. Both Gast and Evans emphasised the importance of the home market and the fact that taxation was checking consumption and so causing distress. They also rejected Malthusianism as implying that distress was inevitable.

Evans also propagated Spence's plan for land reform, drawing like him on Dissenting ideas concerning the law of the Jubilee in the ancient Hebrew state, which had been an agrarian republic. He asserted that the Spencean system had previously existed under Moses and Alfred and among the early Christians, Spenceanism being in fact true Christianity.

Spence's real importance in radical history lies in his pioneering of new methods of propaganda—cheap tracts and verse, slogans, tokens, wall-chalkings, free-and-easy and so on. He is best known however because his advocacy of common ownership of land guarantees him a place in the 'history of socialism'. He was therefore no 'typical' plebeian radical, but he was undoubtedly part of the plebeian radical movement and expressed all its basic attitudes. His polity would carry decentralisation to extreme lengths, with the old parish as the basic unit. He lamented that an unpleasant commercial spirit was spreading in society and disrupting more traditional and more just relationships. His advocacy of expropriation of land fitted in very well with current attitudes over the parasitic character of landlords, land monopoly, Norman yoke, and waste and common lands. The rent from this land would effect the radical aim of abolishing existing taxes. And though the land would be communally owned it would be let to individuals. Here was no concept of collective agriculture but the traditional ideal of a society of independent small producers. Over the means of effecting such changes, Spence stressed not a high degree of organisation but a general mobilisation of the 'people'. Once enlightened as to the true nature of society and injustice, the people would unite and irresistibly demand their rights from the small band of oppressors. Violence might well be necessary, but only if the oppressors sought to check the people by force; they might see sense and not try, but in either case the victory would be sudden and quick. In this Spence was generalising from the usual eighteenth-century forms of popular protest, which were not organised in any formal sense but came about spontaneously on the basis of shared values and information. These protests, food riots or strikes, and especially the 'insurrections of the people' of 1740, 1756, 1766, 1795 and 1800 took the form of mass action which never disavowed the use of violence but which rarely resorted to it, real violence being nearly always due to the authorities.

Evans also had connections with a group who practised fraud, perjury, swindling and extortion.[28] One of the Spenceans, Arthur Thistlewood, might also seem to be of this type. After a chequered career, including a visit to revolutionary France, and being persistently rumoured to have taken part in Despard's conspiracy in 1802, he had by 1813 ruined himself by gambling and was making a living as a common informer profiting from successful *qui tam* prosecutions.[29] By the end of 1812 he was also a member of the group of revolutionary democratic 'Patriots' around the veterans of the Corresponding Society, Thomas Hardy and Maurice Margarot. They wanted the abolition of nobility and clergy, confiscation and sale of the great estates, the provision of a plot of land for everyone, and the revival of the old Anglo-Saxon laws. They pinned their hopes on a French invasion under Napoleon, whom they revered as the child of the French Revolution. In December 1812 Margarot was planning to visit France in a smuggling vessel, the money to come from Thistlewood. But Thistlewood failed to raise it, though Margarot did visit France in 1813.[30] With the end of the war

Thistlewood went to France with Evans' son, £600, and a letter of
introduction from Galloway to Richard Hodgson, one of the members of the Corresponding Society who had actually gone to France
in the 1790s. Hodgson found Thistlewood a scoundrel and a gam-
bler, and he lost nearly all his money gambling in the Palais Royal.
Thistlewood stayed in France for nearly a year, but sent young
Evans back with 'crackers' for his own illegitimate son, in the
'Service of the British Republic'.[31]

> He was a stout, active, cheerful-looking man, with something of a
> fearless and determined cast of features. His deportment at that time
> was free and unembarrassed, with much of the air of a sea-faring man.[32]

But it was with prophetic insight that in 1813 an informer
remarked:

> In short from his past life, his present pursuits, principles & low connec-
> tions &c he seems to be a Second edition of Colonel Despard.[33]

In 1816 the Spencean society had tried to capitalise on the
widespread distress and unemployment. Their committee of agitation, under Watson and Thistlewood, arranged a public meeting at
Spa Fields, while Thomas Preston organised support in Spitalfields
from unemployed weavers and the disbanded Tower Hamlets
militia, and Watson's son, who had returned from sea, canvassed
sailors. Hunt agreed to chair the meeting but insisted they delete
from the resolutions any proposals for land reform, abandon their
idea of a mass march to the Prince Regent's residence at Carlton
House, and concentrate on legal political demands like universal
suffrage. Watson readily agreed, but Thistlewood did so reluctantly,
for he and young Watson were planning a rising and hoped the mass
march would have begun it. The Spenceans now split because Evans
strongly disapproved of their agreement to shelve land reform, and
he refused to have anything to do with the conspiracy. The Spa
Fields meeting was a great success, attended by huge numbers and
brilliantly managed by Hunt, who prevented any disorder and so
thwarted Thistlewood's and young Watson's hopes of a clash and
insurrection. Towards the end Hunt proposed that the meeting
adjourn until Parliament assembled, but young Watson carried an
amendment that they meet again on 2 December. His motive
became clear on that day. He and Thistlewood still hoped that a
rising could develop out of a mass meeting, but it was now clear that
this would not happen when Hunt was in control. And so, well
before Hunt arrived, young Watson harangued the crowd and got

some to follow him to take over the City. The attempt was fairly easily dealt with. It is doubtful whether the elder Watson was a party to this conspiracy at all; certainly he did not join the actual attempt, to Thistlewood's fury.[34]

Watson, Preston and Thistlewood remained at the head of a group of radical revolutionaries for the next couple of years. They saw the people as exploited by the small number of persons who staffed the political system, and robbed and oppressed by unjust laws and taxation. The interests of the people were directly opposed to those of the system. The group were revolutionaries in their belief in the right of the sovereign people to change any political system and resist oppression, and the conviction that there was no obligation to obey orders and laws from rulers in whose choice they had no say. They were thus committed supporters of the idea of a National Convention. This revolutionary inclination was heightened by a conviction of the basic weakness of the government, a conviction stemming from their political analysis of society and its antagonistic interests, and from a sense of the basic isolation of the government and authorities in the post-war years. Although the bulk of the population was not radical but neutral, there was such a widespread feeling that the government was useless that the radicals felt realistic in hoping to achieve their aims, especially as they believed some parts of the country were ready to act. Moreover these authorities, in their alarm at their isolation, were becoming repressive. The London revolutionaries shared in and tried to foment a growing sense of crisis, a feeling that the outsome could be only despotism or liberty. They were appalled by and tried to arouse anger against the corrupt Parliament that ignored the people's interests and appeals, the standing army that was retained in peacetime to put down protest whereas it should be replaced by the 'ancient civil force', the use of spies, the Corn Bill (product of a conspiracy between great landowners and ministers to tax the poor), and the Bank of England and its reckless issue of paper money. Remedy would come through universal suffrage, annual parliaments and the ballot. There was a variety of other aims and projects among the group and some, including Preston, were committed Spencean land reformers. There were also disagreements over methods, though all thought violence would be necessary in the end.

Preston and Thistlewood favoured determined action by a small, resolute group to deal decisive blows against the tyrants. In September 1817, when the depression had lifted and there was little political excitement, these two headed another conspiracy from which Watson was excluded, with a secret committee of seven, including a number of Irish, trying to win over the 'distressed mechanics' and planning to rise on 11 October, set up a Committee of Public Safety and declare the land the property of the people.[35] In February 1818 Thistlewood had a plan to murder Sidmouth, Ellenborough and a few other ministers.[36] This was not the way of Watson, who favoured building up a mass popular movement among the non-represented, 'industrious classes', especially the labouring classes who produced the wealth of the country. This meant public meetings, publications, organisations, in short open activity, but this meant it had to be legal to be at all possible. And so Watson pushed Hunt's line, to claim no more than the three basic points so as not to break the laws.[37] They could not anyway have successful meetings without Hunt. In February 1818 Watson persuaded Thistlewood and Preston to agree to a British Patriotic Association, organising subscriptions throughout the United Kingdom, but they were not on good terms.[38] However in May Thistlewood went to prison, leaving Preston eclipsed and confined to private conversations with a trusted few. Watson was left the dominant figure, especially as he was the best writer and public speaker. He was able to set aside plans to attack the Tower in favour of building up a movement through propaganda and organisation. But he often had trouble with more impatient members of the group.[39]

The man who drew these various groups together was Henry Hunt. He had by 1810 made the acquaintance of many of the London reformers, was elected in 1815 to the new Westminster Committee, and became a frequent speaker at Westminster meetings. In 1815 he also became a London liveryman and regular speaker in Common Hall.[40] His ideas were basically the commonplace ones of the established reformers in Westminster and the City, yet he became the foe of Burdett and the section of the Westminster Committee known as 'the Rump'. This stemmed in part from the growing moderation of the Westminster leaders, as parts of the constituency became more prosperous, even opulent, which was reflected in Burdett's decline as a demagogue and closer relations with liberal Whigs. Even such men as Francis Place or Alexander Galloway, veterans of the Corresponding Society (hereafter LCS), still republicans and mostly atheists, contemptuous of tradition and of aristocratic selfishness, inefficiency, indifference to (or failure to comprehend) the true needs of the country and indeed general ineptitude, and consistent in opposing any alliance with the Whigs, had no great respect for 'the mob'. They were serious-minded men who had made their way by self-discipline, and in the heroic and dangerous days of the 1790s had been very conscious of being a rational minority to whom 'the mob' was hostile. This attitude never left them, and they always distrusted demagogy and demagogues. They saw reform as the implementation of reason, and radicalism as something intellectual, not emotional. Though they pressed for a full radical programme, and at different times probably all of them were willing to achieve it by insurrection, this did not demonstrate a faith in the ability of the masses; rather, it would destroy the power of aristocratic factions and remove the corruption that degraded the moral tone of the whole population and prevented the knowledge of reason. This, in conjunction with the spread of education, would ultimately lead to higher morality and political virtue generally, but it would take the form of following the lead of the intelligent and rational part of the community. This belief that reform resulted from the spread of reason was seen at its strongest in Place's Godwinian beliefs, but in general these ex-Jacobins retained a rationalist democratic ideal that was not founded on a belief in abstract popular rights but on a confidence that the masses would follow the lead of the middling classes.

In contrast, Hunt was one of those who gained importance through their popular appeal and links with the radicalism that at the end of the wars had so rapidly struck deep roots in the manufacturing districts. This radicalism of the handworkers of the villages around Manchester, in the West Riding and in Nottinghamshire and Derbyshire was different from that of the Londoners', based as it was on communal solidarity and the weakness of the authorities. The veteran Major Cartwright regained importance after 1811 through his provincial tours. He affronted many London reformers not so much by his belief in universal suffrage, for he was willing to moderate this for reasons of expediency, but by his belief that mass support was needed to gain reform and his readiness to work with people of all social levels. Cobbett's ideas were basically the same as Burdett's, but he came to aim at a different audience. For by 1816 he was despairing of any action by the higher classes against the political establishment. In the autumn he began a special twopenny edition of his *Register*, which had an unprecedented and instant success in the provinces. He thus had a key role in arousing provincial radicalism, but it was the provinces that gave him such importance. In this situation Cartwright was able to convert him hesitantly to universal suffrage, and Cobbett, who saw Burdett as delegate of the people of England, became critical of the baronet's lukewarmness. The delegates who came to the 1817 Convention, especially William Benbow and Samuel Bamford, were insistent on universal (manhood) as against Burdett's household suffrage, and Cobbett came over to their side. Moreover Burdett refused to attend the Convention, and offended many of the delegates by his attitude to their petitions. In the course of 1817, then, Burdett lost his position as popular hero and was subject to increasing criticism by Cobbett in the name of universal suffrage and for his weakness in the cause of the people.

But in March 1817 Cobbett fled to America and his *Register* lost its dominant position for ever. The Westminster reformers tried to make Hone's *Reformists Register* replace it and draw popular discontent back under their influence. But the chief successor was in fact Thomas Wooler's *Black Dwarf*, strong supporter of Cartwight and universal suffrage. The main rival to Burdett's popularity was now Hunt, close associate of Cobbett whose ideas, whether on politics, taxation or currency, he completely followed. Not surprisingly, he was disliked by many of the London reform leaders for, like Cobbett, his tone and appeal were much more popular and coarser. Hunt had become used to crowd activity in Bristol, and in the 1812 elections had received large working-class support and revealed a gift for public speaking, acquiring a taste for it. He was a brilliant showman and excellent at handling a crowd. The necessary arts of the demagogue—the emotion, the personalisation of politics—repelled Place and his sort the more successful they proved. 'Bristol Hunt' became a disruptive force in Westminster and City politics, upsetting the leading reformers there. He consistently assailed any ideas of rapprochement with reforming Whigs, and since the classic Whig claim for support was based on history, much of the attack consisted of demonstrating their base record, beginning with the Riot and Septennial Acts. His popular inclinations involved him in a serious policy difference with the London reformers in 1815 when, in alliance with Cobbett, he totally rejected their agitations against the income tax, arguing that they were selfishly seeking something that would benefit well-off people but be of no use to the poor, who would in fact suffer because other taxes would have to be raised. And he clashed with them over his wishes for an increase in popular demonstrations—in 1816 they rejected his plan for a procession for the imprisoned Westminster MP, Cochrane. So by the end of 1816 he was accustomed to vilifying moderate and 'sham reformers' and washy milk-and-water orators.

The Bristol elections of 1812 had given Hunt a national reputation, but it was the Spa Fields meetings that established him in importance as a rival to Burdett. Several leading reformers had been invited to speak, including Burdett, Cochrane and Cobbett, but Hunt was the only one to accept, and his credit was only raised when, despite the disapproval of Westminster reformers, the first meeting was a huge success, brilliantly managed by Hunt. The meeting approved a petition which Burdett and Hunt were to present to the Prince Regent, but Burdett refused to have anything to do with it and Hunt questioned his commitment to the people.

At the convention at the Crown and Anchor in January 1817 it was Hunt who allied strongly with the northern delegates in favour of universal suffrage and secret ballot, against the wishes of Cartwright, Cobbett and the absent Burdett. He controlled the highly successful demonstration that brought the reform petitions to Parliament and made Cochrane present them. And so the decline in Burdett's popularity was accompanied by a rise in Hunt's in the country, especially Lancashire. For the rest of 1817 Hunt stood out as the advocate of universal suffrage, annual parliaments and ballot against the baronet and the Rump. And while the Westminster reformers would have nothing to do with those involved in the Derbyshire Insurrection of June, Hunt went to the trial and his friend William West organised a subscription in London. Hunt therefore gained from the revulsion at the exposure of Oliver the spy. Cobbett joined in the running campaign against Burdett, and early in 1818 advocated Hunt's adoption for Westminster instead of Burdett at the next election. Burdett therefore tried to restore his popularity by declaring for universal suffrage, annual parliaments and, later, the ballot, but many did not believe him, and in May, with an election near, Hunt announced his candidacy specifically in opposition to Burdett. He received support from Bamford, who set about raising a subscription in Lancashire.[41] When Cochrane announced that he would not seek re-election for Westminster, the Burdett group would not accommodate Hunt but tricked Cartwright's supporters and chose Kinnaird as Burdett's running mate. And so while Cobbett announced his candidacy for Coventry, Hunt persevered in a candidacy in clear opposition to the 'little faction', the 'secret junto' who claimed the right to choose Westminster's representation. 'My course is plain and direct, and disdains all subterfuge or studied ornaments of speech—universal suffrage and annual parliaments, and an opposition to all laws that have a tendency to curtail the liberties of the people, and oppress and starve the poor.'[42] The show of hands was won by Hunt and Romilly (the Whig candidate), and unlike Romilly, Burdett or Cartwright, Hunt appeared at the hustings every day and drew large crowds behind his blood red colours, caps of liberty and cry of 'Universal Suffrage, Hunt and Liberty'.

However much opposition and disgust he raised among some, Hunt had solidified his reputation with others. Employing self-praise and personal abuse he continued to elevate himself in popular esteem as the man who 'will not flinch'. In the Westminster election of 1818, he received great support from Gale Jones, and was backed to the hilt by *Sherwin's Political Register*. W. P. Washington acted as his poll clerk, and his committee included Dr Watson, who led a group to protect him at the hustings, and Thomas Preston, with his placard 'Suspension to Taxation and annihilation to Bank-notes'.[43] The Watsonites were avid readers of *Sherwin's* and since 1816 strong allies of Hunt. One of them was asked if they were 'Hunt's men'.

> No! not his men; yet they always launched out in his praise, saying, that he was the only Gentleman in England, and they looked up to him as their leader.[44]

It was a group without any inherent strength of its own. Watson and his associates had made extensive contacts in the terrible winter of 1816–17, were familiar and welcome figures at trade lodges, exerted influence and had successfully called large numbers to Spa Fields. But in 1818, though their names were well enough known, this was no longer the case, and a public meeting in May was not a success. Perhaps they welcomed Gast so readily because of the contacts he had. But because of this situation, they always looked outside London for signs of mass support.

The provincial radical movement had been broken up in the spring of 1817 by disagreements, repression and arrests. But in January 1818 most of the political prisoners were released, and they resumed their activity. In South Lancashire in March and April a series of meetings were held. These demonstrated the continued support for radicalism, and a letter from Stockport described the 'uneasiness' of the area. Of all the manufacturing districts, this was where Hunt was most respected, and where Watson's group had their chief contacts. Watson was working for a widespread movement that would proceed towards a confrontation, and his reputation made radicals elsewhere willing to follow his lead. The meeting on 4 May 1818 near Spa Fields passed strongly-worded resolutions, including one not to pay any more taxes until the people were fully represented in Parliament, and adopted a petition to the Prince Regent instead of to the corrupt House of Commons which had ignored the million and a half signatures to the 1817 reform petitions.[45] One of the speakers, Dugdale, was a Manchester man. There was excitement in Lancashire at this meeting, and it was intended that the country should follow London's lead. At the same time Hunt and *Sherwin's* were urging tax refusal. In Lancashire Bamford was telling his listeners to be firm for the day, and Benbow was talking of marching on London. At Saddleworth on 4 May Ogden told them, 'I therefore recommend it to you, to Unite in a General Union, and you are sure of success.' In June, there were plans for a 'grand general meeting' in all parts of the country, a tactic that had been canvassed in 1797.[46]

National movement in London and country, tax refusal and simultaneous meetings—these were the concerns and hopes of the group Gast joined.

By the end of 1818, Gast supported the full radical programme. Moreover, though the whole nation would benefit from Reform, experience had convinced him by 1818 that the masters and employers, instead of uniting with their workmen against the ruinous political system, were subservient to it, and in the difficulties that inevitably resulted, tried to maintain their situation at the expense of their workmen, even to the use of legislation like the Combination Acts. It was therefore only by their own efforts that the mechanics could gain justice at the hands of employers and 'every jack in office'. But the extent of distress meant that trades could no longer protect themselves singly, and so they must copy their employers and unite. Once united they would achieve their aims, for masters and men could not do without them. Their skill and industry were the source of all wealth, and they were largely themselves to blame for their plight through their failure to think for themselves and unite to show their power:

> You have it in your own power, the wealth of the empire centres in your skill and industry; you are the granary from whence the NATIONAL PAUPERS and DRONES of SOCIETY draw their succour and support: You are powerful beyond your own calculation, yet you are weak, decripid, dejected, and despised; you are rich in all the materials that constitute wealth, yet you are poor and wretched. Your families are in rags, and destitute of the necessaries of life, your habitations are the scene of misery and want.

The realisation of this power was prevented by the mechanics' disunity, apathy, indifference and lack of self-respect, for 'they have lost sight of their own value and respectability'.[47] And these were mostly due to an addiction to the taproom, the pipe and pot.

> It was their own jealousies and divisions which had deprived them of their proper weight in the state. They had the club of Hercules in their hands, and they might thank their own want of concert and self-respect if they had not wielded it. Disunited they were like bits of broken glass.[48]

Gast urged them to unite for both industrial and political aims, regain their forefathers' spirit of resistance, 'show the world that you are valuable members of society', and 'recover your rights and respectability'.

Spurred no doubt by bitterness at his own personal disappointments, Gast could speak as violently as anyone else.[49] But he differed from Watson and the others in his emphasis on the mechanics as an order and in some notion of politics as the balancing of interests rather than the mere once-for-all implementation of justice. He never ignored the realities of power.

By 1818 at least Gast had developed the basic ideas to which he held for the rest of his life. Their essence was conveyed in his first major public speech.

> The chief object of his speech was to urge the mechanical, the manufacturing, and the agricultural part of the community to think respectfully of themselves—to feel that those who arrogantly called themselves the higher orders, owed all that they possessed to the industry of the people whom they affected to despise. These haughty personages were, in fact, the mere drones in the hive, where the industrious bees collected their produce; and it was the duty of the bees to drive these drones away, especially if they were troublesome. If men were to be estimated or respected from their usefulness, it was clear that the people, whose labour was the source of public wealth, were entitled to the highest consideration. Yet these were the people least considered in this country; but why? because those people did not duly regard themselves. For those people were not attentive to their interests. Their highest interest was the examination of the conduct of the Government of the country, which took away half of the produce of their industry. Yet they rarely attended to this important object until the distress of the country excited them to think, and compelled them to feel. The change was fortunate, for the people now considered politics, upon which they were quite as competent to judge as those who presumed to regard themselves as the highest order. But why should any man of any mind shrink from forming an opinion upon political questions? For the great Locke had observed that political knowledge was nothing but the fruit of common sense applied to public affairs. This was the language of a genuine Englishman, who felt that all rational Englishmen could and should understand their public duties.[50]

6
FROM PALACE YARD
TO CATO STREET

Gast was actually drawn into ultra-radical politics through his trade union work, when he responded to one of the very early attempts at a general union of trades. The impetus for this came from Manchester, where a series of well-organised strikes took place in the latter half of 1818, some, like the weavers', involving a delegate organisation covering a wide area. The authorities were all the more worried because of the involvement of some of the radicals of 1817. In the numbers involved, level of organisation, and length and bitterness of the dispute, the cotton-spinners' strike stood out. Through this experience, they seem to have taken the lead in the movement for a general union of trades. This led to the meeting at Manchester on 10 August 1818, of delegates from nineteen trades in a number of towns who formed a 'Philanthropic Society' to resist reductions.

The cotton-spinners sent delegates to various towns to appeal for financial help, and they met with a very sympathetic response. They succeeded in winning the support of the London *Gorgon* which, in contrast to the uniform hostility of the rest of the press, came out wholeheartedly in support of the strike and went on to condemn the slavery of long hours, the Combination Laws and the employers' excessive profits. 'It is by trading in the blood and bones of the journeymen and labourers of England, that our merchants have derived their riches, and the country its glory and importance.'[1] Though Wade was a Benthamite and clung to the belief that wages depended on supply and demand, he saw high wages as beneficial to industry in that they enlarged the home market, and followed Ricardo's argument that the price of goods did not depend on wages. His appeal for information from the London trades on wages, prices and strikes gained information for articles by Francis Place, on tailors, type-founders, saddlers, printers, opticians and pipemakers, which showed that combinations did indeed affect wages. And so the *Gorgon*, with a circulation in London and Lancashire, became a champion of trade unionism.

Early in September the spinners were beaten and went back to work, but in the meantime their delegates had been pressing for a general union as well as for financial help. At each town, they called a meeting through a printed circular:

> Gentlemen, Two Delegates from Manchester having arrived in   at the request of the different Trades in that Town and Neighbourhood, to solicit your kind assistance and support in forming a Union of the operative Workmen, Mechanics, and Artizans of the United Kingdom, to support each other in all Difficulties, which may occur between them and their Employers, for the mutual Benefit of the labouring People. They do hereby request that you will send a Delegate from your Trade to   where every information will be given.[2]

What success they had is not known, but such general unions were formed in Nottingham and London.[3] The London contacts were made through the Watsonite group of radicals, several of whom were natives of Manchester and Stockport. The chief of them was W. P. Washington, a leading Lancashire 'Luddite' in 1812 who had been indicted twice before coming to London in 1818 and becoming a leading figure in Watson's group. He had kept up a correspondence with the north and the group was visited by a man from Manchester in July.[4] On 12 August Washington arranged for the Watsonites' committee to hear two Manchester delegates, Henry Swindell and William Jones, and for the committee members to distribute to their particular trades the circular calling a trades' meeting on 21 August. The delegates had a thousand copies of the *Cotton Spinners' Address to the Public* printed in London, and distributed them to the hundred-strong general meeting of the Watson group on 16 August.[5] Watson and Washington took them to address a meeting in Spitalfields, while Waddington introduced them to the shoemakers. It was therefore through the Watsonites that the contacts with the trades were made, and the two delegates (Matthew replacing Jones later in August) remained in London until 14 September, when they left for Norwich, and several times addressed the Watsonites' meetings and made small collections.

The trades' meeting on 21 August at the White Lion contributed £30 to the Manchester spinners.[6] At their next meeting, on 28 August, Gast attended for the shipwrights. Thereafter the 'friends of the Manchester Cotton Spinners' seem to have met regularly on Fridays in an upstairs room at the White Lion, while Watson's committee met in the parlour downstairs. But early in September the landlord lost his licence because of these radical clients, and so the Watsonites moved to the George, in East Harding Street, while the trades' delegates met at the Craven Head. Gast was soon a prominent member. 'The Deputies for forming a union of Journeymen (as suggested by the Manchester Men) meet at the Craven's Head in Drury Lane. They have appointed Gast their Chairman, who has issued a circular for them to meet there next Friday.' By October the organisation was strong enough to interest the authorities, and a meeting was invaded by the police. But in November, after a visit from another Manchester spinners' delegate who circularised the trade societies, they issued *An Address to the General Body of Mechanics* in favour of a general union, vigorously written in Gast's typical style; this was reprinted in the *Gorgon*. And on 2 December the union was finally instituted as the 'Philanthropic Hercules', with Gast as President.

Despite its debt to Manchester initiatives, even to the extent of its title, which clearly borrowed from the Manchester 'Philanthropic Society', this union was not such a new departure for the London trades, for it merely sought to formalise, in a period of trade union difficulties, the established procedures of inter-trade assistance. It was to be a federation of trades, each of which had its own committee and held its own funds gained from the penny a week subscription. There was also to be a general committee of delegates chosen for six months from each trade, one for the first hundred members, and one more for each further 250, to which all disputes must be referred. The campaign over apprenticeship had already shown a willingness and ability to engage in joint action. But, as was so often the case, the impetus to this formalisation came out of sympathy for a large strike; in this respect the Manchester cotton-spinners in 1818 were like the Bradford wool-combers in 1825 and Derby silk-weavers in 1833–4.

Late in December an informer reported: 'I understand there are between 30 and 40 Delegates from Different Trades who meet regularly at the Craven's Head under the Direction of Gast and that they mean shortly to Publish such part of their proceedings as they deem proper should appear before the Public.' Indeed the articles of the society were then published, along with a further appeal, and in January the *Gorgon* welcomed its formation.

Events thereafter are obscure. Gast and the new union aided the campaign, organised by Washington and two Manchester spinners, Hollis and Boslom, to have the trial of fifteen arrested cotton-spinners moved to London, the outcome of which was that

Washington spent five months in prison for debt. And the fact that Gast attended none of the Watsonites' meetings between 10 January and 4 July 1819 suggests he was busy with the Philanthropic Hercules up to the latter date. Around June he issued an *Address to the Mechanics and Labourers of the United Kingdom,* reprinted in the ultra-radical *Medusa,* which referred to the Philanthropic Hercules. And at the end of July an appeal on behalf of the newly-released Washington was issued by Gast, Boslom and a millwright, Miles Hopson. Since subscriptions were received at the Pewter Platter, where the Philanthropic Hercules' committee had met, this was probably the last act of the union, which had proved a transient one.

Eighteen years later Gast stated:

> He wanted to see, not merely isolated unions in the several trades, but a general union made up out of the whole. In 1818, he proposed a society which he had called the Philanthropic Hercules; it being, in fact, a Parliament of working men. He proposed that each trade should elect delegates, in proportion to its extent; and that the delegates thus elected should constitute a working man's Parliament.[7]

The Hercules was one of the very earliest attempts at a general union of trades, a cause to which Gast was devoted for the rest of his life.

> He would never be satisfied until he had seen that project realized; for then, and then only, should he feel assured of the complete emancipation of the working classes.

In 1818 Gast had also become a leading member of Watson's group.[8] Following the trades' meeting on 28 August, he came to the general meeting of the group at the same public house on the following Sunday, 30 August, and immediately became one of the leaders, alongside Watson and Blandford. Following Watson's lead, the group had accepted a strategy of propaganda and organisation. Watson wanted to publish a series of strongly-worded pamphlets, but was unable to find anyone to print or publish such works for him, not even Sherwin, so he had to turn printer and publisher himself, and on 29 August appeared the first number of an intended twopenny monthly, *The Shamrock, Thistle and Rose, or the Focus of Freedom,* the title indicating an appeal to the three Kingdoms. It was meant to be the organ of communication for the non-represented people. In August the group also agreed to follow this publication by a public meeting, as the Seditious Meetings Act expired on 24 July, and a committee was set up to arrange this, with Blandford as chairman, Washington as secretary and Watson as treasurer.[9] Inevitably they thought of Hunt as the chief speaker, for there was no other comparable figure likely to agree. Hunt was definitely working in alliance with them, and often requested their help at some event or election, though on the whole he avoided going to their meetings (whenever he did attend one of their private meetings he was silent through all the seditious talk). He readily agreed to chair the intended meeting as long as he was not seen to have any part in arranging it.

The group intended this meeting not only to help arouse interest but to be a further stage in the stepping up of demands. Much of the first number of *The Shamrock* was devoted to the Spa Fields meeting of 4 May. The Prince Regent's answer to the May petition was now declared unsatisfactory and the projected meeting was instead to adopt a 'remonstrance' to the Regent calling on him to impeach and punish the ministers, abolish the boroughmongering system and 'restore' manhood suffrage. Hunt agreed to this, and as part of this line Watson drew up for the meeting twenty-six very strongly worded resolutions (though Hunt and Gale Jones toned them down) and a declaration of rights.[10]

The group also agreed to Watson's idea of organising the radicals in groups of ten, and the public meeting was therefore also to launch a Universal Union Fund of the Non-Represented People of the United Kingdom of Great Britain and Ireland, with Watson as General Secretary and Hunt Treasurer (though his friend William West was appointed as Assistant Treasurer to do the real work).[11] (But the Lancashire contacts soon changed this organisation into the more familiar groups of twenty-five.) This union was to group the people in support of the three radical aims, with a subscription of a penny a week to be paid to the leaders of each group of ten, by him to a hundredth collector, by him to a thousandth collector, and by him to the assistant treasurer, but the revolutionaries clearly also saw this organisation as enabling them to call everyone together at very short notice when the confrontation came about.

Behind all the publications, declarations of rights, refusal to petition, and organisation lay the ultimate aim of radical Reform through a national convention, when the unfranchised, now enlightened and united, should elect their own representatives who would go to Parliament and claim their rightful place.

The meeting was finally fixed for 7 September to suit Hunt's convenience, and invitations were sent to Gale Jones and a certain Bryant to speak. Spa Fields being no longer available, an attempt was made to use the Palace Yard in Westminster but the High

Bailiff refused, and so they had to meet nearby and erect their own hustings in the street. Placards were set up to advertise it, and one of the men went all round London with a tilted cart covered with notices. Gast had made such an impression on the group on 30 August that he was immediately asked to be a speaker at the public meeting. And so on Monday 7 September, 'the non-represented of London and Westminster' met round a rickety hustings composed of a few planks and poles lashed by ropes to the iron railings on the footpath just by the entrance to Westminster Hall, and on this was placed a chair.[12] Only a few hundred attended, owing to the lack of political interest and the greater attractions of Bartholomew Fair. Hunt presided, and the resolutions were to have been proposed by Gale Jones, but neither he nor Bryant arrived and the group felt bitterly that Jones had let them down. And so Watson had to move both the declaration of rights and the resolutions, Hunt moved the remonstrance and Gast seconded instead of Watson, and Gast then had also to move the establishment of the Union Fund, which Blandford seconded. Gast was therefore really substituting for Jones, an unenviable position for a maiden public speech in view of the surgeon's eloquence, and as he was following Hunt and Watson it was difficult not to repeat their points. Yet he made a long speech, in very strong language, with severe attacks on ministers and Wilberforce (a favourite target of his), but the chief feature was his stress on the importance and role of mechanics. It was very impressive and a great success, so much so that after the meeting the group decided to print the remonstrance and Gast's speech.[13] The meeting had made his reputation and introduced his name to the press.

But as a whole, in view of the poor attendance, the meeting was not a success, though it did mark the renewal of public agitation by the Watson group and a new phase in activity, and it was extensively reported in the newspapers. But the group failed to follow it up. Sidmouth refused to receive the remonstrance, so it was never presented to the Regent. Thirty to fifty men came to the regular Sunday meetings, but with Washington preoccupied with the business in the north, Watson, Gast and Blandford were the leading figures. They tried to keep up a flow of publications, but they had hardly any money, always dependent on last-minute *ad hoc* subscriptions. The Westminster meeting had cost £7, leaving a deficit of £4. The second number of *The Shamrock* did appear at the end of September, including the declaration of rights, and they also issued a halfpenny pamphlet by Watson, *The Rights of the People, Unity or Slavery*. But the cost of a further number of *The Shamrock* was too

great and none ever appeared, though in December Watson published a second edition of his *Rights* and a *Letter to Sidmouth*.[14] They
had failed in their plans, and so had to rely on the other radical
press, especially *Sherwin's*, which continued on its uncompromising
way, was often read aloud at Sunday meetings and occasionally
contained articles by members of the group.

The group had decided immediately after 7 September to hold
another meeting before Parliament met and could pass new legislation against meetings, something the group constantly expected.
Gast took the lead here in insisting that this time they should, for
once, have a big name other than Hunt, and accordingly early in
November they wrote to Sir Charles Wolseley and Thomas Northmore, two members of gentry families and reformers of several
years' standing, supporters of the radical demands of universal
suffrage and annual parliaments, who had both recently been active
in favour of radical Reform. An interchange of letters finally elicited in December that Wolseley would have nothing to do with
Hunt but that Northmore was willing to take part.[15] However, in the
meantime the question had become academic, for the group simply
could not afford another meeting, being chronically short of money.
Yet by the end of the year there was strong agricultural agitation for
greater protection and Gast insisted that the presentation of the
Agricultural Petition and the presumed outcome, a more stringent
Corn Bill, would so inflame public opinion that the radicals could
profit from it, and a public meeting must then be held. The group
agreed with Hunt's advice that the strategic time for a successful
meeting would be after the Bill passed the Commons and before it
passed the Lords.[16] But no such bill did appear and so, in view of the
shortage of funds, the public meeting was dropped.

Meanwhile Watson was making strenuous attempts to further the
union, with sections of twenty-five and penny subscriptions. Nineteen sections were said to have been formed by early October,
nearly forty by the middle of the month, and fifty-four by the end of
November, by which time six hundredth-collectors had been chosen. But Wooler was very sceptical of these claims, and certainly the
penny subscriptions were slight. In mid-November £2 13s. 7d. was
paid to West, and by the New Year they seem to have dried up. Only
seventeen members of the intended general committee of thirty-six
were ever appointed, and at a meeting of the collectors in July 1819,
fourteen or fifteen attended and it appeared that a total of only
£8 4s. 0d. had been raised.[17]

By the end of 1818 the group had thus achieved very little. Their weakness and disorganisation was highlighted when on 3 December Watson was arrested and held for a couple of days for debt. Their meeting on 17 January was invaded by the police, so the group decided to move from the George to the Jacob's Well in the Barbican, which had a room twice the size. They always preferred meeting at a public house in the City, as they felt that in the event of prosecution they would do better with a City of London jury. But the landlord was told that his licence was in danger and so made the group leave. They moved to the Ben Johnson, though its room was very small, but the magistrates told this landlord his licence was in danger and so they had to leave again, and finally settled in the Crown and Anchor in King Street.

The group felt restricted and watched, depressed that the authorities clearly knew so much about them, and in constant expectation of a Corn Bill and bills to restrict the press and public meetings. When in January 1819 they sent an account of their proceedings to Wooler's *Black Dwarf* and invited him, Sherwin and Carlile to join their committee, Carlile and Sherwin refused while Wooler did not even reply. Instead, in the *Black Dwarf*, he had expressed doubts about their strength, and urged all monies raised by penny subscriptions in provincial sections to be retained locally and not sent to West or Hunt.[18] Wooler distrusted Hunt and also, as a Yorkshireman, saw quite clearly that the main hopes of radicalism lay in the country and not London. Yet the revival of provincial radicalism and other developments in 1819 were to increase the importance and raise the hopes of the Watsonites, mainly because of their contacts with the Lancashire reformers and their alliance with Hunt.

South-east Lancashire had been the leading radical area in 1816–17, and the revival of public activity after February 1818 was a clear sign of support for radicalism and of a level of organisation. The series of strikes in and near Machester from June to September, of bricklayers, carpenters, dyers, spinners, weavers and miners, were independent of this, but inevitably some of the radicals, notably Bagguley, Drummond, Johnstone and Healey, tried to profit from them, capture them and canalise them along seditious lines. On the whole these efforts remained peripheral, but they did have some success in gaining support, particularly with the bitterness of the spinners' struggle, and the failure of both this and the weavers' strikes. The clearest example was the formation on the very morrow of the strikes, of the Stockport Political Union, led by Bagguley, Drummond, Johnstone and Moorhouse. But late in 1818 several other radical groups appeared in Manchester and nearby parts of Lancashire, and, as with the Hampden clubs, forming societies and unions. The period of strikes was thus succeeded by a period of political agitation, and in 1819 London finally lost its leading place in radical movements.

But through the strikes the Lancashire radicals had strengthened their contacts with the Watson group. The cotton-spinners' delegates had regularly addressed the meetings in London, and on their return to Manchester brought with them copies of Watson's *Shamrock*, which was reprinted and extensively circulated, as was later his *Rights of the People*.[19] Watson's message in his *Shamrock* was twofold—the importance of rank-and-file support and consequent need for mass mobilisation, and the need for organisation on a national scale in his proposed general union. Despite his union's limited success in London, there was a response in the Manchester area and the idea of the union was copied and adopted, with sections of twenty-five under quarter-hundred leaders. The formation of societies in Lancashire at the end of 1818 was therefore partly in response to Watson's union, though, as Wooler advised, the money from the penny subscriptions was retained and not sent to Hunt. And the Rev. Harrison, leader of a group in Stockport estranged from the Political Union there, was trying to build up national contacts through subscriptions for Bagguley, Drummond and Johnstone, who had been arrested.

By early 1819 there was a substantial ultra-radical movement, to which Watson and Thistlewood were familiar names (partly also because of general notoriety and earlier personal contacts) and there was regular correspondence between Watson and James Wroe, one of the Manchester leaders.[20]

These developments could not but encourage and help the Watsonites, and the numbers at the Sunday meetings in November and December were very large. Throughout 1819 they were to see the provinces, especially Lancashire, as the main hope of radicalism, and generally to believe in its vast support in certain areas, a belief strengthened by Wroe's statement in January that 30,000 men there had pikes.[21]

With the New Year, Hunt received invitations from Manchester, Birmingham, Leicester, Stockport, Leeds and Shields to attend public meetings, a clear sign of a new level of activity. It was to Manchester that he went, apparently officially as treasurer of Watson's union fund. Though the visit was not very pleasant or a great success, especially as the hustings collapsed when he spoke, he was beaten up in the theatre and in his hotel, he came back with no subscriptions, and his criticism of Wolseley for refusing to act with him was condemned, he was clearly the chief radical figurehead, and was breaking new ground outside Bristol and London.

Apart from the Manchester meeting there were also large successful public meetings for reform of the franchise and repeal of the Corn Laws in January and February at Stockport, Royton and Oldham. At these the speakers like Knight and Saxton were making calculated references to violence; the Stockport meeting at Sandy Brow led to fights over a Cap of Liberty that had been displayed at Spa Fields, and ideas of simultaneous meetings and, especially, a national convention were expressed.

The Palace Yard meeting in September was therefore important in marking the return to public activity by the Watsonites, and it also stressed their alliance with Hunt and separation from the Westminster reformers, both of which were to gain them credit in town and country. In January 1818, with the release of all the political prisoners, the leading reformers in Westminster and the City had at last bestirred themselves to do something, and at a great meeting at the Crown and Anchor had launched a fund for the relief of the late prisoners. The leading figures of the committee were Brookes (the treasurer), Galloway, Wooler and Cleary (the secretary). It was a cause that could, and did, rally all shades of reformers—Burdett and Cochrane gave £120, and J.G. £1—so that by April £1,200 had been collected and all but £200 distributed, to 50 victims. But trouble began in July, as the committee had given £75 to Benbow and £300 to the Evanses. These were the three who, when in December 1817 all the prisoners were offered release on certain conditions as to future behaviour, had been the only ones to refuse, and had thereby become radical heroes. But the disproportionate money to the Evanses aroused strong opposition, especially as it was attributed to the presence on the committee of Evans' brother-in-law, Galloway. Thistlewood, in contrast, was deemed ineligible to receive anything. The Watsonites had been enemies of the Evans group ever since the first Spa Fields meeting. The Evanses had also denounced Watson's meeting of May 1818. Hunt particularly hated Cleary since their clash at the 1818 Westminster election. The four men who had actually hidden young Watson and Thistlewood after Spa Fields in 1816–17 wrote two letters to the committee on the matter but received no reply, whereupon Watson, Preston and the other Huntites seceded from the committee and the two letters were published in *Sherwin's,* Cleary replying in the *Black Dwarf.*[22]

In November 1818 the suicide of Sir Samuel Romilly threw the whole question of Westminster representation open afresh.[23] Hunt was ready to stand again, but the Burdett group decided on the young J. C. Hobhouse, secured the withdrawal of Kinnaird, whom Place favoured, and arranged Hobhouse's acceptance at a public meeting, despite attempts by Hunt to nominate Cobbett and by the reforming Whigs Sturch and Wishart to have a reforming Whig like John Russell. Brookes organised Hobhouses's committee, Burdett contributed £1,000, and for three months Hobhouse canvassed unopposed, anxious to avoid any Whig opposition. But all the democrats opposed this choice and supported the cry of Hunt, Gale Jones and Watson that there was a plot to fill the vacancy with a tool of Burdett's, and in the end Cartwright was put up as a candidate. Hobhouse completed the breach just before the election when he disavowed universal suffrage and even signified support for a franchise that, it transpired, would exclude many existing Westminster electors. This disunity, the absence of a Tory candidate and Place's provocation led to a Whig candidate, George Lamb. The election was very violent, with constant uproar at the hustings, cries of 'No Rump!', 'Turncoat' and 'Hunt a mad dog', and ended with Lamb's victory and Huntite rejoicing at the defeat of Burdett and the 'Rump'. The Watsonites were active on Cartwight's committee, and Wolseley, Northmore and Wooler all strongly backed Hunt and Cartwright against Hobhouse, and so all the leading democrats were united. Wolseley and Northmore chatted on friendly terms with Watson during the election, agreed to a public meeting in London and then engaged in propaganda in the country.[24]

The Westminster election had a great effect also among radicals all over the country and produced a reaction against the self-appointed clique who were trying to make Westminster into a pocket borough, had betrayed radicalism in running Hobhouse and had treated Cartwright so dirtily. Hunt's exposing himself to danger every day at the hustings won him great credit in the country, and the Watsonites also gained credibility from their role and alliance with Hunt.

They took up the idea of a public meeting again, but decided to delay until Parliament had dispersed, and then to meet in favour of a national convention. They were also strongly attracted by a suggestion by Cobbett, in his *Register* which was sometimes read at the Sunday meetings, to flood the country with forged Bank of England notes to create a financial panic and collapse of the system. Waddington printed a handbill on this and the group distributed hundreds of them in the hope of thereby achieving a panic.[25] Meanwhile a rupture between Evans and Wedderburn broke up the Spencean society. Wedderburn opened a chapel in Hopkins Street where he and Allen Davenport made very violent, seditious, and bitterly anti-Christian Spencean speeches, and his group became part of Watson's following.[26] Thomas Davison was publishing Volney's works and had in February begun a Painite republican journal, the *Medusa; or, Penny Politician*, which publicised Spence's plan and had frequent contributions from Davenport and Blandford. And when Carlile was prosecuted for publishing Paine's political works, Watson helped him prepare a defence that was to last three days and take the form of a political manifesto which could itself be published.[27]

By May 1819, then, things looked more hopeful. The Watsonites were the chief ultra-radical group in London, where there was a flourishing democratic press. They were close allies of Hunt, the chief national figurehead, who in June presided at their dinner to celebrate the 1817 acquittal of Watson and his colleagues.[28] And in that month the Huntites called a public meeting to consider the handling of subscriptions for political prisoners, with Galloway, Wooler and Bowrie in attendance on behalf of the committee. They received a powerful onslaught from Gale Jones and Gast, and Hunt followed this up by writing a long article containing a document given him by Burdett, which he took to be by Oliver, on the events up to the Derbyshire Insurrection, and accusing Cleary of being a spy. This was too long for the *Medusa* so was issued as a pamphlet, to which Cleary, backed by Evans, issued a reply, Hunt being supported by Cobbett and Watson.[29] The alliance with Hunt was thus solidified. In March they were even asked by the landlord to use the White Lion again.

The Watsonites were also encouraged by a sense of participation in a national movement, centred on national periodicals like Cobbett's *Register* and especially the *Black Dwarf*, and were in contact with Lancashire through correspondence, reading the *Manchester Observer* (which Wroe and his group took over in June) and visiting delegates. After the meetings in January and February radical activity in Lancashire continued, and there are clear signs of rank-and-file arming in March. But radical activity was not confined to Lancashire. In Yorkshire societies spread based on the Political Protestants of Hull, which opened reading-rooms and held political discussions, an open activity in contrast to the Watsonites' way. Yorkshire in fact probably became in 1819 the strongest radical area of all, mainly in parts of the West Riding and Barnsley. And thence societies grew up in the north-east (where there was a dramatic upsurge in radicalism), Carlisle (a centre of handloom weaving) and Glasgow (which became one of the strongest centres). These were all in contact with one another, but though in September 1818 a society of Political Protestants was formed in London and Watson was very anxious to make contacts with them,[30] the Watsonites' provincial links were basically confined to the Manchester area.

In the middle of the year, a new round of public meetings began, attempting to harness discontent at unemployment to radicalism. The two Stockport groups united in a remodelled Stockport Political Union, and a set of rules was drawn up adopting the Hull model. From this spread a movement over the whole of south Lancashire to unite all shades of radicals in unions on the Stockport model. Whatever the differences over the use of violence, all united in an open, constitutional campaign. This coming together and the strength of the movement were shown in a well-attended delegate meeting held at the very strong radical centre, Oldham, early in June. Here, despite the impatience of some, it seems to have been agreed to launch a wave of large public meetings which would elect representatives of the people who would go to London in January 1820 to try to take their rightful seats in Parliament and so provoke the final showdown. Though the movement was not monolithic and there were great differences over tactics and dates, there was great general support for this strategy, especially as there was no clear commitment to violence. Basically the public meeting campaign was seen as arousing and mobilising the people so that in the end they would confront their oppressors in an irresistible show of strength. Whether there would be any violence or not basically depended on the responses of the authorities.[31] The strength and possibilities of radicalism seemed demonstrated by the public meetings at Stockport on 28 June, and Nottingham, Hunslett Moor and Rochdale on 19 July with their large attendance and tremendous press publicity. The government was isolated, it was realised how very weak the authorities were and how helpless to prevent the radicals' controlling many areas, and it seemed obvious that open activity and progressively bigger meetings would in the end prove irresistible.

> The effect on the reformers' morale of each successive demonstration was instantaneous . . . If the open organisation of the people had continued on this scale it would have become impossible to govern . . . The

policy of open constitutionalism was proving more revolutionary in its implication than the policy of conspiracy and insurrection.[32]

It is not clear how far the London Watsonites were a party to all this. In April they formed a new London Union, divided into sections, but in June the articles of the Stockport Political Union were circulated.[33] Delegates from the country made it clear that radicalism was much stronger there. At the end of June, presumably in connection with the Oldham conference, three delegates came to London from St Helens, Leeds and Huddersfield dressed as gentlemen and seeking to form parish unions all over the country.[34] There was regular correspondence with Lancashire through parcels or messages in rolls of wallpaper sent by the paper-hanger John George, who headed a section of Watson's Union.[35] Watson composed the resolutions for the great Stockport meeting of 28 June.[36] They knew of the plans for a 'general union', simultaneous meetings (Preston was a strong advocate of this) and a national convention (Birmingham was planning a meeting on 12 July to elect a 'legislatorial attorney' and Evans wanted one at Westminster to elect himself).[37] In June a Union Society was formed in London on the northern pattern, by a branch of the White Lion group, and in July new societies were formed in Spitalfields and Southwark.[38]

In this context the Watsonites resumed their efforts to have a public meeting, but lack of money always prevented both this and the sending of delegates to the country, though Preston was always advocating a bank robbery and in June even reconnoitred a house.[39] In May Thistlewood was released from prison and immediately resumed political activity. Yet he and Preston supported the idea of public meetings as this might provoke a clash. It was therefore agreed to hold a meeting at Smithfield on 14 July, the anniversary of the French Revolution, and then send delegates to the country to organise a 'general meeting' over the whole country a fortnight later, a total mobilisation of the people.[40] The Smithfield meeting was therefore to adopt a tone of strong defiance towards authority, to be a move in the run-up to a confrontation and revolution, for there would be only one more meeting after it, and then the people would 'demand their rights'. The resolutions therefore not only included familiar radical phrases and points, but concentrated on the point that laws and taxes were not binding on anyone without a vote. And so resolution nine ran:

> That from and after the first day of January, 1820, we cannot, conscientiously, consider ourselves as bound in equity by any future enactments which may be made by any persons styling themselves our representa-

tives, other than those who shall be fully, freely, and fairly chosen by the voices or votes of the largest proportion of the members of the state.

And the next resolution was that books be opened in each parish in London to enrol the names and residence of every man of mature age and sound mind, to enable the holding of their own elections. The 1818 remonstrance was also to be readopted. They were encouraged to do this by the fact that Parliament was in recess so could pass no coercive acts. And since it was essential to pass these resolutions, Watson and Thistlewood urged peaceable behaviour at the meeting and no arming until after.[41] But some were impatient in the general air of excitement, especially with rumours of plans to seize arms depots near Derby and Birmingham. George's section included a gunsmith who made pikes for some members, there were plans for converting chisels to use for pikes, and talk of assassination to effect the revolution. And Preston was quite ready for the clash to begin at Smithfield and lead to the seizure of arms and ammunition at the Artillery Ground and the East India Company depot near the City Road.

It was during these preparations for Smithfield and perhaps as a result of feeling that the Watsonites were at last achieving something, that at the Sunday meeting on 4 July Gast reappeared on the scene, though he had already been in contact with the Huntites at least. Shortage of money forced the postponement of the meeting to 21 July, and Gast urged them to invite speakers from Manchester, Stockport and elsewhere, and unsuccessfully pressed for Wolseley or Northmore as chairman instead of Hunt. Gast was one of the select committee which arranged the meeting, invited Harrison of Stockport, Edmonds of Birmingham, Cartwright, Wooler and Wolseley, and from 12 July met nightly, secretly, at different places. Printers would not print advertisements until in the end Davison did a hundred in the name of a fallacious 'Committee of 200' and also a thousand copies of an address to the people, which were sent to places in the country. Attempts were made to win Irish support—one resolution supported Catholic Emancipation—there were to be addresses to the Roman Catholics and to O'Connell, the head of the Catholic Board, and a tailor made a tricolour whose colours, red, green and white, stood for the three kingdoms. The chief speakers at the meeting were to be Hunt, Wolseley, Gale Jones and 'Mr Gast'. Some members were to become enrolled as special constables. If the meeting were attacked, they would retreat to Moorfields or Finsbury Square to make a stand. And immediately after the meeting the next one would be planned.

As the day approached, excitement grew. Sometimes 300 came to the White Lion meetings. The sense of crisis was heightened by Sidmouth's circular of 7 July to Lords Lieutenant to act to preserve order and keep the yeomanry in readiness. There was interest and expectation in the country, and some came to London, notably Harrison, and Ward of Nottingham. The London coachmakers agreed to go to the meeting as a group. By noon on the day there was a solid mass in the square, all windows, roofs and balconies were full, and the crowd was variously estimated from 10,000 to 60,000. Men carried boards about marked 'Order'.[42] Gast was one of the chief speakers. Wolseley had not come, but Harrison seconded the resolutions as 'the strongest ever proposed'. With consummate showmanship Hunt unfurled at a strategic moment the tricolour as the 'Union flag of England, Scotland, Ireland' and a red flag with the motto 'Liberty or Death'. Though Harrison was arrested in the middle of the meeting for a speech made earlier at Stockport, Hunt prevented any violence, and when later he saw part of the crowd trying to kick up a row he cut the meeting short by reading extracts from the recent *Black Book*, urged them to refuse taxes, and the meeting dispersed peacefully, a huge success and very well publicised in the press.

The following week, while in the City Wood and Waithman led attacks on the Lord Mayor for calling troops for the Smithfield meeting and the provocative way of arresting Harrison, there were moves to propose Hunt as Sheriff, and Hunt engaged in a row with Waithman, the Watsonites sought to keep up the momentum. Copies of Hunt's address to the Irish were printed as the *Address from the People of Great Britain to the People of Ireland*, and Thistlewood sent 4,000 to Dublin and Cork and got Wooler and Carlile to send others to the provinces.[43] Davison printed the proceedings of the meeting as a pamphlet.[44] Thistlewood and Watson drew up a twopenny address, 'The Reformers' Gazette', aimed at soldiers and sailors, and persuaded the Union Society at the Crown and Anchor, King Street, Seven Dials to pay for the printing of copies. Two societies, one of them Irish, applied to enrol. A new ultra-radical periodical appeared, the *Theological Comet*. And Blandford was preparing to become a publisher should Carlile be imprisoned.[45]

In response to urgings from the country, Watson got the group to agree to organise each parish in London, Westminster and Southwark under a committee and a secretary, with a general committee at the White Lion having Blandford as secretary. Thistlewood supported the plan as enabling them to call their whole strength together within twenty-four hours. Soon about seven parochial districts were formed, at Seven Dials, Cripplegate, St James's, Shoreditch, Clerkenwell, Wedderburn's chapel in Soho, and the Irish group in Lambeth who included Webb, a veteran of the LCS and mainly consisted of Irish labourers at the engineering works like Maudslay's. Some of the most violent members, like Harrison and Hartley, attended Wedderburn's chapel, and looked to Thistlewood rather than Watson as leader. Their mood was enhanced by their growing numbers (over 200 attended on 18 August) and Irish support, by the royal proclamation of 30 July ordering sheriffs and magistrates to proceed against fomenters of disorder and by the threats to the landlord of the White Lion of loss of his licence, so that they had to move to the George, in East Harding Street. Several of the group supported Hunt's plan of tax refusal, strongly advocated as it was in the *Medusa* and *Black Dwarf*. Wooler's advocacy arose out of the great Birmingham meeting of 19 July which had, in a direct challenge to Parliament, elected Wolseley as 'legislatorial attorney'. Though Thistlewood and the rest thought this was premature and preferred simultaneous elections to hurry on the confrontation, they agreed with the plan and wished to hold one in Westminster just as Manchester and Leeds were planning.[46] Watson was equally revolutionary, and thought the favourable time was soon coming. On 15 August he and Thistlewood wanted to plan a rising in London in four different places—Gast to lead one from Deptford, Thistlewood in Spitalfields, Preston on the north shore and Watson across the river.[47] Since Gast was present he presumably approved the idea. A very violent speech by Gast on 8 August was characteristic of the group's mood.

But Watson was still constantly speaking against premature action, and was pushing for district meetings. He and Thistlewood failed to get any response from the Spitalfields weavers, but the Irish group in Lambeth, who were steadily distributing the address to the Irish, agreed to form a Surrey Committee under Dennis Shaw, a veteran from the 1798 rising, and to hold a meeting for Southwark and Surrey on Kennington Common. This was provisionally fixed for 23 August, but had to depend on Hunt's convenience (Gast again vainly pressed for different speakers) and Hunt was in Manchester for the great public meeting there. Despite shortage of money (Thistlewood collecting £7 from prisoners in King's Bench prison), a great attendance was anticipated for this Kennington meeting, especially as it would follow the Manchester meeting which was expected to be the greatest ever, and at which Preston and Thistlewood thought there might well be violence.[48]

On 18 August news of the Manchester massacre reached London. That night a crowd thronged both the room and the passage at the George (including sixty Irish from across the river). In fury they heard Gast read a newspaper account of the massacre, and there were many calls for violence.[49] But that night the committee decided to call off the Kennington Common meeting. This was on the advice of soldiers who pointed out how vulnerable the crowd would be to an attack in the open fields, with no place to retreat and the bridges two miles away. And so, wiser than Chartists twenty-nine years later, they decided instead to hold a meeting on 25 August at Smithfield, where there were many places of retreat.[50]

The next day feelings were heightened by Carlile's eye-witness account of Peterloo in *Sherwin's*, and Peterloo clearly had the effect of increasing extremist opinion. Carlile, who had taken over *Sherwin's*, changed its title to the *Republican*. In September two new ultra-radical papers appeared, the *Briton*, strongly Huntite, and the *Cap of Liberty*, run by James Griffin, which supported the Watson-ites to the hilt. Many of the Watsonites now acquired arms, mainly pikes, despite Watson's doubts but to Thistlewood's delight, but these were mainly for the purpose of defence against any attack by the authorities. Their intense hatred and suspicion of the rulers generated the belief that Peterloo was the start of a 'reign of terror' when the government would act as a member of the sinister 'Holy Alliance', and this feeling was heightened by arrests of Blandford, Wooler, Carlile and Waddington for placards they displayed. It seemed that an armed clash was now inevitable, and the only possible outcome was despotism or revolution. Elaborate precautions were made to prevent arrests from disrupting the Smithfield meeting, the site of the stage was chosen to enable retreat and resistance in case of the attack that Preston confidently expected and wanted, about fifty men had grenades, and Preston told them all to bring a stone wrapped in a handkerchief (for Thistlewood wanted no open display of arms to provoke attack).

The hardening of democratic feeling seemed accompanied by growing unity. On 19 August the Watsonites welcomed the suggestions in the *Statesman* of a reconciliation between Carlile, Wooler, Burdett, Cartwright, Hunt and Cobbett, though they had doubts over Burdett, and they went on 20 August to a meeting at the Crown and Anchor called by Cartwright and Wooler on the Manchester massacre and to effect a coalition of all democrats. This meeting was clearly an attempt to capture for radicalism the general outrage at Peterloo and at the government's congratulations to the magistrates. But though the strength of feeling was shown by the more than 3,000 respectable people who attended and agreed to the sending of the lawyers Harmer and Pearson (who was already a reformer of note in the City) to Manchester to investigate, they rejected the violent speeches by Watson, Gale Jones and Thistlewood's friend Lawson (who proposed they be armed at all future meetings).[51] That this feeling was not so easily capitalised on was also shown by the Smithfield meeting on 25 August which Wolseley declined to attend and which Cartwright criticised in a public letter as harmful. The speakers were Watson, Preston, Thistlewood and Walker.[52] Gast was not there, and in fact hardly ever again came to the group's meetings and was never again to speak at one of their public meetings. It is very possible that he was alarmed at the dangers involved and at the revolutionary elements, or that his allegiance was to Hunt rather than Watson. But, as we shall see, he did not break connections with Watson and Thistlewood.

Considering that the Smithfield meeting was fortuitously the very first open-air public meeting in London after Peterloo, its relatively small numbers (8,000 to 20,000) and very mild and orderly character were a bitter disappointment to the Watsonites. It was quite clear that the outrage over Peterloo was not the same as radicalism, and that far more success was attending the tactics of Henry Hunt.

Hunt towered. He did not put a foot wrong in the weeks after Peterloo. He gained very widespread praise for his efforts before the great meeting to ensure peace and order, and for his steadiness under arrest. His letters to London were regularly printed in the papers and convincingly portrayed the attack as totally inexcusable. The original charge of high treason seemed monstrous. It was the reformers—Hunt, Wolseley and Pearson—who were vainly seeking redress through the law, against authorities and ministers who blocked these efforts, increased the army, and seemed bent on illegal rule, terror and civil war. To support Hunt was to support the laws of England. Invitations came to him from scores of towns to speak. He seemed fully aware of the responsibilities of his position, and exerted himself in favour of united protest. The prospect opened of a vast, unanimous campaign. And because press and public opinion seemed so strong and unanimous, it did really seem that Parliament would be quite unable to refuse redress, and indeed even that the system of corruption might at last come to an end. And so Hunt, Wolseley and the rest, influenced no doubt also by their coming trials, exerted themselves in favour of a united constitutional campaign.

The Watsonites regarded all hopes of legal and parliamentary redress as futile. But they were determined to take advantage of the general feeling, especially as they had a special relationship with Hunt. They clung to the old Spa Fields tactic—the best chance of a successful confrontation lay in the course of a public mass meeting. If they could not get up the meeting themselves, they should profit from others. The Westminster meeting called for 2 September promised to be much larger than the Smithfield one, especially in view of Burdett's open letter denouncing the ministers and his consequent indictment. In the morning four of the group toured Spitalfields with bugles urging attendance, and Thistlewood and Hartley hired a band and led an armed group to the meeting behind the Universal Suffrage flag. The meeting at Covent Garden was certainly huge, the biggest Westminster meeting Place had ever seen, but the Thistlewood group failed to provoke a clash, and their disappointment was complete when the landlord of the White Lion refused them the use of his room. The Surrey Committee, however, wanted their own public meeting immediately after the Westminster one to capitalise on the enthusiasm.[53]

Watson did not agree with these tactics, and strongly opposed Thistlewood's behaviour on 2 September. He was encouraged in this by news from the country. After Peterloo the radical movement naturally lost coherence, for the campaign of public meetings clearly had to end, and a variety of tactics were proposed. An informer reported that on 22 August three delegates came to London, from Nottingham, Leeds and Birmingham.[54] They brought the message that the campaign of mass meetings must end, that radicals should concentrate on 'General Union Societies' throughout the kingdom, and that simultaneous delegate meetings were to be held at Coventry, Nottingham, Leicester and Sheffield, all at 9 pm (a very improbable occurrence). The union societies were to be on the Stockport model, with small divisions of 25 under a leader, regular penny weekly subscriptions, a grand overall committee, a central meeting place in the form of a reading room, and a small secret managing committee of five. This would all be legal, but the Birmingham delegate, George Edmond's son, made it quite clear that this should be accompanied by arming so as to provide an effective organisation for 'the day'. *Sherwin's* took the cue and published information on the Stockport organisation, and Watson revived his efforts to form parochial organisations. The next week a lady came from Manchester to advocate the plan and form a society of female reformers, while young Edmonds stayed on and at the end of September became editor of the new, violent, *Democratic Recorder, and Reformers' Guide*, which carried articles by Watson. But Preston opposed the policy of replacing the London sections, which he saw as military organisations, by district unions, decentralised and operating openly.

The chief preoccupations among the Watsonites were therefore the extent of feeling over Peterloo, the approaching reign of terror, the tactic of public meeting clashes, the need for arms, the connection with Hunt, the need for organisation, and a belief in very extensive radical support and arming in the country. An extraordinary session of Parliament was called for 23 November, and it was obvious that coercive legislation would be passed. This introduced a sense of urgency which set them against the tactics of Hunt and Wooler. These wished to build up a great, irresistible pressure of opinion, and so opposed any activities that might alienate some reformers. They opposed any new initiatives before Parliament met and passed coercive legislation, for it was important that government and Parliament should make the first move towards a further divide in opinion, towards confrontation and so further strengthen the moral case of the reformers. Then new actions would be needed, but in the meantime the people must act moderately and peacefully, yet show their unity and moral determination. This was best done by abstaining from exciseable articles as it would also weaken the government through loss of revenue. This meant the initiative should be left to Parliament. The Watsonites saw this policy as bankrupt and pathetic and wanted to take the initiative themselves while feeling was still high, and bring things to an issue *before* Parliament could meet. This would include public gatherings. Watson therefore supported a policy of organising in parochial unions on the provincial plan, a public meeting to agree again to a remonstrance to the Prince Regent and, when this was rejected, arming.[55] It was a policy founded on common action over the country, and indeed the London group were well aware of their own weakness, and through his correspondence Watson urged that there be simultaneous meetings all over the country. This was an extension of the mass meeting tactic, and was meant to effect the final mobilisation and provoke confrontation. But it must be arranged *before* Parliament met and passed measures preventing public meetings.

In the confused situation after Peterloo, when the bankruptcy of a policy of legal and parliamentary redress was increasingly apparent and a policy had to be agreed quickly before Parliament met, this idea met a widespread response.

In the meantime there was the chance of arousing enthusiasm on the occasion of Hunt's entry into London, which the Watsonites intended to make a great occasion. When Hunt wrote to Blandford that he would arrive on 8 September, Thistlewood formed a committee to arrange a triumphal welcome and then another Smithfield meeting on 9 September. He was still hoping for large crowds and a clash. This was upset when Hunt postponed his entry to 13 September, but the committee arranged a procession, route, band, dinner at the Crown and Anchor and publicity. It was to be their great occasion, and again Thistlewood urged them to come armed. But the Westminster reformers had recently formed a committee under Brookes to raise subscriptions for the victims of Peterloo and the defence of those up for trial, and young Evans persuaded them, despite the reluctance of some, to arrange a dinner to welcome Hunt. Approaches were therefore made to Watson's committee and though some were against co-operation Watson persuaded them to agree, and a joint, cheap dinner was agreed to as was, despite the opposition of Galloway and his *Statesman*, a triumphal procession, arranged by a 'united committee of 500'.[56]

The crowds which greeted Hunt were huge, and all the papers agreed that it was a sensational triumph for him (and open disapproval of the ministers). At last he had replaced Burdett as the popular hero, and this beat the crowd which gathered in 1810 to greet Burdett on his release from the Tower. But as the hero of Lancashire, the country generally, and now London, he was affronted by the assumption by Watson, Preston and Thistlewood that he was their man. He no longer needed their alliance, and in any case his policy of unity among reformers forbade too close an identification with a particular group, especially this group, and in view of his approaching trial it was impolitic to identify himself with them. He made sure the triumph was his alone, and took care to distance himself from Watson and his friends. The route they had fixed was too long and very tiring for him. The committee had bungled the invititation to Wolseley to chair the dinner and so Watson proposed the rather insignificant figure of Gale Jones, which seemed an affront to Hunt, especially as in 1810 Burdett had chaired his dinner. Since Jones had not arrived in time Hunt took the chair and emphasised the need for unity and warned against any riot or disturbance. But then, as if as a slap in the face, Jones arrived and criticised the managing committee for their treatment of Watson, Thistlewood and Preston. The dinner was not a happy occasion, and next day Watson and his group complained to Hunt of his behaviour, whereupon he dropped all communication with them and they completed the breach.[57]

Hunt kept up the momentum of the agitation, appearing at meetings in Southwark and the City, and accompanying Carlile to his trial, but the Watsonites had no share in it. It was a cruel blow to their hopes of mass action in alliance with Hunt, and they felt very bitter at him. Yet Watson persisted in his policy, and there were several delegates moving around the country in support of an insurrection arising out of simultaneous meetings early in November. One of them was Tetlow, one of the chief rank-and-file organisers in Manchester, and he came to London on 17 September under the alias Westwood, changing his lodgings every night, and supporting Watson's efforts.[58] Walker therefore rented a room in Spitalfields capable of holding four hundred as a reading and central meeting room, and a number of branch union societies were formed, themselves containing sections. The most violent was led by Wedderburn, Davenport, Harrison and Hartley at Wedderburn's chapel in Soho; the largest was the St Giles union, in King Street, numbering 140, with Palin as secretary; Waddington led one in Snowhill, and also opened a shop selling coffee-substitute, pike-heads and second-hand firearms; and there were also unions for Cripplegate, Marylebone, Somers Town, Southwark, and Fleet Market.[59] This meant some degree of decentralisation, which was acceptable to Watson but resented by Preston who wanted a small resolute minority able to take decisive action.[60] Then in October the select group or division started meeting privately at Watson's dwelling off Fleet Street, to concert plans for the coming rising. It was attended by Watson, Thistlewood, Edmonds of Birmingham, Gast, Banks and perhaps sometimes Gale Jones.[61] As far as one can tell, Gast was privy to the insurrectionary plans. Several people were acquiring arms, but shortage of money hindered purchases. Thistlewood continually went round collecting money, his main source being prisoners in King's Bench, while Hartley led a footpad robbery.[62] And on 17 October began a series of Sunday dawn drill-meetings at Primrose Hill, Islington, Harrow Road and Brixton.[63]

Early in October they decided on a further Smithfield meeting on 20 October while Habeas Corpus still held, but Watson was corresponding with Tetlow through parcels and was daily expecting a letter from the country to fix the date of the simultaneous meet-

ings.[64] Thistlewood went ostensibly to Leicester and came back with
money and the news that Derby, Nottingham and Leicester were
well prepared and that thirty towns were ready to act. He also went
to Manchester, but had a cold reception from Wroe.[65] Presumably
as a result of some communication, the Smithfield meeting was
postponed to 1 November to be one of the simultaneous ones.
Watson drew up thirty-eight very strong resolutions (many of them
based on those of the July Smithfield meeting) which were to be
identical at all the meetings. The plan was for all the meetings to
send an address to the Prince Regent in favour of enfranchising
every man, wait for a fortnight for his answer, and then meet again
simultaneously at the same places on 15 November, before Parliament met and before Holy Alliance troops arrived.[66] Clearly the
rising would start then.

But this plan was struck a resounding blow when in mid-October
the Manchester group running the *Observer* printed a letter from
Hunt attacking the idea of simultaneous meetings and suggesting
that the idea had originated with government spies who wished to
provoke a clash; public meetings were not safe, they should wait to
see if Parliament did introduce repression, and meantime weaken
the government by abstaining from beer, spirits and tea. Hunt's
letter was widely reprinted in the press, and Watson and Thistlewood were very bitter, the latter especially feeling he was being
accused of being a spy. Angry letters passed between them, Hunt
and Blandford, which the newspapers gaily reprinted. The plan was
damaged not only by this vituperation, but because of Hunt's position as the national hero, and because several of the London unions
looked to Hunt rather than to Watson, as Preston had foreseen. The
chief radical periodicals including the *Black Dwarf*, supported
Hunt's opposition, and it was really only the London papers, *Republican*, *Medusa*, *Cap of Liberty* and *Democratic Recorder* that persevered with tax-refusal and simultaneous meetings to mobilise the
people and overawe Parliament.[67] And the suggestions about spies
had the usual paralysing effect.

The Watsonites nevertheless persevered with their plan. The
White Lion, now licensed as a preaching room, was their centre
instead of Walker's coffee-house and reading room, and delegates
from the union societies planned the meeting, posted hundreds of
placards, had Davison print 20,000 copies of their resolutions and
appeal, hired a wagon and made a new tricolour.[68] Gale Jones and
Gast both declining, Watson was to take the chair and he, Davison
and Gast were to take to Sidmouth the Address for the Prince

Regent. Watson sent the copies of the resolutions to the provinces, but by the end of October had received communications from eleven places, including Manchester, that because of Hunt's letter they would not meet on 1 November. The whole scheme had therefore misfired, and though the London meeting was persevered with it was a solitary affair, and even before it was held the hopes of Watson and Thistlewood were focused on 15 November, when simultaneous ones might still take place. But, as always, some of the group hoped for a clash on 1 November, mainly Hartley, Davenport, John George's son Robert and others of Wedderburn's group, though they were opposed as being premature by Wedderburn himself and Edmonds. On the morning of the meeting a group led by Thistlewood made arms which they took along; Hartley was openly selling pike-heads at 1s. 3d. each, and there was an arms depot in Spitalfields. But the meeting, in Finsbury Market, was a very tame affair, held in a sea of mud and attended by a mere 1,500 to 2,000. The resolutions and address were very inflammatory, though when Davidson (a relatively new member, and as violent as the other mulatto, Wedderburn) proposed they come armed at the next meeting, this was rejected. It was agreed that Watson, Gale Jones, Davison and Gast should present Sidmouth with the 'Appeal of the People to the Prince Regent'.[69]

The meeting did not make a great impact, was poorly reported, and seemed to show the group's isolation. Nevertheless that very evening preparations were begun for a Smithfield meeting on 15 November, especially as a letter came from Manchester saying they would meet then.[70] On 5 November Watson and Gast delivered the Address at Sidmouth's office, and it was expected they would both soon be arrested.[71] But the news from the country was confusing, and on 9 November, though a Manchester delegate, Bradbury, was in town, Watson announced that communication with the country places had dropped as they had sided with Hunt. And so simultaneous meetings on 15 November were off, and the London meeting was therefore postponed until 24 November, the day after Parliament met, when it was expected feelings would be high after the speech from the throne promising coercion.[72]

In the meantime efforts were made to build up strength in London. A delegate organisation of the union societies was arranged, Walker forming one at his coffee-house.[73] Watson seemed to have wished to aim specifically at working-class support. In August he had been denouncing the plunder of labourers and mechanics by their employers, and one of the Finsbury resolutions had run:

it is the bounden duty of all industrious Men, especially Mechanics, Artizans, and Labourers, who by an oppressive system are brought to the verge of famine, (amidst plenty and profusion) to exert themselves by all possible means to elect persons more inclined to preserve their liberties and happiness.[74]

Watson now proposed circularising all the houses of call. Thistlewood went to the Spitalfields weavers, and efforts were made at the very radical shoemakers, who had begun a special subscription for the victims of Peterloo, and indeed a union of shoemakers was formed with Black Davidson as secretary.[75] The Sunday meeting on 21 November was larger than for some time.

The Smithfield meeting was publicised by Waddington's going round in Finsbury with a board, two horn-blowers touring Spitalfields, and a band hired by Walker, while the lack of money was overcome through a visit by Thistlewood to Jeremy Bentham, who had often given the group money in the past. Gast was invited to take the chair but presumably declined as Watson was again the leading figure. This was expected to be the last meeting that would be allowed, and so their last chance of a row (on 8 November they planned to interrupt a Middlesex meeting, but that turned out a very tame affair, and on 9 November, Lord Mayor's Day, Thistlewood led a group to hoot the old Tory Mayor, Atkins).[76] An inflammatory placard was composed, and Watson and Thistlewood expected the meeting to be dispersed and were determined to resist. They each had a sword and told everyone to come armed, while Davidson, Harrison and Harland built up a store of arms and ammunition, and issued a list of gunsmiths and sword cutlers to be raided if necessary.[77]

But before the meeting took place the situation was changed by further news from the country. In Manchester the radical leadership had been taken over from Wroe and his group by Tetlow and, above all, William Walker, the 'sailor boy', who emerged as a great public speaker and the dominant figure in the whole area. He and his followers had bitterly opposed the wrecking of the simultaneous meetings on 1 November by Hunt, Wroe and the *Observer* group, and now, in concert with other areas, were planning a national meeting of delegates on 23 November (the day Parliament met and heard the speech from the throne). This, when it was confirmed that repression was planned, would organise an insurrection. Delegates were moving around, and a radical employed by Pickford's collected money as he toured the country in his removal van.[78] On 21 November Watson received a letter from Manchester that made it clear there was a lot of activity in the north (aided by Wooler's tour), and that said the Manchester Union subscriptions brought in £6 a week (which meant 1,440 members), that Hunt's influence was fast declining, that there were delegates from Nottingham and Glasgow then in Manchester, that the radicals had organised in five districts—Scotland (centred in Glasgow), the four northernmost English counties (centred in Carlisle), Yorkshire, Lancashire, and the Midlands (centred in Nottingham), that there were hundreds of thousands ready to fight, and that a general delegate meeting would be held at Nottingham on 23 November and when the content of the Prince Regent's speech was known it would adjourn to a more secret place and decide on 'ulterior measures' and a general rising by means of simultaneous meetings.[79] They looked to Watson and Thistlewood for support in London. And on 23 November William Walker left Manchester for London to find out the contents of the Regent's speech so as to take the news direct to Nottingham.[80]

The London group responded eagerly. Placards for the Smithfield meeting were sent in parcels to such places as Manchester, Derby and Nottingham. They supported simultaneous meetings and suggested 13 December, and Edmonds got Carlile to advocate them in his *Republican*. All this was to devalue the Smithfield meeting, but Watson drew up a series of inflammatory resolutions which proposed they go in a body to present a petition to King, Lords and Commons and that, if no redress were gained, they should refuse taxes, refuse to acknowledge the legitimacy of either House of Parliament and call simultaneous meetings over the country on 13 December.[81] And so were combined the fundamental revolutionary tactics—simultaneous meetings, tax-refusal and national convention.

But the preparations for a fight were too far advanced to be abandoned, and Thistlewood would never let an opportunity pass, especially as he thought that by 13 December coercive legislation would have made all public meetings impossible. The authorities assembled horse in readiness and seditious handbills were distributed at the meeting, but a mere six or seven hundred attended and it passed off without incident and with very little press publicity.[82]

Watson's hopes were now pinned on simultaneous meetings on 13 December, and Walker went on to Nottingham (the money provided by Bentham) where, on 29–30 November, the conference decided on 13 December. Travelling delegates then organised the simultaneous movement.[83] But after the Smithfield meeting Watson was arrested for a debt incurred on Hunt's welcome into London, and so he was removed from the scene and Thistlewood was left as undisputed leader of the group.[84] The failure of the last two London meetings and of Watson's plan of parochial societies (Wedderburn's group had quarrelled and broken up),[85] convinced Thistlewood that there was no hope of building up a mass movement in London. Walker's information convinced him that the lead must come from the country, and he visited Manchester early in December, so talk of a London meeting on 13 December was now dropped. But the strategic position of London meant that something must be done, and Thistlewood always thought that London could in some way give the lead for a rising that would nevertheless depend basically on the provinces. This lead could perhaps come in the traditional Spa Fields way of large crowds and a clash, but more and more Thistlewood was now reiterating his long-held belief that a few determined men could 'do it'. In this he was seconded by his friend Preston, who now became prominent again, and the meetings of the inner circle now took place at his house.

Two last attempts were made to rouse a crowd. On 30 November they agreed to a meeting on 2 December on Clerkenwell Green while public meetings were still allowed. Waddington went to ask Gast to take the chair, and Thistlewood and Palin toured the unions and coachmakers to get support. But as Watson was not released it never took place, and Thistlewood finally decided that it was pointless to arrange meetings of their own.[86]

He had hopes of the Westminster meeting to be held on 8 December, and it was decided to attend, interrupt, erect their own stage and propose their own resolutions. But a complication arose in connection with Hunt. Cobbett had now returned to London and joined Hunt and Wooler as leaders of a campaign to promote 'frugality, temperance, and sobriety' by giving up tea, spirits and all exciseable articles, while Cobbett and Benbow were also believed to have brought back plates to forge Bank of England notes. The White Lion group recognised the feebleness of this policy—they 'would not Fight for Cobbett & Hunt Would Recommend them to Drink Water for 2 or 3 years and Wait for his puff out'.[87] Hunt was also working to gain Roman Catholic support. But Hunt had wanted Burdett to fight the six acts clause by clause, and was disappointed when he worked closely in concert with the Whigs. He was now denouncing him and the Westminster reformers again. So he agreed with the Cripplegate Union to hold a meeting at Smithfield in rivalry to Burdett's at Covent Garden, and the Marylebone Union also gave its support. The White Lion group was furious at this attempt to reduce the numbers at Covent Garden, but on Wednesday 8 December Robert George and James Wilson carried a black flag with skull and crossbones and Gast's motto of June—'Let us die like men and not be sold like slaves.' Protected by Davidson and about forty men armed with bayonets and some firearms, it was intended to be a call to rise (as had been suggested for the 1 November meeting). The group first took it to Hunt's Smithfield meeting, a legal and very ordinary affair, attended by about 1,800 with a very mild speech by Hunt, and one by W. G. Lewis of Coventry. The group barracked and made violent calls, which only aroused the crowd's displeasure and condemnation from Hunt.[88] They then went on to Covent Garden, to the joint Whig–Westminster meeting, attended by about 5,000, but again met disapprobation until in the end the black flag was torn to shreds, all that was saved being the fragment bearing the word 'die'.[89] That evening twenty-three of the group met at the Black Dog and then at Preston's, very depressed at the day's events. It was obvious that there was no chance of rousing the metropolis, and so, at Thistle-wood's suggestion, they divided up into groups of four, each under a captain—Hartley, Palin, Bradburn, Cooke and Davidson—with Thistlewood and Preston under George Edwards as captain.[90] The failure of all public meetings, whomever called by, to lead to a rising, the failure of parochial unions, Watson's imprisonment, the 'treachery' of Hunt and Wooler, the six acts, Thistlewood's ascendancy, his implicit confidence in the violent George Edwards, the growing isolation of the group and the demise of the ultra-radical press all helped produce the final abandonment of Watson's strategy of mass organisation and action in favour of secret activity. The White Lion meeting on the 12 December was the last of its kind.

At the weekly captains' meeting on 9 December Thistlewood got them to agree to his brilliant plan to act when their number reached 200 by attacking Parliament dressed as soldiers; he also suggested attacking the Bank of England to achieve the same effect as Cobbett's puff-out.[91] But on 13 December they decided to abandon these plans as they only numbered forty-seven, and instead adopted Thistlewood's suggestion to assassinate ministers when they attended a cabinet dinner. They decided they were not ready to attack the one due on 15 December but to wait until they numbered fifty.[92] It was a logical step, as it would be a crushing blow to tyranny, the people of London would then rally to democracy, and they were confident that thousands in the country were only waiting the signal to rise. The legitimacy of killing tyrants was a cardinal article of faith, and idea had been mooted early in 1818, and had by November 1819 become a common idea among the London radicals. That night they were all given numbers to use instead of names, and the next day organisation was completed under eleven captains, with the password 'die' (taken from the fragment of the flag saved at Covent Garden).[93]

There remained the possibility of the simultaneous movement in the provinces on 13 December, and so every night from 13 to 16 December they met armed with cutlasses, pistols and ammunition in case there was news that Manchester or Glasgow had risen. But by now the movement in Lancashire had fragmented into weakness, and though the authorities there took the threat very seriously, the meeting was called off. The same happened elsewhere, with the sole exception of Glasgow, where a 'holiday' was held. A renewed attempt was made in Lancashire to act on New Year's night, and Thistlewood and his men again met every night after Christmas, but nothing happened. Lancashire was now a broken reed, especially after arrests on 22 December for conspiracy, and Yorkshire and Glasgow were left the chief radical centres.[94]

The group now began to suspect Hartley of being a spy, and he first tried to emigrate to the Cape, and then went into hiding. Williamson warned Banks that he was also suspected; Williamson was C, and now sailed for the Cape, while Banks, who was BC, ceased mixing with the group, especially after Robert George on 29 December shot at him, but missed.[95] The government was therefore suddenly completely dependent on the reports of 'W—r', George Edwards, who Thistlewood later said was the most sanguinary of all, an *agent provocateur*.

On 23 December they agreed that one man should be in charge, not a committee of captains. Thistlewood was naturally chosen, and made Edwards his 'aide-de-camp'.[96] They now numbered fifty-one, and their main activity consisted of the accumulation of weapons and looking for an opportunity to use them, preferably before Parliament met on 12 January so that there would be a power vacuum. They still had provincial contacts, letters coming from Ireland and especially Leeds, with Tetlow to make another visit on 10 January.[97] But they decided their tactics themselves. They did accumulate arms, though they were wretchedly poor. Thistlewood

had been seen constantly in the streets, dressed in a shabby manner, his countenance squalid and emaciated, and his whole dress and the expression of his features, denoting a man who was reduced to a state of extreme indigence. He was generally observed walking or running through the streets with eager impetuosity, and his shoes and an old surtout coat, which he generally wore, bearing all the marks of the poverty and distressed circumstances of the wearer.[98]

Though at times they considered acting at the Spanish ambassador's fete on 29 December, George III's funeral in February when the troops would be at Windsor, or even when the Regent's wife returned to England to claim her rights, basically they stuck to the idea of assassinating ministers, singly or collectively. At the end of January they got Watson, still in prison, to draw up a proclamation to the people to be issued after the blow was struck, and sent immediately by the mails to the country; it announced that the tyrants had been destroyed, a provisional government had been established at the Mansion House, a convention of the people would meet in a month elected by all adult males, and declared void every act passed by the boroughmongers in the last hundred years. Watson also prepared an address to the soldiers, announcing the killing of the tyrants, calling on them to make common cause with the people and wait for instructions from the provisional government, and promising them, if they rallied to the people, discharge with full pay for life and a gift of £10. Davison promised to print both but never did so.[99]

Thistlewood seems not to have intended to take power himself, but to retire once the system was overthrown.

> Thistlewood then began to mention the persons who would be the best to form the new Government, he said there was Gale Jones although he was a timid Man that he must be fetched, there was Lawson of Spital Fields he was a most excellent Man & there was also Mr. Gast of Deptford, as good a man as any in London, & there was the Doctor who would do to be set to legislate.[100]

In response to a letter Gast came to see him on 30 January, and according to Thistlewood fully supported him.[101] Total reliance should not be placed on Thistlewood's statement, but it is difficult not to believe that Gast knew of his plans and in some way approved of him. The Marylebone Union, which met at the schoolroom run by the cripple Thomas Hazard, gave 10 lb. of gunpowder to help Thistlewood, a group of Irishmen were contacted and signified their readiness to act, as had also a group of navvies using a pub in the Edgeware Road. The shoemakers seem also to have been favourable, Wilson had support in the Bear Street tailors' society, and contact was maintained with people in the north.[102]

A plan to attack the Earl of Harrowby's house on 2 February was not carried out, but on 19 February it was decided that something must be done the following Wednesday, 23 February, whether there was a cabinet dinner or no.[103] The government therefore had inserted in the *New Times* of 22 February a false announcement of a dinner at Harrowby's that night. The group were overjoyed, and finally agreed on the plan that had been drawn up some time before.[104] There were to be three groups, who would each act simultaneously at 8.30 pm. One group would meet at Hazard's house or in the loft of a stable in Cato Street hired by one of the conspirators, Harrison. They would then go to Harrowby's house, rush in on the dinner, led by Ings, the butcher, and Adams, the tall ex-soldier, and kill all men present but leave ladies unharmed. The second group would meanwhile have met at Cooke's, in Shoreditch, and at 8.30 pm would capture the Artillery Ground and take the cannon there. The third group, led by Palin, would meet south of the river, at 8.30 pm fire the large oil warehouses at Horsley Down, and then cross over and start fires at Funivals and Staples Inns. The murder party would then, with the exception of Harrison who would go to set fire to the King Street barracks, meet Palin's party at Cavendish Square, storm the Bishop of London's house there and take the weapons it contained, and then capture the artillery pieces at the Light Horse barracks in Gray's Inn Lane. They would then go to the Artillery Ground to combine with Cooke's party and Harrison to take the Mansion House for the provisional government, and seize the Bank, its books and its money. The two proclamations would then be posted.

On the evening of 21 February Thistlewood had gone to the Marylebone Union and told them of the attacks planned for the Wednesday, and to be ready to act when they saw fires lighting the sky. The Cripplegate Union was also expecting the time for fighting.[105]

The rest of the story is familiar enough.[106] Only eighteen eventually gathered in the Cato Street loft, the police stormed them but bungled it and in the confusion only caught nine, and Thistlewood escaped after killing one policeman. Brunt and Thistlewood still hoped to succeed, but the lack of light in the sky soon told them that Palin's group had not acted, and Cooke was not at home when his party arrived. 'We then went on towards the Artillery Grounds passed the Gates & looked in & Thistlewood said all quiet here too we have been sold by all parties.' The enterprise had failed, they split up, the leaders were soon rounded up, the press was full of the sensational news, and public revulsion was intense and helped the government overcome some of the opprobrium of the six acts. Groups had been waiting in the north, hourly expecting the signal to rise, but the London arrests destroyed the move. But efforts persevered in the West Riding and Glasgow and Paisley. It seems that the date set was 1 March, but arrests in Glasgow on 22 February deranged this, and it was postponed to 1 April. That night a rising was attempted at Huddersfield, while in Glasgow and Paisley perhaps 60,000 obeyed the call to stop work. But both were dispersed, though unrest continued in Yorkshire, especially at Barnsley on 11 April. The movement then collapsed.

The Cato Street sensation damaged the reformers' cause and unity, and helped the ministerialists in the general election. Though Hobhouse was fairly easily elected alongside Burdett at Westminster, Wood was the only reformer elected in the City (though later in 1820 Waithman was elected sheriff and Thorpe Lord Mayor). The government took pains to secure a successful result at the conspirators' trials, but were unable to use most of the evidence they possessed, fearing that the evidence of Edwards, as a paid informer would have an adverse effect. Luckily Robert Adams confessed and was the chief witness at the trial of Thistlewood, Davidson, Brunt, Tidd and Ings, and Abel Hall was also willing to testify.

Some were willing to make efforts for the prisoners. A committee to collect subscriptions for their defence included members of the group like Walker, Whittaker (another coffee-house keeper, who had been an active Watsonite in 1816–17), Denis Shaw, Dwyer (who became a paid informer), Griffin and Edmonds (now editor of *Cobbett's Evening Post*), and also Wooler, old Evans and Hone, while the London and Westminster divisions of shoemakers both gave £50.[107] Their main efforts were concerned with propagating the idea that Edwards had been the main instigator and Thistlewood was his dupe. Harmer was retained as counsel, and help came from ex-sheriff Phillips, Wood and one of the current sheriffs, Parkins. They managed to secure a true bill against Edwards for high treason and a warrant for his arrest, but he could not be found, even though Wood went to France in search of him, for he had been hidden in Guernsey. But the result of the trial was a foregone conclusion.

The group was depressed. Some retired from politics, Waddington becoming porter to a tallow chandler. On 10 May, the day of the executions, about twenty gathered at Whittaker's coffee-house to hear Preston's funeral oration.[108] They were in disarray, and it was Gast who was to gather them together again.

7
QUEEN CAROLINE

Thistlewood's failure, and the defeats in Glasgow and the West Riding left the London ultra-radicals depressed and fragmented. And this was in a context of a general fragmentation of the radical movement, discredited as it was by failure and conspiracies, demoralised by arrests, betrayals and the six acts, its leaders removed by imprisonment and its press killed off by the new legislation. At a few places in London—the Spotted Dog in St Clements Lane, Walker's and Chapman's coffee-houses in Shoreditch and Whittaker's in the Borough, and the Cross Keys in Brown Street —small groups met, debated and toasted the five martyrs. Before his imprisonment Hunt also sometimes went to Whittaker's and the ultras went to cheer him at his judgement. Hunt's friend, West the wire-worker, also put the first floor of his premises in the Strand at their disposal.[1]

Early in 1820 they concentrated on collecting subscriptions at these places for the defence of Thistlewood and the others, sedulously insisting that the conspiracy was mainly Edwards' work. They received help from Wood and Wooler, and Wooler then took the lead in organising relief for political prisoners generally. Until his trial in August he was the active democratic leader. At his main centre, the debating rooms at the Paul's Head in Soho, which Gast was probably attending, he organised a 'permanent fund' for political prisoners, and in May he, Gale Jones, Edmonds and Lewis launched the 'Liberal Alliance'. Wooler's aim was quite clear, to provide, as in 1817, a means of organisation and communication under the cover of relief funds and so defeat the blows delivered to public meetings, the press and political associations by the six acts. There were to be a managing committee and monthly meetings of subscribers; it urged the formation of provincial societies, and had a committee of correspondence. The idea spread. The ultras tried in March to start their own fund at the Spotted Dog, but probably merged with Wooler's, and in the provinces, where similar moves had already begun, permanent patriotic funds were set up at such places as Manchester, Birmingham, Glasgow and Nottingham.[2] These efforts at recreating radical organisation had some success, and by the autumn there were travelling delegates again in the north and a conference took place at Manchester.[3]

The sale and consumption of radical tea and coffee to avoid the excise duty, begun in 1819, was thriving in 1820, with Wooler again the leading advocate. But vendors of roasted grain were being arrested, and so in July Wooler, Lewis, Griffin, Gast and Waddington tried to organise protection for such people and resistance to harassment.[4]

But what gave the organised groups a common issue was the return to England of Caroline of Brunswick.[5] In 1813–14, largely through the work of Brougham and Whitbread, she had become the target of enthusiastic support against her highly unpopular husband, the Prince Regent, the 'Pig of Pall-mall', and this was heightened by her apparent alliance with her daughter, the very popular Princess Charlotte. Caroline had now been abroad since 1814, but immediately George III died in February 1820, the problem of the position of the new Queen was raised, for George IV wished to divorce and depose her. The radicals saw the opportunities of the situation and the prospect of a confrontation between Queen on one hand and King and ministers on the other. This could only discredit the latter in view of the popularity of the Queen and vast dislike of George IV. On this the radicals could capitalise. Even in January, when the death of 'the damned old King' was imminent, 'Thistlewood said, we shall now see when the Princess arrives if the Whigs or the Tories are strongest—and then will be the time for the Radicals to come in', though next month he decided the matter was irrelevant for republicans.[6] Before the old King's death she had made a move towards England. Even before his funeral the ministers had created an issue by agreeing to the new King's wish to omit a reference to her from the Liturgy. On 13 February a man went round with a horn selling papers and announcing the arrival of the Queen; the *Morning Chronicle*, *Cobbett's Evening Post*, *Statesman*, *Black Dwarf*, Thelwall's *Champion* and Wooler's *Gazette* all took up her cause; Hume raised her case in Parliament; colours and emblems were bought and worn; and radicals were planning great triumphal demonstrations should she come to London.[7] This was all before the Cato Street sensation. By March radicals were pinning

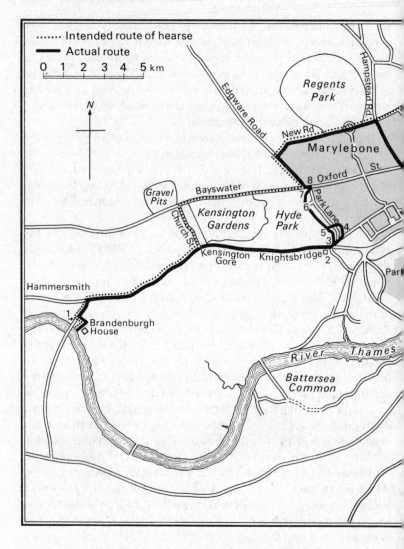

their hopes almost entirely on 'a general row' over the Queen and on 4 June, persuaded by Wood, the Queen dashed all the hopes of a compromise shared both by the ministers and her legal adviser, Brougham, and sailed for England.

The reception she received was sensational, from her landing at Dover and her journey through Kent to the solid crowds that stretched from Greenwich all the way into London. Here radicals

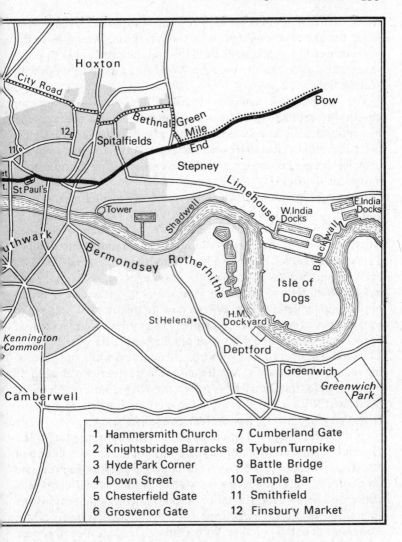

1 Hammersmith Church   7 Cumberland Gate
2 Knightsbridge Barracks 8 Tyburn Turnpike
3 Hyde Park Corner   9 Battle Bridge
4 Down Street   10 Temple Bar
5 Chesterfield Gate   11 Smithfield
6 Grosvenor Gate   12 Finsbury Market

had prepared horns, flags and music, and for a while great crowds
gathered each day and insulted and molested any who did not cheer
or take off their hats. In the night time they broke the windows of
unpopular ministers, especially Castlereagh. In contrast, when the
new King went to the House of Lords to give personally the royal
assent to the first bill passed in his reign, he was greeted by crowds
shouting, 'The Queen! Where's the injured Queen?'[8] The Queen

was at first cautious in her utterances, and stressed her loyalty to the King. But she also sought popular support through her gifts to the poor, refusal of a guard, appeals to the populace and public appearances when, ever accompanied by Wood, she was always met with acclamations.

The enthusiasm comprised many emotions—excitement, chivalry towards an injured woman, admiration of her courage (she had refused to be bought off), a sense of justice (given the King's behaviour), belief in a foul conspiracy against her, disgust at the use of 'spies' on her behaviour, a delight in embarrassing the ministers, hatred of George IV. Some were alarmed at the government's intentions in a situation where the most recent precedents were alarming ones from the reign of Henry VIII. It was expected that in both Houses of Parliament there would be secret, biased enquiries where her side of the case would not be heard and then a Bill of Pains and Penalties to depose her without a proper trial. Such an achievement would mean that the boroughmongers would have asserted their right to declare by themselves any individual or group outlaw and liable to death; as Place saw it, 'this alone should make every man a Parliamentary Reformer'. The radicals were overjoyed at the issue and settled on it with relief after the dangers of 1819. They could in safety condemn King and ministers while still protesting their 'veneration' for royalty, and were further encouraged by the support for the Queen from reforming Whigs like Grey Bennett, Sir Robert Wilson and Creevy, not to mention Burdett, Hobhouse, Hume and the Queen's law officers, Brougham and Denman, while even the Whig magnates attacked the ministers' proceedings. The Queen Caroline affair nullified the effects of the six acts and their attempts to check the independence of public agitation in press and on platform, for it produced mass demonstrations and a virtually unlicensed press. And it confirmed the basic unpopularity of the rulers. The sale of the *Black Dwarf* and the *Champion* rose, and the Commons deputation led by Wilberforce to arrange a compromise was mobbed.[10]

Support was now being organised. Reformers were in the ascendant in the City of London, having done well in the ward elections. Both Common Hall and Common Council declared for the Queen, and late in June she was welcomed officially on her visit to the Guildhall. An address to her was approved in Southwark, and Francis Place gave his support to those working for an agitation in Westminster.[11] His radicalism made him indifferent to the fortune of Whigs or Tories, and his republicanism forbade any concern over the Queen herself, but he wanted to prevent the ministers' passing such a bill against an individual, and was all for using the affair to discredit royalty.

> When in 1820 the Queen came from abroad, I set myself zealously to work to procure addresses to her. I set on foot the first public meeting, and wrote the address and resolutions. I cared nothing for the queen as the queen, she had been ill used by her husband, had left the country to him and his mistresses, and all that could be said against her was that she kept a man, a fine handsome fellow, this was no concern of any body's and if she liked to do so, it was a matter in which she ought to have been indulged without scandal, without reproach, while she could be no bad example at home. She however received 40.000£ a year of the people's money which she wasted and I could have no respect for a receiver of the plunder of the people but I saw very plainly, that if a public meeting was held, it would be followed by many others, and thus nearly the whole of the unprivileged unfrocked unpensioned unofficered part of the people would meet and address the Queen and go to the queen in thousands. I knew very well that the consequence would be a familiarity with the Royalty highly injurious to its state, that the mystification of the throne would be greatly impaired, the 'Divinity which doth hedge a King' would to a great extent be set aside and that many thousands of people would lose their reverence both for Royalty and Aristocracy and this I assigned as the reason for my *interference* in favour of the Queen, as it was called. I doubted whether or not so much stupidity existed amongst the Lords and especially in the Privy Council as would induce them to push the matter to extremities. But, when I saw them all commit themselves as they did I was exceeding pleased, and worked the harder on this account. I was now sure that the excitement would be general and that the consequence would be, such a falling off of respect for Royalty and Aristocracy as had never before existed amongst the people in this country. I saw that to immense extent this falling off would be followed by contempt.[12]

The result was a great Westminster meeting on 4 July, and Wood, Waitham and Wooler now worked hard to crown these big efforts in the City, Southwark and Westminster, so that on 6 July three great processions all came to the Queen's residence, Brandenburgh House at Hammersmith, each bearing an address to her. Already places in the country had voted addresses and the procedure was now established of regular days for the presentation, by procession or deputation, of addresses to which Wood gave the Queen's prepared reply, and the whole press, even the most loyalist, had to give the texts of both and details of the processions.

Alongside the periodicals and public meetings a third form of activity was started by Benbow, who had come to London with Cobbett and set up as his publisher. At the end of June he printed and had posted hundreds of copies of a bill, *Proposal to Murder the*

Queen!!, a violent accusation that her life was in danger from her enemies, and followed this up by a regular series of violent placards.[13] Dolby and Fairburn followed suit, paying boys to circulate their bills in vast numbers all over the metropolis. And soon these three, Griffin and others were publishing tracts and pamphlets, often in verse, all grossly insulting to the King, though none did as well as the hugely successful *Non mi Ricordo!* and *The Queen's Matrimonial Ladder* by Hone and Cruikshank.[14] The authorities seemed powerless.

The 'Queenites' were further encouraged by the government's granting of an open enquiry, to begin on 19 August, in connection with their bill to divorce and depose the Queen, and the postponement of the coronation, for they hoped to achieve maximum impact by disrupting that splendid affair. Excitement grew as the 'trial' approached, fed by xenophobic contempt for the foreign witnesses. The Queen seemed to be moving in a radical direction, especially in her reply to an address from Wakefield which raised such a storm in the loyalist press. With Cobbett now writing her replies and her famous letter of remonstrance to the King in August, she had become the 'Queen of the Radicals', leader of the 'Seditious rabble'.[15]

All this encouraged Gast to move. His view of the whole tangled negotiations was that the Queen had not been treated fairly, had been made to suffer by the King, and been subjected to spying. He admired her courage, and her fortitude in face of the very scurrilous and vituperative attacks on her. He thought her reply to the Wakefield address admirable and making her worthy of support. But apart from all this, he saw the issue as one between ministers and people. If the ministers prevailed in this contest they would be immeasurably strengthened, 'for if they succeed in their machinations against her, we, who are now only tied by one leg, shall be completely double-ironed upon both'.[16] The ministers must be checked. It was therefore in their interest to support the Queen, and she could only win in the boroughmongers' Parliament if there were a massive arousal of public opinion out of doors. This was possible and, given that liberty was now spreading on the continent, could well go on to result in political reform and the ending of corruption.

And so, helped by West, Waddington and Griffin, Gast led a rump of the 'out-and-out' radicals in arranging a meeting to address the Queen. Bridges, the Tory Lord Mayor, reacted to the revival of this group with alarm. When a warning to the landlord of the Jacob's Well that his licence was in danger did not work, the City Police occupied it on 31 July to prevent the meeting, and it was held instead at the Cart and Horses in Goswell Street, outside the City. The presence here of a strong party of police officers did not prevent the meeting or Gast's hour-long speech. Gast had himself composed the resolutions and the address to the Queen, but though the address was pure royalism, the resolutions were regarded as the strongest yet passed at a 'Queenite' meeting.[17]

In his speech Gast made many of the familiar points, and took care to praise 'Brave Alderman Wood' and condemn the system of 'spinnage' (espionage). But his was basically an attack on the upper classes generally. His address and resolutions 'was wrote in language which the "higher orders" was by no means capable of', and he particularly fastened on Castlereagh's reference to the Queen's appeal to 'a base populace'. They were, he said to shouts of applause, the nerve and sinew of the State, the industrious bees who created all the luxuries of the higher orders (who were idle drones) and the ministers (who were caterpillars). He stressed that the affair gave a good chance of achieving reform through mass agitation, and reiterated his standard view that public opinion was an Herculean club which would eventually destroy the Hydra of corruption.

> If WE say we will defend our Queen, I should be glad to know who will resist us? They dare not attack a hair of her head, if the public voice is raised against it, for the public voice is political power, and it is the public voice alone which had preserved to this country, even a shadow of its liberties.

But Gast's outlook and connections made this meeting an artisan affair; the appeal was to the 'thinking, working, and industrious classes of the country, in London and its environs'. About 400 artisans came to the meeting, several journeymen spoke, and copies of the address were given to two people in every mechanical trade to procure signatures. True to form, Gast urged them to accumulate funds for a demonstration to present the address by giving up both pipe and pot, and urged them to conduct themselves on that day in such a way as to demonstrate their superiority to the higher orders, not only in usefulness but also in behaviour.

It was a campaign quite clearly organised through the trade societies, and the organisation, whether purely *ad hoc* or not we do not know, was extensive enough to gather a claimed 29,786 signatures, a very large figure if true.[18] And though this number cannot be checked, the size of the artisans' procession on 15 August is not really debatable. It was well organised, and exemplified the trade societies' liking for show and pageantry. They assembled at 11 am at

St Clements' Church in the City, marshalled into groups by men with white wands. The address was borne between two people genteelly dressed in mourning, but wearing white silk rosettes. These white ribands, symbolising innocence and purity, were Gast's idea. Behind the address walked in pairs about a hundred men dressed in the same way, and then another hundred dressed in coloured clothes, some with aprons, others with silk coloured hand-kerchiefs and, like the rest of the procession, many wearing sprigs or leaves of laurel. These were nearly all clean and 'the better-class of journeyman mechanic'. Their numbers swelled as they marched. In Knightsbridge they caught up with the Middlesex cavalcade and were then themselves caught up with by the Hammersmith and Shoreditch processions, to make one continuous line from Hyde Park to Hammersmith. Only fifty went up to the drawing-room behind Gast, who made a long speech before reading the address, all then kissed her hand and she appeared at the window to cheers from the rest outside. The whole business had revealed impressive organisation by Gast's group, and the wearing of white favours was adopted generally by supporters of the Queen.[19]

On 19 August the trial really opened and the hearing lasted until 8 September, and then again from 3 October until 25 October. All the details of the evidence were carried by the press unchecked, and the nation wallowed in obscenity. Excitement and agitation con-tinued unabated, and London had a mass of ward and parish meet-ings (with the same people participating in several different gather-ings), and, mainly on Mondays, processions carrying the addresses to the Queen. At length on 10 November the ministers gave in and abandoned the bill, and jubilation was immediate. Mobs marched up and down shouting 'light up' and enforced a brilliant illumination all over London that lasted three nights, the biggest since the one at the Peace of Amiens. People were forced to shout for the Queen, in the poor areas of Seven Dials and St Giles there were bonfires, fireworks, lights and shouting, the Strand was a blaze of light and a great crowd gathered there, the main centre being Benbow's large shop. Stones and bricks showered on the offices of the ministerialist *Courier* and *Morning Post*, and the Police who tried to disperse the crowd were put to flight. The Life Guards were called, and even they seemed in favour of the Queen. It was a time of triumph of radicals and people over King and ministers.[20]

Yet this agitation is often seen as a diversion of radicalism from reform into the side-issue of the Queen's rights, which proved a dead-end when she died, and a blow to ultra-radicalism in that the popular movement was led by parliamentary radicals and Whigs like Hobhouse, Hume, Wood, Wilson and Noel, forging the alliance that carried the day in 1832.[21] There is a danger in being too intellectual here, for it may be that the fact of agitation was more important than its ostensible aim. The affair was crucially important in dissipating the constrictions of the six acts and re-establishing open political campaigning. Further there was 'never an episode more damaging to Royalty and its claims',[22] and it did much to discredit the political system. It did involve many artisans in open political agitation. And the movement was not in fact wholly under the control of the parliamentary reformers; this is especially true of the latter part of the affair, after December 1820. But most accounts concentrate on the events up to the abandonment of the bill in November, and treat what followed as a postscript. This is a mistake.

The climax to the first phase of public meetings came with an indoor one at the Freemasons' Tavern at the end of September, crowded and highly successful, with the amicable participation of Peter Moore, Wood, Hobhouse, Hume, Thelwall and Wooler stressing a united front.[23] The following week their address was presented, but on the same day there also came to the Queen a procession of the shipwrights and caulkers of the Port of London.[24] This was a very impressive affair, that must have taken a lot of trouble and expense. It is known that some shipbuilders donated. No names were mentioned, but Gast must have been one of the organisers. Three thousand assembled in Stepney and proceeded on foot, and there was full expression of their love of pageantry and a show to express pride in their crafts, and benefit society rituals and decorations were drawn upon. The order was thus:

> Two men on white horses.
> A blue flag with the motto 'Address of the Ship-builders to the Queen'.
> A model of Noah's ark, carried on a pole.
> A blue flag, fringed with silver lace, motto 'Hearts of Oak'.
> Blue flag with a portrait of the Queen, 'God protect the Innocent C.R.'
> Model of the head of a ship, inscription
>   'Long may our wooden walls defend our native land,
>   May innocence and truth break the tyrants' band!'
> Blue flag, 'Hail! Hail! Star of Brunswick'.
> Model of a first-rate ship of war.
> White flag, highly decorated, 'We maintain and protect the innocent'.
> Union Jack, 'What we have we guard'.
> White flag, four hands united.
> Blue flag, side view of ship's keel, 'Let Justice guide the helm'.
> Blue flag, 'The Wooden Walls of Old England'.

Blue flag, 'The Ship-caulkers' Tribute of respect to insulted Majesty'.
Blue flag, 'Ship-caulkers of the Port of London'.
Two small blue flags like Persian standards, 'Cheer up virtue'.
Two more, 'Oppressors are cowards'.
Large flag with picture of Noah's ark, 'Ezekiel, chapter 28, verse 4'.
Union Jack.
Flag, arms of the ship-caulkers, 'Sons of Freedom and Justice'.

The men marched six abreast, were all, the press agreed, very clean
and respectable in appearance, and all wore sprigs of oak or laurel,
or white favours. They had at least four bands, and when they
reached the house they drew up in almost military precision. It was
the most imposing procession to date and was greatly applauded.

On the next presentation day the Thames watermen and lighter-
men came up with their address, and the river was filled with their
boats. In the following weeks this lead was followed, and many
trades held meetings to approve resolutions and addresses in support of the Queen and elect committees to organise a presentation
by deputation or procession.[25] These were the coachmakers (in
twenty carriages), glass-blowers, bakers, Spitalfields weavers (their
address signed by 40,00), carpenters and joiners, coopers, sawyers
(with thirty-two flags), stay- and corset-makers, printers, cabinet-
makers, chairmakers, carvers, musical instrument makers, upholsterers, curriers, leather-dressers, silver-workers, paper-hangers
and bricklayers. One of the most splendid was the brassfounders'
and braziers', but best of all was the 4,000-strong procession of the
London benefit societies, in which 54 societies took part, each with
its own flag, representing 25,000 members. A few trades and
benefit societies also took part in the procession that accompanied
the Queen on her visit to the City to celebrate her 'acquittal', one
bearing the banner with the immortal lines:

Vouchsafe, Disposer of all Human Good,
Save Caroline, and prosper noble Wood.[26]

The artisans played an important part in the campaign, and the basis
of their organisation was the trade societies. The Queen Caroline
affair thus promoted open, political demonstrations by the trade
societies, as opposed to petitions alone, and established a practice
that was maintained throughout the decade.

Moreover, Gast was still active in building up an organisation of
mechanics, and meetings were held late in October to plan another
mass procession to the Queen. Gast's group was the only one that
worried the authorities, and indeed troops and Horse Guards were
held in readiness. It seems, though the evidence is not very clear,

that some sort of permanent organisation, a Mechanics' Committee, was set up. It is possible that the Philanthropic Hercules had provided some basis for it, as at least two people, Gast and the millwright Miles Hopson, were in both. Soon there was to emerge a Mechanics' Union, with its Union Flag.[27]

At the same time the democrats, led by Cartwright, Wooler, Pearson, Benbow, Lewis, Dolby, Griffin, West, Whittaker and Davison were active again. On 23 August they launched a committee to collect subscriptions (not exceeding a shilling) to replace the Queen's plate seized by the King.[28] They secured a sensation in October when Pearson exposed a man Franklin, alias Fletcher, who had issued an unauthorised seditious placard in the name of this Queen's Plate Committee and was found to have composed in the last two years a series of incendiary radical placards in the name of groups who had had nothing to do with them. When a magistrate and Sidmouth prevented legal proceedings against him, the democrats convincingly portrayed Franklin as an agent employed by the ministers to foment sedition, another Edwards.[29] The democrats took heart, and also persisted with the policy of Hunt and Watson of an Irish alliance. The two Irish leaders in London were R. Hayes, a Roman Catholic priest, and W. E. Andrews, who ran the *Catholic Advocate*, both of whom had been in contact with the Watsonites in 1819 before the rift with Hunt. They and Thomas Murphy were all on the Plate Committee, and Cartwright, Wooler, Hayes and Andrews soon formed the 'Friends of Civil and Religious Liberty' in favour of Catholic Emancipation and in touch with Daniel O'Connell. This was to be the main radical organisation in London in the 1820s. Also, a Scotch group under Dr Gilchrist united with these under the motto of 'Shamrock, Thistle and Rose'.[30]

The 'Queenite' agitation was much stronger in London than anywhere else, but the democrats also had contacts with the country, with London delegates going to Yorkshire, the four northernmost counties, Scotland and Wales, while Saxton, the Manchester leader, went on a tour in support of the Queen. In December 1820 fifty delegates met at Manchester, and the authorities heard of revolutionary plans again in connection with the Queen's affair, and for a move in May 1821.[31] If this is so, it was probably meant to be in conjunction with the disruption of the coronation.

The democrats knew of their differences from the other reformers. Pearson had tried to interrupt the Freemasons' Tavern meeting in September but failed, even Wooler insisting on a united front.[32] Radicals were worried when the Queen ceased receiving addresses in November and was visited by the Duke of Sussex and Prince Leopold; they feared that Wood was trying to dampen down the agitation and that 'the Queen is ratting'.[33]

It is doubtful if they were right. A sort of co-ordinating committee for the campaign had emerged, consisting of Hume, Noel, Thelwall, Wilson, Hobhouse, Barber Beaumont and George Rogers (a tobacco-manufacturer prominent among the Westminster reformers).[34] Early in November they decided on a new phase in the agitation. This was before the bill reached its second reading in the Lords, but it was assumed that it would pass in the upper House and then go to the Commons, where the whole process would be gone through again, but with much more emotion. And so they called a meeting for 15 November of the chairmen of all London meetings that had been held in support of the Queen, and prepared an address to be passed at a second round of meetings, probably simultaneously, for 'there would be nothing so effectual in preventing its [the bill's] further progress as to call forth the combined and simultaneous action of all the Committees from which Addresses to the Queen had proceeded, so as to bring forth an unequivocal declaration of the opinions of the whole population'.[35] But by the time this meeting was actually held, the bill had been dropped, and some felt that the matter was now settled, though most wanted to press on with other issues (liturgy, allowance, residence). The fourth person who spoke was Gast, and he sounded a note of discord, for, true to form, the theme of his speech was pride in the working mechanics, and an emphasis on the role of the radicals. 'Had it not been for the Radicals, who had stuck to her like her back bone, her polite aristocratic subjects would have sacrificed her long ago.' He insisted that agitation must continue, and told them he would propose to the Mechanics' Committee an address to the Queen, and an address or petition to the Commons to make the ministers bear the cost of the proceedings 'and to cause their estates to be confiscated if they were unable to pay it from their other property', and perhaps also make the King pay something. Gale Jones then tried to argue, in characteristic radical fashion, that the meeting was not merely advisory but was a decision-making delegate body, but was opposed by Richter and Wilson. In the end they all agreed on a resolution welcoming the dropping of the bill, and to call further meetings to deliberate on measures to secure the rights of the Queen and recover the country's constitutional liberties. This was widening their aims, but when Cartwright introduced a typically long resolution in favour of parliamentary Reform and received support from Edmonds, Wooler and Jones, it was opposed by Hume, Thelwall and Wilson as irrelevant and easily voted down.[36] The differences within the agitation were clear.

But the agitation went on. A new round of meetings adopted addresses congratulating the Queen on her 'acquittal' and calling on the King to dismiss his ministers. Occasionally democrats tried to move a resolution calling for the impeachment of ministers, as did Benbow at the great Westminster meeting.[37] Again, from December to February, these addresses were taken to the Queen by deputations and processions. And the co-ordinating committee, having so well organised the Queen's visit to the City in November, became the Queen's Cavalcade Committee and organised these demonstrations.

Gast called a meeting of course. By now Waddington and Griffin were both in prison, and it is not clear who was on his Committee of the Industrious Classes, probably some Watsonites, like Walker and Moggridge, and delegates from trades. With the reformer Thorpe now Mayor they met unmolested on 11 December at the Jacob's Well, and again Gast stressed the Queen's dependence on popular support and the important role of the mechanics, and voiced his suspicions of Brougham. The address of the 'Artisans and Industrious Classes' gained perhaps 20,000 signatures and was presented on 23 January 1821 by a procession behind a large flag inscribed 'The Union Flag' in gold lettering and probably also already behind the emblem of a bundle of sticks on a pole, Gast's idea to symbolise strength from unity. There were also a number of other flags, curious devices in iron and wood, and specimens of mechanics' skill.[38]

The individual trades also responded. The shipwrights were again the first, for on 18 December about three thousand marched to seven bands to present the address of the shipwrights, caulkers, joiners, sailmakers, shipsmiths and mastmakers. Again there were splendid silk flags, banners, bannerets and streamers, and there were also many models of vessels in every stage of building. Other trades followed suit—Spanish and Moroccan leather trade, fell-mongers, kid and lamb dressers, furriers and skinners; curriers; printers; bricklayers; coopers; glass-blowers; bookbinders; sawyers (2,000 marched); coachmakers; cabinet-makers, chairmakers, car-vers and musical instrument makers; tin-plate workers (in four barouches); goldsmiths, silversmiths, and jewellers; calico-printers; carpenters and joiners, painters and glaziers; Camberwell labour-ers. The most splendid were the brassfounders, braziers and coppersmiths, with several suits of fine armour, and the benefit societies put on another good show. But most attention was drawn by the seamen's procession. The climax came on 23 January, just before Parliament met, when 63 addresses were presented and many trades marched. 'The zeal of the Mechanics is beyond all precedent.'[40]

The ultra-radicals worked hard to keep up the pressure and gather large crowds to meetings, processions and the opening of Parliament. A number of petitions were presented in favour of the inclusion of a reference to the Queen in the Litany, but when motions to this effect in January and February were lost, the parliamentary opposition largely dropped the Queen's case and turned to other issues, leaving the agitation high and dry. Public demonstrations continued, especially on the King's visits to the theatres,[41] but the Queen ceased public appearances and her acceptance of a government grant disillusioned some supporters. The agitation was running out of steam, and the radicals' hopes of a grand climax at the coronation were waning.

The ultra-radicals were not inactive. At the end of December Gast, Walker, Blandford and Benbow led the formation of a committee of 'Patriotic Benevolence' to aid political prisoners, basically a revival of Wooler's earlier attempt, with district sections, a general committee whose weekly meetings were open to all, and penny a week subscriptions from working-class members. In February 1821 Gast and Benbow publicly launched the Patriotic Benevolent Institution.[42] The group also formed another extremist organisation. Through press reports on the Italian revolutions, they had become interested in the Carbonari, who were seen as like austere Scotch Presbyterians, foes of gambling and advocates of continence and a primitive Christianity that rejected the Roman Church. In March they formed in Soho an Anglo-Carbonarian Union, which merged the outlook of mechanics, radicals and Spenceans in its Creed and Catechism that, in the name of true Christianity, asserted the unity and equality of all mankind and strove 'for the attainment, establishment and security of the just right of all men, to the *full* and *whole* produce of their labour separately and collectively in the equal power of use and enjoyment, together with an unabridged and just share of the whole abundance and fruits of the Earth, arising out of the combined powers of Nature, Art and Manual Toil'.[43] Thus was Gast's basic philosophy encapsulated in the programme of this 'Carbonaria'.

All this encouraged Dr Watson to re-enter politics, joining the

Patriotic Benevolent Institution and interrupting a meeting called in favour of emigration to the Cape.[44] By May placards were appearing over his name, for interest in the Queen revived as the coronation drew nearer and the radicals hoped she would go to enforce her claim to be crowned and would receive support from the crowd. Addresses had continued intermittently from some of the trades, and she now made public appearances at the theatre.[45] The Gast–Watson group was planning what they saw as the last effort. On coronation day, 19 July, the illuminations were poor and crowds gathered at the Queen's lodgings and the Abbey. They were generally sympathetic to her when she arrived and tried to go in, but no move was made to help her when at each door she was refused entry because she had no ticket. No row ensued. As their last effort the group began plans to arrange a separate coronation of the Queen,[46] but this was ended when she died on 7 August, to the joy of the King and relief of many people.

The whole business seemed to be over.

> Poor Queen! I thought her heart was broken the last time I saw her, but did not expect the catastrophe so soon. For her it is well over . . . Her best friends, if poor thing she had any, must be glad it is well over. Peace to her Ashes.[47]

Burdett was wrong. The most dramatic events were yet to come. Caroline's wish was to be buried in her native Brunswick. London wanted a public funeral, and the government feared the crowds would give it the character of pageantry and suspected the City magistrates of favouring the same. The government and court wished to rush the corpse abroad as soon as possible, and announced this would be done on 14 August, by their nominees and not by her executors, and that only members of her actual household could accompany it, not men like Wood. The 'Queenites' wished for delay to give more time for demonstrations, and so her executors continually protested at the haste in removing the body.

The obvious way to convey the corpse was by water, but this the government dared not do as the City magistrates' authority extended over the stretch of river next the City, and they had many large barges, so could easily stop the conveyance of the body. The government well remembered how at the opening of Waterloo Bridge the Lord Mayor's barge, though forbidden to do so, had broken in on the royal procession and for a while cut off a whole line of royal barges; the government had had no legal remedy at all. They feared that the City authorities might stop the transport, land the body and lay it in state at the Guildhall. Moreover, the transport would have to pass through miles of shipping, and they feared that the seamen would stop it, for of all the addresses that had poured in on the Queen the government had been most worried at that from the merchant seamen, said to have been signed by 10,000. The body must therefore go by land to Harwich, and thence by sea to Germany.[48] But to avoid demonstrations, it must not go through London but be taken north to the City Road and so skirt north London to the Harwich road.

The press publicised all the protests at the haste, and it was clear that crowds would turn out and follow the hearse in a procession. Some trades, including carpenters, coopers, brassfounders and Morocco leather dressers, decided to go in a body.[49] There might even be attempts to make the procession go right through London. Many welcomed the chance of a row, and some even wanted to force the procession into the City to deposit the body by force in St Paul's for a day, but the Lord Mayor would not countenance this.[50] The government determined to proceed and kept the intended route secret, so that when the Queen's Cavalcade Committee met on the night of 13 August, Thelwall could only go out to tell the crowds outside to assemble at Brandenburgh House, where the body lay, at 6 o'clock the next morning.[51]

The next morning the appointed Conductor of the Funeral Procession, Bailey, came to Brandenburgh House before six, to find there were already crowds there, as there were also at Hyde Park Corner.[52] At six o'clock Clarenceaux King of Arms and a herald arrived with the order to take possession of the body, and with them a squadron of Oxford Blues. These formed a line in front of the house facing a hostile crowd, while a Bow Street patrol guarded the gates. A few minutes later arrived some of the Queen's executors and chief supporters, and an official from the Lord Chamberlain's office to take possession of the body in the name of the Lord Chamberlain. Outside, soaked in the pouring rain (which lasted all morning), waited the Cavalcade Committee on horseback, led by Hume and Hobhouse, and the Hammersmith Committee, led by one of the churchwardens. With the arrival at 6.50 of the hearse and eight, with thirteen coaches and six, excitement had become intense. The whole of Hammersmith was crowded, every house and shop was shut, every available vehicle had been requisitioned, and the turnpike-gate was removed. The church bell tolled minute time, and across the river minute guns fired.

At 7.30 Bailey took possession of the body, to strong protests from the executors, and revealed the route—to Hammersmith, then towards Kensington, turn at Kensington gravel pits into Uxbridge Road, and thence to Bayswater, Tyburn Turnpike, Edgware Road, New Road, Islington, City Road, Old Street, Mile End, Romford, Chelmsford, Colchester and Harwich. The carriages began to set off at eight, and the executors, committees and crowds fell in behind. The head of the procession reached Hammersmith Church at 8.55 and here the crowds were very dense, and charity children strewed the road with flowers. They moved on to Kensington and reached Kensington Church at 9.30 to find Church Street blocked by two vehicles in an effort to cut off the intended route and force the procession to go through London and the City. No sooner was one of the vehicles removed than it was replaced by another, and carts were steadily added. And so the procession waited, and by luck or judgement the hearse stood right in front of Cobbett's house, covered in black, while the crowd yelled 'Through the City!—through the City', and others broke up the gravel pit road to make sure no procession could pass along it.

Word reached the Home Office straightaway, and Sir Richard Baker, the chief magistrate at Bow Street, summoned the Life Guards and was told by Lord Liverpool to go and get the cortege to the New Road by a different route, through Hyde Park and out at the Oxford Street end by Cumberland Gate. He went, and so at 11.15, having waited since 9.30, the procession moved on again having given up the intended route, to cheers and shouts of 'City, City!'. But when the hated Life Guards arrived they were greeted with 'Blues for Ever, No Reds, Piccadilly Butchers, No Butchers, Kill the buggers'.

But when the procession reached the Kensington gates into Hyde Park it found them shut, for the crowd was determined to prevent its missing out the City. Repeated attempts by the Life Guards to open the gates, amidst a shower of stones and mud, failed. And so the procession gave in again and went along Kensington Gore and Knightsbridge, all the while to shouts of 'City!', with the Life Guards at the rear of the procession receiving a stream of abuse and missiles. But at Hyde Park Corner the Park Gate was barricaded with market-carts, and so Baker at the head of the procession moved on, amidst shouts, mud and missiles, intending to go up Park Lane. But this was also blocked by carts, and though Life Guards were sent to remove them and much fighting and many wounds resulted, they were unable to do so and at the request of their commanding officer Baker halted.

Meanwhile at 11.30 Henry Hobhouse, Under-Secretary at the

Home Office, had asked the magistrate William White to go and help the procession. When White joined it he found it surrounded by carriages and a huge crowd but he managed, perhaps taking the crowd by surprise, to force the Hyde Park Gate after very great resistance, and the hearse and the part of the procession behind it then went through, leaving the front part outside. A race for Cumberland Gate now developed, the crowd running to shut it to prevent access to the Edgware Road, the hearse and the procession going at a trot while White and the Life Guards galloped ahead to keep the gate open.

Meanwhile Baker heard the news, turned along Down Street with the front part of the procession, got into the Park through Chesterfield Gate, and rushed across the park. Half-way between the Grosvenor and Cumberland gates he caught the other half of the procession up, only then to hear pistol shots towards Tyburn Turnpike.

White had succeeded in reaching Cumberland Gate first, and placed Life Guards at the end of Cumberland Place and Oxford Street to keep the way open. By now the park was filled with crowds streaming across, and when the first carriage went through the gate a great struggle began. There were very few constables, so a few Life Guards helped the carriage through by hitting at the crowd with their sabres, but some of them were hurt by the bricks and stones and they were now exasperated and very angry. The crowd broke down twenty foot of the park walls and made a barricade of timber, iron and posts on the Edgware Road. This delayed the procession and the attacks on the soldiers continued, but they forced a passage, lined up six on each side and the procession got through. But still the crowds in the streets and behind the park threw bricks and stones, and some of the guards now fired their pistols, several people were wounded and the crowd scattered in all directions, but stones and bricks were thrown again and White forbade any more shooting. Foot Guards now arrived, the Riot Act was read, and after five minutes' more struggle the gate was cleared and the procession succeeded in reaching the Edgware Road. The crowd had been defeated.

On the Edgware Road the procession was reunited, and the Life Guards and the front half of the procession resumed their places in front of the hearse. But huge crowds lined the road and pelted the Life Guards so that the officer asked White for permission to withdraw them, as he feared in their anger they would shoot again. White agreed, but kept the Blues as they seemed less unpopular.

The procession proceeded along the New Road between huge crowds but without hindrance until they reached the junction with Tottenham Court Road and found the way on to Islington blocked by a massive barrier of coaches and carts chained together, and an enormous crowd very angry at the shootings. Baker therefore did not try to force the barrier, especially as he was told that there were still more barriers and even trenches further along the road. Tottenham Court Road led back into town, so White wanted to turn left up Hampstead Road and rejoin the New Road further along, but this would take time and Baker felt the return to the New Road at Battle Bridge would easily be blocked at the turnpike gates. And so he turned down Tottenham Court Road to St Giles, and White left.

Every side-road to the east was blocked to prevent the procession's turning to avoid the centre. Baker hoped to go along Holborn, but two wagons piled with huge loads prevented it, and he had to give in completely and lead the very bedraggled and dirty procession along Broad Street, Drury Lane and the Strand to shouts of 'Victory! Victory!' The gates at Temple Bar were open and the procession proceeded in total disorder into the City, through Fleet Street, St Paul's Churchyard, Cheapside and Leadenhall Street. At Bridge Street, having failed totally in his task, Baker heard that the Lord Mayor was on his way and he then left the procession. It was met by the Mayor, Marshals, City officers and Sheriffs, and joined by two small groups of tradesmen with banners and proceeded on its way. At five o'clock it reached Mile End and was joined by a crowd of seamen. Most of the crowds dropped off before Bow and Stratford, but many continued as far as Ilford.

The Queen's final exit had been the most dramatic event of all, with a clear expression of popular feeling and successful defiance of the government. But there was more to come. Baker had to resign in disgrace, Sir Robert Wilson was dismissed from the army for his behaviour on the day, and the entire liberal press condemned the government for its handling of the funeral and especially the shooting at Cumberland Gate. It soon transpired that not only had several men been wounded there but two had been killed, a carpenter, Richard Honey, and a bricklayer, George Francis. Normally the burial of these two would be arranged by their respective trade or benefit societies, but immediately Gast, Watson, Waddington, Gale Jones and their Committee of the Industrious Classes saw the possibility of a public funeral to the two men. On the very day after the Queen's 'funeral' they circulated a handbill calling for a public funeral for the two men to repeat the crowds of 14 August. Watson and Gale Jones persuaded Mrs Francis to agree, tempting her with the prospect of a public subscription, while Galloway, apparently in charge of the corpses, advised leaving it to the bricklayers' society.[53] Gast both called and presided at a meeting at the Bear and Ragged Staff in West Smithfield on 21 August, very fully attended by deputies from the trades, and urged a public funeral for the following Sunday.[54] The committee proposed that the trades march as groups, each carrying the tools of their trade, via Cumberland Gate to Hammersmith Church. The two men had actually lived in Bloomsbury, but the Queen had attended Hammersmith Church and the plan was to take the officiating curate there by surprise by arriving at 4 pm, the usual time for Sunday funerals. The aim was purely political, and the proposal to carry tools ominous, but though this latter idea was rejected, it was agreed to have the funeral, and sawyers, bookbinders, weavers, compositors, seamen and calico-printers agreed on the spot to attend.

But during the week the respective carpenters' and bricklayers' societies disassociated themselves from the plan and arranged the funeral themselves.[55] It is not clear what was involved here, as the burial was still to be at Hammersmith Church, and so the cortege would follow a route which, though it missed out Cumberland Gate, still went right through London. Gast's committee went ahead in planning a mass turn-out. It was a most serious and critical project, far more so than the events of the Queen's funeral. The Cavalcade Committee and every one of the papers that had supported the Queen, except the *Examiner*, condemned the idea as provocative and bound to lead to more deaths. The rift among the 'Queenites' seemed complete. Waithman, as Sheriff of London and Middlesex, had a responsibility for keeping order and was particularly worried because the planned route went past the Knightsbridge barracks of the hated Life Guards who had killed the men. He issued a public letter appealing for the funeral to be called off, in vain.

But the press gave full publicity to the plans, and the liberal papers especially gave very full reports of the two long inquests, the first verdict being of murder by troops unknown. Excitement grew during the week, and the day was a great one.[56] Crowds began to gather in Smithfield in the late morning including the sawyers, coopers and braziers as trades. At one o'clock they were led by Watson and Waddington behind the symbol of unity, the bound sticks, to Francis' house and there joined the hearse, four mourning coaches and two hundred 'decent, orderly' bricklayers. All then went to Oxford Street to join Honey's benefit society, the Provident

Brothers, and their flags, and at Grosvenor Square met Honey's hearse. So began the most impressive of all the Queen Caroline demonstrations, with carpenters, bricklayers, mutes, lids of feathers, band playing the Dead March in *Saul*, the great crowd gathered by the ultra-radicals, and preceded by Waitham and his deputy on horseback. There was a long line of vehicles, and the procession was huge, all the press agreeing that nearly all the participants were workers. It marched in complete order between vast crowds of spectators, and another great mass was waiting at Hyde Park Corner to join in.

The commander of Knightsbridge barracks had shut the gates and all the soldiers were inside. Waithman had also posted some officers there, and arrived there ahead of the procession, only to see a little girl standing with her mother hit by a brick thrown over the wall from inside. When the procession reached the barracks hardly any soldiers could be seen, but there were a few at the windows provocatively pretending to be overcome with grief at the bodies. There were a few hisses and shouts of 'Butchers' but they were immediately stopped by the majority and Waithman rode about checking for any sign of disorder. For the most part they passed in complete silence, the numbers now completely thronging the road.

By brilliant organisation they reached Hammersmith exactly at four, when the church bell began to toll. The curate met the coffins at the gate, and every head was uncovered in total silence; into the church went the coffins, mourners and as many of the crowd as could get in, all trying to touch the coffins, while the crowd outside swarmed over yard, walls and trees. The plan for a mass, orderly demonstration had succeeded.

But as the crowds dispersed and passed the barracks on their way back, they hissed and booed, while some troops laughed at them through the window. A cornet was spotted passing through the crowd and beaten up, soldiers rushed out to save him, fighting resulted and there was nearly an ugly clash between Waithman and Sir Richard Phillips and some of the troops before the latter were all got inside. But the crowd was now thoroughly inflamed and a shower of stones broke 282 windows, and in the end the magistrate Conant had to come with police officers to restore order. This was not achieved until 10 o'clock.

Despite the ensuing recriminations between City and government, the Queen Caroline affair was really over. Yet it had further shaken the prestige of monarchy and government, restored freedom of political agitation, brought trade societies into open political activity, and enabled Gast to build up a radical trade organisation. It was therefore an important episode in London working-class politics and had ended with a rupture between ultra-radicals and the rest with the former making the running, and a very impressive overwhelmingly artisan demonstration. It can hardly therefore be seen as a 'diversion'.

Yet an attempt at a further meeting by Watson failed,[57] and the movement did seem to lead to a dead end. This was not because of its aim so much as the dropping of activity by members of Parliament or more respectable ranks. The Queen Caroline affair showed, as did the Reform crisis later, the reliance of the radicals on a general air of political agitation created by those in much more influential situations. Only in that context could large numbers be attracted into political activity. Despite very widespread radical notions among the artisans, the radicals of themselves could not attract large numbers into activity—they needed a context of general political excitement.

There were still many groups of radicals. A convention was called early in 1822 in Manchester, but had to be postponed because of lack of funds, and both Permanent Fund and Great Northern Union were declining.[58] Small groups of freethinkers were kept in contact by Carlile's *Republican*. In London the 'Carbonaria' still existed in 1822, and there was a new violent conspiracy led by Towler and Potter, two of Thistlewood's group.[59] Many of this group kept in informal contact around Preston and Blandford in the East End. The Committee of the Industrious Classes seems to have continued, and in 1822 still had a Mechanics' Union and its Union Flag, and a motto:

This Union shall live when tyrants are dead;
This Union's so firm it strikes tyrants with dread;
This Union so friendly it joins hand and heart,
Nor dungeon nor axes this Union shall part.[60]

But this was the motto of the Cripplegate Union at the end of 1819,[61] and we must assume some continuity and transformation of the 1819 union, or a merger with it, to form a political artisans' organisation in Clerkenwell. Its activity may have been continuous, and in November it was circulating a handbill, said to have been composed by Bentham, justifying manhood suffrage, annual parliaments and the ballot as true Christianity, Christ having been a great Reformer, and advocating an organisation into 'trithings' and so on.[62] Its chief members alongside Gast were Washington (now active again), Whittaker the coffee-house keeper, Sadgrove, a sawyer (whose trade was suffering greatly from the spread of sawing machines), and Raven, a cooper. On 28 October they met and decided on a procession and dinner on 11 November to welcome Hunt on his arrival in London after release from prison. The brass-founders, morocco leather dressers, carpenters, shipwrights and sawyers all agreed to attend. A 'trades' committee' met nightly and soon grew to fifty members. The continuity of this group is shown by their use of the same flags and banners used in the processions to the Queen. A separate group under Galloway was also arranging a more expensive dinner, but the two were merged at the lower price. And so Hunt was welcomed by the trades' committee, wearing green and white cockades and medals struck for the occasion and bearing wands; Gast delivered an address of welcome in the name of the tradesmen and artisans of the metropolis, and a procession began in which the sawyers were prominent. Quite large numbers gathered, especially as it was a Monday, but the hopes of vast crowds were not fulfilled, and there were no efforts to enforce an illumination.[63]

Thereafter the Mechanics' Union may have carried on, and there may well have been some continuity with the groups around Gast later in the decade. But it made no more public appearances, and indeed the general lack of political excitement precluded much radical activity before 1829.

Part Three
ARTISANS IN BOOM AND DEPRESSION

PROLOGUE

After Hunt's re-entry into London, Gast was not involved in radical activity again until 1830. But that event had been arranged by a mechanics' committee, and Gast remained at the heart of artisan movements for the whole decade. Meanwhile he did not cease to earn his living as a working shipwright, and the condition of his trade was always his chief concern. His only writings between 1822 and 1825 were two articles in the new *Mechanics' Magazine* suggesting how to cut timber to avoid dry rot and wastage, and four in the *Public Ledger* on the state of shipbuilding on the Thames. When he next achieved notoriety, in 1825, it was as 'Gast, the destroyer of the Thames shipping trade', a leader in shipwrights' trade unionism.

In 1825 the newspapers drew public attention to the strikes of the Thames shipwrights, north-east seamen and Bradford wool-combers. Yet these were only the greatest in what was a year of strikes. These conflicts were the result of economic fluctuations.[1] Steady recovery in the early 1820s led to a fall in unemployment and a number of strikes for wage rises, including two by Tyneside and Wearside shipwrights in1824 and a flurry of successful ones in the Manchester area at the end of that year. New extensive unions appeared, as among the cotton-weavers of Glasgow, Manchester, Bolton and Stockport, and the northern sawyers. In 1825 industry moved into full employment and this, together with the rise in food prices from 1823, created the classic context for trade union action in London. Wage-rises were achieved by carpenters, carvers and gilders, coopers, ropemakers and upholsterers. Price-lists were presented by braziers, coopers, line-and-twine spinners and sawyers. New unions were formed by bedstead-makers, bricklayers, sawyers, seamen and silk-weavers. Strikes were organised by carvers and gilders, ropemakers, tin-plate workers, carpenters, cabinet-makers and ladies' shoemakers, and violence against blacks characterised the last three, especially among the carpenters on strike at Buckingham Palace where the Coldstream Guards were called to restore order.[2]

Nearly all the demands for rises were to make good previous reductions, mostly made in 1816, and illustrated the traditional artisan conception of a customary level of reward rather than a rising standard of living, evidenced also by the shipwrights' proposal of wages rising or *falling* with the price of bread.[3] Yet observers thought there was something unprecedented in the events of 1825, and they were probably right. Trade union action had replaced food price agitation in the activities and attitudes of skilled artisans, and a trade union consciousness had most clearly developed.

For it was not only the extent of trade union activity. Demands and strikes for higher wages persisted right through 1825 and even into 1826, but the boom had broken in the second quarter of 1825 and depression followed. In this unfavourable situation struggles grew fiercer and failures frequent, most notably in the total defeat of the strike of the Bradford wool-combers and stuff-weavers which, led by John Tester, lasted from June to November 1825. Alongside growing trade union bitterness against employers went greater trade union solidarity. This was seen in the close links between shipwrights in the different ports, the joint campaign of the five London carpenters' societies, the London sawyers' federation of the different branches (moreover sending delegates through the country to unite the provincial societies and allying with the northern sawyers' union).[4] It was seen most of all in the sympathy and support from all over the country for the strikes of the Leicester framework-knitters and Bradford combers. The latter especially received an impressive amount of aid and aroused a feeling of a common cause. The greatest London contributions came from hatters and carpenters, but it was a measure of feeling that money came from the distressed and striking ladies' shoemakers and the very depressed Spitalfields weavers and dyers. 'It is all the workers of England against a few masters at Bradford.'[5]

In all this unprecedented activity, organisation, militancy and unity, contemporaries sensed a new spirit of insubordination among working people. *The Times* fulminated against 'Gast, Tester and Co.', while the shipbuilder Young tried to alarm the public at the new doctrines:

> capitalists are represented as useless drones; and a settled conviction is entertained that the time is rapidly approaching when the labouring classes will claim by force a large participation of the good things of this

life, which have been too long witheld from them by the cupidity of the
higher ranks, and their own want of intelligence.[6]

Felix Farley's Bristol Journal blamed the 'spirit of combination' on
Owenism and its 'doctrine now so industriously propagated, that
the profit of the cápitalist is the idle man's share of the industrious
man's earnings'.[7] Such assertions reappeared in the next trade
union wave of 1833–4, but completely missed the point, for in 1825
Owenism most certainly did not determine the growing concentration of popular protest on trade union activity against employers.
There was no new inrush of ideas of replacing the employer class. It
was hardly a big step for workmen on strike to regard their labour as
essential to the employer—this is the very *rationale* of a strike—but
the attitude did not necessarily last. It was natural during his strike
for Gast to warn Young that 'I can assure the ship-builder of my own
knowledge of working mechanics (and that's not very limited), the
far greater part know capital is of no use without labour.'[8] The
essential point was not new ideas but the *organised* strike itself, and
herein lay the reality that others sensed, a growing insubordination
and determination, and a sense of acting within a common trade
union movement. This was powerfully delineated by an anguished
master cabinet-maker. The journeymen had successfully adopted
the tactic of striking at one shop at a time, so that the strikers were
easily maintained by the rest at work. When his turn came one of the
men

> in order to show the feelings, and spirit by which they were activated,
> deliberately put on his cap, and sat down upon a couch which happened
> to be there, and in a menacing attitude told me they would now be their
> own masters, the reign of tyranny had lasted too long, and that they
> would not be tyrannised over by anyone, adding in an insulting tone, he
> would shew me, he had as good a right to speak to me, sitting with his hat
> on, as in any other way.[9]

As well as Owenism, contemporaries blamed the repeal in 1824
of the Combination Laws. This was again to miss the point, for it was
the combination of economic factors that produced the concentration on industrial action. But what is certain is that a great spur to
trade union solidarity and stridency was given by the threat in 1825
of the *reimposition* of the Combination Laws, a situation to a large
extent due to the shipwrights' union. And out of the campaign
against this legislative threat arose a trade union newspaper, in
which Gast and the shipwrights had a leading role.

But the activities of the shipwrights between 1822 and 1830 were
not confined to conflict with employers over wages, apprenticeship

and union recognition. Particular economic circumstances led to the
concentration in 1824–5 on industrial action, but this was only one
of several courses of action also followed at different times. The
same is true of other artisans. They engaged in a great variety of
activities, concerned with the questions of legislative interference
with their clubs, education, machinery, competition and free trade.
In particular, the depression after 1825 discouraged industrial
action and there was more recourse to political action. Because of
the general political situation before 1830 this did not take the form
of pressure for parliamentary Reform. For after 1822 the Liverpool
administration was unassailably strong against Whig opposition and
threatened middle parties, and had dealt successfully with such
problems as a break with the King, the 'revolt of the landed gentlemen', and near-rebellion in Ireland. It absorbed the reforming
pragmatism of Peel and Huskisson, secured co-operation from liberal members of the opposition, and gained popular appeal through
Canning. This was a very different situation from the post-war
period. The artisans' political activity after 1825 concerned issues
like the Corn Laws, currency, tariffs, and legislation over wages,
machinery and hours. Direct industrial action was thus one alternative among many other complementary ones, but all of them, especially in the case of trades with special problems, expressed rejection of the assumptions of the dominant political economy.

8
THE THAMES SHIPWRIGHTS' PROVIDENT UNION

The shipwrights' union formed in 1824 was an attempt to profit from the industry's recovery and remedy the sufferings of its work-force since the end of the wars. The post-war depression in British shipping, due to over-capacity, lasted basically until 1835, and in the 1820s was made worse by the government's weakening of protection through its reciprocity treaties and alterations to the Navigation Laws. The shipping depression meant a depression in shipbuilding, and the Thames builders suffered especially from the decline in building for the East India Company and the navy. Late in 1822 there was no building *at all* on the Thames and very little repairing. The wartime prosperity of the shipwrights, caulkers, sail-makers and the rest had gone, and the peacetime discharges from the public service only heightened the sufferings from unem-ployment and builders' competitive efforts to cheapen costs.[1] The sail-makers had a number of strikes.[2] The number of shipwrights on the Thames fell.

This depression led to competition among the builders for orders, and the men suffered. Prices were reduced, which was made much easier by the absence of fixed piece-work prices, apprentices were used to the detriment of the journeymen, the autonomy of the gangs was infringed, all of which embittered and soured relations. These abuses were made possible by unemployment and competition among the men for work, which put them at the mercy of the builders and led them to work longer hours and hoard work, and so increase unemployment and the general competition.[3]

These features were common to many trades, and there seems to have been general agreement among the shipwrights over what was wrong, both with the industry and the situation in the Thames yards. Gast's own analyses were characteristic of these general views, if expressed more clearly and cogently, but were perhaps also more political. He blamed the government for much of the suffering because of the admission of India-built ships, the short-sighted run-down and dismissals in the royal yards, the building of warships in India, the refusal to help the Spanish constitutionalists against France and the 'Unholy Alliance' (which would have meant more naval work) and the Reciprocity Treaties. He attributed this to a defective political system in which the interests of the workmen were ignored; 'the Agriculturist, the Manufacturer, and various other branches of Trade, have their Advocates and Protecting Duties—all have their shields of defence but the Operative Ship-wright and Caulker.' And he reiterated the radical view that the main general causes of distress were the growth of the National Debt and taxation. But over internal conditions on the Thames he directly expressed the general view that it was competition between the men that increased their sufferings, and made them hoard work at the expense of others to the ultimate detriment of all, and accept damaging innovations. A lack of unity put them at a disadvantage before their employer, and it was essential to have common purpose and action. As always, he blamed the men themselves for their disunity: 'the employer holds a most decided advantage over the employed, through their own improvident measures'; 'the working classes are weak and impotent from their own divisions, and that is occasioned by their too free use of the pipe and pot'. But he also blamed the employers for taking advantage of it. And he persisted in his under-consumption argument, whereby if distress were ended, 'then every man could obtain the means to purchase all the necessary articles of life and comfort; and would not this be a good thing; it would give fresh impulse to consumption, and of course to manufacture and trade'.[4] These themes he had all expressed in 1819, and a conviction of the evils of competition, the need to check this both by unity among men and by legislative regulation, the importance of the home market and the beneficial effects of high wages was to dominate his trade union activity in the 1820s. But his views clearly grew out of the conditions and attitudes prevalent in his own industry.

In a period of depression industrial action was unlikely to secure changes, and the shipwrights sought political remedies. In 1823 they protested against foreign competition, and petitioned against the India Trade and Reciprocity Duties Bills, receiving help from one of the builders.[5] In the same year they also petitioned the Commons for legislation to regulate their trade and fix prices.[6] But the situation changed dramatically when after 1823 the general economic recovery and increase in trade now at last affected shipbuilding. After seven bad post-war years there was now plenty of building work on the Thames, in fact an over-demand for men.[7] The shipwrights could now hope to remedy their grievances by industrial action, and in 1824 secured changes in several yards. But this led to resistance, and in this context was founded on 16 August 1824 the Thames Shipwrights' Provident Union, under the leadership of Gast (the secretary), Nathaniel Clark, Benjamin Lomax, John Purdy and John Grieve.

This union was therefore only one of the courses of action on which the men concentrated at different times, and indeed in the discussions preceding its formation several courses were proposed. Some wanted a fund to relieve shipwrecked shipwrights or a fund to support aged shipwrights at the level to which respectable men were entitled, both of which the new union provided for. Others favoured a fund to set up a mould-loft to teach their sons to draft. All insisted on defending the dignity and independence of the shipwrights against inroads on the freedom of gangs. And the union must remove the unrestrained competition that was so detrimental to their respectable position.[8]

The union was very similar to most London trade societies in its rules and organisation. It also expressed very traditional ideals: 'it is the intention of the members of this society by a moral union to support their respectability in society.' It was also characteristic that the actual impetus for its formation came out of support for disputes in the country, in this case in the north-east.[9] A further factor encouraging it may have been Hume's act of 1824 repealing the Combination Laws and freeing combinations from prosecution for comspiracy, for the meeting that established the union also passed a resolution thanking Hume.

The aims of the union were to be expected: to lessen unemployment and share work by reducing hours, preventing hoarding of work and by gang-leaders' always giving preference, when making up their companies, to those longest out of work; to end misuse of apprentices; to enforce pay for all work done; to preserve the freedom of gangs; to secure uniform prices; and only to work in proper yards.[10]

But this did not at all imply class hostility to the builders, for the union, 'by duly appreciating the interest which does exist between the employer and the employed, will, by every act of their future conduct, endeavour to establish that reciprocal confidence which at all times is so essential between master and men'.[11] There were good grounds for believing that the builders would welcome an end both to competition and to the uncertainty over prices that had led to so much ill-feeling. Since their profit was a percentage of the total bill, it was not inevitable that they would oppose higher earnings, as only competition had led them to cut labour costs. It was a widespread attitude, even in the cotton industry, that most employers reduced wages reluctantly and only because of competition from others who had already reduced. It was the initial reductions by a few masters which triggered off reductions by the rest, so if the original reductions could be prevented, wages would generally be maintained. This could be done by legally established tribunals, or by strong unions which were not seen as taking on all the masters at once, but only the few 'unscrupulous' ones who caused all the trouble. The shipwrights hoped that, as in many London trades, the builders would co-operate in the drawing up of a book of prices (in 1825 a select committee found that three builders at least favoured fixed prices).[12] Initially, to conciliate the builders, the union forbade working for masters who were not regular shipwrights or did not have proper premises, that is shipowners and a number of little men (some of whom had been in business for a long time).[13]

Once formed, the new union spread very rapidly to include nearly all the Thames shipwrights in the merchants' yards, and even some in the King's yards, to a total of 1,300–1,400. It amassed funds, was able to enforce many of its aims, and conducted a long strike. This ease of organisation, strength and achievement all seem remarkable, but are explained by the secure basis of existing solidarity and common attitudes among the men. Where there were already clear, established practices on which the men were agreed, they needed no union to be able to defend them. They allowed no reduction in the 5s. day-rate, the traditional price for running work (stripping off and putting on planking) was maintained, they excluded shipwrights who had not served a full apprenticeship (and this put them in a stronger bargaining position once the union was formed). The gang system provided an existing authority structure: 'we generally leave those things with the leading hand of the company'.[14] It was where practices were *not* clearly established that there was 'ambiguity', over such things as docking or prices for old work. But there was general agreement that all prices should be standardised between yards so as to prevent reductions, and by far the most common concern voiced in the discussions prior to the union's formation was the clear mode of payment or price-book so often sought in the past, and this was the chief aim of the union. The unity of the men was furthered by the constant mobility between yards.

There was thus a very solid foundation for the union, and its structure was obvious, a committee of delegates from the different yards. This must have been the basis for previous, more informal action like the demonstrations for Queen Caroline. It enabled the committee one morning to call a meeting for 4 o'clock that day and have a thousand attend.[15] These committee-men were the real basis of the union; they collected subscriptions in the yards, acted in each yard as negotiators between people and builder, and on the whole only informed the general committee if the matter was important. They were elected in the yards, could not be dismissed by the committee, and many of their actions never needed to come to its notice.[16] Thus the employers' complaints about the committee's power and 'interference' in the yards completely missed the point, for the yards had great autonomy and most of the disputes in 1824 and 1825 were actually purely internal affairs in which the committee was not involved. 'Every yard is a sort of republic in itself, governed by its own rules and its own regulations.'[17] Purdy even claimed that if the committee agreed on a matter, each committee-man then had to take the opinion of his yard on it and report at the next committee meeting, and only then did the committee come to a decision.[18] The committee in fact hardly needed to exert power. What the men wanted from it was a clarification of many matters and establishment of clear practices, alongside the existing ones over day-rate, running work, apprenticeship and gangs. Once this were done, they would implement them as they had the others. The committee was thus in a very real sense a tribunal. Its other main function was to build up a fund, and this it did through a subscription of a penny for every day in work, the fund not to be drawn on during the first year.

These features point to a common defect of many trade union histories, namely excessive concentration on formal structure and events at the top. Unions were very often episodic formalisations of the much more important continuous informal practices. In 1825 the Bristol seamen had no 'union', but met regularly and had common policies.[19] Cotton-spinners' unions were often totally destroyed by long disputes, but new ones were easily formed. 'Trade union history' should concentrate much more on workshop practices than on formal organisation. What the formation of a union usually meant, in fact, was the accumulation of a *fund* to enable the more effective implementation of policies *already* pursued. The shipwrights' union is an example.

At first the union was busy arranging demarcation with other trades and developing contacts with other ports. In Bristol 'we have had a man down by the name of Gast, who has caused a great deal of mischief among them'. A sub-committee also began work on a price-book. But hopes of co-operation from the builders were on the whole disappointed. The great competition between them precluded a general agreement over prices, but the chief factor was the common reaction to a new union, fear of its power rather than its policies; 'they had forebodings that we had some secret measures behind'; each master 'discovers, as he thinks, some formidable army marching to decompose all his internal regulations'. The much talked-off price-book they feared would be not merely standardisation but a claim for higher wages. And they resented the general insubordination of the men, and the familiar sight of the committee-men 'in their usual posture, across the road, with their hands in their pockets'.[20]

Several disputes arose, usually confined to a single yard, and attempts by one firm to recruit blacklegs from Southampton were foiled.[21] A dispute at Blackwall yard led Wigram to secure discharges of shipwrights from the royal yards at Deptford, Woolwich and Chatham to replace the unionists, but this was foiled and the discharged men were paid by the union not to replace them, and were soon absorbed into existing companies. This led to clashes with another builder, Young, over the autonomy of gangs and he called a meeting on 23 February of the chief builders. They agreed on two things—to oppose the union and to seek help from the government. Their strategy over the next months became clear. They despaired of being able to crush the union by themselves and so wished to do so through legislation. They directed their pressure on Huskisson, the President of the Board of Trade, to secure a new coercive enactment. In March they agreed to hold no communication with the union, and to sack all committee-men. The union believed, rightly it seems, that the latter measure was done to provoke a general strike so as to gain unfavourable publicity for the union and influence Parliament in favour of legislation. The union therefore did not strike.

In March the battle arena shifted. Already in January Gast had been aware of feeling in Parliament in favour of restoring the Combination Laws, and, as in 1802, the shipwrights sought to conciliate public opinion through publications.[22] The shipbuilders were putting pressure on the government, and had willing allies in the shipowners, alarmed at the seamen's unions. Though Huskisson had not quailed before their opposition to his reciprocity treaties, the shipping interest was powerful and influential, and had close connections with *The Times* which campaigned against unions and in favour of new legislation. Francis Place was alive to the danger. In March he urged Hume to contact both shipwrights and builders, and himself opened a correspondence with Gast. A further deputation of shipbuilders saw Huskisson and pressed either for the repeal of Hume's act or the enactment of another for which they provided an outline. One of its provisions was that no money could be subscribed to any such association without the consent of a magistrate, who would be the treasurer. Amid a growing outcry against combinations Huskisson, on 29 March, asserting that the 1824 repeal had produced dangerous combinations, secured a select committee of the Commons to enquire into the effects of Hume's act. Supporting him, the Home Secretary, Peel, singled out the seamen and shipwrights for attack.[23]

Following this victory the shipbuilders moved further towards confrontation by issuing six regulations to govern all future contracts and work. Two of these were unacceptable to the union and a confused period followed, during which the union gave up efforts at conciliation. Both sides were manoeuvring for the select committee, which began sitting on 18 April. Petitions and counter-petitions were presented, and the builders distributed a copy of their proposed bill to every MP. They also elicited from the Shipowners' Society a condemnation of the shipwrights' combination. It is surely no coincidence that just before the select committee began hearing evidence from the shipbuilders, they provoked the final showdown. On 27 April they resolved that unless by 29 April the shipwrights returned to work in all the individual yards where they had struck, and all shipwrights agreed wholly to the builders' regulations, they would not employ any members of the union. It was an open declaration of war, and the strike began.

The builders were confident of gaining the legislation they wanted, and in May both sides' attention was focused on the select committee. Many trades petitioned in vain to be heard, but because of the many accusations against them by the builders the shipwrights were heard so that, to Place's contempt but the historians' gain, the committee went into the dispute in great, if confused, detail.[24] Gast managed the presentation of evidence very well indeed, supplying witnesses to rebut every charge made by a builder, and was himself examined at length. The builders meanwhile consulted the government on the presentation of their evidence.[25]

In general the shipwrights could be pleased with a campaign that cost them over £46.[26] But the committee's report was hostile to combinations and the shipwrights were among the trades singled out for censure.[27] This encouraged the builders to persist with their regulations. But the actual bill was not very sweeping, and though the builders and others continued to press for coercive clauses, the eventual act changed the legal position but little. However on 24 June Huskisson secured agreement by the Commons to suspend for two years the regulation whereby ships must be repaired only in Britain to stay on the British registry. It was a move avowedly to break the shipwrights' strike.[28]

The struggle therefore shifted back to the Thames, and the builders' failure to secure the legislation they wanted led some of them now to consider compromise. But most of them still hoped to defeat the union through government help, and they gained permission to engage strike-breaking shipwrights from the royal yards at Portsmouth and Plymouth. Deputations of builders set off for both places and new crisis had arrived. Gast rushed to Portsmouth, managed to swing the shipwrights over to his side and prevent the recruitment of 'yellows', and even negotiated a settlement with the three builders there. Agreement was reached on the composition of gangs, the builders at last recognised the union, and they even agreed to the shipwrights' earlier proposal that in each yard the builder would discuss with his men there the union's new price-book with a view to fixing prices for that yard, for they still rejected the idea of a uniform price settlement. This agreement was ratified in London by both builders and union, and work resumed. But difficulties arose in the discussions of the price-book, some builders were now favourable to a general price settlement, the union thereupon revived this claim, quarrels arose and a general strike seems to have began again. The hard-line builders appealed to the shipowners for support and applied to the Navy Board to order men from their yards to go to work in the private ones. Instead, the government agreed to open the royal yards to any ship needing repair.

This meant that the strike was doomed to fail, men returned to work, and the union agreed to a settlement on the basis of the Portsmouth agreement, which did recognise the union but did not establish uniform prices. The masters congratulated themselves on the defeat of the union, and tension continued. But despite its debts the union did survive.

So ended what was long remembered on the Thames as 'the great strike', which 'lasted so long, that the grass is said to have grown up in the building slips'.[29] It was not just the biggest strike in the whole history of the union, and the biggest in London between the ship-wrights' in 1802 and the tailors' in 1834. It left Gast and the shipwrights more than ever convinced of the need for unity among the trades. It was intimately bound up with the struggles in 1825 over legislation on combinations, in the course of which Gast led the formation of a permanent trades' committee and a trade union newspaper.

9
THE COMBINATION LAWS

The repeal of the Combination Laws was mainly engineered by Francis Place, and there seems little reason to doubt the main lines of his account.[1] Place was one of the group of Westminster reformers who had been prominent in the Corresponding Society and as such remained strongly opposed to any moves towards alliance with the Whigs. Place himself was the greatest organiser, hardest worker, most rationalist and toughest-minded of them all, extreme in his atheism, antagonism to the aristocracy and contempt for royalty. Himself capable of persistent action, he had very high standards and was continually disappointed by the political figures he had to work with. This tended to isolate him, though he was widely respected. In general he disapproved of the compromises of the Westminster reformers and was only spasmodically active, in 1807–8, 1809–10, 1812, 1814 and 1818. His isolation was increased when in 1811–12 he was accused by Evans, Thistlewood and their blackmailing associates of being a spy. Matters came to a head when in 1814 Burdett ordered the committee of the West London Lancasterian Association (WLLA), an educational body run by the Westminster reformers, to expel Place and his friend Richter, and replace them by Evans, Thistlewood and two others. Place resigned and stayed out of politics until 1818, reflecting on the ingratitude and dishonesty of public life.[2]

On the other hand, Place's rationalism and non-popular approach led him to support a wide range of practical, specific reforms empirically based on factual information, whether over law, police, benefit societies, education or morality, and to a willingness to co-operate with all sorts of people on such specific matters. Around 1813 he also began to find in Joseph Hume a politician after his own heart, ready to work unstintingly and with perseverance at important matters.

Men of Place's outlook easily adopted utilitarian arguments, and Place became a friend of Mill and Bentham and a convert to their views. Rational progress now became for him the diffusion of utilitarianism. But however narrow his social vision, Place never forgot his working-class origins or lost his sympathy for working men. For him Malthus' argument that population tends to increase faster than the means of subsistence unless checked was a revelation, but he had doubts over his actual figures and so in 1815 began trying to collect information on the wages of London trades since 1777 to relate them to population figures. Then the issue of the Corn Bill intensified his collection of details on prices and wages, and so began his statistical and economic studies on the condition of working men.[3] But having no real contacts with artisans, he found out far less on wages than on bread prices.

One feature of his sympathy for working men was revulsion at the blatant injustice of the various legal restrictions on journeymen's combinations. He believed the laws produced secrecy and 'outrage', and since the power of the London trade societies did to some extent affect levels of pay, laws which applied only to workmen were particularly unfair, as they meant that levels of wages to some extent depended on breaches of the law. Since the laws did not *prevent* trade unionism but merely created bitterness, illegality and secrecy, they should be repealed. On the same lines Place and his radical associates were later to urge the abolition of a newspaper stamp duty which did not prevent a cheap press but made it illegal and extreme, and of the monopoly of the two Patent Theatres which did not prevent the flourishing minor theatres but brought the law into disrepute. The Combination Laws led to unnecessary antagonism between employers and employees, and since they and trade unionism could have only a marginal effect on wage levels they, like any laws interfering with wages, merely hampered rational industrial relations and diverted attention away from the real factors governing labour.

And so in 1814 Place set to work to achieve their repeal, expecting it to take many years. His methods were to contact the parties in any industrial dispute in town or country, to approach the London trades, and to send letters to the press.

In 1818 John Wade, with financial help from Bentham, began his small weekly periodical, the *Gorgon*. This was profoundly Benthamite and voiced the outlook of the Westminster reformers. Yet it was unusual in being aimed at a working-class readership, and it campaigned against the Combination Laws as blatant examples of legal repression that moreover ruined industrial relations. As such it attracted Place, who saw it as a two-way channel of information. Wade included Place's very detailed and accurate information on tailors' wages, trade unionism and the price of bread in support of his arguments on the bad effects of the Combination Laws and the necessity for, but general lack of aggression of, trade societies which alone prevented wages lagging too far behind the rising price of bread. Place also provided information on the compositors and type-founders.

By 1819 things had gone surprisingly well, with the commitment of the radical MP Joseph Hume to the cause, and the organisation of a petition from London artisans. Place now had hopes of a bill fairly soon and through a friend in Edinburgh, Thomas Hodgskin, tried to enlist the support of M'Culloch, the prestigious writer on political economy.[4] But artisan support was not forthcoming, the *Gorgon* folded and Place had as yet failed to make the working-class contacts he wanted. He was not the man to give up, and by 1822 he had established contacts with some of the London trades: compositors (from the time of his post-war researches on the relationship between wages and the price of corn), hatters (from 1821 when an effort to secure a wage-rise resulted in the conviction for combination of twenty-five of them, including the new secretary, John Lang), and carpenters (from their efforts in 1818 and 1822 to undo the 1816 reduction and restore wages to the 1810 level). He also had provincial contacts, mainly with cotton-weavers in Manchester, Glasgow and Bolton. His links with one of the Bolton leaders, William Smith, were particularly important when Smith later became one of the conductors of the *Bolton Chronicle* which gave Place a provincial platform. It may have been through Bolton that Place also made links with cotton-spinners, for early in 1823 a long strike of the Bolton spinners was defeated by the arrest and imprisonment of their leaders; certainly by 1824 Place had contacts with cotton-spinners in Manchester and Stockport. Place wrote articles in provincial newspapers and through M'Culloch and the *Scotsman* secured further press discussion, and gained the support of some MPs, including Hobhouse and Grey Bennett. Hume moreover secured from the Attorney-General and the two specialists in the government on economic affairs, Huskisson and Wallace, promises not to oppose a select committee on the Combination Laws. Huskisson recognised that the many existing laws were complicated and contradictory, and he favoured consolidation on the lines of his and Peel's reforms in fiscal and criminal matters; but he also accepted that their inequity created unnecessary distrust and strife. And so when in 1822 Hume presented further petitions, including a London one signed by 15,000, and gave notice of a bill the following session, Place thought success was near.[5]

Their plans were interrupted by an alliance between Gravener Henson, the former leader among the Nottingham framework-knitters, with George White, a clerk at the House of Commons, to draw up a bill which would not only repeal a mass of acts against combinations, many of which were obsolete, but would also, following the lines of Henson's bill of 1812 and the demands of outworkers generally, set up a complicated machinery to regulate wages, conditions, hiring and firing, and hours, settle disputes and abolish truck.[6] One of the Coventry MPs, Moore, informed Huskisson of his intention to introduce the bill, secure a thorough examination of the evidence at the committee stage, and then leave the bill over until the next session. But though Huskisson and Peel were in favour of condensing the laws and removing injustices, they were hostile to the introduction of a whole array of detailed policies and measures. The bill in fact attracted very little support, nearly all the mere eleven petitions in its favour coming from the Leicester–Nottinghamshire–Derbyshire area and the Norwich weavers. But from Place's point of view the bill was unfortunate in that it aroused opposition among MPs and ministers. So little support did it receive that Moore agreed to Huskisson's request to withdraw it in return for a select committee early in the following session. But in September he called for petitions, and William Longson, a weaver's leader, was active in support in the Manchester area and a campaign was begun in Sheffield.[7]

Place's strategy was to act as soon as Parliament reassembled in 1824 in order to forestall Moore. An article by M'Culloch in the *Edinburgh Review* in January 1824 converted many MPs. Place had a circular printed calling on workmen to petition for repeal and including a suggested form of petition, copies of which he took to London trade societies and sent to his provincial contacts, and he also had it inserted in the *Black Dwarf*. Hume was to move for a committee to enquire into the laws forbidding the export of machinery and emigration of workmen as well as those governing combinations, and after some difficulty Huskisson agreed and supported Hume's successful motion on 12 February.[8]

Place was not at all confident that he could get any journeymen to come to give evidence and so he prepared a number of his associates to give evidence on the lines he wanted, employers like the printer

Richard Taylor and the engineers Maudslay, Galloway, Donkin and Martineau (these were just as interested in the export of machinery as in the Combination Laws). But he and the *Black Dwarf* did arouse some response, while Hume as chairman of the committee circularised towns for information. The Mayor of Stockport, for instance, called a meeting where a crowd, led by Harrison, virtually ignored the question of machinery but bitterly assailed the Combination Laws and the employers and set up a committee to agitate for repeal.[9] Working people in the area organised correspondence, subscriptions and delegates, MPs were lobbied, and over a hundred petitions came from the country and nearly thirty from London.[10]

Much of this does seem to have been promoted by Place and Hume. All the London petitions seem due to Place, as no petitions came from trades other than the fifteen he visited (of which nine did petition, some of them several times). The first seven petitions that arrived do seem to be due to Moore's appeal (mechanics of Barnsley, Tewkesbury and Sheffield, weavers of Norwich and Wymondham, shoemakers of Loughborough and Derby), and the same is probably true of eight others from the Midlands. But Place probably had a hand in the six from cotton-spinners (he certainly drew up the Manchester one) and three from cotton-weavers. And there was obviously an organised, concerted campaign among the boot and shoemakers, based on their well-established communications network, which produced nearly forty petitions from all over the country. Together these all amounted to over ninety of the total of 130-odd petitions for repeal of the Combination Laws.

In the end Place did manage to arrange evidence from some Londoners—Lang of the hatters, George Crowhurst of the Original Friendly Society of Carpenters and Joiners, and two City men's shoemakers, as well as a number of masters and ex-journeymen. Delegates also came from such places as Manchester, Stockport, Glasgow, Hawick, Dublin, Macclesfield and Yorkshire and contacted Place, who carefully arranged the evidence for the committee.[11] Place had foreseen that repeal would be desired by work people and opposed by masters in the belief that it would lead to wage rises. He tried hard to convince the men's delegates that the laws hardly affected wages, which were governed by supply of and demand for labour. Few were convinced. How much tension there was we do not know, but there was a split among the Bolton weavers, one group, led by William Smith, loyally co-operating with Place's strategy, the other led by James Barnett, a radical in 1819, and Richard Needham, who was to remain prominent among the

weavers and be in the 1830s a leader of the Operative Conserva-
tives. The latter pair went to London and came back denouncing
Hume's 'Humbug Committee'.[12] In London they had associated
with a pair called Marshall and Powell. Marshall seems to have been
quite well known in the north and was said to have devised an
infallible way of doubling or trebling the weavers' wages; he was
probably the Francis Marshall later prominent in the National
Association for the Protection of Labour. Powell was probably the
John Powell who was soon to be an ally of Gast.

White soon became an ally of Place, and the committee was very
well managed. In June, instead of a report, the committee agreed to
a series of resolutions, and in accordance with these Hume introduced three bills. Two were to repeal the prohibition of emigration
and to consolidate and amend the arbitration laws. The third concerned combinations. In Place's view, the Combination Act of 1800
was now not the worst of the legal restraints on combinations. In
particular, a law of Edward I against conspiracy had in recent years
been construed by judges to apply to journeymen's strikes and
meetings. To prevent such new developments in judge-made law,
which in Place's eyes was synonymous with prejudice, Hume's third
bill, drawn up on his instructions alone, apparently even before the
committee agreed on its resolutions, went further than them and not
only repealed a large number of potentially dangerous statutes but
also freed combination from liability to prosecution at common law
for conspiracy. The question of export of machinery was left over to
the following session. Between 25 May and 5 June all three bills
passed the Commons without any serious opposition, real discussion or realisation of how much further the bill on combinations
went than Hume had originally advocated. The only attempt to
whip up alarm came from *The Times* whose proprietor, John Wal-
ter, was offended by Taylor's evidence on the 1810 prosecution of
the paper's compositors.[13]

'The fact that the Combination Laws Repeal Bill was passed
during the late session of parliament, does not seem to be generally
known.'[14] The *Mechanics' Magazine* warned workmen that if they
tried to take advantage of the repeal to raise wages the result would
be their reimposition or even a more stringent measure, and Hume
later echoed this when in the ensuing period of high employment
and rising food prices the inevitable wage demands and strikes
occurred. Place himself strongly backed the cotton-weavers' efforts
to raise wages.[15] There were many strikes in Lancashire—in Hyde
alone in January there were successful strikes by weavers, colliers,

dyers, farriers and shoemakers.[16] The larger Lancashire manufacturers were soon pressing for the repeal of Hume's act, a panic
attitude developed in some of the press, accusations of crime and
even murder were levelled at trade unions in Dublin and Glasgow,
and opinion both in and outside Parliament was aroused. In this
context, with strong rumours that the Combination Laws would be
restored, the Thames shipbuilders made their approach to Huskisson, and Hume and Place prepared for battle. On 28 March, despite
Hume's opposition, Huskisson secured his select committee,
chaired by Wallace, apparently with the aim of pushing through a
bill on the lines suggested by the shipbuilders.[17]

But the situation in which this committee operated was quite
different from that of a year before. The trade unions were now
much more active and alarmed, as there was a great difference
between the removal of statutes under which for some time they had
learned to live, and the enactment of new measures probably much
more coercive and effective. Early in 1825, amidst the rumours,
many trade societies had contacted Place and he now strengthened
his connections in the cotton industry and formed new ones with the
Sunderland shipwrights, Shields seamen and others. Moreover, the
Thames dispute put Gast at the forefront of the battle, and he was
uniquely qualified to concert united action among the London
trades. We cannot know much about inter-trade links in the early
1820s but they certainly existed, and Gast was leader of the
'Mechanics' Union' which organised the demonstrations over the
Queen and Hunt's entry in 1822. This may have been the same as a
society in Clerkenwell that Gast belonged to in 1822.[18] The Thames
shipwrights also had contacts with nearly all ports in the kingdom.
And there was a lot of dockside solidarity; a coopers' strike in 1821
had received support from caulkers, shipwrights, sawyers, lighter-
men and watermen.

Gast accepted Place's offer of help and on his advice circularised
nearly forty trades and secured the formation on 18 April of a
general committee of two delegates from each trade to watch over
the proceedings of the select committee and resist any change in the
law.[19] The committee seems to have included shipwrights, ship
caulkers, hatters, brassfounders, silk-weavers, silk-dyers, sawyers,
carpenters, ladies' shoemakers and ropemakers, but what others
there were we cannot say. Place made efforts to secure provincial
delegates, and soon there were in London Woodruffe, Beveridge and
Hodgson of the Shields and Sunderland seamen, Nesbitt and Rippon
of the shipwrights of those ports, Taylor from Birmingham, Thomas

Worsley of the Stockport cotton-spinners, and others from Glasgow, Sheffield and other parts of Yorkshire. These joined the London trades' committee to form a group of men whose intelligence and ability even the demanding Place found very impressive, though he singled out the shipwrights above the rest. The committee employed George White as parliamentary agent and collected money for expenses. Place wrote a reply to Huskisson's speech and the trades had 2,000 copies of it printed as a pamphlet and carefully distributed, especially to MPs.

In their apparent desire to agree on a bill quickly, the select committee proved very biased, willing to hear all sorts of accusations against trade unions and paying for such witnesses' time and travel, and refusing to hear the unions in defence. The trades' delegates met at the Red Lion in Parliament Square, saw Place daily and petitioned the committee to be heard, but usually in vain. At length the committee had to agree to hear representatives of some of the trades that had been accused, but of all the London trades on the trades' committee only the shipwrights were heard. The select committee also heard two representatives from the coopers, who probably took no part in the trades' committee but had presented their employers with a price-book which would increase task-work prices (as new design, more iron and fresher timbers meant it now took longer to make casks) and equalise earnings, and with demands for shorter hours, pay for stowing, and limitation of apprenticeship, which finally resulted in a general strike.[20] Because of the committee's attitude, Place and Hume prevented delegates from being sent from such places as Manchester and Leicester. The committee was also incompetent in that it misunderstood much of the evidence, spent a lot of time on the details of petty incidents, and hardly examined the effects of Hume's act at all. It thus totally failed to justify a bill such as the one the shipbuilders wanted, but the government was committed to a bill of some form.

Despite 97 petitions against reimposition of the Combination Laws, signed by over 100,000, as against a mere seven from employers in favour, the final report and Wallace's speech on its presentation aroused serious alarm.[21] But it now became clear that the ministers were not against trade unions or wage negotiations as such, but disapproved of their restrictions on the free movement of labour through apprenticeship, the obstacles they placed in the way of mechanisation, the coercive power they exercised and the federal organisations they were believed to be developing. They were worried, that is to say, at possible threats to order and to economic progress. So the bill which the Attorney-General presented on 17 June was not nearly as outrageous as expected.[22] It did not restore any of the statutes Hume's act had repealed. It made all associations illegal except those of persons

> who shall meet together solely for the purpose of consulting upon and determining the rate of wages or prices, which the persons present at such meeting or any of them, shall require or demand for his or their work, or the hours or time for which he or they shall work in any manufacture, trade or business.

This expressly made trade unions legal as such and free of any liability to prosecution at common law. However the repeal of Hume's act seemed to put the legality of a delegate organisation in jeopardy, and there was a long second clause against intimidation, threats or coercion of employer or fellow-workman which could make almost any form of pressure an offence. It laid down summary jurisdiction by magistrates, made provision for compulsion of offender and witnesses to give evidence, and allowed conviction on the evidence of one witness instead of the two stipulated in Hume's act. Hume was ready to accept this last provision, but disliked the clauses concerning information on oath and absconding witnesses, the vagueness of the intimidation clause, and the confining of activities 'solely' to questions of wages and hours, for this excluded equally important matters like apprenticeship and contracts.[23] The trades' delegates equally disliked the last three, and objected to the lack of recognition of delegate organisation.[24] Still, all were willing to accept the bill if these matters were remedied, and friendly meetings between Hume, White, Wallace and the Attorney-General secured some agreement to these changes, Hume promising not to oppose the bill and to try to prevent opposition out of doors. Place was satisfied, persuaded the trades' delegates not to oppose the bill, and got the country delegates to return home.[25] But many, including the shipbuilders, wanted a much more coercive bill, and perhaps because of this Peel suddenly told Hume on 23 June at the second reading, which Hume did not oppose, that unless the Thames shipwrights went back to work on 25 June he would introduce two clauses on 27 June to put combinations under common law again. The shipwrights of course did not return to work, and Place now rallied Burdett and threatened a mass lobby of Parliament.[26] At the committee stage on 27 and 29 June there were very stormy debates with Peel becoming very nasty indeed. There were many attacks on Hume, but he was never the man to give way, and he was strongly supported by Hobhouse and Burdett. Hobhouse also presented a petition from Gast's committee protesting at trickery. The ministers tried on 27 June to add 'insult' in the second clause to the forbidden means of inducing men to leave work. Hume strongly opposed 'insult' as too vague, so that the Attorney-General gave in and proposed instead 'molesting or obstructing by threats, intimidations, or any other means'. Hume strongly opposed 'molest' as far too vague, but lost by 90 to 18. Denman's amendment to substitute trial by jury was lost by 78 to 53, and an amendment to the clause on absconding witnesses was also defeated. However, Peel did not carry out his threat, the clause on informations on oath was amended, and the Attorney-General promised to add a provision for appeal to Quarter Sessions.[27] This was done at the third reading, as also were changes concerning the time-limit after an event for which punishment was allowable and prescribing prison for witnesses who did not appear. Hume now declared the bill much better than before, except for the molestation part.[28] Despite the satisfaction of Hume and Hobhouse, Place and the artisans were still angry at the restrictions on their activity 'solely' to wages and hours and a last effort was made in the form of petitions to the Lords from the trades' delegates and others. Place and a shipwright, Philip Hardy, and a deputation of silk-weavers convinced Lord Rosslyn of the injustice of the 'solely' limitation, and White prepared an amendment for him to propose to allow action on matters other than wages. Through incompetence the Commons had also failed to fill some blanks in the extra clauses to the bill and Place hoped this would prove a loophole, but the Lords spotted them and filled them in.[29] But when Rosslyn suggested his amendment

> —The LORD CHANCELLOR said that the clause as it stood would bear the very interpretation which the noble earl desired, and if it were brought before him, sitting as a judge, against any party applying for his *habeas corpus*, in a more oppressive sense, he would discharge the prisoner.

The Prime Minister agreed and the Chancellor repeated his statement. With this explanation Place considered the final act satisfactory.[30]

It seems clear that on the whole the trade union leaders were relieved at the outcome, for they had feared legislation much nearer to what the shipbuilders wanted. Gast immediately stressed to the shipwrights the legality of their proceedings and the need to obey the law, and in accordance with the new act spoke out against molesting yellows.[31]

This Combination Laws struggle of 1825 was very important

because, superimposed as it was on a wave of trade union activity that was already reaching out towards wider contacts, it was bound to provoke greater trade union solidarity and organisation and to underline the importance of political activity. In Manchester the threat of new legislation had led to a meeting of trades on 14 April that set up a Manchester Artizans' General Committee which co-operated with the London delegates and which Doherty, who was closely involved, later described as an attempt at a general union of trades.[32] Trades' committees were also formed in Birmingham and Sheffield, while in Sunderland was formed a body of 'Associated Trades' which, most remarkably, actually took the name Philanthropic Hercules, which suggests greater contact with Gast and the London shipwrights.[33] Missionaries also went from Manchester to such places as Staffordshire and Birmingham, and at the former persuaded the potters to join the 'Grand Union of England'[34]—'union' not in the formal sense, but in the sense in which the shipwrights' societies in the different parts were 'in union' with one another. In London, Gast's group launched in July the *Trades' Newspaper*, run by a permanent committee of trades' delegates.

10
THE 'TRADES' NEWSPAPER' AND FRANCIS PLACE

The 'Trades' Newspaper'

The very existence of the trades' committee over the Combination Laws led naturally to ideas of making it permanent. Already during the campaign the committee had become a forum for discussion on trade matters, such as apprenticeship.[1] This was a repetition of the apprenticeship campaign, when that artisans' committee had sought to become 'the means of keeping up the Spirit of the Mechanics, by having an Opportunity of meeting Monthly'.[2] The establishment of a newspaper was an extension of this system of communication and co-ordination, another means of conveying information on matters of concern to trade unions and of developing feelings of common interests and solidarity. The fact that the paper would be run by a committee of shareholding societies meant there would be a permanent organisational focus; 'the mode by which the affairs of the *Trades' Newspaper* are conducted is the means of concentrating in one Committee the deputies of several Trades of London, and thereby establishes a system of communication not less desirable than the existence of the paper itself.'[3]

For Gast this question of unity between the artisans' trade societies was of overriding concern. From at least the time of the Philanthropic Hercules, and very likely before, he was a consistent advocate of a general union of trades until the end of his life. It was obvious to him that the living standards of the London mechanics bore a direct relation to their level of organisation, and so a general union of trades, by providing financial support, would further strengthen the position of each. Basically he was proposing to replace the long-established London practices of *ad hoc* financial aid by a formalised structure, and so he placed his greatest hopes among the London trades. But though his concern was always to be with the mechanics, to defend their position and obtain from society at large a recognition of their value, his vision was large enough to desire a national union of trades, a desire reinforced by the perception that several London industries and their workmen were suffering from competition with cheaper country goods.[4] A general union was urgently needed, and Gast hoped the new paper would help promote it.

Though Gast was ready to condemn the 'grinding employers', 'the locusts devouring the product of the hardworking and industrious mechanic',[5] he was equally outspoken in his strictures on the artisans, who were themselves largely to blame for their plight. Their labour was indispensable, so they could easily restore themselves to an honoured position in society by common action. 'The industrious classes are the wealth and strength of nations, and nothing but their own conduct makes them poor and impotent.'[6] Though always grumbling about their employers, and even their fellow workmen, they would do little about it. He condemned in a very high-minded way their addiction to the pipe, pot, bull-baiting and 'gratifying sensuality'. Because he saw that utter poverty made collective resistance impossible, he was doubly angry that the London mechanics, who did have the means of collective action, failed to give a lead to the country. He attacked the trade particularism of the London artisans, their 'presumptive self-consequence'. He saw signs that this particularism was being eroded by the problems the London trades were encountering; 'the present pinching times will teach the Working Classes that their only remedy is in their own Union & Reciprocal, Co-operation'.[7] But he placed his main hopes of change in education. As much as Place he saw education as an antidote to drink, and he supported Lancasterian education, mechanics' institutions, the *Mechanics' Magazine* and so on. True to the spirit of the age, he believed that as education replaced 'sensual indulgence', mechanics would recognise their true value to society and their potential power;

> once a man get a relish for mental acquirments, and begin to see and feel he as a stake in Society, and that knowledge affords him a variety of enjoyments, he will employ his leisure hours to an advantage, and keep such company that will tend to improve his condition in Society; his example will soon attract the attention of his fellow workmen even in spite of themselves.[8]

Workmen thus gave in to the capitalist because of ignorance, poverty and division. Union would remedy division, but the two chief obstacles to this union were ignorance and poverty. The mechanics at least were as yet free of grinding poverty, and so could unite when ignorance was dispelled. Gast thus saw much of his work as educational, as in the Clerkenwell society he had belonged to. In 1825 he was a leading figure in the Mutual Improvement Society, founded by the shoemaker Rider and including many of the London artisans' leaders, like Lang, Wallis and Knight.[9] In its discussions of matters of interest to artisans it was, as much as the *Trades' Newspaper*, a logical outcome of the late struggle, and in December it resolved unanimously in favour of a union of trades. But in Gast's eyes the newspaper would reach a much wider public and its educational role be correspondingly greater.

In securing the establishment of the paper, Gast was also trying to bring the trades permanently into politics, not in the sense of adopting a particular political stance or programme, but in the much more fundamental sense of becoming a permanent part of the political nation. The political nation bore little relation to the electorate, for everyone recognised that 'public opinion' was an essential component of the political system; though it should never dictate to Parliament, it was quite legitimate for Parliament to amend a bill out of recognition in response to expressions of public feeling, as in the case of the friendly societies' bill in 1828.[10] The means of mobilising public opinion were well established—press, public meetings and petitions. The establishment of the new paper was thus a political act. Gast saw the mechanics as one of the important 'interests' in the community, but the government and Parliament paid much more attention to other interests—landowners, capitalists, anti-slavery lobby, and so on. It was essential that the mechanics be heard and become an important part of public opinion through the platform and the press. Throughout the 1820s the trades showed they were fully conversant with the techniques of public meetings, petitions, lobbying, newspaper articles and letters. But public meetings were of little use if not reported, and notice and understanding in the press were often difficult to secure. Again and again mechanics complained that they were not given a fair hearing, and so the new newspaper was an assertion of their political existence as an interest.

Of course, Gast was also political in the other sense; he was to show again that he was still a committed radical. He certainly believed that artisans' needs would be better met if a change in the representative system admitted a number of them to Parliament. Suffering would have been less 'had one half of the house of Commons, consisted of the best Informd, of the working Classes; & I believe they would have cut a better figur there, than some that is there; They would found out means to protect their Br, Workmen from the direfull effects of any change of Circumstance that may have operated to their Injury'.[11] The *Trades' Newspaper* was certainly in favour of parliamentary Reform and condemned the existing system. But at this time Reform was not practical politics, and the trades and their paper did not spend much time on abstract issues.

Gast, then, sought to promote the artisans' respectability, a consciousness of their value to society, and a recognition of this from society at large in status, pay and treatment. This would be achieved by unity, the removal of ignorance and influencing public opinion. These three aims are clearly set out in the manifesto of the new paper, in a style that is very much Gast's.

> A new and important era has commenced in the history of our class of society. We have become universally weary of the state of ignorance in which we have been so long sunk; we are grown sensible of the inefficacy of all attempts to better our condition, either extensively or permanently, until we better ourselves; we have begun to call up the power of our *minds* to assist in the improvement of our humble lot, and to cultivate and improve these by all possible means; and now it may be safely predicted that the day is close at hand when by Reason alone, we shall assert, successfully, our rights and interests at the bar of Public Opinion.
>
> But it is not enough that Mechanics should have begun to exercise, like other men, the right of thinking, and acting for themselves; it is necessary, in order to the achievement of any general good, that they should *think and act together*, not, however, by any secret or mysterious confederation; not by delegating to a few the privilege of thinking for the many (a concession excusable only when it cannot be helped); but simply by availing themselves of the same public medium to which other classes of men have recourse to make their sentiments known to, and respected by, the public. What the British Mechanics still want, is a Press—a Newspaper of their own—a common organ which may give better effect to their common appeal to the hearts and understandings of men, and which may, under all changes of circumstances, through good and through evil report, advocate and uphold the interests of the working classes, as before all others entitled to consideration and protection.[12]

The new venture was certainly a trade union paper, with a regular section on wages and combinations, regular reports on the activities of all the shareholding London trades, and much news on trade unions in the provinces (much of it drawn from provincial papers). 'It throws a flood of light upon the strength of trade unionism which, until this time, one must follow through the shadows of the Courts

and the Home Office papers.'[13] It strongly championed Gast and
the shipwrights in their dispute. It promoted trade union solidarity
through its advocacy of 'the cause of Union', reports on the Mutual
Improvement Society and extensive coverage of the Bradford dispute; it was indeed the main agency for co-ordinating and transmit-
ting subscriptions for that strike.

But, of course, a newspaper would not have been launched without expectations of commercial success. It was widely recognised in
the 1820s that a working-class reading public existed, and this was
underlined by the success of several new periodicals. The most
spectacular was John Limbird's *Mirror of Literature, Amusement
and Instruction*, a sixteen-page twopenny weekly begun in 1822
with a miscellaneous content and believed to sell 10,000 weekly.
There had also been a number of periodicals aimed specifically at
artisans, beginning in 1821 with the *Labourer's Friend and Handicraft Chronicle*, a sixpenny monthly with technical and general
information; the most successful was the threepenny monthly
Mechanics' Magazine launched in 1823 by Joseph Robertson and
Thomas Hodgskin. Alongside articles on the latest inventions, science and more general matters, this had contributions on industrial
conditions and the state of the Spitalfields weavers and campaigned
in 1824 for the repeal of the Combination Laws. Even before the
Black Dwarf finally ended in 1824 Wooler was planning another
paper, and in 1825 he issued a short-lived *Mechanics' Chronicle*,
while in April 1825 the ultra-Tory *New Times* began to carry
reports on the activities of trade societies.[14] The *Trades' Newspaper*
would never have begun without this belief in an artisan readership,
and it was appropriate that Robertson was its editor and Limbird
the publisher. Limbird also provided a reminder that workmen who
worked long hours on weekdays were most likely to read Sunday
newspapers and Saturday miscellany-cum-fiction, and so the
Trades' Newspaper came out on Sundays and tried to include all the
usual material of such a paper—general news, crimes and offences,
chapter of accidents, London markets, naval intelligence, sports
and pastimes, literature, art and science, natural history, theatres,
and foreign events.

The idea of a paper seems first to have been mooted by Edmonds
at a meeting early in May, those attending including a few trades'
delegates. These then informed the main trades' committee under
Gast that met at the Peacock, and they decided to begin a separate
paper of their own. The first suggested titles were *Genius of Industry* or *Workman's Advocate*. It was then agreed that £1,000 would

have to be raised, by £5 shares which could be held only by trade societies over 25 members. The rules and regulations were not finally agreed to until a general meeting of shareholders on 12 July. The paper would be run by a committee of management of eleven representatives of shareholding societies plus a secretary. Half of these would go out in rotation every six months, their replacements elected at a general meeting of shareholders. Gast was chairman of this committee until he went out in rotation in January 1826. The editor was appointed at a salary of £6 a week, the usual payment in London for reporters of morning papers.[15]

On 12 July it was decided to begin the paper on 17 July. The publication was thus begun rather hastily, and it seems that efforts in the two preceding months to sell shares had not been very effective.[16] It was, of course, only a limited number of trade societies that had participated in the trades' committee, and though several of these took a number of shares (the Original Friendly Society of Carpenters took fifteen), these alone could not take all the 200 shares. Efforts to involve other trades were, understandably, not very systematic, especially as leading figures like Gast had other commitments. In July the editor claimed that the £1,000 had been raised, but it is much more likely that Place was correct in stating that only £500 came in.[17] This was a missed opportunity, for the country delegates had been enthusiastic over the proposed paper and found a similar enthusiasm on their return home. A systematic use of these influential country contacts could have involved a number of trades in the large towns, but this was never done and the paper began with insufficient capital.

It also achieved a very limited circulation. It began with hardly any advance publicity, and most of the country contacts did not know beforehand of the date of the first number. As Henry Woodruffe of the South Shields seamen commented, they should have appointed an agent in each town to print handbills and advertisements and collect names of likely subscribers to contact by post. On 27 July Woodruffe did not know of a single copy in his town, while on 18 September Knowles in that place would not have known of the paper's existence had he not seen it referred to in its rival.[18]

The fact that there was a rival only made matters worse. Edmonds, the radical publisher of 1819, had persevered with his scheme and began in June his *Journeyman, and Artizans' London and Provincial Chronicle*. George White was hoping to become editor of Gast's paper, but the delegates decided not to appoint him, mainly because of the objections of Thomas Foster of the Manchester spinners, who had been antagonised by White's behaviour as their agent for the 1825 Factory Bill. White thereupon went into partnership with Edmonds and exploited all his provincial contacts on behalf of the *Journeyman*. He wrote systematically to such men as Rippon, Beveridge, Hodgson, Tester in Bradford and Clarke in Leicester, and even visited Leicester and Nottingham. He met with a loyal response—Rippon pushed the sale, Hodgson circularised the houses of call, Clarke distributed numbers, and Woodruffe had 300 handbills printed which he distributed at every public house. These men were naturally confused and dismayed when the *Trades' Newspaper* began.[19]

Yet even with its superior organisation and sale, the *Artizan* folded in September. The prospects for the *Trades'* were bleak, as it had failed to achieve a general readership and only sold a few hundred through the member trades. Things were made worse because the editor, Robertson, confined himself wholly to the content of the paper, leaving all else, including finance and publicity, to the committee of management. This was a large task for men working at their trade who were also active trade unionists at the time of industrial problems, and they were not able to do it properly. The main work fell on Gast, who was in effect manager of the paper, Purdy, and Lang (who in December became secretary for a while and improved their efforts). 'Had it not been for the zeal of the indefatigable Lang, Mr Gast, and a few others, not half those now acquainted with the paper, would have known any thing about it.'[20] Yet all were also busy officials in their own trades. There were complaints of irregular delivery in the provinces; as late as January 1826 it had virtually no sale in Birmingham, and at the first quarterly meeting that month there were errors in the accounts. Robertson was a poor editor, indolent and lacking application (he also greatly annoyed Tester by delays in sending on subscriptions for the strikers), and the paper often did not appear on time.[21]

'The Trades' paper was an abortion from the beginning.'[22] In Place's view, the conductors did not understand the business of running a newspaper, while Lang admitted that 'all new enterprises, however promising and well contrived, being necessarily doubtful in their results, it rarely happens that they are conducted in their commencement with all the vigour and judgement which they afford an opportunity of exerting'.[23] Given this, as Place said, its mere survival was remarkable; so also were the perseverance of its organisers, loyalty of the trades and the decision in January 1826 to set up their own printing establishment to print the paper and any other trade work. This would cost £500, a further appeal was launched, the trades took over both printing and publishing the paper in March, and soon adopted a new format.[24]

The London trades involved are easily known, but this is not so with the provinces. The links with the shipwrights in the outports seem to be revealed by shareholders in Bristol, Southampton, Yarmouth, Shields, Sunderland, Leith, Dundee, Dublin and Cork. The paper carried a fair amount on provincial shipwrights, while Gast, Purdy and Grieve were leading organisers and contributors. Shares were also held in Manchester, Cambridge and Carlisle, and by Oldham and Liverpool sawyers, but it remained very dependent on the London trades, some new ones joining in 1826, such as the line-and-twine spinners (experiencing reductions) and carvers and gilders. Sales fell early in 1826 (no doubt reflecting the depression and unemployment); by July all the original capital had gone and Place lent £20 one week to pay the printers.[25] But with the end of the Thames shipwrights' strike Gast was able to contribute to the paper and devote more time to its affairs. In June 1826 he went as a guest to the Liverpool shipwrights' anniversary celebration, and sold over twenty shares and boosted sales; Purdy had visited Manchester in March for the same purpose.[26] Place was also by now contributing articles, some of which increased the sale. From July the sales rose steadily for six months to reach 500 in December. But additional financial aid was needed in August from the silk-dyers and brassfounders; in December, when there were rumours it was to be dropped, it was rescued by further help from the carpenters' societies, and it soon received more help from the sawyers.[27] In October efforts to increase London support were begun by Gast and Jackson, a leader of the West London sawyers. In November and December they organised a series of public meetings, at which several shipwrights were prominent.[28] Early in 1827, with sales under 700, they still felt confident enough to have three editions, and new shares were taken by two societies of coopers (a trade suffering severe unemployment).[29]

The valuable help which Francis Place gave in 1826 was in contrast to his hostility when the paper began in 1825. This was due to the choice of editor. Place had warmly encouraged the idea of starting a paper, for the contacts made in 1824 and 1825 had at last given him the position of respect and influence among working men that he had so long sought. He had high hopes of at last removing the misguided and prejudiced attitudes he discerned among working men and opening their eyes to the true laws of political economy, especially that wages could only rise with an increase in capital or decline in population, and to the clear benefits that resulted from machinery in the form of cheaper production and therefore wider sale and therefore greater production and employment. These ideas he sedulously propagated among the working men he knew and in tracts. The newspaper would be a 'teaching paper', doing the good work of enlightenment alongside mechanics' institutions. When they rejected White the trades consulted Place over appointing the editor, and Place proposed the younger Baines, son of the proprietor and editor of the *Leeds Mercury*. This was on personal grounds (he was a gentleman, industrious and trustworthy) and qualifications (he was experienced in newspapers, had liberal views, was well informed on morals, legislation and political economy, and knew most of the literary men in London favourable to workmen).[30] Place was cruelly disappointed when instead they appointed J. C. Robertson, a journalist who with his *Mechanics' Magazine* had already succeeded in gaining an artisan readership and had campaigned in 1824 against the Combination Laws. His magazine was read by Gast and no doubt others on the committee, and Gast had contributed a couple of technical articles.[31] But the main reason for his appointment must have been that in June he also had decided, in conjunction with Limbird, to cash in on the supposed new artisan market and was advertising a new paper, and so his appointment thus avoided another rival.[32] The *Trades' Newspaper* even had the same motto as the *Mechanics' Magazine*. Place deplored the choice because he considered Robertson untrustworthy, dishonest and malicious, a man in whose hands the newspaper could never perform the work of enlightenment and effacement of prejudices.[33] He refused to co-operate with the new paper, contributed to the *Journeyman* instead, and did his best to mobilise his contacts in support of it. Given his ascendancy over Woodruffe, Rippon and others, this further damaged the *Trades'*.

Mechanics' Education

To understand Place's attitude we have to go back to the founding of the London Mechanics' Institution in 1823. The main course of events is familiar.[34] Robertson, a patent agent, and Thomas Hodgskin, a journalist and writer, had met in Edinburgh but both returned to London in the early 1820s. Robertson conceived the idea of a literary miscellany on the lines of Limbird's *Mirror* and approached the publishers Lacey and Knight who, however, insisted on a more scientific and technological basis, as in the *Labourer's Friend*. The outcome was the *Mechanics' Magazine* owned by Robertson, Knight and Lacey, and edited by Robertson and Hodgskin. Educational standards being higher in Scotland, Robertson had also been inspired by the Andersonian Institution in Glasgow and the Edinburgh School of Art to advocate an institution of adult scientific and technical education for artisans in London. The Andersonian had had a very successful mechanics' class, centred on the great lectures of George Birkbeck. But controversies had arisen after Birkbeck's time and in July 1823 some of the mechanics had seceded to found their own institution. It was therefore essential that such mistakes should not be repeated and that the proposed London institution must not offend the mechanics' susceptibilities—they must feel it was their own institution, run by them and catering for their needs, and not a boon conferred by patronising gentlemen. Hodgskin was a very close friend of Place who was a fervent believer in education and knew Birkbeck's successor Ure at the Andersonian, and Place warmly joined forces with them to compose an address published in the *Magazine* and distributed as a leaflet. A tremendous response came from a large number of liberal figures, including Brougham, Bentham, Burdett and Birkbeck (now in London), while Place worked tirelessly to locate, visit and circularise a large number of trade societies, benefit societies and houses of call. Two successful preliminary meetings of influential people led to the launching of the institution at a public meeting attended by over two thousand, mainly working mechanics. Place was the chief figure in drawing up the rules, one of which was that of the elected committee two-thirds should be mechanics.

The new institution was to flourish and stimulate a number of others. These were the results of the trend, clear by the 1820s, in favour of education at all levels. This stemmed from a variety of religious and philanthropic impulses and a belief in education, especially scientific, as the great means of human progress and perfectability, the advance of civilisation, the triumph of the rational over the 'animal'. Education would counteract wicked thoughts, improve morals and manners, reduce crime and drunkenness, and make people more orderly both in life and work. It would make workmen more productive (economic progress was one aspect of this progress) and produce subordination and respect on the part of inferiors to superiors and the laws, and so be a safeguard against blind revolt and rebellion. Given that more and more people were acquiring education and desiring it for their children, the question in the 1820s was not whether they should be educated or not, but what sort of education they should receive. It is therefore not surprising that there were already some institutions of adult education in London nor that the London Mechanics' Institution received such strong respectable support in the press, gifts of books and money and so on.

But among the group that actually launched and developed the institution, there were also more specific motives. Place and his group were certainly passionate advocates of education at all levels, and in the WLLA had specifically sought, through establishing schools on the system initiated by Joseph Lancaster, to check crime and destitution and civilise those groups whose ignorance seemed a menace to society. But the association had folded up in despair at the vast amount of ignorance and illiteracy they discovered and the marginal impact they were making. Where Lancasterian schools succeeded was by attracting the children of higher social levels, and for Place's group in the 1820s there were powerful influences in favour of concentrating on artisans as much more promising material. But they still hoped thereby to put an end to irrational activities, make artisans honourable members of society, and benefit worthy workmen by enabling them to improve their condition and rise to the level they deserved.

They also recognised that an industrial nation needed literate workers, that the country depended on the skill of her mechanics yet was very deficient in mechanical education. Technical instruction would therefore benefit the country as a whole. Early supporters of the institution included Galloway, Maudslay, Donkin and Martineau, the great London engineering employers who desperately needed better technical instruction for their workmen.

The group were also reformers, who wished for progress and social change, including the removal of absurd religious animosities and the securing of rational industrial relations through knowledge of the laws of political economy. They were also radicals, who saw society in political terms as a small number of parasitic rulers robbing and oppressing the vast majority, the people. The people must be made aware of the true state of affairs, and so radical reform was basically the removal of ignorance. Education would end oppression, destroy ridiculous veneration for royalty and aristocracy, and sweep away the irrational political system and its monopolies. And so the reform of manners, advancement of technical skills, widening of opportunities for men to better their position, and reform of the governing system would all be forwarded by enlightening artisans through the teaching of chemistry, mechanical philosophy and economics in the mechanics' institution.

But mechanics' institutions were not pushed at an unreceptive public—they offered the opportunity of gratifying widely-felt needs. There was the hope of rising socially, for with industrial and commercial expansion there was an ever-growing need for educated people, not only clerks and supervisors but also manual workers. Changes in technology militated against learning in the traditional way by precept and working by the eye and necessitated the use of plans and scale drawings. In Gast's own industry a science of naval architecture was growing, on which there was a fair amount of discussion in the *Mechanics' Magazine*,[35] a periodical whose very success demonstrated this desire for technical instruction. For many, membership and attendance in the institution also offered respectable activity free from the public house. Place deplored drunkenness as much as anyone, but unlike most others he did not go in for high-minded denunciations, for he had every sympathy with young single men who *had* to lodge at public houses, benefit clubs who *had* to meet there, married couples who lived in one room from which they *had* to go out to keep their sanity.[36] His concern was always to encourage alternatives to the pub, and he helped any kind of educational activity he met. His perception was acute, and many working men who were trying to resist the pub settled with relief on the mechanics' institution. Many were also attracted through interest, for we must remember the rapid spread of popular scientific lecturing from the later eighteenth century. And there was a strong ultra-radical current in favour of adult education, seeing, as much as did Place, the end of oppression in education, a 'rationalist illusion' only intensified by governmental efforts to restrict the press, whether in the persecutions of Carlile and his group in the 1820s or of the unstamped papers of the 1830s.

All these motives had produced a variety of educational activities among artisans—individual acquisition and reading of books, often entailing most heroic sacrifices, membership of local subscription libraries, small informal reading and study groups. These were forms of self-help and self-improvement that often provided companionship and enjoyable respectable activities away from disreputable places. Drawing on these, the London Mechanics' Institution aroused great hopes and evoked a great initial response, as did the number of others formed in 1825–6, usually with Birkbeck's help, in Spitalfields, Deptford, Rotherhithe, Southwark, East London (Stepney), Camberwell, Hackney and Hammersmith. Gast himself helped establish the one at Rotherhithe in November 1825, and somehow found time to participate in it, though by 1827 he could only attend the lectures, not evening classes.[37]

To the historian it seems obvious that contention was likely to rise over democratic control and the type of education provided. Right at the start Place clashed with Robertson and Hodgskin over the rules and was outraged at their dishonesty. Quarrels continued in the early years of the institution. Many artisans soon expressed disappointment and criticism in this and in the succeeding institutions, and so many left in disillusion that these institutions generally failed in their hopes of attracting large numbers of artisans. Often the majority of members were non-manual workers like clerks, a fact which might be recognised in changes of title from 'mechanics' institution' to 'literary and scientific institution'. Mechanics preferred their own, smaller and less formal study groups and mutual improvement societies, whose membership was confined to their own social group and where politics was often discussed, whereas in many mechanics' institutions it was excluded.

But we must not assume that the disappointments and criticisms were the expression in cultural and educational terms of two opposed class outlooks. These mutual improvement societies did not necessarily purvey a counter-culture or ideology. The education they provided was on the whole knowledge of the dominant culture, and was another facet of the artisans' quest for respectability. Since the education would confer self-respect, especially as it was an alternative to the pipe and the pot, and secure respect from society at large, especially as the prestige of education was growing, these societies performed an integrative function. Education was socially desirable, and could provide the means of rising socially. Place stressed this latter point in his replies to those, like Thomas Single, who poured scorn on the artisans' quest for education:

I was a journeyman at eighteen years of age, having no relation or patron able to assist me in any way. I got married before I was of age, and soon had a family. My business was one of the worst in London, both as to uncertainty of constant employment, and as to wages. I soon experienced the terrible evils of poverty. It may be fairly said, that I had no other prospect than that of living a life of misery myself, and of turning loose into the world a large number of wretched children. From this I was saved by precisely such teaching as journeymen may receive in Mechanics' Institutions. My school learning was merely reading, writing a bad hand, and arithmetic to vulgar fractions. But I had a good worthy man for my last school-master, who, during the half year before I was put to a trade, taught me a little geography, and thus excited a desire in me to know more of my own and foreign countries, the shape and motion of the earth and of the solar system: thus my ideas were somewhat enlarged. He showed me also a book of anatomy, and thus further excited my curiosity; and poor as I was, and as I for several years continued to be, I always found the means of procuring books on various subjects, and these I read diligently. Thrown out of employment by no fault of my own, and kept out of employment for several months, I employed my time in learning arithmetic, some geometry, and in reading a portion of Euclid: this I did without any assistance. 'Oh!' say all the Thomas Singles in the world, 'yours is not a common case; and of what use, after all, could these branches of learning be to a poor leather breeches maker?' True, Messrs. Single, mine is not a common case, and this is a conclusive reason for supporting Mechanics' Institutions. They will make such cases much more common among the most repectable journeymen; and these are they who will in the first instance become members of such institutions. As to the use of this kind of learning, we shall see that presently. While struggling in poverty to maintain my family I was joined by four other journeymen, each of whom paid sixpence a week to a poor French emigrant for a lesson in his language. A desire for knowledge had been excited in each of us by different causes, and the more we knew the more we desired to know; and this desire never ceased in any one of us, and is as strong in me at the present moment, as it was at any period of my life.

Increase of knowledge produced increase of self respect. I had never since the day of my marriage drunk so much as a pint of porter at any one time, and had scarcely ever spent so much as sixpence at any one time on myself, except to the French teacher;—my coadjutors were as poor, or nearly as poor as myself, and equally sober and industrious. And now, Messrs. Single, mark the result—every man of us flourished; one only did not become a master, because his business was a secondary business, but all became respectable men, and nearly all became men of property. Had we had the advantage of the London Mechanics' Institution—could we have had knowledge imparted at such an institution, our poverty would have been of short duration—our success earlier, and more certain—our cares, anxieties, and fears would have been lessened, and our families benefitted much earlier. Every man cannot succeed in the same way, and to the same extent as I and my fellows succeeded: but a great number may, and, by the aid of the Mechanics' Institutions, most assuredly they will succeed. Let then the Messrs. Single preach for ignorance, the parent of vice, and crime, and misery to the working people; heed them not—go on—get all the knowledge you can;—no man can tell how much any kind of knowledge may aid him hereafter.[38]

How revealing this is of Place's outlook! As Lovett later commented, 'you think the course you have pursued may be followed with advantage by others'.[39] But the attitude was by no means peculiar to Place; it struck the deepest chords among those who wished to be members of respectable society. Carlile, who so accurately expressed their outlook on many matters, supported mechanics' institutions because they would increase the amount of knowledge and raise the labouring man to a sense of his importance to society.[40] Gast identified the same two benefits—they would be agencies of technical progress, which would benefit the whole country; and they would (like the *Trades' Newspaper*) give artisans a pride in themselves and a consciousness of their value to society; from the latter would come an assertion of their right to recognition, and a refusal to accept degradation: 'the growth of knowledge was quite consistent with the proper performance of mechanical labour, and the due subordination of the workman to his employer. At the same time he admitted the modern plan of diffusing scientific education was calculated to impede the growth of oppression, and to make men more tenacious of their just rights.'[41] The emphasis on improvement by self-help did militate against anything smacking of charity or paternal supervision, though those willing to make great efforts often reacted against those who did not. We see 'the self-made man's contempt of the feckless, and the autodidact's impatience with those who did not take up the opportunities of self-improvement which were offered'[42] in Place, Carlile, Lovett and Gast.

The quarrels in the London Mechanics' Institution did not therefore reflect diametrically opposed views on education. They arose over the institution's scale. Robertson and Hodgskin had fairly modest ideas and were thinking along the lines of the mechanics' societies that already existed, 'a mere club' as Place viewed it. They were unprepared for the great response they met. But Place knew from bitter personal experience the daunting obstacles and great sacrifices that usually faced those seeking to acquire even the most modest materials for educational advance. He was determined that this institution should free its members of such problems and would have only the very best—a large building that could adequately house a big lecture-room, laboratory, museum, experimental workshop, schools, furniture and plenty of books and apparatus. He may also have envisaged a correspondingly high standard of teaching probably beyond the grasp of most working men. He certainly always supported small educational societies run by artisans alone[43] but seems to have seen them as recruiting grounds for mechanics' institutions which would be at a higher level and to which would come men who had already secured a fair degree of educational development, men like himself or William Lovett. But the expenses of such an institution would be too great for artisans alone to bear, and aid from wealthy sympathisers would be essential. Robertson

198 Artisans in Boom and Depression

and Hodgskin reacted with dismay to Place's vision and proposed expenses, and clung to the view that the costs should be borne by mechanics themselves. They were much more optimistic over mechanics' readiness to subscribe a high fee than was Place, whose scepticism had been increased by the poor response he had as yet received to his efforts to repeal the Combination Laws. At first Place gave in, but with the widespread response he prevailed in his view, large donations came in, and men like Birkbeck attained predominant positions on the committee. From this situation stemmed the problems of who should be in control and whether the institution under such management would meet the needs of its clientele. Failure over the latter made the former issue more acute.

The chief failure lay in the lectures. These were on a wide variety of topics and were desultory and not organised in any systematic course. The lecturers did not understand the needs of their audience and pitched the lectures at far too high a level, assuming a familiarity with science and an understanding of technical terms that simply did not exist. The audience's boredom was increased by the fact that far too many lectures were on subjects like chemistry and algebra rather than on mechanical arts that were within the experience of the artisans. Lacking in elementary education, the students needed not long lectures but regularly organised class instruction, yet this was not at first provided. The disappointment and disillusion were great.

The misguided concentration on lectures was particularly damaging since it led to the leasing of a large building in Southampton Row and the construction of a splendid lecture-theatre. This absorbed so much of the funds that the library, museum and elementary classes were neglected. The remoteness of the managers from the artisans was underlined by the appointment of a full-time secretary with an office open at hours (10 am–4 pm) totally unsuitable to working men, in stylish apartments into which humble mechanics were loth to venture. This self-consciousness was also felt in relation to the number of non-artisans who joined right from the start.[44]

Small wonder that many mechanics quickly withdrew and returned to their own informal efforts. This was recognised in perceptive articles in the *Mechanic's Weekly Journal* which urged artisans to continue to form small societies to buy books and to borrow books from lending libraries, to meet weekly and introduce discussion in turn. It condemned the Mechanics' Institution, with its long lectures, as the contrivance of a few master tradesmen out of touch with the artisans' needs.[45] Robertson was by now making equally cogent criticisms in his magazine, concentrating on the very slow progress which had lost membership, the misguided expenditure on a lecture-theatre which had necessitated a loan from Birkbeck and loss of independence, and above all the lack of control by working men themselves.

In the first preliminary committee the mechanics had clearly been suspicious of the intentions of the employers and had approved of Robertson and Hodgskin's opposition to the role of non-mechanics. Later on, discontent at the committee and its power (the decision to take the Southampton Row building was made by the committee without the consent of the membership) fomented criticism of the lack of democratic control and the committee's composition. It was a natural response to unsuitable tuition and a policy out of touch with their needs to blame the fact that the artisans did not have a sufficient say. By the rules, two-thirds of the committee had to be working mechanics, but after the elections of September 1824 (when only a small number voted), only 23 of the 36 were classed as 'working mechanics', and one of them was Place's son, who had taken over the family business. 'Mechanic' had been defined at the start as any man who earned his living by the work of his hands, but there were soon complaints that too many working masters as opposed to journeymen sat as mechanics on the committee.[46]

Robertson did not, however, stand for a different educational ideal. When a correspondent came near to criticising the whole scheme on class lines, namely that all the benefits from economic progress and efficiency would go to master manufacturers and capitalists because of the glut of workmen, Robertson replied that knowledge was better than drink, that wages would rise if there were less drunken cheap labour and less competition for work between hungry, ignorant, licentious workmen underbidding one another, that allowing the free emigration of men would raise wages, that everyone gained from an increase in national wealth, and that all machinery, by increasing capital, led to rises in wages.[47] It could almost have been Place. Robertson was mainly criticising details of policy, and here showed how close he was to mechanics' views.

Yet even he agreed with the managers that political topics should be excluded from the teaching. It was an ironic illustration of the viewpoint of the gentlemen, that though the theory of mechanics' institutions was to cultivate the minds of artisans through education concerned with objects within their daily experience, this tended to be seen in terms of subjects directly related to material pursuits and so excluded one topic that greatly interested many of them—politics. There was persistent criticism of the exclusion of politics in the early mechanics' institutions and both they and the later Lyceums declined in membership if they had nothing on politics or current affairs. This was not in itself a sign of artisan radicalism. Politics was easier to follow than algebra or chemistry. Politics and contemporary events were of more direct interest than many scientific subjects. They were also more interesting, because like religious topics, they were controversial. These were the three main reasons for the popularity of politics. The thriving Saturday and Sunday papers should have been a reminder that there were limits to what a tired man could cope with on a weekday evening (many of the most serious mutual improvement societies met on Sundays, but respectable opinion would have been offended if the Mechanics' Institution met on the Sabbath), while the high political content in newspapers showed the extent of interest. The spread of coffee-houses which took daily and weekly papers which could be read free with a meal, and the political discussions at public houses, were other signs. That politics was entertainment was evident from the attendances at debating clubs where performers were paid a fee to argue for or against a motion, institutions that Carlile was convinced were of absolutely no politically educative value, though his associates Gale Jones and Robert Taylor were often star performers.[48] Such emotions also no doubt characterised the welcome to radicals at trade club meetings in the post-war years, and later to Chartist lecturers at public houses.

> He was convinced that the agitation, as carried on in London this last year or two, had been useless, they met and lectured to the same Chartist audience in the fumes of smoke and liquor; it seemed that the only object in lecturing was to afford them amusement; they could not thus create Chartists.[49]

When Lyceums and many mechanics' institutions did open newsrooms, these were often the most popular part, though educationalists deplored the fact that newpapers and partisan or sectarian tracts drove out 'pure' educational magazines.

But we should not make impossibly high demands of political sophistication. It remains true that the basic tone of debating clubs was radical, and that many mutual improvement societies were radical and anti-Christian, like the 'Liberals' in Long Acre whom William Lovett joined.[50] And there *was* a radical critique of mechanics' institutions that was not confined to their constitution. While Carlile sniped at them as all-male establishments,[51] many

more agreed with his condemnation of the exclusion of political and
religious topics as preventing the people's gaining knowledge of
their true rights. Carlile's life was devoted to providing this knowledge.

> The first principle of this paper, springing from the prevailing passion of
> its editor, is to communicate knowledge, in a sort of political reading
> made easy, to that portion of the people which is suffering injury and
> oppression, in want of that knowledge.[52]

They saw mechanics' institutions providing the *wrong* kind of knowledge, not of man's rights and place in society, but of geology,
natural history and harmless, miscellaneous, entertaining, scientific
facts. And, as we shall see, those who opposed political economy
suspected the institutions as devices for inculcating its tenets, a
motive Place frankly avowed.[53]

The influence of Birkbeck and the other non-artisans thus led to
misguided policies that overrated the artisans' educational abilities,
followed the wrong priorities and clashed with deeply-held feelings.[54] The dislike of charity, of which benefit and trade societies
were an expression, included an aversion to charity education and
therefore the free lectures. 'The provident and industrious
mechanic wants not charity but justice!'[55] They disliked the
middle-class managers' condescending and patronising attitude,
preference for the 'showy', and desire to limit the scope of the
education to what they themselves deemed 'useful'.

> But it is predicted that 'at no very distant period, the best informed
> among them will be instructed in every thing *which relates to their
> condition in society*;'—this is 'an ill phrase' an aristocratical, *Courier*-like
> way of speaking; if you really wish to bring important information within
> the reach of the working people; in the first place enable them to get
> their living by industry; do not when they ask for bread give them a
> stone; then, I would say, advise them to study men, as well as books; and
> instead of confining your instructions to their 'condition in society' strive
> to teach them their duty as members of the body politic, and their civil
> and religious rights as Englishmen and citizens of the world.[56]

The artisans' wish to run things themselves, as in their preference
for benefit societies over savings banks and insurance schemes
offered by employers, led to a preference for mutual improvement
societies over mechanics' institutions. The latter, of course, spread
both in London and the provinces to become an educational
development of national importance, and not all repeated the mistakes of the first ones. 'The movement found, not an eager adult

population, ready to learn the wonders of science, but a semi-literate population of youths, needing the most elementary education.'[57] The lessons were often learned, elementary classes were provided, the concentration on lectures dropped and newsrooms opened. But their role in the education of artisans was much less than that of the private clubs, where people discussed common reading and spoke in turn. These remained a persistent feature of artisan society, and cropped up in every artisan movement, whether political or co-operative.

The history of the London Mechanics' Institution thus estranged Place from Robertson, who kept up a running war in his magazine. The group around Place who had such a great share in its foundation and development also played a key role and gave evidence in the repeal of the Combination Laws in 1824.[58] Moreover Place's tireless work on behalf of the Institution at the houses of call and trade societies meant that now he did at last make the contacts that had hitherto eluded him, and this was the beginning of his influence among London artisans. Important artisans in the Mechanics' Institution were Tongue of the bookbinders, Johnson of the whitesmiths and Whittaker of the painters and glaziers. When early in 1824 Place sought to organise petitions for repeal of the Combination Laws, he visited several houses of call.[59] But on the whole these were *not* of the trades that banded together in 1825 under Gast to campaign against new legislation and found the *Trades' Newspaper*, the exceptions being hatters, carpenters, silk-weavers (who refused to help Place in 1824) and brassfounders. Place in 1824 was therefore probably visiting not the trades most worried about Combination Laws but those connected with the Mechanics' Institution, and since they included such superior and aristocratic trades as compositors, millwrights, bookbinders and smiths it may well be that the chief artisan response to the institution came from the superior trades.

Robertson supported repeal of the Combination Laws on basically the same grounds as Place, and declared that working men should not exercise undue power or coercion,[60] but he carried on his vendetta by singling out Place's evidence for attack. It was not surprising that when he became editor of the *Trades' Newspaper* Place was offended, or that the paper contained frequent attacks on mechanics' institutions, especially the parent one, though he admitted improvements had occurred.[61] In 1825 a group of non-operatives formed a provisional committee to found a mechanics' institution for Rotherhithe, and proposed that only half the committee be working class, which produced an outcry from Robertson and a correspondent until it was changed.[62]

But the paper's attitude to mechanics' institutions was not solely due to Robertson, for the criticism continued after he ceased to be editor.[63] The membership of most of them fell away in the 1826 depression. The London Mechanics' Institution therefore increased the quarterly subscription to the high level of 24s. which led to a further decline which continued until 1830, and to an increasing proportion of clerks. Several members resisted a policy that would exclude mechanics, and when in July 1826 the committee proposed that anyone not employing journeymen should be regarded as working class (which would make working masters eligible), this was rejected at a general meeting. In the committee elections, four of the working-class section were working masters who employed journeymen, and it was now that George Adam was elected and emerged as the leading critic of the mechanics' lack of control.[64] Adam was secretary of the First Society of Carpenters and, from late 1826, on the committee of management of the *Trades' Newspaper* in which he was soon a leading figure. He sought to have 'working class' defined so as to exclude employers but failed, though in March 1828 the quarterly meeting rejected proposals that would specifically include working masters. Meanwhile the membership of the Rotherhithe Institution had also fallen off in 1826, and the resultant raising of the subscription to 16s. was a recognition that it would not be one for mechanics. At its peak membership was 300, of whom only half were working class, but by April it had fallen to 100. Proposals were made to alter the name to Rotherhithe and Bermondsey Literary and Scientific Institution, or Institution for the Diffusion of Useful Knowledge, and Gast opposed the change, calling on mechanics to rally to its support and prevent its being taken over.[65] When in April 1826 Place wrote an article for the *Trades' Newspaper* in favour of mechanics' institutions, several of the managing committee opposed it, while in September 1827, long after all connection with Robertson had ceased, the paper was still regularly condemning the gentlemen governors, free lectures and the exclusion of political economy and politics.[66] Indeed in 1827 the paper's committee regarded the London Mechanics' Institution's committee as its chief enemy.

Malthusianism

It was not only Robertson's attacks on the mechanics' institutions

which Place thought mischievous, for in the paper he also condemned Place's population theories and gave publicity to his friend
Hodgskin's book *Labour Defended against the claims of capital*.

Respectable opinion was moved by the spectre of over-
population, Malthus having proved that population had a natural
tendency to increase faster than the means of subsistence, being
checked only by such disasters as war, disease and famine. The
pessimistic conclusion was that any increase in the amount of food
merely meant that more people would survive and the masses
always remain at subsistence level. To those who refused to accept
this fatalistically the remedy lay in checking population growth by
artifical means. The most common way, recognised by Malthus
himself in later editions and by influential writers like M'Culloch,
was 'moral restraint', sexual abstinence. Another idea was emigration schemes, State-assisted or otherwise, to send unemployed to
the Americas or Australia and effect a fall in population. Place,
while rejecting much of Malthus' argument, especially his calculations, was fully convinced of the correctness of the basic principle,
and throughout the 1820s persistently tried to get over his case,
concentrating on the connection between population and wages.[67]
Any increase in wages reduced profits and would therefore drive
capital from the industry to more profitable areas of investment,
and thus decrease the amount of capital and therefore employment
in that industry. The amount that went on wages could only be what
was left after the employer had received a profit equal to others'.
Wages could therefore only rise in one industry if they rose generally, which could only happen if demand for labour grew, for the
market price of wages was determined by supply and demand. Since
population was in excess of the number that could be employed,
wages were very low and many were half-starved even when in full
employment. Excessive population produced poverty, misery, vice,
crime, disease and premature death. This must be understood by
working men so that they would not follow red herrings. 'The
operation of the laws against combinations of workmen had drawn
off the attention of the working people from all other causes of low
wages, and had induced them to conclude that the sole cause was the
law.'[68] Trade union action could itself achieve little. Well established and organised societies which by regular contributions could
amass funds with which to support unemployed members could
affect wages, but though many of the London trades had these they
were impossible for the bulk of working men. In any case trade
unions, however strong, could never keep up wages for a length of

time if there was always a redundancy of hands that furnished starving men who were ready to break any strike and take work at any price. The success of some London trades in keeping up wages rested on the fact that they were seasonal—every year there was a period when business was so brisk that demand for labour exceeded supply. But this could not last for long, and in other industries, such as cotton, where supply of labour always exceeded demand, trade unionism must be ineffective.[69] Employers were not to blame for low wages, and appeals to their humanity Place treated with derision. Wages could only rise if there were a change in the labour supply–demand ratio. Demand could rise from industrial expansion due to increased markets, and Place thought that this was happening, especially when machinery cheapened production, so that the overall standard of living had risen in his lifetime. But this could all be wiped out by population increase, and so Place concentrated on the need to contract the labour supply by checking the growth of population, a benevolent activity to avert potential disaster.

In most of this Place was in agreement with M'Culloch but he had nothing but contempt for those who unfeelingly preached 'prudential restraint' through sexual abstinence, a mockery akin to preaching abstinence from eating. Nor had he much patience with emigration schemes which at vast expense would have a marginal effect and were anyway misguided in seeking to send industrious men abroad. The only remedy lay in physically preventing conception, and so this 'fierce Malthusian with a large family'[70] courageously set out to publicise contraceptive techniques.

In 1822–4 he distributed tracts and handbills anonymously.[71] In 1825, as a result of his Lancashire contacts, especially the Bolton weavers, and of his meeting the delegates who came to London in 1824 and 1825, he had great hopes of at last exerting a powerful influence over working-class opinion and securing recognition of the laws governing population and wages. Over some of these men, like Woodruffe and Rippon, he achieved a great personal ascendancy and they became willing allies. He made a summary of a lecture by M'Culloch in favour of higher wages, which could only follow an acceleration in the increase of capital or a check in the increase of population. Thousands of copies were printed and distributed—Rippon took 500, Tester distributed 2,500.[72] Place continued to write on these lines in the *Morning Chronicle*, the *Artizan* while it lasted, and the *Bolton Chronicle* (edited by William Smith). He received strong support from Richard Carlile, to whom Place gave a great deal of help in the 1820s, and to whose periodicals he contributed. Carlile completely accepted the economic theories of 'his old tutor',[73] was equally horrified at Malthus' view that the poor should be left to starve, and was not in the slightest afraid to advocate contraception openly. He ran a series of articles in the *Republican*, presumably written by Place, under the title 'What is Love?', which he reprinted as a book, and Place used his contacts to circulate it.[74]

Given the horror such proposals aroused, it was inevitable that Robertson would seize the chance to attack Place where he was most vulnerable. In the *Mechanics' Magazine* he condemned the 'crooked opinions which Mr. Place entertains', and the *Trades' Newspaper* continued to assail 'the efforts without a name'.[75] He employed the argument that God could never have allowed more births than could be fed, a reasoning that filled Place with fury. And he poured scorn on the idea that it was possible to gauge the population needed in twenty years' time. 'How can any man possibly tell when, by adding one or two more to the mass of the population, he will help to overstock, at some future day, the market for labour?' It was ridiculous to expect him to 'consult the population tables every time he goes to bed'.

But in his attacks Robertson came to take a wider view and moved towards alternative analyses that were close to the attitudes of his artisan employers. Many of these were aware of the ideas of 'Malthus, that enemy to procreation among the labouring poor',[76] and there is no doubt that they resented being told that their sufferings were their own fault and that they were breeding too much. Believing that their skill was of value to the community and that they had a *right* to a respectable position, they were deeply offended by schemes cooked up by unproductive rich men to remove 'surplus population' by emigration, to 'transport' industrious men who merely wished to work for a decent reward. Emigration projects were fashionable in the later 1820s, but to Gast it was a 'cruel and senseless scheme' which ignored all the basic grievances of the mechanics.[77] And contraception aroused as much horror among them as in other levels of society.

It was not at all that they denied what Place said about the surplus of hands, one of their basic problems. They saw the accuracy of his comments on the wretched Spitalfields weavers, into whose trade there was always an influx of hands when trade was brisk, leaving it overstocked when demand slackened. Some even accepted Place's argument as far as a general tendency was concerned, but what they could not accept was his almost exclusive concentration on this issue. Basically he seemed to offer a gospel of fatalism—present poverty was unavoidable. In 1829 Place told Doherty that trade unionism could achieve nothing. 'Is there then no remedy? Yes, one, and only one, ceasing to produce hands faster than there is a demand for hands. There is no other.'[78] This was a message of despair. William Longson, with whom Place engaged in controversy in the pages of the *Bolton Chronicle* in 1826, pointed this out. 'F.P. contends that every effort for arresting the progress and alleviating the distress of the working classes must prove abortive, except a diminution of their numbers. Under this idea, he deprecates the remedy I suggest, and must, for the same reason, discourage every other that can be devised.'[79] Longson sought to redirect attention to the problems of *fluctuations* in employment.

Trade unionists could not accept this fatalism, and it was in the 1820s that 'Malthusian' became one of the dirty words of popular radicalism. In articles, letters and editorials in the *Trades'* paper and elsewhere, a critique was developed. How was the theory reconcilable with any improvement in the past? There were other reasons for unemployment—competition from women and children, machinery that displaced human labour, high taxation that reduced spending power and therefore demand, and therefore employment. Malthusianism was therefore diverting attention away from events that were remediable. And, as so often, this chimed in with radical arguments, for it wholly left out of account the questions of political power, 'the badness of government', Corn Laws and currency and reform.[80] Place's approach therefore served a reactionary function:

> Tom Paine-burnings, volunteer-playing-at-soldiers, Bible Society speech-making, and other scenes of farce are over; population is now the raw-head-and-bloody-bones set up to frighten political babes from the forbidden fruit of the tree of knowledge.[81]

Restriction of numbers would bring no improvement if the distribution of political power were the same. Artisans like Gast warmed to Robertson's cry that 'there are other ways than that of making workmen scarce, to enable them to obtain a due share of the fruits of their labour;—for example, a better knowledge of their importance in the scale of society, union to uphold each other in the assertion of their rights, habits of saving, and that degree of independence which is their necessary result.'[82] The standpoint adopted in the *Trades'* differed from Place's in not being completely imprisoned within the existing economic system. First, population was *not* excessive, because there was in the country enough food and clothing for all; some went without because others had too much, and the evil lay not in total numbers but in the unequal distribution of wealth. 'To tell men that their bad pay and poverty arises from there being too many people will never be believed while there is in the country far more than a sufficiency of food for the whole.'[83] Secondly, they rejected the assumption that wages should fluctuate with supply and demand, for everyone willing to work had the *right* to good wages, irrespective of the demand for labour. This provided a yardstick against which to measure society and find it wanting.

The *Trades' Newspaper* also published letters from Thomas Hodgskin and extracts from his book.[84] Hodgskin's secure place in the history of socialist thought tells us nothing about his contemporary influence. That he had an impact is mainly attested by Francis Place, but Place had special reasons for exaggerating Hodgskin's role, namely close personal friendship and disagreements in the Mechanics' Institution over policy and economic theory.[85] Moreover in his disdainful attitude to working men Place shared the assumptions of respectable society that workmen could not by themselves have developed aggressive or anti-capitalist tendencies out of their own experiences, but must have received them from outsiders, like Owen or Hodgskin. The mere fact of publishing the passages from Hodgskin's book in the *Trades'* paper is no sign of any widespread interest, but was due to his connection with Robertson. But it is worth noting in passing that many of Hodgskin's ideas did correspond with those of London artisans. He asserted the overriding primacy of labour in the creation of wealth, as without it capital was useless, but that for historical reasons the owners of capital took the greatest share of the product while labour received the least. The result was an unjust and growing contrast of wealth and poverty. Active employers were workers, though too highly paid, but as providers of capital had interests opposed to the men. The poverty of labourers was not due to an overall shortage of wealth but to the organisation of society, and he rejected current theories that the reward for labour should merely cover subsistence and reproduction, and a political economy confined wholly within established property-rights. This struck a chord among artisans who encountered capitalism in the form of shipbuilders or clothing, footwear and furniture warehouses. The structure of the shipbuilding industry was that the builder took orders for work from the shipowners, provided the premises, materials and equipment, and gave out, or sub-contracted, the work in parts to self-recruited gangs at agreed prices. The gang then did the work subject to the supervision of the builder and foreman as to quality of workmanship and completion of work on time. So though it was a capitalised industry, the workmen practised a large degree of freedom and control. They regarded themselves as the true workmen, the builders' role being merely supervisory, provision of capital and taking of orders. Such capitalists merely owned the means of production which were put at the disposal of the producers, and their profit was a deduction from the product of labour; they were seen as middlemen or monopolists.[86]

But with the failure of the *Artizan* Place needed an outlet, and in November 1825 became a regular contributor to the *Trades'*. Reconciliation was made easier when in March 1826 Robertson went to King's Bench prison for debt and ceased to be editor, so that changes in editing, printing and publishing all occurred at the same time.[87] Place again had his candidate for editor, a radical attorney's clerk in Bradford, Squire Farrar, with John Tester to be his assistant, but the trades ignored him again and appointed John Anderson.[88] But the personal problem had been removed, and Anderson in fact very regularly consulted Place.

Place maintained his regular contacts in Glasgow, South Shields, Bolton and Manchester. He helped Benjamin Lomax in his attempt to set up in business, and was consulted by London trades like the hatters, carpenters, silk-weavers, seamen, shipwrights and coopers.[89] In 1826 he read the memoirs of Robert Blincoe concerning the treatment of children in cotton mills, and had Carlile publish them in 1828.[90] In 1827 he helped the Shields seamen petition against pressing, and in 1829 drew up for the Manchester spinners a new factory bill which, after he consulted Peel, was passed into law.[91] Anderson's editorials had much in common with Place's views in their attacks on the wealth and ceremony of the monarchy, the attitudes of the aristocracy, the riches of the Church, the Corn Laws, large army, National Debt, high taxes, sanguinary criminal code and game laws. Both saw the remedy in wider parliamentary franchise and more frequent elections, supported Catholic Emancipation while disapproving of O'Connell's rabble-rousing and intolerant Catholicism, and expressed contempt for sham-reformers like Brougham. But the *Trades' Newspaper* was never a simple purveyor of Place's views, and events after 1825 threw into prominence a number of issues on which many artisans took a line opposed to Place's.

11
THE TRADES IN DEPRESSION

Trade, Wages and Machinery

In 1825 the boom ended and the year closed in financial panic. The depression deepened to make 1826 a terrible year of falling wages and widespread distress. Some recovery from the end of 1826 into 1828 was followed in 1829 by sudden relapse into deep depression, and the mild recovery of 1830 ended in 1831, so that overall the period 1826–32 was one of high unemployment and distress made worse by the high food prices after bad harvests in 1829–31.[1] The weakness of trade unions led to wage reductions and the failure of their strikes, from the Bradford combers in 1825 to the Lancashire spinners in 1829–31. The London trades also had their reductions and unsuccessful strikes, but the main effect of the depression was to aggravate the long-term problems of some of them. There was no uniformity here; while the coopers maintained strong apprenticeship regulations, shoemakers and tailors were succumbing to the swell of cheap labour. Everyone agreed the silk-weavers were at one extreme.

The number employed in the Spitalfields silk industry continued to grow after the terrible year of 1816, but this merely meant a deterioration in their general conditions. New businesses arose in places like Macclesfield, Sudbury or Manchester and competed with Spitalfields. In the 1820s weavers in full work often toiled fourteen or sixteen hours a day for 16s 0d. a week, but many earned as little as 6s. or 7s. 'I can safely say that in intelligence, in form, in size, in cleanliness, they are far below every other trade in the metropolis. They are now what some of the other meaner trades were 40 years ago.'[2]

On the top of this situation, the Spitalfields weavers received two further blows. The first was the repeal in 1824 of the Spitalfields Act which regulated apprenticeships and provided for the agreement by committees representing masters and men on prices which were approved and enforced by the magistrates. This at least maintained the *rates*, but of course unemployment reduced earnings. In 1823 a united weavers' campaign secured the rejection in the Lords of a bill to repeal this act, and led on to a revision of the prices agreed with the employers in 1824. At the same time a general union of all the Spitalfields weavers' societies was agreed. As a result, they refused to help Place against the Combination Laws. But later that session the Spitalfields Acts were repealed, despite a mass lobby of Parliament, leaving them defenceless against price cuts. They now joined in 1825 with the other trades to oppose reimposition of the Combination Laws and to found the *Trades'* paper.[3]

The second blow was the abolition in 1825 of the prohibition of foreign-wrought silks, to have effect from 5 July 1826, when a 30% duty would apply instead. This was a disastrous blow, for by late 1825 there were few orders, buyers all waiting for the influx of French goods which were cheaper because wages there were much lower. In January 1826, when the silk-dyers were usually very busy in anticipation of spring orders, they had no work. Masters now began to reduce prices below the 1824 list, sometimes by as much as 30% to put them actually below the 1774 list. Some of them, like Newbury, the last to reduce, did so reluctantly but felt forced by competition. The new year saw the return of starvation, soup kitchens and mass applications for parish relief. Even Robertson, who strongly supported free trade, grew so appalled by their sufferings that his faith in the ending of prohibition was shaken.[4]

The weavers were therefore fighting against the repeal of wage-fixing, the ending of prohibition, and wage reductions. For the rest of the decade they shifted desperately from one course of action to another.[5] Late in 1825 they memorialised the government against the impending introduction of foreign silks, appealed to the masters' humanity and charity, and contested the reductions in a series of bitter individual disputes. When all these failed they reverted in 1826 to trade unionism. William Wallis had emerged in the early 1820s as one of their leaders, and was prominent in the 1825 Combination Laws struggle and the founding of the *Trades'* paper. In May 1826 Place urged him to organise the weavers and offered his help, and Wallis secured the formation of a General Protection Society with weekly subscriptions to build up a fund and secure a return to the 1824 prices. Most masters agreed to this, but only on condition that all the rest did, and the weavers were not strong enough in that year to enforce it. At the end of 1826 they therefore humbly petitioned the Royal Family, nobility and gentry for patronage. But the masters' response had emphasised that the basic problem lay in competition, for if a few masters refused to agree to list prices, the majority were forced to reduce as well. This was recognised by artisans generally. In 1827 the Spitalfields weavers therefore petitioned Parliament for a new act to regulate wages and so check this competitive wage-cutting, and sought a united campaign with the masters. When this failed they reverted to industrial action, as there had been some recovery, and in April 1827 struck for rises up to the 1824 level; 10,000 were thus idle. Many small masters gave in immediately, and others followed, so that by May nearly all masters agreed to the rise. But distress deepened in June and reductions began again in July. Trade unionism having failed, the weavers in 1828 again petitioned Parliament in favour of wage-fixing, but in their anger also added demands for parliamentary Reform. This failed, so in July 1828 they agitated for tariff protection, efforts which were intensified when in February 1829 there were proposals to *reduce* the duty even further. With failure here, the return of widespread distress and relief committees, the weavers returned to industrial action but not this time in the form of strikes, which had failed, but of threats of destruction of masters' looms made, it was said, under the direction of a secret committee. In their fear many masters agreed to pay the 1824 prices, but serious riots broke out in June. When these ended, attempts were made to establish a national trade union. In despair they then asked the government to transport them to a new Australian colony on the Snow River, and when Peel refused, Wallis came forward with the idea of settling the unemployed on the waste lands of England. In October 1830 they were again begging the new King and Queen for relief, in 1830–1 trying to form a trade union, in 1831 supporting parliamentary Reform and petitioning for a bill to fix wages, in 1832 seeking prohibition again. In following a variety of courses in connection with a constant outlook, they were typical of the London artisans.

The shoemakers were also preoccupied with difficulties and memories of better times.[6] Their industry was increasingly characterised by competition for work and lower earnings. In response to this men worked longer hours to compensate, which only resulted in even greater competition and still lower earnings. The men's shoemakers, weakened by the division between West End and City, were facing growing competition from the warehouses in London selling shoes made cheaply in the country, especially Northampton, and merchants were having export orders made there too. Though on the whole they maintained the 1812 rate, the regularity of work and therefore earnings were declining. The City men had a strike in 1825. In ladies' shoemaking, of which there was little in the provinces as London set the fashion, while superior shops in the West End supplied high quality, bespoke goods and paid skilled men accordingly, the society men working for other respectable masters found themselves in growing competition with the haberdasher shops and warehouses selling cheap shoes made at the lowest possible prices, especially for the country and export markets. The women's shoemakers had greater difficulty in keeping up earnings, especially those in the City working for the 82 fair shops there. Journeymen in distress and out of work were tempted to make goods on their own account, and many became 'chamber-masters', making cheap, inferior shoes at a faster pace and lower prices, often employing lads cheaply. When trade revived they often became journeymen again, but they were helping to effect a general cheapening of labour and were often regarded as the journeymen's worst enemies;

> they change from poor miserable journeymen to poor miserable masters; they must sell low to enable them to get rid of their goods, and more respectable masters must, as a matter of course, reduce their profits to be enabled to compete with them.
>
> To this source, Mr. Editor, we may trace all the misery which exists among shoemakers, and, I have no doubt, many other trades. Journeymen are oppressed, and they become masters; the increase of masters reduces profits; the reduction of profits causes the employers to continue the course of oppression until oppression can no longer be borne.[7]

In 1825, when all other trades were pressing for rises, the City ladies' shoemakers were striking against reductions and faced the formation of a masters' association to beat them, and there were further strikes in 1826.[8]

The shoemakers' decline continued throughout the 1820s, and was paralleled by the much more dramatic collapse of the tailors, who for long had had the strongest union of all.[9] Since the end of the war competition from the less skilled dungs, doing piece-work and longer hours, was reducing their earnings. By the early 1820s much of the trade was in the hands of 'show-shops' and 'slop-shops' selling cheap, inferior articles, to order or ready-made respectively. Some of them employed cheap labour directly, including females, but most gave work out to small masters who competed with and undercut one another, either working at home as chamber-masters and often using the labour of their families, and women and children, or acted as middle men, 'sweaters', giving work to journeymen to be done at low rates at their homes. As among shoemakers, low earnings led to overwork to compensate and therefore greater competition for work all round. The flint tailors in bespoke shops naturally suffered from the growth of the ready-made sector, and unemployment grew. Moreover in many houses of call there were two books for names of members seeking work, and those on the first book, reserved for senior members, always received priority. The result was that newer members often in desperation took work below the fixed rate. The 1826 depression drained their unemployment funds, and in 1827 a strike against female labour was beaten, the first strike lost in over sixty years. In 1830, on the death of George IV, the employers refused to adhere to the old custom of double pay during court mourning, and defeated the tailors' response of a general strike. The rapid spread of piece-work instead of day-work then opened the way to cuts in earnings and the growth of outwork.

The disasters in these three trades in the 1820s were extreme cases, but similar developments occurred in others. By the later 1820s the carpenters were already suffering from greater competition for work, while linen-drapers and other firms were beginning to sell cabinet furniture and force small trade, working master cabinet-makers into active competition.[10] In this decade the latter began to go down in the face of middlemen using cheap, unskilled labour, and unemployed and inferior workmen who set up in the East End as garret-masters working themselves, their families and lads and selling at low prices to the 'slaughter-houses'. All these five trades were facing the problem of greater competition for work due to an influx of workers into the trade, a large portion of them women and children except in the case of carpenters. And they were not alone. Even the hatters in 1824 were experiencing a decline in work for this reason, and the situation was much worse in the 1826 depression.[11] The silk-dyers had an influx of women and children, and the line-and-twine spinners suffered from female labour, while the ropemakers struck at the end of 1825 against a flood of apprentices.[12]

The response of most trades to this labour surplus was to try to maintain a rigid system of apprenticeship, to keep out the tide of unskilled labour, which often provoked conflicts with employers.

No doubt one of the causes of the prevalence of combinations, and indeed one excuse from [sic] them, is the feeling entertained by the workmen in almost every trade, that they are surrounded by a pauperized and almost servile population, towards whose condition, if labour found a common level, they might be reduced. They are naturally tempted therefore to erect and strengthen artificial barriers, to insulate themselves as much as possible in their particular crafts, and to restore in effect the guilds, and the apprenticeship laws which have been abolished, or have lost their efficacy.[13]

But as the hostile *New Times* commented: 'But the possessors of skill, and education, and capital, constitute an aristocracy: the carpenters are aristocrats compared with the canal diggers . . . In fact, the higher classes of mechanics are peculiarly liable to suffer in any convulsion. Those below them will, in a scarcity of work, undersell them in labour.'[14]

The London trades were also aware of three other weaknesses in their situation. The first was country competition, for wages in London were much higher. And the more production was for export and not the home market, with attendant emphasis on cheapness, the more London industry was at a disadvantage. The second was foreign competition, more important now with the growth of international trade and the tariff reductions. While the shipwrights and caulkers feared Baltic and Indian shipbuilding, the silk-weavers were threatened by French, Indian and Chinese silks, the shoemakers by cheap French shoes, and the ropemakers by foreign cordage that was sold at a price lower than that of the raw hemp on which they worked.[15] Thirdly, technological changes posed problems, such as the use of different timbers and more metal that threatened coopers' earnings, while the hatters had several disputes over 'yeoman crams'.[16] In a few trades machinery threatened employment. Since 1820 the ropemakers had been suffering from a new machine called 'Devil', which nine men could operate to make a ship's cable which formerly involved over eighty men.[17] At the same time the sawyers suffered from the extension of steam-sawing from veneers to the cutting of deals and timber, which it could do much more quickly; in their discontent they had been active in the Queen Caroline agitation and in support of Hunt. Their last good year was 1825, for 1826–7 saw a rapid spread of sawing machinery.[18] Silk-dyers were being hit by a machine that crushed the skeins, pressmen were being displaced by printing machinery, and machinery was also apparently causing problems among the brassfounders.[19]

Though mechanisation was not typical of London trades, it should be remembered that it is with the differing experiences that we are concerned. For apart from the tailors, cabinet-makers and pressmen, all the other eleven of these trades came together to take shares in the *Trades' Newspaper* and indeed the seamen and cork-cutters are the only other London trades known to have done so. These artisans had the same ideals as the compositors, bookbinders or engineers, but whilst these latter were more secure, the former felt the need to act together to combat threats to these ideals. The threats had been less serious in the boom of 1825, but the depression of 1826 underlined their gravity. Yet while 1825 had fully revealed the development of trade union consciousness, circumstances in 1826 did not favour industrial action. The later 1820s saw the exploration of alternative courses of action.

What courses were available? Gast's consistent answer was —general union of trades.

> I have often told you, and I now repeat it, that the antidote is in your own hands. Throw away your sotting, your pipes at improper times, your jealousies and divisions, your over-reachings of each other, your under-selling your labour—let all the useful and valuable members of every trade, who wish to appear respectable, unite with each other, and be in friendship with all other trades, and you will render yourselves worthy members of society, at once respectable and respected. You need not care for Blacks or Scabs, Jackdaws or Yellows. The industrious classes are the wealth and strength of nations, and nothing but their own conduct makes them poor and impotent.[20]

And again:

> borne down by excessive taxation, and exposed, by their poverty, to the rapacity of those employers, who have lost sight of their relationship to their poorer brethren, what can they do? I will tell them what to do. Get rid of that spirit of selfishness and jealousy which unhappily prevails amongst them—make common cause—cultivate union of sentiment, and form that union which will afford protection to every working man in the Empire.[21]

By 1826 he saw his case vindicated as in the changed economic climate strike after strike failed, even the one that had received such generous, nation-wide support. 'The Bradford combers and weavers were much better supported in pecuniary assistance to obtain justice of their shameless oppressors, than any other trade, and yet even they failed in obtaining it.'[22] The urgent need for general union was emphasised by the increasing vulnerability of London industry to country competition. But he recognised that in 1826 industrial action alone was not likely to succeed.

> The Unions would not be equal to the task, from the impoverished state of the manufacturing population, who have been labouring for a long

time under reduced wages, and are now suffering great privations, that render them very inefficient auxiliaries in a union war for keeping up the prices of labour.[23]

He therefore looked to legislative remedies as much as anything, to be worked out by a central directing committee that would focus all the great talent that existed among the working classes.

> Its not improbable that by collecting to gather in one focus, the Wisdom and talant of the great mass of the Working Mechanics; through the medium of Deputation; that on discussing the principles of cause and effect, they may discover some new principle, which by a Judicious application might as effectually throw into their hands the power of Changing the then existing system, in their favour & Interest; as the present is against them.[24]

He saw his general union not merely as a means of arranging financial support for trades on strike, but as a means, alongside a working-class newspaper, of uniting the working men as a political force.

In looking to political action, Gast was reflecting a tendency among the shipwrights and the London trades generally. The 1825 strike left the shipwrights' union suffering financial weakness, defeats and a reduction in membership, and Wigram was confident that its power was destroyed.[25] And things got worse, for the ship-building boom did not survive 1825, and by late 1826 there was high unemployment everywhere among all artisans involved in ship-building and repairing. The continuous decline lasted until 1830, with no real recovery before 1834.[26] Many of the shipwrights' unions in the outports seem to have collapsed and there were many strikes. On the Thames the years 1826 to 1828 were three disas-trous ones, and as trade union action could no longer be effective, there was reversion to pre-1824 activities. When at Blackwall Yard Green forced several of his companies to sign a document abandon-ing their union and promising not to join another, the union's response was to consider legal redress, not industrial action.[27] In 1827, when there was a barrage of petitions from the depressed shipowners against Reciprocity Treaties, the Thames shipwrights again added their own petition.[28] Many other trades were resorting to political rather than industrial action, but this political action did not, as Carlile noted with interest, take the form of a revival of efforts at radical political Reform, though veteran radicals were active again in the distressed manufacturing districts of Lanca-shire.[29] The artisans were no less radical than before, but parliamen-tary Reform was not practical politics and they concentrated on more specific matters.

The first of these was the Corn Laws. Shipwrights, silk-weavers and others supported protection and opposed the tariff reductions of the 1820s. This was because foreign goods were cheaper which was because wages there were lower, and the reasons for this were lower standards or costs of living. Any attempt to compete with such foreign goods would result in wage reductions. This would be very unjust because of the high English cost of living, for which they saw three reasons. The first was the high level of taxation which, being mainly indirect, pressed unjustly on a vast number of goods and redistributed wealth from the useful to the rich who battened parasitically on the State, and, by forcing up the cost of living and therefore wages, made English goods uncompetitive. 'Before Ministers launched into this sea of unexplored free trade, they should have brought the country to the state of taxation and expenditure of 1790.'[30] The second was inflation due to excessive issue of paper money, and the sense of the unfairness of currency fluctuations was intensified during the speculation and financial panic of the winter of 1825–6. 'The paper panic of the last fortnight has superseded every other consideration; and the death of the Emperor of Russia is made subservient to it.'[31] Many, like Gast and Purdy, denounced the currency system, and 'those who *gave encouragement* to the too general circulation of *paper currency*'.[32] But this question was more complex than taxation and many, like Grieve, did not feel competent to pronounce on it. This was not true of the third factor, the Corn Laws, uniformly resented as a blatantly selfish measure which taxed the rest of the community to the advantage of the lightly-taxed landowning holders of political power. It is no surprise that artisans supported a radicalism which sought, through political Reform, the drastic reduction of taxation, removal of parasites, abolition of self-interested bodies like the Bank of England that determined the currency system, and the end of the Corn Laws. As they saw it these three factors, all in themselves unfair, made any moves towards free trade unfair, as free trade meant foreign goods underselling British, and consequently unemployment and wage cuts. It was totally unjust to reduce tariffs *before* dealing with taxes and Corn Laws, a viewpoint widely shared among the public in connection with the unfortunate silk-weavers. The artisans clearly preferred protection, but since the tariff changes were a fact, as were wage reductions, they agitated for the removal of these three evils. The London artisans were confident enough of their skill not to fear competition on equal terms, and were often actually prepared to consider wage reductions if the cost of living fell (as the shipwrights had proposed in 1825),[33] an example of how they thought in terms of a traditional level of reward and position in society, and not in terms of ever seeking improvement.

With the end of the financial panic and an agricultural campaign to raise the corn duties, attention focused on the Corn Laws. Early in 1826 petitions for their repeal came from the sawyers, ladies' shoemakers, united carpenters, and shipwrights.[34] A similar agitation in Lancashire produced excited meetings, sometimes also passing resolutions against taxation or the currency.[35] Place was writing regularly in the *Trades' Newspaper* on the issue, sometimes linking it to the need for parliamentary Reform, and calling for a wave of petitions. He helped the London carpenters and silk-weavers over further petitions, and through his provincial contacts secured petitions from workmen in Macclesfield, Manchester, Blackburn, Oldham, Leeds, Bradford, Bolton, Sheffield, Glasgow, Shields and elsewhere, while Hunt helped organise one in Common Hall. As a climax, Place told Hume to bring in a bill to repeal the Corn Laws, but in March 1827 Hume only gained sixteen votes.[36] Following this, a number of Anti-Bread Tax Associations were formed in London (George Adam being secretary to one) and one in Manchester, and occasional meetings and petitions continued.[37]

Several correspondents in the *Trades' Newspaper* agreed with Place that the repeal of the Corn Laws would remove a great injustice, be a blow to unproductive landlords and enable a reduction in wages which would increase overseas sales and therefore employment at home. They preached harmony between employers and employees.

> The mechanic and the ploughman exert themselves to add something to the general wealth of the community, and do it at the expense of much sweat and toil. The master manufacturer and the farmer superintend the labour of their assistants, and by their superior education and judgement render their labour more efficient and productive.[38]

Allen Davenport, the Spencean, no doubt generalising from his experience in the shoemaking trade, saw trade unions as totally unable to prevent wage reductions because of the surplus labour; 'for no Union, however organised, can prevent the poor half-starved man, with his children's cry for bread ringing in his ears, from working for whatever wages he can obtain, be they high or low'. If wages could not be kept up, the price of bread must be brought down. He saw employers and employees as natural allies against landowners, and even believed the landowners had cunningly repealed the Combination Laws to foment industrial strife.[39]

This was not the general view. The silk-weavers had only petitioned for repeal of the Corn Laws when they had lost prohibition, and were ready to keep both, so that Robertson criticised them for their 'monstrous coalition of bread eaters and bread tax-gatherers'.[40] The shipwrights were well aware that the repeal of the Corn Laws alone would not reduce the cost of living enough. Thus it was the Gast came forward as the chief opponent of those who believed 'that the repeal of the Corn Bill would be a *panacea* for all our wounds'. 'I am for a free trade, not only for corn, but every other commodity', but he reaffirmed that the reduction of National Debt and taxation, and reform of the currency were also essential, before foreign competition would cease to be a threat. In opposition to Davenport and 'Justitia' (whom he suspected of being one and the same), he emphasised the power that employers had over wages, and could not accept that working men should meekly accept wage fluctuations. Against natural forces he posited workmen's rights, and challenged 'what right any man or men has to fix wages of labour, without the consent of the labourers'.[41] He therefore took up Burdett's consistent view that the distress of workmen had nothing to do with the Corn Laws, as cheaper bread would merely mean lower wages, which was why manufacturers wanted repeal. Gast claimed that supporters of repeal had not 'pointed out the means, how the working classes of society will be able to protect themselves against reduction in wages by their employers, which of course would follow, should the present Parliament repeal the Corn Laws'. Any wage reductions should be controlled, and since this could not be done by the trade societies, the remedy lay, of course, in a general union. 'I trust they will see the necessity of petitioning the Commons against a reduction in wages, so that in turn, the poor, half-starved ox, that treadeth out the corn, may have his protecting bill.'[42] Gast was thus, like the silk-weavers, favourable to legal intervention over wages, and indeed some sort of minimum wage. But above all he was against wage reductions, arguing as in 1819 and 1822, that higher wages would increase the market for British products. The present crisis of 'over-production' he saw not as one in terms of need, for many Britons needed the products of British industry, but in terms of spending power, for they could not afford them. Increased spending power would be achieved not only by higher wages but by reducing the huge, unjust inequality of wealth through slashing total taxation, abolishing all existing taxes that pressed unjustly on the poor, and replacing them by an income tax which above a certain level would be 100%.

Gast was saying that British industry should concentrate on the home market and not exports. This was natural for shipwrights, for whom there was little question of building ships for other countries, and many other London trades produced for the home market alone and realised that it was manufacturers producing for export who were keenest to reduce costs by wage cuts or mechanisation. Free trade seemed to mean competition between British artisans and miserably-paid foreign labour, to the detriment of the former and benefit only of the capitalist.

In 1827 these attitudes were heightened over the question of machinery. At the end of 1826 the pressmen began a campaign against the spread of steam-powered printing machines (they received no help from the superior compositors who, secure from any threat of mechanisation, favoured the machinery as helping expand the industry). But Adam, Wallis and Gast came to a meeting in December, and Gast's proposal to adjourn so that other trades could involve themselves was agreed. In January 1827 the sawyers, long very militant against machinery, agreed to join with the printers in a joint campaign, and their leader, James Beale, called for a general union of trades.[43] Out of this arose a series of meetings which began in February at the Golden Lion at West Smithfield on the subject of machinery, led by Gast, and attended by representatives of the silk-weavers (led by Wallis), shipwrights, sawyers (led by Jackson), printers, watchmakers, bookbinders, coopers and brassfounders.[44] The concern was increased by the publication that month of a pamphlet by the weavers of Frome, part of the decaying West of England woollen industry, which illustrated the displacement of human labour by machinery, blamed exports for mechanisation, and emphasised the primacy of the home market.[45]

Gast who, with Adam and Wallis, took the leading part in these meetings, was convinced that mechanisation often caused unemployment, while also recognising that it had good effects in some industries and that potentially it could reduce physical effort and shorten working hours. But in practice it produced poverty and unemployment and therefore contracted the market, which therefore outweighed its cheapening of production. Machinery would increase productive power far beyond what overseas markets could take. He was not against the machine as such but its abuse, whereby the benefits went to the few and the many suffered. The evil lay not in the machine but the structure of power in society and the neglect of Parliament. In the meetings and in letters in the *Trades'* paper others agreed, and a petition was approved calling for a tax on machinery to slow down its introduction and to provide funds from which to relieve those it displaced, so that workers as well as capitalists could share in some of the gains.

If machinery did not lead to wage reductions, it could be of benefit to all. How then could this be achieved? Despite the small numbers regularly attending, numbering at the most 500, Gast, strongly supported by Wallis, whose trade, acutely conscious of their weakness, was favourable to unity with the other trades, secured approval for another of his attempts at a general union. A 'General Association' was formed, a central committee elected with power to add to its members, and trade societies were invited to send delegates.

The meetings also supported proposals for a law that would make wage agreements between masters and men legally binding. This would prevent the situation whereby wage-cuts by a few masters forced the rest reluctantly to follow suit. It was in accordance with Gast's view by 1826 that industrial action alone was inadequate and that legislative remedies were essential, and was strongly influenced by the silk-weavers, who had never ceased to regret the repeal of the Spitalfields Acts. The idea had also received support in the north.

The Lancashire cotton handloom weavers found the long-term worsening in their situation accelerated in the 1820s by the spread of power-looms and consequent adult male unemployment. Faced with this and the competition that forced masters to reduce wages, they agitated for a tax on power-looms and 5,000 signed a petition by William Longson in favour of legal backing for wage agreements made by a committee of masters (a regular aim from the end of the previous century).[46] During the appalling distress of 1826 (which produced machine-wrecking in April), Longson regularly advocated the idea. In April the Bolton weavers and masters agreed on a wage-list, but in August, when many were paying 30% below this, the Bolton weavers' committee began a campaign in favour of wage-fixing. This was to be by a committee not solely of masters but of delegates of both masters and men, and it would be a legal offence to pay or receive below the rate. Despite Huskisson's hostility, several masters were favourable, the *Bolton Chronicle* gave publicity, support spread, and the following year Longson's book put the case.[47] Wage reductions were bad because 'this diminishes the home consumption and demand to the same enormous amount; and finally drives us to seek a foreign market for those commodities which we render unsaleable in the home market'. These reductions were due to competition: 'they have been effected by a few out of the many employers reducing the workmen's wages for the purpose of *underselling* all the others . . . these others perceiving the means whereby they are undersold, are obliged to reduce wages in their own defence'. This could only be rectified by legislative means: 'wages cannot be equalized, even by the general consent of masters and men, unless a legislative enactment be obtained to give legal validity to the general assent of the parties'.[48]

Place, of course, saw machinery as beneficial in that, by cheapening production, it increased consumption at home and sale abroad and so led to industrial expansion and increased employment. The cause of distress lay in over-population. The idea of wage-fixing he regarded as absurd; as wages were governed by supply and demand any attempts to control them were futile, any minimum wage would become also a maximum, and if wages were kept artificially high the fall in profits would drive capital away from that industry. But in view of the widespread support for the idea among the cotton- and silk-weaving workmen and employers he urged them to petition, not for an act but for a select committee, which was much more likely to be gained. He was, of course, so sure of his case that he had no doubts over what the findings of the committee would be. Longson and the rest welcomed the idea, a campaign was started and strongly backed in the *Trades' Newspaper*, petitions came from Lancashire, and in March and April 1827 Place worked very hard to gain support from MPs for a committee. Only Hume was much use, but he did try very hard, yet Peel secured the rejection of his motion.[49]

In this context it was no surprise that Gast's group resolved:

> That the prevailing disposition of unprincipled, needy, or mistaken employers to speculate at the expense of the labourer, and the competition of Machinery with the Wages of Manual Labour, render a law to protect agreements made at any meeting of Masters and Journeymen valid and binding on all parties in such trade, in any district, and thereby prevent individual reductions taking place, and also protect the fair-dealing employer from unprincipled and ruinous competition, and ourselves from pauperism and starvation.[50]

The meetings were virtually unanimous in favour of the idea, but there were one or two dissentients—Gast's old radical associate West thought it impracticable, and a coopers' society rejected the idea of state control of wages as a form of slavery. This was to misunderstand the plan, which was certainly *not* that 'the State' should regulate wages—all London artisans, including Gast, would have rejected the idea with horror.[51] In the *Trades' Newspaper* in

1825–6 there was a controversy over suggestions that wages should be tied to the price of bread.[52] Gast rejected the idea of a uniform wage for all absolutely tied to the price of bread as a form of slavery, especially if controlled by a Parliament in which working men had no voice.[53] He supported pay variations to maintain differentials between mechanics and others, reflect the differing kinds of work and allow workmen to participate in any rise in the prosperity of their industry. He accepted that wages could rise and fall, supported free collective bargaining and indeed competition within limits. The artisans never supported mathematical equality and were ready to see a more skilful or harder worker earn more than his fellows as long as he did not thereby harm them. But this proviso was crucial, and unchecked competition was seen as the basic evil. In international trade they were willing to accept *fair* competition, but competition between appallingly paid foreign workmen and British workmen burdened by Corn Laws and high taxation was not fair competition. Artisans complained about 'unfair competition', 'excessive competition', 'unscrupulous competition'. The idea of legally-binding wage agreements was consistent with all this. It followed the principle of the Spitalfields Acts whereby, as Hale explained but the public did not always grasp, the magistrates did not actually decide the wages but merely ratified a wage agreement made by masters and men. The scheme was not to give the State any say at all over wage levels; it was one of free collective bargaining where the bargain was enforceable through the law courts. It would allow masters and men to negotiate wage rises or reductions according to the fortunes of their trade, and so would give the men a legal say in wage levels, but would prevent the wishes of the majority of employers from being frustrated by a few employers indulging in 'unprincipled competition'. Place's argument that if wages were kept too high capital would be driven away was to miss the point, as the plan was merely to make effective the wage agreements acceptable to all but a few masters.

One of the influential figures at the Golden Lion meetings was the very interesting man John Powell, a Clerkenwell watchmaker who was active among the silk-weavers. In pamphlets and in articles in the *Trades' Newspaper* he developed in a striking way all the above ideas, to the extent of analysing the role of money, condemning free trade under any circumstances (pointing to the steady decline in the value of cotton exports), and seeing a growing polarisation into rich and poor and immiseration of the majority, with society reduced to a system of purely monetary relationships.

Nothing can be more conclusive of the fact of prevailing ignorance on this subject, than the incontrovertible tendency of the existing order of society, and of the doctrine *called* political economy, to produce a convergence of money influence, or despotism, which is the worst of all despotisms, as it weakens the bonds of society, by reducing the affections of human nature to a money value on the one hand, and a divergence of poverty and misery on the other; or in other words, increasing wealth in few hands, and extending privation among greater numbers, the unerring indicators of national decay according to all experience and all history.[54]

Against political economy he upheld the 'immutable laws of social economy'. It is not surprising that he admired *Labour Defended*, but unlike Hodgskin he was a genuine working mechanic and had a greater influence.

The other influence at the meetings came from representatives of a society that for years had campaigned in favour of wage-fixing and settling the poor on waste lands.[55]

Gast's 'General Association' was joined by the sawyers and silk-weavers, but the other trades involved are not known. The committee circularised the trade societies, co-opted some 'influential gentlemen, manufacturers and others' and chose a small executive of 'Directors'. But it did not make a great impact and its members were mainly silk-weavers, though it survived into 1828.[56]

Political Economy

We have now explored the different preoccupations and attitudes of Gast and his artisan associates, and must draw them together. Gast saw the causes of poverty not in over-population but in competition between employers and the employers' power over their workmen. This power was due to the moral shortcomings of the people, their jealousies, exclusivism and selfishness, and to the heavy burden of taxation due to the National Debt, which pressed unfairly on the poor and led them in despair to take work at any price. Of all this the employers took advantage. The employers' power meant that all the benefits of mechanisation went to them, while the workmen actually suffered as cheaper production was no gain at all when accompanied by wage reductions and unemployment. He therefore sought a union of mechanics to put them in a stronger position than their masters and make them able, through reducing hours, to spread work and reduce unemployment. But labour, the creator of wealth, must also be recognised politically so that its interests would be attended to. It would then gain a drastic reduction of taxation (necessitating the abolition of all places, pensions and sinecures) and the replacement of existing taxes by an income tax; it would repeal the Corn Laws; it would prevent an unfair free trade system that was ruining industries like shipping, shipbuilding and silk-weaving and ensure that any competition with foreign producers was on fair terms; it would secure legal backing for wage agreements and so end, not competition itself, for differences between trades and the ability to prosper through superior skill and harder work should remain, but evil competition; and it would see, by a tax on machines, the preventing of wage reductions and the reduction of hours, that workmen benefited from mechanisation. He totally rejected leaving wage levels to be determined by free market forces; he stood for the *right* of working men to protection and a fair wage as the guiding economic principle, and their right to a say in determining these.

> Is not labour the productive source of wealth; and have not those that produce it a right to enjoy it? Is labour rewarded in proportion to that of its transfer? and are there not too many who *live* out of the profits of transfer? Do not Land Owners and Tradesmen of every description, do every thing they can to reduce the rewards of labour? And does it not behove the Labourers themselves to obtain as many of the comforts of life, in exchange for labour, as they can obtain?[57]

Like Place, he thought the more capital that circulated the better, as wages would then rise, but whilst Place sought this by reducing the wealth of landowners through repeal of the Corn Laws, Gast also placed emphasis on a confiscatory income tax and, above all, on the need for high wages which would give an impulse to consumption and the flourishing of trade and industry, and thereby give employment to the surplus of labour.

> If every man in the country had received, and did receive a just remuneration for his labour, it would increase the quantity of labour, and give employment to thousands. Let the agricultural labourer receive 14s. per week, instead of 7s., and every other class of society, whose wages are a disgrace to the country, rise in the same proportion.—Let the unproductive classes of society forego part of their useless capital, and they will find that by giving the operatives the means to purchase, it will give a great stimulus to trade. Having the means, they will endeavour to furnish themselves with some of the little comforts of this life, which they have been so long robbed of; the baker, butcher, shoemaker, carpenter, cabinet-maker, cotton-spinner and weaver, in fact, every other trade would partake of the happiness. It would be a spur to industry, and the great capitalist would find an increase to his capital, and a much happier security in the enjoyment of his capital, than he enjoys from the present state of society. A measure of this kind would considerably counteract

the effects of the late panic among the working classes. I think no better means can be pointed out for the employment of the working classes, than by giving the means to create consumption: consumption will create labour, and the country would be ultimately the richer. It is repugnant to every feeling of human nature, to allow the unfeeling and unproductive consumer to swallow up that which in justice belongs to the operatives. It is owing to this deprivation of means, that the labourers have not been able to purchase; consequently it is one of the many causes that has produced the late distresses in the manufacturing and commercial departments. In my humble opinion, all the nonsense which has been uttered about pawnbroking palliatives will never effect a cure. England must be restored to a healthful currency more equally distributed, the over grown capitalist must be more liberal with his means, and allow the increasing population of the country a chance of purchasing the comforts of life. The 'bold peasant' must again become his 'country's pride', pauperism become hateful in the minds of labourers, the dead weight cut adrift, then (and not till then) England will again be a pattern for the world and the envy of surrounding nations.[54]

He rejected the 'Ricardo system', that what is taken from wages is added to profits.

This was all to take a stance opposed to the theories of political economy now becoming orthodox and widely publicised, by Place among others. A convenient summary has been given by Professor Webb.

(1) A mechanistic 'Newtonian' view of economics, without human or social dimensions, and with a full complement of abstractions like 'labour', 'capital', 'free contract', and so on. (2) A supreme concern with problems of production, and as a corollary the absolute benefit of machinery, notwithstanding any temporary distress caused by its introduction. (3) The canon of freedom—freedom of trade, freedom from government interference, and, above all for the working-class audience, freedom of the labour market, with particular reference to the restrictive effect of trades unions. (4) The Malthusian theory of population in its simplest form: population tends to outrun subsistence, the former increasing geometrically, the latter arithmetically; from this follows the necessity of the limitation of numbers, by moral restraint, birth control, or emigration. (5) Stemming from Malthusian teaching was the theory of the wages fund—the so-called 'iron law'—in its crudest form, that there was a fund, fixed in amount, out of which wages were paid, and that the wage level varied as the proportion of this fund (and so of capital) and the supply of labour. (6) Finally, as both basic assumption and final deduction, the proposition that the interests of the working classes and of the middle classes were the same—the

forwarding by all possible means of the interests and increase of capital, with the middle classes as the suppliers of the all-important capital in control of economic development and society.[59]

It is immediately apparent how different Gast's attitude was, and Gast was not alone, for the *Trades' Newspaper* contained many other expressions of the same views. In nearly every point Place took an opposing stand, and Place was increasingly aware of his failure to secure trade unions' acceptance of political economy. In 1824 the smiths' petition in favour of repeal of the Combination Laws had blamed low wages on the drive to export goods which British workmen were unable to buy. In that year Place had failed to convince the trades' delegates of the truth of political economy.[60] And he grew increasingly disillusioned by the views expressed in the *Trades' Newspaper*. No-one put them more forcefully than Thomas Single:

Wages, in most cases, are regulated in a great degree *by the power* the men have to oppose their masters. This is one reason why in some trades they are well paid, in others badly . . . Among masters there exists one general feeling to get work done as cheap as they can . . . To tell men that their bad pay and poverty arises from there being too many people will never be believed while there is in the country far more than a sufficiency of food for the whole.

The object of making machinery is, to perform labour at a less expense, and with a less number of hands. All kind of machinery, which assists men to do labour with more ease, and in half the time, ought to be a benefit, and one which none should feel so much as the men themselves . . . But if the poor are no better clothed, no better fed, and no better housed, there is no national improvement. All the (what is called) improved science of machinery is a humbug—a delusion set up to trick them out of the value of their labour . . . To prevent such an evil, and to protect the working classes, the number of hours for a day's work should be reduced in a ratio that machinery is made to supply the place of men . . . Could all the working classes of England at this time get a sufficient quantity of food to eat—could they all get a sufficient quantity of clothes to cover their backs, and furniture for their dwellings, there would (and everybody knows it) be a much greater demand for all our manufactured articles, and therefore a greater demand for labour.

Were we, at once, to leave off some of our machinery, and lose some (nay almost all) of our foreign trade, and give working men the necessaries of life for a day's labour, our home trade would increase, quite as much, or more, than our foreign trade decreased. At all events, we should not then be living in the midst of starvation in a land of plenty . . . What! are thousands and millions in this country to starve for the sake of commerce—for the sake of enabling a few great capitalists to carry on a system of trading with foreigners by machinery, which has no other earthly tendency than to enrich hundreds and starve millions?[61]

In vain Place opposed these tendencies and told them 'that all the good that has of late been done in the way of free trade, that all the useful information, which is now so widely spreading itself over the country and tending to elevate the class to which he [Wallis] belongs far above the rank they have hitherto held in society, is the work of *Political Economists!*'[62] The rejection of political economy was quite explicit, not only on specific issues but in general approach:

> The great evil with men who have written on what they term political economy is, that they never take into consideration the habits and customs, and all the natural passions and propensities belonging to human nature.
>
> They overlook the immense power which the capitalist has over the labourer, and the manner in which the conduct of the former influences the fate of the latter. They also have in general this radical evil at the bottom of all their systems. They consider man as a machine, and the labourer as a commodity.[63]

The belief that mechanics' institutions were inculcating political economy, an aim quite openly avowed by Place, fuelled the attacks on them.

But we must not generalise from these opinions expressed in some trades (though they included all the largest in London) as to the ideas of 'the artisans'. All had similar aims of respectability, securing and preservation of their position, but some found these in danger and sought out remedies. Though their aims were modest, the course of economic and social development meant they might take up positions that challenged the existing structure. Others were secure, so did not. It depended very much on circumstances, even with the same people. In the 1830s William Vialls was active, with Place's help, in two projects designed to promote artisan respectability—a small coffee- and reading-room where workmen could relax away from the pub and educate themselves; and a society to make loans to artisans in difficulties. But in the 1820s this same William Vialls, ladies shoemaker, reacting to the degradation of his fellow workmen, became assistant secretary of Gast's 'General Assocation'.[64] The same social ideal could at times lead to 'revolutionary' conclusions. It is essential to recognise that some artisans, defending a way of life under attack, adopted social critiques at least equal to and probably greater than any factory workers'. In the words of Gast's ally Jackson: 'Every industrious man ought to receive a remuneration proportioned to his usefulness, and if this was not done, there must be something wrong in the system.'[65]

The dominant influences in the *Trades' Newspaper* were now the shipwrights Gast and Grieve, the carpenter Adam, the ladies' shoemaker O'Neill, and the watchmaker Powell.[66] The editor, Anderson, wavered between them and Place, but on the whole it was their view that the paper expressed. By October 1826 Place felt that the paper 'in the hands of Mr Anderson is becoming any thing but a teaching paper to the people and will shortly be extinct'.[67] His last article in it was on 5 November, and by now he was supporting a new venture.

In October he had met a friend of Hume's, Northouse, editor of the *Glasgow Free Press*, in London to draw publicity to the terrible distress of the cotton-weavers of south-west Scotland and to his plans to relieve this by state-assisted emigration. To Place, the scheme was, to use one of his favourite words, 'absurd', but he gave help to Northouse, and when Northouse and Hume decided to start a new paper, the *London Free Press*, Place gave him support. The paper began in February 1827 and expressed the ideas of Hume and Place. But its sale was small and it folded after twenty-four weeks.[68] The *Trades' Newspaper*, with sales of under 700, was also in difficulties. In December 1826 Lang had consulted Place and received the dispiriting advice to sell it to Northouse while it was still worth something. In March Lang and Adam came again, with the result that in June 1827 Place arranged an amalgamation of the two as the *Trades' Free Press*, to which he contributed articles.[69] In fact, since the opinions were the same as in the *Trades' Newspaper* and the committee consisted wholly of trades' delegates, it seems that the *Trades'* paper had taken over Northmore's.

But financial problems remained, and the paper survived mainly through continuous help from the carpenters' societies. Indeed the committee now consisted of six carpenters, plus Grieve and one other.[70] Finally in December the paper was sold. A trades' interest remained in that half of any profits were to go to certain trade societies, and Lang remained publisher and secretary to the committee but management and editor were different.[71] The paper was jointly owned with a religious paper, and the new editor of the *Trades' Free Press*, who seems also to have a share in the ownership, was William Carpenter, a popular writer and lecturer on religious topics. Accordingly, the paper changed to a Saturday one so as not to come out on the Sabbath, and religious topics came to occupy a prominent place. Carpenter was a striking example of a self-taught man; first errand-boy and then apprentice to a bookseller, he had by great efforts mastered a number of ancient and modern languages and become a very fluent writer and speaker. His politics were very liberal, and he was both secretary to an anti-slavery committee and founder of an anti-Corn Law society.[72] In 1828 the paper still had a fair amount of information on trade unions, but this amount steadily declined, and in July the name was changed to *Weekly Free Press* to win more non-working-class readers, and its sale probably rose to about a thousand.

With this change in ownership Place gave the paper up for lost and even ceased taking it. The views of Gast and Adam also found little expression, and there is very little information on Gast's 'General Association'. This did survive in some form, led by Gast, Adam, Powell and Wallis and consisting mainly of silk-weavers (Gast was now fairly active in Spitalfields).[73] It emerged again to notice in its efforts to collect trade subscriptions in support of the twenty-one-week strike of the Kidderminster carpet-weavers, a strike that aroused a fair amount of emotion, characterised as it was by the recruitment of strike-breakers, use of troops, blacklisting and arrests of strikers for begging. Gast and the other speakers now reached new heights in their attacks on employers. By July 1828, the aim was again a general union of the trades, and alongside the existing members were delegates from the coopers and carvers and gilders. The *Trades' Free Press* under Carpenter reported these meetings but its attitude was very hostile, though sympathetic coverage was given by Anderson who was now editor of the *Morning Advertiser* and the *Sunday Herald*. But only £196 was collected in London for Kidderminster and the strike there failed, and though this vindicated Gast's case for a general union and the same lesson was drawn by the Kidderminster weavers themselves and by a delegate meeting of fourteen Nottingham trades, the general union faded again from view.[74]

On one hand, then, 1828 saw Gast and his associates more bitterly outspoken than ever, and even more committed to the idea of a militant general union of 'the labouring, wealth-producing classes' to defeat the 'conspiracy against the working classes'. Yet in the same year some of them were also involved in another activity fully approved by Place and Carpenter, an agitation that was a classic example of the artisans' readiness to defend their societies, in this case the benefit societies. It was in many ways a repeat of 1825.

12
THE BENEFIT SOCIETIES' CAMPAIGN

T. F. Courtenay was a Tory sinecurist MP with connections with the government.[1] He was one of those who strongly approved of benefit societies as a means of reducing poverty and easing the burden on the poor rates, and also of improving the morals of working men. But he shared the common opinion that they were often badly and wastefully managed, through incompetence or dishonesty, and so failed to fulfil their functions. Magistrates were very familiar with cases of societies that ran out of funds to pay benefits, and were wont to comment on their failure to conform to the law.[2] Courtenay had promoted legislation on the matter in 1819, but was still concerned that benefit societies did not have a realistic ratio of benefits to subscriptions and that monies were not always in trustworthy hands, both causes of financial disaster. He therefore secured and chaired select committees in 1825 and 1827. The latter especially reported in favour of new legislation and recommended a particular set of tables containing calculations of the right ratio of benefits, membership and subscriptions.[3]

The furore raised was a striking example of the artisans' suspicion of Parliament's intentions and their refusal to allow any interference in their own affairs. They suspected that Savings Banks had been started as rivals to their societies and, since they invested their deposits in government funds, to support the system. Others believed 'that however beneficent the professions of Parliament might be, its Acts had generally a tendency to abridge the liberties of the working classes, and that it therefore behoved every one to arm himself against a sinister attack'. 'There were some who had objected to petitioning, on the ground that nothing tends to flatter the vanity or confirm the obstinacy of the Legislature more than by doing so.'[4] Their attitude was similar to that over wage-fixing; they were very desirous of receiving legal sanction and support for what they did, but refused to have any interference by the government in their affairs—their negative view of government persisted. In general, as in mechanics' institutions, they were grateful for help, but resented paternalistic direction. Gast felt this and strongly supported benefit societies' independence, 'for his part, he should never wish to see them, however ill they might at present be managed, under any other control than that of their contributors'.[5] Just as in mechanics' institutions philanthropic gentlemen wished to confine subjects to what was 'useful' instead of what the mechanics wanted, so they disapproved very strongly of the convivial aspects of benefit societies that were so important to their members, and wished to limit them to strictly utilitarian purposes. Similar suspicions and controversies arose in both cases, the artisans preferring educational and benefit societies under their own control; but these were no less integrative self-help instruments of respectability.

When the 1827 Select Committee was set up, some immediately feared the worst, for they were sure that in 1825 Courtenay had wanted a bill adverse to benefit societies. By May a number of societies had joined in a delegate organisation under a provisional committee of eight led by Gast and with a secretary, John Hunter, an East End baker who had been an associate of Thistlewood's and was now active in some of the silk-weavers' campaigns.[6] Suspicions of Parliament were expressed in declamatory speeches, and many felt that if any more restrictive acts were passed they should cease to enrol. A circular was sent to all known societies in London, and in September a permanent committee of twenty-one was formed under Gast and Hunter and including Gast's allies in general union, Adam and Vialls. But for the rest of the year this did not meet regularly. Place had, of course, been consulted early on and he vehemently confirmed their views that the aristocracy were opposed to friendly societies because of their democratic self-government and so wished to take them out of the hands of their members and turn them into charity concerns.[7] The societies were very angry that Courtenay's committee did not hear representatives from any artisan societies at all, confining itself to evidence from some of the large metropolitan friendly societies on the best way to calculate benefits. And their fears were confirmed when it reported in November in favour of restricting societies purely to benefits for infirmity, old age, funeral expenses and the endowment of children. Gast's organisation held a large public meeting in December, and by January 1828 the committee was meeting every evening and opened a systematic subscription.[8]

The bill that Courtenay introduced in 1828 was as bad as they expected, seeking basically to take control away from members so as to establish financial rectitude.[9] First, like the 1819 Act, it gave wide powers to the trustees, especially the power to appoint the treasurer without consulting the members; this was totally opposed to the democratic structure of the societies, whereby all officers were elected by the members, subject to their control, and removable. Secondly, before societies could be enrolled, their proposed articles had to be sent for approval as to their soundness to the only government office in London which, in Courtenay's view, had the properly qualified actuaries, the office of Commissioners for Reducing the National Debt; this was greatly resented, especially as the artisans had no confidence in the competence of these men or the soundness of the calculations recommended by the select committee. Thirdly, there was no clause such as the 1793 Act had contained whereby all disputes between members could be settled by arbitration, the award of the arbiters being final. Reliance on arbitration procedures, as a sort of informal law separate from the official legal system, was very deep-rooted among artisans; the shipwrights and builders had well-established arbitration procedures to deal with disagreements over prices. Arbitration allowed benefit societies to settle affairs in their own way, and they were greatly opposed to the power the bill gave to biased and unqualified magistrates to decide in such disputes and impose fines. Fourthly, they disliked the bill's provision for fees to the clerk of the peace for enrolment. Finally, the bill would affect existing societies, even if already enrolled, as if ever they made a change in their rules, they would come under the new act.

The resultant campaign was very impressive.[10] In all, 108 London societies subscribed to the metropolitan delegate committee which, in close alliance with the *Trades' Free Press*, co-ordinated agitation of national scope. Hundreds of petitions bore down on the astonished House of Commons from all over the country. Opposition MPs, notably Brougham and Hobhouse, used the familiar tactic of initiating debates through the petitions to argue that public opinion and especially the lower classes were all against the bill. The House was impressed. The bill was now at the committee stage, and the petitions were referred to the committee on the bill. Courtenay acceded to the delegates' request to be heard. The committee agreed to drop the retrospective classes whereby old societies would come under the act. Carson of Birmingham convinced them of the injustice of the trustees' clause, so there was not much of the bill left when they admitted Gast and the other four metropolitan delegates, though in fact only Cotter and Hunter, the chairman and secretary, needed to speak. Courtenay was isolated and the committee decided the bill should be dropped and that instead Courtenay should bring in a modified bill the following week. But he was so fed up that he refused to do any more; the benefit societies had won.

Courtenay, with some justice, claimed that the object of his bill had been misunderstood. It was merely intended as a supplement to his own 1819 Act which itself, in order to prevent societies' functioning on the basis of faulty calculations, had ordered that a magistrate could only approve a society if its tables of payments and benefits were approved by two competent actuaries. His 1828 bill merely sought to replace them by the more competent actuaries at the National Debt Office. He pointed out that many of the petitions against his bill were also in fact opposed to provisions in the 1819 Act.[11] His perception was sound, for the societies did indeed dislike many of the provisions of that act, but many had not known of its existence. Now that they had become aware of it, they particularly disliked the vesting of all the society's property in three trustees, who had to be householders, which nearly all members were not; these trustees appointed the treasurer, independently of the members, and their consent was needed to any change in the bye-laws so that, since the trustees could not be replaced, they could thwart the wishes of the membership. They also disliked the long delays and fees involved in having any new articles enrolled. They now looked back favourably on the 1793 Act which had forbidden any fee or reward, had not had such powerful trustees, and allowed for arbitration. And so the London meetings saw attacks on the existing acts as well as the new bill, and Gast drew up a resolution in favour of the repeal of every act except the 1793 one.[12]

When Courtenay washed his hands of the matter, some of the bill's committee thought that something should be done to meet the societies' wishes. One of them, the Dorset magistrate Portman, therefore suggested that the societies themselves frame a new bill and so, in the knowledge of support from Portman, Hobhouse and others, the meeting called to celebrate the defeat of Courtenay's bill actually decided to draw up a bill of their own to replace all the existing acts and make the whole situation clear.[13] A committee was set up to do this, including Gast and the other four of the deputation, plus Vialls, Adam, William Lovett (who had come to prominence in this campaign) and four others. By December the bill was drawn up, and was then printed, circulated free to every society, and sold publicly for 1s. It advocated the repeal of six previous acts, including Rose's. It did not provide for powerful trustees, and enrolment did not at all depend on the soundness of a society's calculations. The rules of societies had to be confirmed by the barrister already appointed by the National Debt Commissioners to certify the rules of Savings Banks and were then to be submitted to quarter sessions, the certificate given by the clerk of the peace being legal evidence of registration. The registration fee was fixed, rules could be changed by a three-quarters' majority at a general meeting, and the magistrates had no obligation to approve the soundness of the tables of payment and benefits. Societies had now to give a financial account to members every year, which strengthened democratic control, and as a guide for calculations in the future, a return of mortality and sickness had to be given every five years to the clerk of the peace for transmission to the central government. It provided for the settlement of disputes by arbitration. The bill thus gave total control to the members, the only restrictions being to prevent abuse of funds and meetings for any other purposes. Portman introduced it in March, and with a few amendments it passed.[14]

The 1829 Act is regarded as a landmark in friendly society legislation, in its appointment of a registrar (Tidd Pratt) and abandonment of efforts at paternalistic control, though the fact that it was the work of artisans is totally ignored.[15] It was a striking illustration of the 'openness' of the British political system in the period of private members' legislation and absence of party discipline, that such an artisan agitation could not only prevent one bill but secure the passage of one of their own. Brought about with the help of Brougham, Hobhouse and Birkbeck, it seemed to dissolve some of the tensions and antagonisms of 1825–7, and the London delegate committee urged full co-operation with the Society for the Diffusion of Useful Knowledge over its questionnaire and efforts to draw up guidelines for tables and rules. This feeling seemed strengthened when the committee went on to try to set up an Asylum for Aged Members of Friendly Societies with Tidd Pratt and Birkbeck as vice-presidents and trustees.[16]

We have seen how security in old age was a cardinal aim among artisans and their benefit societies.[17] Often societies existed specifically for this purpose, like Gast's Hearts of Oak Society (which took part in the 1828–9 campaign) or the Printers' Pension Society. Sometimes this aim was concentrated on when times did not favour other efforts, such as among the shipwrights in 1811 and the early 1820s, or the establishment of a pension society in the depression of

1817 by the watchmakers, among whom trade unionism hardly existed.[18] Gast, naturally, approved of the new suggestion. 'This is noble! it is grand! for who has so great a claim on society when past labour, as the man whose life has been devoted to the production of that which constitutes the wealth of the country.'[9]

But in 1829 the bill had only passed Parliament because it fitted in with the predominant concerns to improve morals and reduce the poor rates, and with the growing current in favour of self-help as against paternalism. And we must not forget the persistent basic suspicion of Parliament and alienation from the political system. Many, like Adam, refused to feel grateful to Parliament, being bitter that it had first been so favourable to 'the attempt made, of invading the sanctuary of their little hard-earned deposits', 'the plans that were in progress, for making the working classes subservient to the interest of aristocratical ambition', 'a blow at the independence of a million of Englishmen, heads of families'.[20] The artisans wanted to be left alone and do things for themselves. As Gast put it:

> I admire those noble institutions that provide for the numerous casualties of life, and old age; but most of those asylums are the productions of persons distinct from the industrious classes, and in most cases are a boon held out by the aristocracy for some special purpose, and to effect some special object. The modes of admission are in general so multifarious in their form, that to many who have seen better days, and deserving persons, whose minds still retain that honourable dignity which characterised them in their younger days, and therefore cannot bend to the required passive submission, they amount to a prohibition.

As the true respectable artisan, he did not want charity, and so warmly supported the proposed asylum.

> To obtain admission there, he will have no occasion to pass through the ordeal of examination by some sprig of aristocracy, or Jack-in-office, bending and cringing with all the obeisance of a slave. No, he will take possession as a matter of right, and this in itself renders the object more desirable.[21]

Respectable artisans wanted recognition, admission to a respected place in society. But they rejected paternalism, whether from Tories or from liberal reformers and 'improvers'. Insofar as there was a growing current in favour of this self-help, artisans could accept liberalism, not because of a swallowing of its doctrine but because it could be compatible with their basic and long-held attitudes. But on the other hand we have seen that many artisans saw changes that eroded their position and threatened their respectability and, in pursuit of the same aims, could adopt stances opposed to the trends in society and to liberal assumptions and this, coupled with the basic suspicion of the political system, could lead to militant class terminology. This again did not arise from the swallowing of any doctrines, in this case anti-capitalist, but out of their experience and a clear perception of what was happening. It is this diversity within the artisan world and the basic autonomy of its ideals and attitudes that is so crucial to the understanding of nineteenth-century England.

13
CO-OPERATION

At the end of the 1820s Gast was caught up in the co-operative movement. In 1829 and 1830 a large number of co-operative retail stores sprang into existence; in 1831 began the series of half-yearly congresses at which Robert Owen figured; and in 1832 appeared a number of 'Labour Exchanges', ambitious attempts to introduce a new system of currency based on labour value. Owenism seemed to have captured organised labour. But to avoid confusion we need to distinguish Owen himself from Owenism, and both from co-operation.

By the mid-1820s Owen was very well known as a successful cotton manufacturer, a paternalistic employer who had wrought such miraculous moral changes among his workforce at New Lanark, a pioneer of striking new educational methods and the foe of religion. Above all, drawing on Godwinianism and his contribution to the post-war debate on pauperism, and in an increasingly millenarian manner, he advocated sudden and far-reaching changes in society. Recognising that industrialisation was ushering in a totally new age where poverty and ignorance could be banished, and believing that as man was wholly the creature of circumstances then entirely new circumstances could produce an entirely different human nature, he proposed that the people should reject the existing competitive system in which true happiness was impossible and all become members of self-supporting communities. Here all goods would be held in common, all would work for the good of all, there would be no rewards or punishments, and a new system of production, distribution and education would equalise and exalt the human race, and end crime, vice and selfishness, the parents of unhappiness. But actual communitarian efforts, either led or inspired by him, both failed.[1]

He had gathered a number of followers, at first paternalistic and philanthropic landowners but by the 1820s also including a number of anti-clerical and radical gentlemen. By the mid-1820s there was a group of 'Owenites' in London operating to a large extent independently of him and not uncritical of some of his utterances and behaviour. The dominant figure among them was the radical Irish landowner William Thompson. On the whole it was not Owen himself but some of his disciples who gave his ideas any popular impact, and these Londoners were an example. And we can see how their Owenism developed into a movement aimed at working-class organisation.[2]

Late in 1824 this London group, under twenty in number, formed a London Co-operative Society. They engaged in propaganda, and in 1825 at last held a successful public meeting. At this meeting Owen, on a visit from America, launched a plan for a new model experimental community within fifty miles of London, needing a capital of £200,000 to be raised by shares of £100, £40 and £10. These London Owenites, who by July 1826 were over 200 in number, had appeared more rational and effective than Owen himself.[3]

But they were short of money and had only sold £4,000 worth of shares, and were beginning to recognise that Owen's efforts at upper-class support were misplaced; 'these individuals were not sufficiently grounded in the principles to render efficient aid, or to second Mr. Owen's views to that extent which was necessary to give the system a fair trial'.[4] They were beginning to look to those who suffered most under the present system. This was evidenced in Thompson's addresses, his massive *Distribution of Wealth*, which in 1825 he carefully distributed to key labour figures like Tester and Longson,[5] and his *Labour Rewarded*, which saw the remedy for the present robbery of the fruits of labour, that Hodgskin had analysed, in a 'co-operative community'. Co-operators sometimes came and spoke at Gast's meetings.[6] But it is doubtful if any of these made much impact. Even the £10 shares were beyond what could be afforded by a working man with wife and children. The London Co-operative Society can have contained few manual workers, though there were one or two, notably James Watson who had originally come from Huddersfield to help run the imprisoned Carlile's business.

One of these worker members launched in 1826 a plan for a small-scale community aimed specifically at the better-off artisans, 'such of the working classes as are not in debt', and by September 1827 Owen himself was in favour of a community of the labouring classes. In this context arose ideas of raising money by co-operative trading. The plan was to raise a fund by subscriptions, use this to buy goods wholesale, sell these retail at a profit and so steadily further augment the fund, eventually use this to employ members to make articles to be sold at a profit, and finally, when the fund was big enough, buy land on which all members could settle.[7] Three gentlemen in the London Co-operative Society, G. C. Penn, the talented P. O. Skene and his brother George, seem to have taken the lead in forming in November 1827, at the society's premises at Red Lion Square, the London Co-operative Trading Association. The first storekeeper proved dishonest and absconded, but enthusiasm kept the society going with Watson and then Lovett impeccably honest storekeepers. The society was well-run and sometimes realised a profit of 20%, but it was dogged by expenses, especially as it had to change premises three times. It employed some members at trades that required little capital such as shoemaking and tailoring, gathered a library of a hundred volumes, held discussions to achieve 'mental and moral improvement', and sold many co-operative works at its store.[8]

In 1827 also a group sixteen strong had formed a Union Exchange Society which held conversation meetings three evenings a week and exchanged goods made by members, either for cash or by barter and divided the commission monthly between members. Its aim was to acquire funds to establish a proper bazaar for exchange of goods, schools for the young and asylums for the aged, with the ultimate aim of employing all members so as to be independent of employers and non-producers.[9]

But it was not these early London efforts that sparked off the national movement. This was done by the co-operative store begun by Bryant early in 1828 at Brighton. This became the model for others elsewhere. Its importance was mainly due to the periodical the *Co-operator*, which under Dr William King conducted steady propaganda in favour of the communitarian ideal and analysed society in terms of competition and the robbery of producers. But it did so in a very down-to-earth manner and disassociated itself from Owen's anti-religious views (indeed it saw co-operation as practical Christianity) and from the extravagances and mysticism of some of his followers. Most important, it gave a good deal of practical information on running stores, and outlined the stages through which to proceed—subscriptions to a fund, retail store, employment of members, acquisition of land.

There is no doubt that King's propaganda was the most effective yet, addressing itself as it did directly to very real problems (high food prices, wage reductions, competition) and to very practical activities, activities which moreover were successful even to the point of acquiring land. Even Carlile, an ardent believer in political economy and the virtues of competition, and full of contempt for the London Owenites, regarded the Brighton *Co-operator* as the best penny periodical that had yet appeared.[10] Societies on the Brighton model were formed at Worthing and Findon, and the 'Brighton scheme' became fashionable. The London group around Penn and the Skenes recognised this, began a periodical, the *Associate*, on the lines of the *Co-operator*, and in the winter of 1828–9 made a determined effort to win over artisans to the scheme of co-operative trading as the way to 'universal plenty'. Their main medium was the *Weekly Free Press*, which under Carpenter and his friend John Cleave achieved by 1830 a circulation of 1,800. Both of them fervently supported co-operation. Carpenter was already active in Lambeth in local politics and in an anti-Corn Law association, and now he and other members of the latter formed in April 1829 a Lambeth Co-operative Trading Union. Cleave was leader of the Westminster Co-operative Society which became the largest in London with a membership exceeding 250. Most important, they opened the pages of their paper to the advocacy and publicity of co-operation. A number of articles by Penn outlining the methods and aims of co-operative societies and announcing their ever-growing number set off a wave of societies in London, Lancashire and elsewhere. A society was formed at Hampstead in March 1829, and by May there were at least fourteen London societies. The Union Exchange Society also started its own *Gazette*, and Carpenter and Cleave began a special co-operative periodical.[11]

The co-operative movement in London thus owed as much to Brighton as to the early London societies, but the fact that the latter already existed put them in a strategic position. The First London Co-operative Trading Association provided speakers and was looked to for advice and information, and so some of its members, notably G. R. Skene, Lovett, Millard, Powell and a clerk, George Foskett, secured the formation in May of a society for promoting co-operative knowledge. Gast early on entered its committee. Its aims were both propagandist and to co-ordinate and assist the efforts of co-operative societies in a practical way by opening a general warehouse in London to supply the different stores, and a general bazaar to exchange the products of the societies. Premises were taken at 19 Greville Street, Hatton Garden, and here the First

London operated downstairs with Lovett as resident storekeeper, and the British Association for the Promotion of Co-operative Knowledge (BAPCK) opened a bazaar upstairs, with Millard resident bazaarkeeper. The latter Association also started a fund to employ distressed Spitalfields weavers and sold their products at the bazaar. Though its plans to start schools never materialised it had great success in diffusing knowledge of co-operation through correspondence, tracts and books on education while some of its members, like Benjamin Warden, master saddler, and Henry Hetherington, master printer, were very effective speakers. By mid-1830 there were over forty societies in London, while the BAPCK had a delegate from each member society on its committee, held successful public quarterly meetings, and began a periodical run by its secretary Skene. It carried on an extensive correspondence with societies in the country, much of which was published in the *Weekly Free Press*. And late in 1829 Watson, who had for long been Carlile's correspondent for his native Yorkshire, went there on behalf of the association and made use of his contacts there to do effective missionary work.[12] The asssociation and the newspaper thus became the chief propagandist and co-ordinating elements in the country, ably seconded by the Birmingham co-operator William Pare through his extensive lecturing and his *Birmingham Herald*. The number of societies with which the BAPCK was in contact rose steadily to nearly 500 by February 1831. It was an impressive and important national movement, and began a series of half-yearly national congresses, the first at Manchester in June 1831, the most successful at London in April 1832. These were attended by Owen (who had returned to England in 1830 after his failures in America) and Thompson, and plans were agreed to launch a new community.

Owen was impressed by the gathering movement and threw himself into renewed propagandist activity. In April 1830 he and Minter Morgan began Sunday morning lectures, at first at the London Mechanics' Institution until there were complaints, and then at an institution in Leicester Square. Here he formed a committee which arranged periodic public meetings. He also joined the BAPCK and occasionally attended its meetings, projected in January 1831 with Carpenter a 'Church and State Society' and in February formed a 'Social Union'. He also revived his earlier proposals to reform the currency by making labour the standard of value.[13] Bromley, owner of the Royal London Bazaar near King's Cross, offered his premises free of charge for a year and here in December 1831 Owen and well-connected sympathisers like Dr Wade, the non-resident Warwickshire parson, and Thomas Alsopp, the lawyer, launched his Association for Removing the Causes of Ignorance and Poverty. An MP opened it, the King and Queen were asked to be patrons, and Owen as Governor and Treasurer had complete control. Here at his 'Institution of the Industrious Classes' he gave weekly lectures to audiences of 1,500, including a high proportion of ladies, and unfolded his plan for a community of 2,000. Later, a series of discussions was held here, at which Gast sometimes participated. In April 1832 Owen began and edited a penny weekly periodical, the *Crisis*, which announced that the old world was falling to pieces, attributed distress to ruinous competition and, at the height of the great political crisis, asserted the superficiality of mere political Reform. His association aimed to have a ballroom and music rooms, monthly festivals, a library, a model of the community, and, ultimately, a self-supporting school of education and industry, and a 'labour exchange'. The 'social festivals' did begin and were a great success.

In the summer of 1832 Owen's son Robert Dale Owen returned from America, took over the editorship of the *Crisis* and headed a new Social Missionary and Tract Society which organised weekly discussions, and had stations at Primrose Hill, Copenhagen Fields and White Conduit House where they distributed tracts and the *Crisis*.[14] In July the association decided to form a 'Bank of Exchange' which Owen saw as a means of reforming the currency so that it would grow in step with increased national wealth. The anticipated vast profits were to be used to replace the poor rates, feed and educate the poor, and pay off the National Debt.[15] After a couple of committees the National Equitable Labour Exchange was finally opened in September and there was an immediate rush of business, so that branches were also opened. In January 1833 the labour exchange and the Institution amalgamated into a national association that was to continue the festivals and the *Crisis*, extend its educational activities and open provincial branches. When profits from the labour exchange reached £2,000 land would be taken to employ members.[16] But that month they quarrelled with Bromley and were ejected. The move to the Surrey branch meant a severe interruption to business and loss of stock. Yet in March Owen leased new premises at Charlotte Street and opened it as his new Institution. At the great public meeting on 1 May Owen delivered an 'historic address' and announced 'to the rapture of the audience' that the millenium began that day.[17] Immediately the Social Missionary Society organised a Social Community of Friends to the

Rational System, or 'moral union', which soon had over 300 members.[18] Owen's Institution became a great centre of activity, with large public meetings and discussions, regular Sunday lectures, highly successful social festivals and a musical department (Social Harmonic Society). This was also the year when Owen toured the provinces and Ireland, made contacts with trade unionists and factory reformers and became a fervent supporter of both. Accordingly at the London congress of co-operative societies and trade unions in October 1833 he launched a Grand National Moral Union of the Useful and Productive Classes to reorganise industry and replace employers with governing boards.[19]

But Owen himself never controlled all these activities. The labour exchange movement, for instance, had developed a momentum of its own to which he merely responded. It was basically an extension of the established co-operative efforts to employ members and sell products at a fair price. The Union Exchange Society had for years been exchanging goods made by members and tried to dispense with money. The coal-merchant James Tucker supplied any member of co-operative societies in town and in 1830 advocated labour notes. The BAPCK's bazaar was to facilitate exchanges between societies and in fact they printed notes with co-operative symbols which could be exchanged for goods in the store. They even tried to increase the store's business by persuading outsiders to accept its notes in payments. George Skene began a society that exchanged goods among members; they were valued according to the materials and labour involved at no profit. This group thus sought to exchange labour for labour and naturally looked forward to labour-notes and a bank of manufacturers. In February 1832 the four societies using the store of the First Western Union opened the First Western Union Exchange Bank, which paid a dividend in proportion to the amount of dealing (as the BAPCK planned to do with their bazaar); though by October it was in difficulties it lasted until August 1833. In May 1832 one William King, who had in 1830 sent three articles to the *Weekly Free Press* advocating labour notes, was the chief figure in a bazaar opened by the North Western Association of the Useful Classes. William Benbow's Central Co-operative Association opened an exchange in August and managed to get tradesmen to accept its notes, as did the Lambeth and Surrey Equitable Labour Exchange south of the river.[20] Owen's labour exchange was built on these, and the committee that set his up included King and Macpherson of the North Western exchange, and James Osborne of the Central one.[21]

We can see a logic in the development of Owenite activities to include workers' involvement. But it would be wrong to see this as a sufficient explanation of the co-operative movement. The artisans were not passive recipients of ideas; they were a social group with certain ideals and interests according to which they moulded the ideas they met. Too many historians share the attitude of contemporaries and see working men not as formulating ideas out of their own experiences but as raw material assimilating ideas provided by outsiders. There was certainly a widespread admiration for Owen, a man who had devoted life and fortune to improving society, but respect does not have to entail acceptance of his ideas, nor must we misinterpret the fact that his institution was a centre for meetings and discussions. There certainly were important working men in the co-operative movement who were Owenites, such as Lovett and Watson, some of whom left important accounts of their activities, which has led to an exaggeration of the Owenite element. The chief society in London, the First London, growing as it did out of the London Co-operative Society, was composed of Owenites, initially at least. And it was some of these who took the lead in the formation of the BAPCK, which emphasised the Owenite communitarian goal in its publications and addresses.

Let us however remember that in March 1830 the BAPCK issued an address emphasising that the aim of co-operative societies should be to raise capital to buy and cultivate land, begin manufacturing on it, exchange the products and form a community. On these grounds it specifically disassociated itself from 'Brighton Co-operation' which merely sought to combine to raise the value of wages by buying and selling at wholesale prices.[22] Yet Brighton was the model for most. A further example of non-Owenite co-operation is the starting, in November 1831, of a co-operative society by Hutchinson at Theobalds Road. As the Central Co-operative Society it grew rapidly under Benbow and George Petrie, a Scotch tailor, to be one of the chief in London. But Benbow was leader of a group of opponents of Owen who clashed with Lovett, Hetherington and Watson. When the third co-operative congress was held in London in April 1832 in Owen's Institution and had a festival there on one of the evenings, Benbow held a rival one which many co-operators attended. And Benbow continued his attacks on Owenism.[23]

The co-operative movement of 1828–34 was in fact a many-sided phenomenon which must not be treated in a linear fashion. It drew together a wide variety of techniques and concerns that were already prevalent in society at large. There was co-operative retailing to buy cheap, ensure proper quality or raise funds. There was the bazaar, growing in importance after the war, where people hired a stall for a time. There was the industrial school, in which the children would receive education and also do work, such as gardening, the produce of which would be sold to defray costs; this was yet another way to secure education on the cheap, and would also inculcate habits of hard work and industry. There was the frequently canvassed riposte to emigration schemes, 'home colonisation' to settle the destitute on the waste lands, supported both by Tory philanthropists and by radicals not loth to attack the landowners.[24] Many of these accepted Owen's arguments that small-scale intensive farming and spade cultivation were more productive and would ensure a more regular food supply. Currency reformers like Attwood (who supported the labour exchanges) saw currency restriction as the cause of distress. Some deplored rapid urbanisation. Concern over the agricultural system, currency, education and destitution were widespread, and the co-operative movement in a sense merely gathered together devices familiar to society at large. It is not then surprising that William Carpenter, who sought to reduce food prices through repeal of the Corn Laws, who supported home colonisation as a remedy for distress, and who planned a self-supporting industrial school for the sons of mechanics, should wholeheartedly support the co-operative movement.[25] But Carpenter was also concerned with the protection of labour, and the BAPCK was composed almost entirely of working men and consciously aimed at societies of working men.[26] It is with the artisan acceptance of co-operation that we must be concerned.

First, as has long been realised, very many members of the trading associations saw no further than retail stores and this is why most societies were confined solely to such activities, the most profitable articles being food (tea, coffee, sugar, cheesemongery, flour and groceries), clothing (linen and woollen drapery, haberdashery, hosiery, gloves and hats) and, to a less extent, general chandlery wares, tobacco and snuff.[27] There were two aspects here, reflecting a consumer-consciousness that was hardly new and which had traditionally focused on food prices and adulteration; indeed there had been over many years, arising out of these attitudes, co-operative milling societies, especially in times of bread shortage, as in 1795. In 1797 the yard-workers at Portsmouth had begun a co-operative mill.[28] But the usual form of seeking fair or low prices was by exclusive dealing. The co-operators of the 1820s knew about these devices, and it was quite logical that Carpenter's Lambeth Union, which included members of his anti-Corn Law society, should plan a co-operative bakehouse.[29] The co-operative societies thus achieved economy by bulk-buying and made sure of having good, pure food, something that Lovett regarded as one of the chief benefits to be gained.[30]

Such activities were well-established and could be very informal, but 1828 saw a fashion for formal societies on the Brighton model, with very often a shopkeeper employed as storekeeper, a simple extension of exclusive dealing. They were intended to be permanent, and often, to increase the use of the store, paid a dividend according to the amount of purchases. In itself there is nothing 'Owenite' here. Carlile saw absolutely nothing in common between community schemes to banish competition, and trading stores competing with shopkeepers.

> The Co-operative inoperatives have, for several years, been carrying on a petty warfare against chandler's shops, have denounced the competitive principle of individual shopkeeping, and have endeavoured to extract this virus from society, by the 'improved' method of having a committee, a treasurer, a secretary, and a storekeeper, to manage a chandler's shop of their own.[31]

Many Owenites shared this view. Owen himself, on his return from America, gave no encouragement to the trading associations, declaring that mere buying and selling had nothing to do with his efforts to transform society. William Thompson warned that they only very partially got rid of the evils of competition, and that they must have aims beyond wholesale purchase and cheap consumption, while Carpenter emphasised:

> The working and dealing of mechanics in co-operation, in the manner adopted by the Westminster and other Societies, although excellent, as far as it goes, falls far short of what may be expected from the *entire* adoption of the co-operative system.[32]

The frequency of these warnings is a sure sign that most societies did have limited aims.

The clearest sign of this is the disillusion of George Skene who, as a leading man in the First London and as founder of the BAPCK, in which he succeeded Foskett as secretary in the summer of 1829, was the Owenite best informed on the co-operative movement in general. He saw a twofold failure in co-operative trading. First, the societies were not succeeding as trading stores. Quite apart from cases of mismanagement, the general no-credit rule meant that members' wives were not keen to shop at the store,[33] while the prices were no inducement because the policy of many stores was to sell at usual prices to make profits, and indeed the food was sometimes actually dearer than elsewhere because it was unadulterated. It required great dedication for men to attend to the society's affairs after a day's work, especially as the profits were often so trifling. Skene had hoped the trading societies would not only amass funds to acquire land but would also, through the joint management, serve as schools in co-operation. But slight profits made the former unlikely, while co-operative principles seemed lost to sight in the bickerings over retail prices and the amount of goods each member bought; buying and selling seemed their sole concern. His criticism was heightened by Owen's on his return, and so Skene proposed to the committee of BAPCK a scheme whereby the goods should be sold in the stores at a price that merely covered costs, so that low prices would increase business and ruin the shopkeepers. Further, the aim should be much more clearly the employment of all the members in production, and since they would now be getting their necessities cheaper their products could also be sold more cheaply to one another and to the outside world. In this way much greater profits to the members, coupled with the cheap goods and the greater likelihood of gaining land, would attract far greater numbers than hitherto. Members should also be made fit for the ultimate community by intellectual improvement and inculcation of co-operative principles.

This represented an Owenite criticism of the co-operative societies, but his scheme, despite support from leading co-operators like Watson, met with opposition. This was mainly because Skene, like Thompson and other Owenites, was ready to see wages fall with the price of food; some artisans saw his plan as indulging in competitive cheapening of labour. The scheme was defeated by a majority of one, and Skene therefore resigned from the committee of BAPCK along with Watson, Wigg, Lowe, Jennison and Voak, and with them founded in April the 'First Manufacturing Community' at Old Street Road. Each member was to pay £5 in instalments, the capital to be used to employ all members, who should all learn two or more trades or skills. All new members must, before admittance, be questioned on co-operative principles, all decisions would be unanimous, there would be committees instead of officers, and regular educational discussions and lectures would be held. Skene also discontinued the *British Magazine of Co-operative Knowledge* and replaced it with his *British Co-operator* which publicised the new society. By August it had thirty members and a branch was being formed. Early in 1831 Gast joined this 'manufacturing community'.[34]

A bi-polar approach to the co-operative movement, retail store or Owenite, will not however suffice. Not all co-operative societies were solely concerned with trading in flour and grocery. Some, like the Hampstead and Second Middlesex societies did not trade at all. Others shared stores—the Metropolitan used the First London's, and First St George's and First and Second Tailors' used the First Western Union's—so clearly had functions apart from trading. Several of them employed some of their members—tailors, shoemakers, carpenters, masons, brushmakers, tinmen.[35]

Self-employment was a natural activity for artisans who were often virtually self-employed or might exchange services. Journeymen carpenters often clubbed together to erect a house in their spare time. So it was not a big step to the idea of employing members of a society. It was in fact a familiar strike tactic among trade societies, as among breeches-makers in 1793, bookbinders in 1794, and tobacco-pipe makers in 1819. In both their great strikes, in 1802 and 1825, the Thames shipwrights tried to secure work direct from shipowners and by-pass the builders, hardly a big step for men already used to taking contracts as a gang.[36] In 1826 the Bristol shipwrights struck against a reduction and with Gast's enthusiastic support decided to start their own business:

> This is as it should be; the men have an equal right with their masters to do work for themselves; the greater part of them are freemen; and if they choose to form themselves into a Joint Stock Company, and make use of the produce of their industry for the purposes of trade, where is the man that could find fault with them? It is a noble example, and worthy of being followed by every trade in England.[37]

In 1828 the Kidderminster weavers, on the defeat of their strike, resolved not only to support a general union but to start production on their own account, and in 1829 George Skene was their accredited London representative.[38]

It seems to have been this employment aspect of co-operation which had great appeal. In 1829 a Brightonian wrote to Gast, in reponse to his call for a general union, commending the Brighton plan for union, namely weekly subscriptions to begin a shop and then employ members; there was no mention of communities. In his propaganda, Penn outlined the stages—weekly deposits, wholesale purchase, selling retail at usual market prices, adding the profits to the stock, and employing members so that all should become so employed and be independent of capitalists or masters; he did not mention land or communities. Carlile described this phase of co-operation as 'Working Unions', distinct from earlier community-building. Tucker, secretary of the First London, thought trading societies of little value unless they went further, but by this he meant employment in manufacturing. Lovett, who knew as much about the movement as anyone, later described its aims as setting up a general store for food, clothing and books, and then the employment of members as 'the first step towards the social independence of the labouring classes', when they would form joint-stock associations of labour and gain control of the country's trade, manufactures and commerce.[39] He did not mention communities. But later in his autobiography he says: 'I must confess, also, that I was one of those who, at one time, was favourably impressed with many of Mr Owen's views, and, more especially, with those of *a community of property*.'[40] Lovett thus distinguishes the aims of the co-operative movement, namely co-operative production, from Owen's ideas.

By 1830 there was growing interest among artisans in co-operative production, no longer just as a strike device but as a remedy for unemployment. Many trades now saw this unemployment as a serious problem, not just a seasonal phenomenon, and while the tailors' unemployment fund was drained in 1826, tramping was also less effective. Co-operative production promised relief to men unable to find work from employers. Already in 1826 some silk-weavers had begun a ribbon manufactory. In 1829 there were six co-operative societies in Bethnal Green, mostly of broad silk-weavers, receiving interest-free loans from the fund to enable them to make goods.[41] By 1832 there were two tailors' co-operative societies, making articles both for the Western Union Exchange and for sale to the public at cheap rates.[42] In 1831 one of the carpenters' houses of call, at the Argylle Arms in Argylle Street, decided to employ its out-of-work members and, on the advice of Hetherington, applied to the committee of BAPCK. They began business in 1832, taking contracts not for *all* members but only for those without work.[43] In mid-1831 another carpenters' society was formed in Pimlico, to build a house.[44] When the labour exchange opened at Owen's Institution, the great majority of deposits came from individuals, made in spare time or because they were out of work, mostly from tailors, cabinet-makers, and shoemakers, three trades experiencing the classic process of degradation of skilled artisans in the situation of labour surplus. In December the managers sent deputations to several trade societies, and the exchange was joined by the two carpenters' societies mentioned above, and one of the tailors' societies formed in 1831. Soon there were several societies, each consisting of members of a single trade, using the exchange, and in April 1833 these formed the United Trades' Association. In May they began a fund to provide loans to member societies to buy raw materials. These societies did not try to employ all their members, only those out of work; their co-operative production was a form of unemployment relief. They might, of course, sell to the public, but in a period of depression or over-production demand was slight. The advantage of the labour exchange was that it accepted goods irrespective of demand and at a fair price, and so provided a guaranteed market.[45] But when at the end of 1833 conditions had improved and it was easier to sell outside, they began to do so to avoid the exchange's commission.[46] Thus, whatever Owen intended, these societies were using the exchange for their own purposes. This was also true of the mass of individual depositors, who in May 1833 were formed into a miscellaneous department, numbering 600.[47]

But by July 1833 the exchange was in a bad way, with losses of stock and bad management, and the producers were keen to take it over. This was done, new notes were issued, and the exchange was now run by a joint committee from the Missionary Society, Miscellaneous Department and United Trades' Association. The new superintendent was Henderson, soon succeeded by the shoemaker William Hoare, with William Peel, of the defunct First London, secretary. The new artisan management paid off the debts and made good the deficiency of stock over notes.[48] But business declined at the end of the year. There was now an accumulation of goods, most of whose value came not from material but labour that was valued at full price, often above its market price. The exchange also failed to supply the wants of all users because it failed to secure an adequate supply of provisions. And so less goods were brought in as people were not sure of being able to take out something they needed, and notes therefore depreciated in the open market.[49]

Artisan support for co-operative production and the labour exchanges was thus on the whole practical and in pursuit of limited aims. And even when co-operative societies did seriously consider taking land, this did not always betoken support for an Owenite community. It could be the familiar clubbing together to buy an area to be divided up among members, a reflection of the persistent interest in small-holdings or weekend summer-houses.[50] Or it could be:

The means of purchasing for every member a small portion of land, whereupon he may erect a cottage, to which, in the evening of his life, he may retire, and by raising provisions for his own use upon the land, find some light and beneficial occupation in the cultivation of his own freehold instead of spending his last days in a workhouse.[51]

The North London Community at Barnsbury Park rented a piece of land, of which each family took an acre, while continuing their urban employment.[52] And very often land could serve for co-operative production to give unemployed relief.

In the co-operative movement, then, artisans took advantage of Owenite facilities in attempts to meet the requirements of respectable artisans—security against unemployment and old age, loans to avoid indebtedness and continue work,[53] education for adults and children. Penn's perception was accurate when he directed his appeals at benefit societies, and indeed some benefit societies did become co-operative societies.[54] We have seen the search for security against unemployment in co-operative production. We see the search for security in old age in the plan for the Lambeth Union to take land on which to erect retirement cottages. We see the loan device in the Spitalfields societies and the United Trades' fund. We see the search for education in the libraries of the First London, First Westminster, First Kensington and First Western Union. In 1830 there was a scheme for a school for the children of co-operators, and schools were opened by the North London society and at Owen's Institution. Several leading figures in the London Mechanics' Institution became Owenites, like Richard Taylor, James Flather and Rowland Detrosier. A leading Owenite, James Horne, was in 1827 president of the Southwark Mechanics' Institution. At Owen's Institution there were regular and well-attended lectures, initially on the social system, mostly by Owen. But by the end of 1832, by popular demand, they were by Robert Dale Owen on physical geography, his brother David on chemistry, and others on geology and astronomy. These lectures were enormously successful because they avoided the mistakes of the mechanics' institutions and were pitched at the right level. In 1833 it was therefore decided to continue with lectures on arts and sciences, and begin a reading-room, library and mechanics' classes. From mid-1833 they had regular lectures by Detrosier, the most brilliant popular educationalist of his day. The Owenite pencil-manufacturer Sampson Mordan also bought a chapel off the City Road for Detrosier and this 'Hall of Science' was run by Watson. At the same time an 'Eastern Institution' was opened near Stepney Causeway.[55]

The 'co-operative movement' was thus a many-faceted affair with a mass of activities to meet the requirements of respectable artisans. It could not appeal to the very poor, whom the no-credit rule totally excluded from the stores; nor could they take advantage of the labour exchange, with its penny rent:

> And it was a most dangerous fallacy to assert that labour exchange was at present, or could be made for a long time, to benefit those who had no money. No, the poor unfortunate wight who was destitute of all means could not benefit by our Exchange at present; but to the poor and industrious mechanic, who could only get a part of his time employed, to him it offered the most decided advantage.[56]

The very poor could not afford the lectures and festivals either, for admission there was not free.

The co-operative movement emphasised respectability. It was categorically opposed to drink and public houses. The BAPCK only admitted persons of 'good moral character'. The movement provided opportunities for good fellowship and recreation of a respectable nature. Cleave ran a co-operative coffee-house. Early in 1831 Gast regularly attended the tea-parties organised by the First Manufacturing Community for co-operators at the East End of town, and Owen often came. The Western Union organised similar ones for the West End, and every year organised a river outing to the Nore and Medway while the Manufacturing Community had an outing to Highbury Vale. The Central society held balls.[57] And the social festivals at Owen's Institution were surely the most successful thing he ever undertook: 'it is the only sign or glimmering of heaven and the millenium, to go to the social festival of the Owenites, and see good sense in a state of hilarity, and good feeling performing all its kind offices'.[58]

That the artisan movement was autonomous is revealed most plainly in artisans' refusal to share Owen's indifference to politics. Gast and his fellows were experienced in political activity and were radical reformers who recognised the importance of political power. Owen's treatment of this as irrelevant could not but seem crass folly, and Lovett singled this matter out as one of the main sources of contention between Owen and his followers. Their adherence to democratic practices also clashed with his paternalism and tendency to autocracy (which he justified by the fact that only he could understand the system). Warden, leader of the Western Union, effectively contrasted the co-operative societies, with their equality of rights between members and election of officers by universal suffrage and secret ballot, with Owen's despotic rule at his Institution.[59] In the 1820s radicalism was not practical politics, but by 1830 parliamentary Reform was a pressing issue that could not be ignored and many members of the BAPCK were involved in radical activity. In April 1830 its committee resolved almost unanimously in favour of radical reform, and the 500 who attended the fourth quarterly meeting adopted a petition containing support for shorter parliaments and manhood suffrage.[60] This political tendency was strengthened when Carpenter left the *Weekly Free Press* and took the momentous step of trying to evade the fourpenny stamp duty on newspapers by publishing a series of 'letters'. He also began a new co-operative magazine[61] but ended it after four weeks and thenceforth co-operative news, including Lovett's extracts from correspondence with provincial societies, featured regularly in the *Political Letters*. The BAPCK fully supported Carpenter, and their meeting in November on the matter, coinciding with a peak of political excitement, was a stormy one with tricolour-waving.[62] Most co-operative stores collected money to support Carpenter. The increase in political interest was reflected in Carpenter's *Letters* and led to a decline in co-operative activity early in 1831. The last address issued by BAPCK was in fact an appeal for subscriptions to help the unstamped struggle.[63] Radicals also defeated Owen's proposal to use profits from his exchange to pay off the National Debt and there were stormy debates at his Institution. At the congress in April 1832 Warden, Lovett, Benbow and Watkins clashed with Owen over his indifference to politics, Cleave called for support for the unstamped war and Watson urged them to read Paine, hardly a co-operator.[64] The topics for the discussions held by the Western Union included, alongside religion, labour exchanges, Owenism and radical Reform, poor laws, commerce and currency, such subjects as the feudal system, Repeal of the Union and Andrew Jackson.[65]

The co-operative movement was an umbrella movement containing a number of artisan activities not one of which was new. The role of Owenites was mainly to provide the facilities to forward these activities, in the form of premises, money, periodicals, publicity and some expertise. But the role of Owenism did amount to more than this, for Owen's superb criticisms of competition and the process of industrialisation did make an impact. But here again what Owen said was already widely recognised among artisans. If we consider Gast's basic ideas in the 1820s—the inadequacy of isolated trade unions; the need for unity among mechanics; the disastrous results of competition in forcing employers to cut labour costs; the accruing of all the benefits of machinery to the capitalist, any gains to the workmen from cheaper articles being wiped out by loss of work; the growing gulf between rich and poor; the poverty of the labourers the cause of fictitious 'overproduction'; labour as the source of all wealth; rejection of Malthusian explanations of distress; the belief that everyone should work; the need for moral reform of the labouring classes—we find these are basic themes in the *Co-operative Magazine* and other Owenite propaganda. We even find, in a petition presented by Hetherington and Gast to the BAPCK, the attacks on privileges and monopolies and the demand for the replacement of all existing taxes by a property tax.[66] It is easy to see how Gast went into Owenite co-operation, for he already agreed with its analysis of what was wrong with the present system. The same is true of other leading trade unionists of the 1820s. Thomas Voak, of the struggling ladies' shoemakers, was on the committee of the BAPCK, joined Skene's Manufacturing Community, and in 1833 led the first shoemakers' section in the United Trades' Association.[67] Joseph Styles, a leading man among the carpenters, was in the First Pimlico and then the Westminster co-operative societies, on the committee of BAPCK, and later one of the chief figures in Owen's Institution and the Social Missionary and Tract Society.[68] William Lawrence, leader of the brassfounders, a trade threatened by machinery, was on the BAPCK committee, and the Hand-in-Hand co-operative society was composed of brassfounders and braziers.[69] One of the attractions of Owenism was that its analysis of the system corresponded with those of the suffering artisans. 'They had learned from it to see capitalism, not as a collection of discrete events, but as a *system*.'[70]

Of course many artisans generalised from small-scale practical endeavours in co-operative production to advocacy of the employment of all workmen in this way: 'as the whole of this mechanical labour will be net profit, they will eventually be able to purchase machinery, and thus drive the monopolising capitalist from the market'.[71] This was not a big step, nor was it at all difficult for many artisans to see their employers as dispensable, for master shipbuilders, bookbinders, tailors or builders were often merely middlemen. Co-operative production was attractive to men who anyway enjoyed some autonomy and collectively often controlled recruitment, pace of work and even employment. It could offer a stable reward for their labour and freedom from wage-cutting without any state interference. The sort of 'Socialism' that appealed to artisans was not state socialism but producers' co-operatives. They were also attracted, in their conviction of the injustice of currency fluctuations, to Owen's proposals to ensure that prices stayed steady so that their reward would be stable.

Owenism did contribute more than this, in that a number of artisans did go the whole way into support for a community, including Gast, Lovett, Styles, Warden and leading figures in the United Trades' Association like Horne of the carpenters and Hoare and Simkins of the shoemakers. But they still retained their same social ideals. A community would ensure a fair reward for labour, security of employment and in old age, education for children and respectable companionship. Gast envisaged a community of mechanics, who would all work for a living.

> They ought to protect themselves when they had the means of doing so in their own power. That protection the Co-operative system was intended to afford them; their motto was, 'those who don't work, shan't eat' . . . He felt assured that if the principles of Co-operation were acted upon to their full extent, a great blessing would be conferred upon the working classes, who would not only be made independent of those who fattened upon their industry, but be prevented from unworthily abusing the talents and skill which they possessed. A Co-operative community would not permit itself to be ridden by great or little beggars, who squandered the earnings of the majority, without adding anything to the general fund.[72]

We should remember that 'community' was a vague term, and might just mean co-operative production in a settlement, which was not Owen's view.

If we look at the committee of the BAPCK and the membership of the Manufacturing Community, we can recognise two other groups drawn into Owenism, namely Spenceans and anti-Christians. The Spenceans included Allen Davenport; Charles Jennison and James Mee, both members of Evans's group in 1819; and John Hunter. Jennison was treasurer to the BAPCK and founder with Skene of the Manufacturing Community, and later became one of the chief figures at Owen's Institution and manager of the Eastern Institution. Davenport also joined Skene's community and composed for it a 'Co-operative Catechism' which is an excellent summary of popular Owenism.[73] The Spenceans were always interested in land reform; Thomas Preston put forward schemes in 1834, 1845 and 1850, and Davenport was to support O'Connor's Land Plan.[74] They were attracted to Owenism mainly through its advocacy of common ownership and its intention to move urban population back to the land. As George Petrie, basically Spencean in his views, put it:

> The great evil to be regretted (and is even acknowledged by legislators themselves) is, that the great bulk of the people have been decoyed from the land and agricultural pursuits into cities and large towns, and there are compelled to submit to their masters' terms, having no other alternative.[75]

The issue of the landed system was a constant one in nineteenth-century British politics, and an essential part of ultra-radicalism was opposition to the 'land monopoly', to be ended by abolition of primogeniture and entail, home colonisation or confiscation. Small land schemes were always cropping up, Owen's and O'Connor's being merely the best known. Hence there was widespread support for co-operative acquisition of land. A correspondent of Carlile's *Lion* voiced the common condemnation of the concentration of landownership in a small number of families who controlled Parliament, government and magistracy and whose oppressive actions led to excessive emigration to the towns, where the workers were at the mercy of employers. 'It is in *the monopoly of the land*, that the misery of almost all the working classes consists.' He wanted to reverse the process and divide up the estates, but, while agreeing with Carlile that the *Co-operative Magazine* and New Harmony were nonsense, he saw the main hope of remedy in 'working unions'. The model was in Brighton where practical men had used the profits from a shop to take and settle land.[76]

The Spenceans were also characterised by their opposition to orthodox Christianity, though they often had substitute forms. In the post-war period the Evanses and Wedderburn ran chapels and sought to prove that Spenceanism was true Christianity. It is well known that Owen's assaults on Christianity antagonised many potential supporters, and both *London Co-operative Magazine* and the *Brighton Co-operator* disassociated themselves from Owen's religious views. The co-operative movement that arose in 1829 included many believers. Yet when Owen returned to England in 1830 and began his Sunday morning lectures he continually expressed his view that all religions were founded on error and, since they were the chief obstacle to that full understanding of the principles of human nature that was essential to the implementation of the social system, especially the fact that character was completely formed by the environment, their annihilation was essential. This alienated many co-operators and led to the collapse of some societies. Carpenter, a popular preacher, was particularly offended and led the attack in the BAPCK, which in vain disclaimed any connection with Owen's lectures or religious views. But the damage was done, members withdrew from societies and the BAPCK, and they collapsed. Looking back Lovett saw this controversy as one of the chief causes of the failure of co-operative societies in London.[77] But in the north the issue seems hardly to have risen, and his contacts here seem to have induced Owen to moderate his views, and by 1832 he was agreeing with Wade that Owenism was practical Christianity.[78]

But though the attacks on Christianity did alienate people from Owenism, it also gathered support. There is a clear connection between Owenism and unorthodox religious ideas. Small religious sects which often included social radicalism or community of goods, were a long-established feature in Europe. In the early nineteenth century they often combined religion with an absorption of the principles of the Enlightenment, and their religion was often a rationalist, undenominational Deism. They were of importance in social movements on the continent and in Britain, and London was no exception. Here was a number of small break-away religious sects and preaching-groups, like the 'Church of God' or 'Freethinking Christians'. Founded in 1798 by Samuel Thompson they were led by him and his fellow brewers Fearon and Coates, and in the late 1820s numbered over sixty. They combined religious and political radicalism, and Thompson, Fearon and the solicitor W. H. Ashurst were leading City radicals. But several of their members went into Owenism, including Ashurst, Hetherington, Warden and the Savage brothers. Hetherington was in 1822 one of the group of printers who, under the inspiration of George Mudie, actually began a community at Spa Fields; Warden was one of the chief London co-operators in the early 1830s; and John Savage, a linen-draper, was one of the original managing committee of Owen's exchange.[79]

The Freethinking Christians believed in the divine mission of Jesus and the resurrection, and regarded themselves as restoring the primitive Christianity that had been corrupted by the Church. But some people gravitated through it into a rejection of Christianity, like Thomas Bayley-Potts who transferred his allegiance to Carlile. In the 1820s Carlile's periodicals frequently quoted Owen. Indeed for Carlile Owen was the greatest man living and though he never wavered in his support for competition, he had to admit that many of his associates had become Owenites, like Watson, Davenport, Millard, Powell, Gale Jones, Julian Hibbert and Medler. It was presumably through Millard that another member of 'The Liberals', William Lovett, came into Owenism.

In 1825 Carlile had become interested in the ex-Anglican

clergyman Robert Taylor, and his Christian Evidence Society, where he, Gale Jones and others expounded their grounds for rejecting Christianity and made a considerable sensation. Money from wealthy admirers maintained the society and enabled them in 1826 to take a chapel for divine service and sermons at which Carlile was a constant attender.[80] This Deism was more popular than Carlile's complete materialism, and many felt the need for some form of service and ceremonial which Carlile did not provide. Taylor's eccentric manner and stream of sarcasm and buffoonery was also more attractive and entertaining than the arid *Republican*. So Taylor's following rose and by 1827 Carlile was almost totally eclipsed.[81]

But in May 1827 Taylor and some of his supporters were indicted for blasphemy. His society ended, and when Taylor received a mild prison sentence many of his followers suspected him of cowardice. He was released in September but in February 1828 sentenced to a year's prison and recognizances. Carlile began a new journal to publicise Taylor's case and work, but its sale was small, and when after a year Taylor paid recognizances and was freed he was widely criticised, and Carlile remained one of his few supporters.[82]

Meanwhile Taylor's group, led by such men as Saull and William Aungier, had formed a new Deist society, under the name of 'Universalists'. They took a chapel in Grub Street, and here a radical ex-schoolteacher and old friend of Taylor's called Fitch secured a licence as a preacher and held divine service for Truth, Reason and Morals. Carlile was affronted, attacked Fitch's beliefs as just as superstitious as Christianity, and opened a rival School of Free Discussion. But whilst his attendance was tiny, Fitch's audience was often 300, and he also allied with a Christian preacher and ex-actress, Miss Macaulay.[83]

On his release and rebuff from his former friends, Taylor attended Carlile's school and attendance rose. At its meetings only two people defended the view that belief in a Deity had beneficial results, one the Freethinking Christian Hetherington, the other an eccentric Frenchman, Pierre Baume, who had had a chequered career and now had his own peculiar views of a deity. In March 1829 he also began speaking at Fitch's chapel and, being a strong republican, was soon hired to speak at the British Forum debating society. He then opened a small bookshop in Windmill Street, Finsbury, where he sold the Sunday papers, all the popular and theological works, and some of his own publications. He then took over in the same street a chapel that had been closed for years but had been used in the early 1820s by a group of universalists, including the master carpenter Henry Medler, who had been one of the Watsonite group in the post-war period. At this 'Optimist Chapel' Baume held Sunday evening meetings and formed a Society for Promoting Anti-Christian and General Instruction. Few attended until the French Revolution of 1830, after which attendance rose as at other similar places. By 1830 there were three meetings a week, three hundred often attended, and there was a regular group of speakers—Baume, Watson, Saull, Medler, Aungier and Gast.[84]

Nearly all these people were involved to some extent with Owenism. Fitch lectured on astronomy to Owenites and gave money to the BAPCK and the use of his chapel for a meeting. Miss Macaulay was one of the group that opened a labour exchange in Blackfriars Road and she also helped set up the exchange at Owen's Institution. Saull became a regular treasurer of co-operative funds and an important lecturer at Owen's Institution.[85] Baume also supported Owenism, often in an eccentric way, and, of course, Gast, Watson and Medler were all Owenites.

Owenism cannot, therefore, be studied in isolation. The group at the Optimist Chapel demostrated a wide range of interests. The prevailing tone of the meetings was anti-Christian—Gast regularly ridiculed the Bible, picking out obscene and immoral passages from it, and advocated Deism as the only true religion of morality likely to lead Man to real happiness.[86] But by January 1831 the group was also discussing co-operation and now included Davenport and the tailor, Lowe (former secretary of the Finsbury co-operative society), who were both, like Watson and Gast, members of Skene's manufacturing association. And soon this association itself began to meet at the Optimist Chapel.[87] The group was thus one of freethinkers and Owenites, but in the circumstances of the time they were also radicals, denouncing state as much as church. In November 1830 Baume's shop was taken over by Watson, who now began his long distinguished career as vendor and publisher of radical and freethinking works. In September 1831 Watson also took over the chapel and systematised its use. The 'Philadelphian Chapel' now had philosophical discussions on Sundays, a co-operative meeting on Tuesdays and a 'theological' (i.e. anti-Christian) one on Thursdays. On Mondays the same group met there as the Finsbury section of the new National Union of the Working Classes (NUWC), of which Gast had early on been a leading member. Watson's class, number 73, the most honourable in the whole union, numbering seventy and including Medler and the spy Abel Hall, also met at the chapel. It was the same group taking part in all these activities.[88] The mixture of interests is seen in Gast's lecture topics—the evils from man prosecuting interests in his own way; 21 Deuteronomy verse 12; the cause of oppression and its remedy; Raphael's Almanack; the treacherous connivance of the parties to the Vienna treaty at the massacre of Poles by the Tsar. Indeed the total of lecture and discussion topics provide a summary of the preoccupations of 1831–2.[89]

But in October 1832 Watson was unable to renew the lease of the chapel and so the group lost their Finsbury meeting-place. Gast thereupon began to attend meetings at a chapel in Southwark that had been used by the millenarian preacher Zion Ward until his recent arrest.[90] Here now were meetings both theological and political (including from June 1832 the NUWC), and Gast naturally spoke at both. In the theological ones he shared the platform with a young new arrival in London, James Smith, originally a Scotch Presbyterian but by the later 1820s a leading member of the Southcottians led by Wroe at Ashton. In London Smith naturally came into contact with Carlile, Taylor, the lady of the Rotunda, and Saull. By October 1832 he was lecturing regularly at the Borough Chapel, preaching Universalism, the identity of the the female God with Nature. He saw established Christianity as the corruption of true religion, and regarded the present as the evil period of the reign of Antichrist, the preparation for the new Christian Millenium. He was even more abusive of Christianity than Taylor, Hibbert and Gale Jones and attracted corresponding notice. Smith became a celebrity, spoke at the Rotunda, and came into contact with the Owenites through Irving, head of a group of dissidents from the Church of Scotland with millenarian tendencies whom Owen allowed to meet at his Institution. Smith's doctrine of the responsibility of Nature (i.e. God) for all human actions merged easily into the Owenite doctrine of circumstances, while his radical Christianity led to a belief in a Social Community free of all distinctions and private property, where woman would be freed from thraldom to man through marriage. By mid-1833 he was lecturing regularly at Owen's Institution and his lectures were published in the Crisis and helped restore its failing fortunes. Soon Smith also took over the editorship.[91]

Gast's involvement with Smith is interesting. He had been some sort of 'Dissenting preacher' in the early nineteenth century. At the end of 1814 he was imprisoned by Deptford magistrates in Dartford Bridewell for fortune-telling.[92] This was regarded as a very serious evil, and was a widespread form of swindling. Offenders were punished as rogues and vagabonds, as was Gast.[93] His aim may have been purely pecuniary, but it was an interest that persisted, for in 1832 he was lecturing on *Raphael's Prophetic Almanack*.[94] Moreover, the arrest in 1814 coincided with Southcottian excitement south of the river and Gast was certainly not ignorant of the events of Joanna's last 'pregnancy'. Though in general full of praise for Smith's lectures, he sharply disagreed with his praise of Joanna, especially over the fraud of the birth of Shiloh.[95] Gast may well have been affected by millenarianism.

These religious and anti-religious currents in Owenism must be borne in mind, and two points in particular need emphasising. The first is the importance of breakaway religious groups in radical movements, even in secular London. The reality of the religion is not always clear, and in Saull's case Deism was a mark for materialism. But very many radicals clearly felt a need to clothe their activities in a religious garb and even ceremonial, and artisans seem particularly attracted to 'rational religion'.

Secondly, the anti-Christian groups of the 1820s are the best examples of those artisans of whom it can be said that 'the works of the Enlightenment came to them with the force of revelation'.[96] Once they felt shaken free from superstition into rationality an enormous feeling of liberation and optimism could result. Having made the one great step, they were willing to make others and consider seriously any new ideas and theories. They were interested in science, Sir Richard Phillip's philosophy of matter, phrenology, mesmerism, evolution or Owenism. Fitch's chapel became an Athenaeum that discussed astronomy and geology.[9] And this was heightened by the fact that this was anyway an age of intellectual ferment, when many old certainties were discarded and a mass of new speculations appeared.[98] Among such radicals in much of early nineteenth-century Europe we find highly individual theories on astronomy, gravity or psychology. Saull rejected Newton's law of gravity. Once people had via free thought entered this world, they were ready to speculate. Not surprisingly they adopted what seem very wild ideas, and could accept the possibility of a totally new society or of total changes in human nature. We must not exaggerate the rationalism of all this—Gast after all, apparently retained his interest in fortune-telling and became an admirer of the millenarian Smith. But equally the seemingly wild nature of some of these beliefs should not be automatically categorised as millenarianism, a concept currently used by historians to evade explanation as much as anything else. It was an age of new theories and systems, and Owenism was one of them.

The final point is that men like Owen and Thompson were not primarily economic theorists. They were moral reformers who saw certain aspects of the current economic system as leading to disastrous moral results. This is true of very much of Owenism, obvious in the freethinking element but just as marked in people like Lovett. The new society would be a new moral world, but in many ways the morality was actually the accepted one. No-one was more respectable than Lovett or Holyoake. We can therefore see how Owenism was accepted by artisans seeking respectability both in the practice of Owenite activities (education, dancing, tea-parties) and in the projected community. Owenites were by no means necessarily extremists. Many of them were the mildest of liberals politically and the nicest of people socially, and this included artisans seeking a way back into respectable society.

And so the co-operative movement attracted artisans and drew on established artisan practices (exclusive dealing, loan funds, exchange of services, retirement schemes, educational, temperance and convivial efforts) and offered relevant responses to a number of pressing preoccupations (unemployment, currency fluctuations, strike power, machinery). It occurred in the midst of widespread discussion of such issues as the agricultural system, currency, commercial and industrial depression, the increase in productive power alongside declining value of exports, urbanisation, poor laws and home colonisation, so that artisans were receptive to ideas of co-operative production in *all* industry and often mixed with agricultural production, of reform of the currency, and of widespread social changes that would guarantee their security in work and old age, their self-respect and morality.

Part Four
FROM REFORM CRISIS
TO CHARTISM

PROLOGUE

By the end of the 1820s Gast and his fellow artisans had developed a combination of viewpoints, aims, policies and analyses which then remained dominant and not greatly changed through the next two decades. The 1820s thus formed a crucial formative decade. However the years 1829–34 seem to have a special character because of the coincidence and extent of a number of artisan movements. Although different forms were emphasised more at certain times according to the political and economic climate—co-operative trading 1829–31, co-operative production 1831–3, political reform 1830–2, trades unionism and trade union rights 1833–4, illegal periodicals 1830–6—the movements were basically simultaneous and overlapping. Fed by the gravity of the Reform crisis and by the confrontation atmosphere of 1834, the sheer concentration, scale, interrelation and intensity of these movements clearly deepened and extended the tendencies of the 1820s. Gast, appropriately, was involved in all of them (except the general unionism of 1834). The early 1830s might in some ways mark the end of his story, especially as he dropped out of prominence after 1833 and from that year the shipwrights were abandoning their leading role in London trades unionism. But London artisan radicalism and trade unionism continued unbroken throughout the 1830s and 1840s, and went into Chartism, that unprecedented national movement of working men. In the 1840s especially, London Chartism expressed all the same preoccupations and attitudes and was characterised by strong links with trade unionism. Chartism is really the culmination of this story, and although Gast died at the end of 1837 he did play some small part in its inception.

14
REFORM

In April 1831 Gast joined a new association and immediately became one of its leaders. It soon took the name of National Union of the Working Classes (NUWC), and during and after the dramatic events of the Reform crisis both the union and its illegal press organs, especially the *Poor Man's Guardian*, were to occasion concern to the government and alarm among the propertied classes. Francis Place, working to create an impressive and unified campaign in favour of the Reform bills, saw them as his chief enemies, sources of extremism and 'no-property' beliefs. This analysis has attracted the attention of historians to both National Union and war of the unstamped, and both have been seen as demonstrating the final creation of an English working class and as the real origin of Chartism.

To understand the origins of the NUWC, we have to understand the situation among the artisans. We have seen that the economic situation after 1825, with frequent unemployment, did not favour trade union action over wages. In the later 1820s, the artisan trades rarely pressed or struck for higher wages, and what strikes there were in London were against wage reductions or changes that resulted in lower earnings, as in the disastrous tailors' strike of 1830. Though there were some moves in favour of general union, in which Gast was the chief figure, the main reaction of the trades was to concentrate on other topics, like tariff policies, bread prices or wage-fixing. The question of limiting hours of work was another such important question, as it was seen as a way of spreading work and so reducing unemployment. Shoemakers and tailors were working longer and longer hours and thus increasing competition for work (during the wars the tailors had successfully imposed a twelve-hour day). In the late 1820s Gast's shipwrights clung to their limitation on hours and so prevented a disastrous decline, and in

1829 his attempted general union supported this tactic.[1] But given the economic situation most of these aims were not sought through industrial pressure on employers. We have seen how some artisans turned to co-operation in their efforts to meet the problems of rising food prices, unemployment and lack of striking power, and how others sought the remedies through political action.

In Lancashire the cotton-spinners, after the series of disastrous defeats and reductions in 1829, developed, through the rallying of Manchester trades to their support, a general union, the National Association for the Protection of Labour; but they also campaigned for effective limitation of hours through legislation. In London the initiative for the new union came from the main house of call of the First Society of Carpenters, the Argylle Arms. In the 1820s there were five main trade societies of carpenters, embracing over twenty houses of call, and their disunity was proverbial, though from 1823 they had held united annual dinners and they had combined in the 1825 strike. By 1830 they were suffering from problems familiar to several of the London trades—capitalism and competition.[2] The building trades were all affected by the continued growth of master builders, who directly employed men in all branches of the building industry and took contracts to do a whole building and so displaced the usual practice of separate contracts with master carpenters, plumbers, bricklayers and so on. The small masters were therefore being squeezed by the forty large London masters who could take big orders but, being in competition, sought to underbid one another and cut labour costs. Moreover, many were speculative builders, with even greater incentives to cut costs. The suffering small masters had likewise to cut their own costs, and so in every case the journeymen suffered. There were also speculative builders who did not have a labour force but, as in tailoring and shoemaking, acted as middlemen and sub-let parts of the work, which led to competitive tendering and even further sub-letting and cheapening of labour. In all the building branches this also resulted in efforts to increase labour intensity by replacing day-work by task-work. In 1827 there was a strike by carpenters working on the new London University against an attempt to abolish their tea-break ('watering time').[3] The worst sufferers in fact were the carpenters, the largest and one of the less skilled of the building trades. They particularly suffered from cheap country labour, and were also threatened by machinery and the growing use of cast iron instead of wood. It was unemployed carpenters who were the most likely to erect cheap houses for speculation, which increased the general competition. By

1831, as with the tailors, though the day-rate was officially maintained, they were suffering terrible unemployment. The carpenters
were the leading group in London supra-trade activities, the chief
contributors to Bradford, the mainstay of the *Trades' Newspaper*.
They were well aware of the threat from unskilled men, and in the
1825 strike had actually organised the non-society men and given
them strike-pay, though they stuck to their view that more skilful
men should earn more.[4] In 1827 a big strike among the Manchester
carpenters received help from the trade all over the country and, as
often happened, this led on to a national union. At a delegate
conference in London the three London carpenters' leaders, Adam,
Maunder and Gotobed, arranged a plan for a new union which was
finalised at a conference in Leicester in 1827. This was the Friendly
Society of Operative Carpenters and Joiners (FSOC), usually
known as the General Union of Carpenters, a federation of existing
societies which arranged tramp relief.[5] But in the desperate situation of 1831 an attempt was made in London to form a new, unexclusive union of non-society men (the Running Horse Society charged
a half-guinea entry fee). The aim of the union was to reduce competition by equalising employment, and securing public building
contracts from the government. These were to be financed from
sinecures, church wealth, public charities, and from a tax on all public
pensions and salaries.[6] This failed, but the moves to general union
and organisation of non-society men led to the rapid growth of the
FSOC in 1833 to become, under such men as Joseph Styles, one of
the chief London unions.

   The Argylle Arms carpenters in 1831 seem to have been aiming
at a plan of co-operative production to meet the problem of unemployment and, under the inspiration of the National Association for
the Protection of Labour, a union of trades. Their application to the
committee of the British Association for the Promotion of Co-
operative Knowledge (BAPCK) which was commonly known as the
Trades' Co-operative Society, resulted in Hetherington, Warden
and Foskett's being deputed to help them. The Argylle Arms carpenters, as we have seen, were eventually to form a co-operative
society which employed its out-of-work members.[7] But the outcome
of the 'British Co-operators'' involvement was a meeting of
'mechanics and artisans' at the Argylle Arms to consider forming a
general union of trades for mutual assistance and protection. A
metropolitan trades' union was then formed, with Warden secretary, Foskett treasurer, and three trustees including John Higginbottom of the Second Carpenters' Society and one of the leading

men in his trade, and F. Rogers, later a leader of the first carpenters' (Argylle Arms) section of the United Trades' Association. A circular was sent to 150 trade, benefit, co-operative and other societies of working men asking them to send delegates, and many did respond, including the musical instrument makers' trade society, and Warden's First Western Co-operative Union. Gast attended the third meeting and was immediately elected to the provisional committee. Two attempts to restrict membership of the committee to 'wealth-producers' were defeated, other members of the nearly-defunct BAPCK joined, including Petrie and Cleave, and in June the rules and regulations were drawn up. This new union drew together the trends of the later 1820s and sought to effect trade union aims through general union and political action. Gast enthusiastically saw it as what he had been working for for years. Its aims were to remedy low wages, end unemployment caused by machinery, competition and the lack of protection for labour, and to secure to the producer the full value of his labour and free disposal of the produce. This was to be done partly by mutual support against wage reductions and by a reduction in working hours. But it was also to be done by the replacement of all indirect taxes by a graduated property tax and by a parliamentary Reform that would give manhood suffrage, secret ballot and no property qualifications for MPs.[8] The political tendencies of the artisans were now in 1831 taking the form of support for radical Reform again, and this was due to the changed political context.

Artisan radicalism was, of course, already well established. The interest of literate artisans in politics and the avidity with which they read the papers were proverbial. The 1820s saw a steady growth in coffee-houses where newspapers were available for artisan clients, and Gast's acquaintances were fully conversant with the policies of Canning, Huskisson or Peel. In 1827 Gast and his allies held a public meeting on the change in government, and it is significant that the chairman they invited was Hume, respected for his incorruptibility, honesty and consequent independence from 'faction', whether Whig or Tory.[9] Gast, Purdy, Wallis and the sawyer Sadgrove were all in favour of a reform that would end political privilege, corruption and the vast taxation. The strength and extent of a generalised support for such reform among artisans was a fact well before 1830, and educational and other cultural activities had a radical bias. But after 1822 this persistent radicalism was also latent, confined to educational or discussion groups and not producing radical campaigns or agitations. This was not due at all to a decline in radical sentiment but simply to the fact that parliamentary Reform was not practical politics. By 1830 this situation had changed.

In the first place, the parliamentary situation was now much more open and fluid after the break-up of the Liverpool ministry and the rifts caused by Catholic Emancipation. There was now a weak Wellington–Peel administration, several likely alternative governments and real possibility of political change. There had been the shock of Catholic Emancipation when a massive popular movement had by solidarity and passive resistance become irresistible and forced a hostile government to give way. The effect of these developments was not confined to London, for in 1830 there was a revival in popular radicalism in many parts of the country, and this owed as much to local as national events. For usually it was preceded and stimulated by a series of local respectable middle-class campaigns, sometimes over Catholic Emancipation, more usually over local government and against the local oligarchies. There was also the encouragement of gentry meetings over agricultural distress, the currency and parliamentary Reform. The sense of impending change was greatly reinforced by the French Revolution of July 1830 and the almost total support for it in the press.

London no less than anywhere else saw an upsurge in reform activity at the end of the 1820s, encompassing a great variety of different groups and views and characterised by alliances on specific issues and by rifts, quarrels and antagonisms. There were the friends of surgical reform led by Dr Thomas Wakley; there was a group led by William Cobbett; among the City of London reformers Wood and Waithman were still important and radicals were strong in Common Hall and Common Council. There were very many Irish in London, and some were inevitably affected by the great campaigns of O'Connell and Sheil, who were also political radicals and friends of Cobbett.[10]

But one of the chief areas of reform activity was in the parishes, for outside the City, Westminster and Southwark, London had no official existence and consisted merely of parishes in the counties of Middlesex, Surrey and Kent. In 1827 a protest movement arose in St Marylebone in favour of an elected vestry, and similar movements soon began in other parishes.[11] In April 1827 an open vestry was restored in Lambeth, and a determined group of reformers emerged there, led by William Carpenter and John Grady, an Irish attorney's clerk. The St Pancras reformers were led by the Irish coal-merchant Thomas Murphy, who had for some time been active in Westminster politics, and by Edmund Stallwood, a recent arrival from the quiet country town of Great Marlowe. The fight against the Bloomsbury select vestry was led by Place's old associate George Rogers, a fairly prosperous tobacco-manufacturer, in alliance with Wakley who was successfully elected churchwarden. Emanuel Dias Santos was a leader of the St Martin's group. By early 1829 there was a strong united campaign for parochial reform, and Hobhouse took the matter up with a select committee which gathered damning evidence of fraud in such places as Marylebone. This, together with the stubbornness of the Marylebone vestry, enabled the democrats, consisting of small tradesmen and mechanics, to take over the reform movement there and demand the vote for all ratepayers. These groups also demanded the repeal of the 'assessed taxes' (on houses and windows) which pressed particularly on householders and shopkeepers. Most of them were non-Anglican, whether Roman Catholic like Murphy, Dias Santos and Grady, or Dissenters like Carpenter, and they campaigned strongly against church rates. This was particularly true in Marylebone where the leaders were the Freethinking Christians John Savage, linen-draper, Thomas Potter, tallow-chandler, and Warden, a saddler recently become a master, alongside the surgeon Thomas Webb, who contributed to Carlile's *Lion* and ran a dispensary for the poor. Peel's establishment in 1829 of the new Metropolitan Police also aroused the opposition of the parochial radicals, because the parishes had no control over the new police yet paid for their upkeep. Since the 'Bourbon police' were regarded by radicals as a political army and a dangerous form of centralisation, and were unpopular all over London, they provided a continuing unifying focus for discontent.

Their object was, evidently, to put down all constitutional remonstrance and free discussion on the part of the people, to suppress public meetings, to shackle the press, and to make each man afraid of his neighbour (hear). The result would be, that no three persons would be allowed to speak together in the streets. Already the ears of freeborn Englishmen were daily assailed with the police mandate of 'Move on there!' a cry that was enough to make our forefathers start from their graves, to reproach their pusillanimous sons for the loss of rights and privileges for which they spent their energies and their lives (hear). The present police had been ordered to provide themselves with watches, for the purpose of making the system of espionage more complete. They were also provided with report-books, in which they entered the names, the ages, the residence, the habits, and everything connected with every man whom they discovered to be at all engaged in public and political meetings. It had been said that even the reporters and conductors of the newspaper press were watched, and the contents of those report-books, some of which he had seen, were transferred to a record at Great Scotland-yard (murmurs of execration.) So much for the public system in its infancy—what would it become when spread throughout the country? People might now walk the streets in comparative safety, but they knew not that the time of their going out and returning home was marked down, if they were at all mixed up in political proceedings. Yet such was the fact, and he feared that at no very distant day it would become known with all its fatal consequences to the liberty, and perhaps the life of those concerned.[12]

The third factor behind the revival of radicalism was, of course, distress. It was not only unemployment and low wages, for, following the poor harvests of 1829, 1830 and 1831, high food prices also created the familiar circumstances that favoured urban discontent. But the political situation was vitally important, as the distress of 1826 had been far worse but had not produced a radical upsurge.

Popular radical movements often followed the failure of campaigns with more limited aims. In London the failure of all the artisans' agitations over tariffs, Corn Laws, price-fixing and machinery emphasised that Parliament as at present constituted did not recognise the importance of the mechanics as an 'interest'. One senses in Gast and others a growing exasperation.

> The placemen, the pensioner, and the landowner, combine together to maintain their standing in society; but when you endeavour to support yourselves by union, you act a wicked part; and when you claim protection, your labour is to find its own level . . . If we are to judge of the knowledge and the wisdom of statesmen, from those effects which result from their acts we shall not give our rulers much credit either for sagacity or kindness.[13]

The sense of frustration is clearest among the Spitalfields weavers, who tried remedy after remedy, to no avail. Formerly loyal and passive, by 1829 they were demanding reform. Place's friend Wallis, though a convinced reformer, tried to limit their demands to specific single ones, but was increasingly opposed by a much more radical group under Clements and Samuel Dean. By 1830 informants were warning the Home Secretary that 'there is not one loyal weaver' and that their meeting-houses were centres of sedition.[14]

Whenever there was revival of radicalism, there were, of course, many veterans around to organise it. Many of the radicals of 1819 became active again, and even the old associates of Watson and Thistlewood were active around Blandford, Preston, Palin, Hunter, Davenport and Neesom.[15]

This changed political context produced clear signs of a revival of artisan radicalism by 1830. Its chief centres were the mushrooming coffee-houses, nearly every one of which not only took the papers but had a weekly debate. The most important of them was Lunt's at Clerkenwell Green, where the British Forum met, and where artisans like Lovett heard Carlile, Taylor, Gale Jones, Henman, George Thompson and Baume expound extreme forms of republicanism.[16] This was the infrastructure of the London artisan radicalism which exploded into agitation in 1830. And the circumstances of the fall of the unpopular Wellington ministry and the fact that the Reform Bill did not pass easily but only after constitutional deadlock and crisis made for vast political excitement (though this was not continuous but ebbed and flowed over a year and a half), unparalleled agitation and an apparently revolutionary situation. Such a situation must have extended political interest and awareness.

And so in both Gast himself and the NUWC we can see expressions of trade union consciousness, an awareness of trade union weakness, support for general union and the limitation of hours, the pursuit of remedies through legislation, and approval of parliamentary Reform. But in the circumstances of 1830–2 political Reform inevitably became the dominant issue. What also happened was that circumstances combined to make the NUWC *the* ultra-radical association in London, attracting many non-artisans and exclusively political figures. To understand this we need to survey the different radical organisations.

Henry Hunt had been removed from the limelight with the eclipse of radicalism in 1820, though in fact he remained fairly active throughout the decade, mainly in the City, where he even became Senior Auditor. He also backed Wakley in the election for coroner for West Middlesex in 1830, and appeared at meetings of the British Catholic Association to support Emancipation. His efforts to ally with Irish groups dated from 1819, and throughout the 1820s the Friends of Civil and Religious Liberty held meetings and distributed thousands of tracts. They were naturally encouraged by the agitation in Ireland, and by 1828 Hunt was in constant attendance. With the passing of Catholic Emancipation, in 1829, in connection with which they condemned the disfranchisement of the 40s. freeholders, the name was changed to the Radical Reform Association (RRA) and Cobbett became a regular member. They were joined by more Irishmen, like John Cleave and the newly-arrived James O'Brien, more members of the Lambeth group like Augero and Carpenter (who reported proceedings in his *Weekly*

Free Press), the veteran Spencean John George, and the Freethinking Christians Savage, Warden and Hetherington (who became secretary). It was presumably through the last two and Cleave that others of the BAPCK joined, notably Watson and Lovett. Only about forty or fifty attended its monthly meetings, and Cobbett soon left after a row, remaining a bitter foe of Hunt's for the rest of his life. But the members were mainly working men, and their programme was the full Huntite one of universal suffrage, annual parliaments and ballot.[17] They followed Hunt's consistent line of hostility to the Whigs as self-seeking hyprocrites, and insisted that 'moderate reform' on Lord John Russell's lines of disfranchising a few rotten boroughs and giving seats to some large towns was no good at all as it would merely make the existing system more secure. Moderate reform was intended to check radical reform. Already the ultra-radical opposition to the eventual Reform Bill was articulated.

By late 1829 meetings were crowded, and they sensed that the growing distress was fertile ground for radicalism. They started a fund to secure the election to Parliament of 'a representative of the people' (Hunt naturally) and appealed to electors in Preston, Coventry and Nottingham. When in January 1830 a political union was formed at Birmingham for 'effectual' reform, the chances of radicalism seemed high. The February meeting was completely filled and many could not get in. Though they were deeply suspicious of the Birmingham leaders and fearful of betrayal, and felt confirmed when the Birmingham union declared for household suffrage only, they decided to form a political union in London on the same model. By now O'Connell had come out for universal suffrage, annual parliaments and ballot, and so on 8 March he chaired the immense meeting, mainly of working people, at the Eagle Tavern, City Road, which set up a Metropolitan Political Union (MPU). The council of 36 included four MPs and Irish and English radicals. The union therefore promised to unite the whole of London radical opinion in one organisation committed to radical reform as against moderate reform, and to a written constitution and a constituent assembly to effect it. In July it began propaganda aimed specifically at the trade societies, and raised money to help a movement among Preston electors to elect Hunt.[18]

The only radicals of note excluded were Cobbett and Carlile and in 1829 Carlile's group was of minimal importance. But this changed in 1830. Hitherto the chief radical meeting place had been the London Mechanics' Institution, and a change in management in 1830 permitted its use even for a meeting under Hibbert,

Hetherington, Warden, Cleave, Carlile, Taylor and Baume in favour of disendowment of the Church.[19] But in May 1830 Carlile leased a building on Blackfriars Road, near the bridge, known as the Rotunda. The smaller of the two theatres was decorated with the signs of the zodiac in accordance with Taylor's interpretation of the Scriptures on the allegory of the two keys, of the mysteries of physical and moral nature. Here Taylor and Carlile regularly deduced the meaning of God, Christ and the rest from the zodiac, claimed to be restoring primitive Christianity, and regularly abused Church, clergy and all religions. Taylor's technique involved his usual scorn and scurrility, with 'vindications of the character of Saint Judas Iscariot' and so on. These meetings had their regular attenders. There were also political meetings, which Place often came to, but these were very poorly attended.[20]

But Carlile also offered both theatres for hire at one and two guineas an evening and the opportunity was too good to miss. In July 1830 both the RRA and MPU began meeting there, and the latter's first meeting was very successful, doubtless owing much to O'Connell's presence in the chair. Then came the electrifying news of the French Revolution, greeted with great enthusiasm, and reform movements were greatly encouraged. Cobbett gave a series of eleven brilliant lectures at the Rotunda on the French Revolution and the English boroughmongers, the burden being that only a thorough-going reform would do, and that the support for reform from great manufacturers, merchants and bankers was self-interested in order to end the burden of tithes and taxes so that they could reduce wages. Political meetings at the Rotunda were crowded for the rest of the year.

But by then the MPU was dead. Hunt was distrusted by many and so his appointment as treasurer was a great mistake. More important were the diverse reactions to the French Revolution and resultant secessions.[21]

Nevertheless the RRA continued at the Rotunda, and political excitement grew in London at the growing support for reform revealed in the press, meetings in the country, and the general election in which the government was believed to have lost many seats. The excitement ebbed somewhat in September but revived with the Belgian Revolution, not only because this was universally popular but because there were widespread fears that Wellington would go to war to help the Dutch against the Belgians and the new French regime. The mysterious rick-burnings in the countryside increased the excitement. By the time Parliament assembled in

October the metropolis was very agitated indeed, and the King's speech was anxiously awaited. But when it came it seemed to deny the severity of the distress and set its face against Reform, arousing incredulity, alarm or fury. But the chief factor in the excitement was that war over Belgium now seemed certain and there were widespread plans to resist it by tax-refusal.[22] The first crisis of the Reform period had arrived.

Attention now focused on the intended visit of the King to the City on Lord Mayor's Day, 9 November. Great crowds were expected and there were fears of riots. The bitterness of sawyers and printers over machinery was noted, especially as in Paris the revolution had been followed by a wave of wage demands and attacks on machinery. The situation was made doubly serious by the great unpopularity of the new police. Radicals were making flags and preparing for the great day, handbills were stealthily circulating urging crowds to come and have it out with 'Peel's bloody gang', and Grady, now much more violent, was in constant touch with O'Connell and Hunt, made a secret visit to Paris and led a group in secret drilling. There was a general panic in London, and the Home Office received reports of plans to cut the gas-pipes, rip up street stones, fire the town and kill Wellington (the 'English Polignac') and Peel.

The Home Office saw the centre of sedition as the Rotunda, where the tricolour was regularly displayed, and Gale Jones was so impressed by the excitement that he came back out of retirement. He and Carlile urged crowds to gather on 9 November and demand from the King that his ministers be brought to trial, while Taylor warned the King to be careful lest he be served as Charley was. Cobbett lectured on Saturday 6 November to a full Rotunda, with a cheering crowd of 300 outside. On the Sunday Gast addressed 400 at Baume's chapel and a thousand attended the Rotunda, the universal topic being the royal visit. But late that day came the news that the visit had been cancelled, and the result was confusion and abuse of the ministers. The government was believed to be moving on to a new coercive course; 'a row was to be kicked up, to give occasion for tyrannical measures'. Carlile expressed the views of many in his expectations of a suspension of habeas corpus, bills against seditious libels and meetings, and massive repression, all of which they must resist. It was this intense suspicion of government and expectation of governmental violence, always shared by radicals at moments of political excitement, that increased the gravity of the crisis. The next day the RRA met under Hunt, with 2,000 inside the Rotunda, while Carpenter, Cleave and Hunter addressed the 3,000 outside, and later Hunt and Thompson spoke from the rails. The tone was of ferocity and fury, with hopes that the next day would be bloody, and though a guard had been placed to stop a mob going to Westminster Bridge, three hundred did go behind a tricolour over Blackfriars Bridge and clashed with police.

The next day, 9 November, groups of labourers came from Greenwich, Clapham and Brixton, crowds of countrymen armed with sticks crossing Blackfriars Bridge and Waterloo Bridge. Around 1,500 youths and workmen gathered in Hackney Road armed with bludgeons, and thousands gathered in the Strand, mostly East Enders especially half-famished Spitalfields weavers. London was witnessing the biggest crowds since 1821. There was a crowd outside Carlile's shop in Fleet Street, the windows of Wellington's Apsley House were broken, a crowd of several hundreds attacked the Watch House in Covent Garden, and in the evening a great crowd gathered outside the Rotunda, where Carlile and Taylor had a meeting, and a couple of thousand marched behind two tricolours into the City. The desired fights with the police came in the evening, with showers of stones.

The next day Cobbett did not lecture as planned, and it was widely believed that the reason was cowardice, so Taylor revived the Christian Evidence Society. But the rain caused the crowd to disperse quietly, though one group did start a fire. The next day was very wet indeed and only 400 went to Gale Jones' lecture. The emergency then passed with the fall of the Wellington government and its replacement by a coalition pledged to peace, retrenchment and reform (the first being equally as important as the others).[23]

But London's radical temper had been unmistakenly shown, and there were several focal points—the British Co-operators at Greville Street, Carpenter's shop off Fleet Street, Carlile's shop in Fleet Street, Baume's chapel and the Rotunda. At the last Carlile issued on 12 November a new periodical, the *Prompter*, to publicise proceedings there, and the pattern for the winter was established. On Sunday mornings and evenings Carlile and Taylor lectured on theology and astronomy; on Mondays the RRA had its meeting; on Tuesdays Carlile and Taylor gave republican lectures; on Wednesdays Taylor led discussions in the Christian Evidence Society; and on Thursdays Gale Jones and Taylor gave political lectures. But a more important development had taken place at Greville Street where Carpenter, having left the *Weekly Free Press* but wishing to continue radical and co-operative journalism, suggested to the group there that a cheap periodical be started by evading the fourpenny stamp on periodicals which had so restricted the sale of the *Weekly Free Press*. This should be done by giving each number a different title and thereby the fictitious appearance of being a separate publication and not part of a series; this would be furthered by issuing the numbers at irregular intervals. The group accepted the idea, and it was agreed that Hetherington, a small printer, using a machine owned by Lovett and with Savage's type, should issue a penny periodical, and Carpenter and Cleave a fourpenny one. And so, starting on 1 October, Hetherington in 53 days issued 28 unstamped papers, mostly addressed to individuals or groups, violent and extreme in tone, edited by a young radical lawyer Thomas Mayhew. Only a few shops dared to sell them, namely Carlile's, Hetherington's, Baume's (soon Watson's) and Strange's in Paternoster Row. But Watson sent thousands of Hetherington's papers to his extensive contacts in Yorkshire. For those willing to risk selling them the financial attraction was strong, for the penny papers were supplied to vendors at 3s. 6d. per 100, which offered a profit greater than that on most periodicals. The circulation seems to have reached several thousand, much greater than radical papers had had for many years. On 9 October began Carpenter's fourpenny papers, 34 appearing in 31 weeks, with an average circulation of 6,000. They had a radical and co-operative content, and were backed by the BAPCK. In December Hetherington re-entered the fray with his *Penny Papers for the People by the Poor Man's Guardian*, more obviously a periodical. Carlile's *Prompter* was also unstamped, with no pretence of not being a periodical, and Carlile's premises were used by Carpenter and by Riley, who began an unstamped periodical of his own.[24]

Most of these radical activities were separate and unco-ordinated. With the demise of the MPU the chief hope of unity lay in the RRA. This held in September a very successful meeting on Kennington Common in support of the French Revolution, and undeviatingly insisted on the full radical programme, refusing to welcome the new ministry. But early in November, no doubt influenced by his parliamentary ambitions, Hunt went out of his way to disclaim any connection with Carlile, Taylor and the Rotundanists, and at the RRA on 15 November he objected to the tricolour and denounced Carlile as a spy. The attacks on him from Carlile and Jones were predictable, but though several of the RRA agreed with Hunt, others, led by Lovett, Watson and Carpenter, greatly admired Carlile and regarded Hunt's action as indefensible. The RRA rapidly declined amidst these quarrels, Hunt's departure from

London and the lull in political excitement. Carlile's decision in December not to let them use the Rotunda any more was the death blow.[25]

When Hunt was elected for Preston in December, a public entry to London was arranged, but the Greville Street group opposed this and it went off at half-cock. As in 1822 the sawyers were prominent, but many trade societies were absent because of misleading placards.[26] And in Parliament Hunt was not the first or last people's champion to disappoint his followers.

Political meetings continued at the Rotunda and Baume's chapel, but by December attendance had declined at both. That month Carlile was indicted for an article in the *Prompter* encouraging the agricultural labourers in their revolt. Though his trial aroused great interest and Carlile went to prison again, exultant at the heaviest libel sentence in living memory, activity at the Rotunda rested mainly on Taylor. On Mondays he and Gale Jones now led political discussions, involving a small group. The star attraction was Gale Jones, and indeed several came specially to hear him and left after his speech. The overwhelming tone was Painite republicanism, and in March 1831 Hetherington began a second unstamped paper, the *Republican*, to report the meetings. But by May attendance had shrunk and in July Taylor was imprisoned for blasphemy. Three meetings were still held on Sundays to discuss Taylor's discourses, and their running was taken over by a sect of Deists meeting at the Borough chapel under the Southcottians Ward and Twort. But the Rotunda now had a debt of £160 and made a regular weekly loss of £5.[27]

The formation of the NUWC in April 1831 thus came at a very opportune time, when there was a medley of active radical groups but no real co-ordination. It therefore absorbed British Co-operators, Rotundanists, parish radicals, Irish, Deists and members of the late RRA to become in July *the* ultra-radical organisation in London. And so Gast, who early in 1831 had virtually dropped political activity and concentrated on Owenism, and who joined the new union for reasons that were not mainly political, soon found himself again involved at the heart of London ultra-radicalism.

In April the union moved to the Castle Street Assembly Room. It was joined by more Marylebone radicals, like John and James Savage and Dr Webb, and a few Rotundanists, like Osborne. It was also joined by William Benbow, now running a beer- and coffee-house which was a centre for debate and political discussion, and here were held the meetings of the union's committee, which any member could attend. The union received favourable publicity from Wakley in his paper *Ballot* and in Hetherington's *Poor Man's Guardian* (as his penny papers were now generally called). It was organised with a general committee, elected quarterly and meeting weekly, branch or district associations each with its own committee, and a weekly penny subscription.[28]

In March Russell had introduced the Reform Bill. This had long been expected, and the ultra-radicals had generally taken a consistent line that the Whigs were not real reformers, as the prosecution of Carlile and executions of argricultural rioters had further emphasised, and that their forthcoming 'moderate' Reform Bill, presumably on the lines of Russell's previous reform proposals, would fall far short of the full radical programme and so would be totally unsatisfactory. It was the standpoint dating from the post-war years. But the actual Bill was nothing like the moderate reform anticipated. It went so much further that it was difficult for radicals to oppose it. Even convinced democrats like Cobbett, Wakley, Carpenter, Carlile and Gale Jones warmly welcomed it, especially as they were confident that it could not be a final measure. The general view was that it was the best that could be hoped for and would lead to further reform. Even the five hundred at the Rotunda meeting welcomed it, a mere handful opposing it in the name of true radicalism (though these did include Taylor, Hibbert and Hetherington).[29] The parish radicals, including democrats like Savage and Murphy, supported the Bill, especially since in February 1831 Hobhouse had introduced a bill allowing for the formation of vestries elected by all ratepayers by secret ballot. It was recognised that the passing of the Reform Bill would guarantee that of the Vestries Bill. Similarly O'Connell and his followers welcomed it as the means of ending the power of the Orange corporations. And so the ultra-radical line was disrupted. Many of the trades held meetings in favour of the Bill, beginning with the carpenters and shipwrights.[30] But the agitation in London was mainly organised by the parish reform committees. Yet as the Bill began to meet with difficulties there were recurrent suspicions that the ministers would not persevere, and the real issue became whether it would be passed unmodified.

Hetherington, however, opposed the Bill from the start. It would make things no better but actually worse by adding middlemen and petty shopkeepers to the ranks of political privilege closed to working men. It would not be a 'first step'. But if it were rejected, a more radical reform might be secured later. Yet he failed dismally to convince the carpenters' meeting of this, and though his *Poor Man's*

Guardian reiterated his attitude it admitted it was labouring uphill
and that many old friends and supporters disagreed. He had an ally
in Hunt who stood out as the lone champion of the full radical
programme in Parliament. But Hunt had earlier disclaimed all
connection with the Rotundanists, after which Hetherington was
the only one of them who continued to have much to do with him.
And in the storm of mockery and abuse that now descended on
Hunt from radicals all over the country for his stance over the Bill,
Hetherington was virtually his only London supporter.[31]

But despite the disagreements, the NUWC was clearly an ultra-
radical body, and this was intensified by the accession of members
of the old RRA. In June its aims were declared, including universal
suffrage, annual parliaments, ballot and no property qualifications,
and these were frequently reasserted. This clearly set the union
apart from the number of other political unions being formed in
London, mainly in wards and parishes, for they had no such precise
aims beyond support for the Bill. The NUWC was characterised not
so much by *opposition* to the Bill as by the fact that it had other aims
and preoccupations, and in fact it often treated both Bill and elections with indifference.

In this union Hetherington steadily grew in stature, especially as
his *Poor Man's Guardian* became its organ. And this importance
was increased by prosecution. In May Carpenter was imprisoned for
publishing his unstamped periodical, submitted, ended his *Letters*,
and from prison edited a stamped monthly. Almost the last act of
the moribund BAPCK was to start a subscription for him. But
Hetherington disavowed Carpenter's defence (that he had not
really broken the law) and when in June he was himself prosecuted
for his *Guardian* and *Republican* he willingly asserted that he had
broken the law but that he was justified in doing so as it was
oppressive and he had had no say in choosing the legislature. His
Guardian was now turned into a periodical quite blatantly defying the
law. Four agents, including Lovett, organised systematic distribution, and destitute people with little to lose by imprisonment were
recruited to sell it in the streets. The NUWC naturally supported
Hetherington's campaign and helped circulate the *Guardian*.[32]

In July delegates came to London from Lancashire. Here, as in
London, nearly all radicals supported the bill, but there were,
especially in Manchester, some groups who agreed with Hunt's
opposition to it. These Huntites were nearly all handloom weavers
and their opposition, like that of Hunt, Hetherington, Hibbert,
Benbow or O'Brien, was not on the grounds of class antagonism and

conflicting interests of middle and working classes. It was in the name of full democracy and the full rights of man, the grounds of 1819. They recognised that the Bill would enfranchise the 'middle classes', and were bitter over the selfish and shortsighted readiness of these people to accept it and exclude the rest of 'the people', to compromise with corruption. But they did not see them as a class with interests opposed to their own. When the Bill ran into difficulties the editor of the *Voice of the People*, Doherty, who supported it, proposed a wave of simultaneous meetings in favour of universal suffrage, from each of which two delegates would go to London with petitions. His aim was to make sure that the Bill was retained, but it was the Huntites who took up the idea. Some meetings were held, and there came to London Brooks and Curran from Manchester, the Rev. Harrison from Stockport, Smedley from Macclesfield, and Meikle from Blackburn. These were very disappointed at the lack of support for Hunt in London, but through Hetherington and Benbow they made contact with NUWC, attended its meetings and tried to bring it over to support for Hunt.[33] The result of this pressure and of Hetherington's stature was that by July members of the union began to support Hunt's stance, and an alliance was formed. At one meeting:

> Gast, Osborne and Cleave were the principle speakers who in great abuse of the Government and the Reform Bill declared it to be nothing but a humbug to gull and would be of no use to the Working Classes without the Ballot and Universal Suffrage which was their just rights and which by uniting in one general union they were certain to obtain in spite of all systems of Government whether Whig or Tory.[34]

This was helped by Hunt's unwavering support for Hetherington, for the union was now fully behind the unstamped campaign and collecting funds to subsidise street vendors imprisoned for selling unstamped papers and to give them more papers to sell on their release. In July a committee was set up to collect subscriptions for Carpenter, including Watson, Benbow, Watkins, Gast, Lovett and Warden, with Saull as one of the two treasurers.[35]

But although Carlile had printed the NUWC's declaration and rules in his *Prompter*, he criticised its pretensions, and the Carlile–Taylor group remained aloof. Nevertheless several Rotundanists did join, the union collected subscriptions for Carlile and Taylor, and Carlile could not but praise the campaign for an untaxed press.[36] In July the Rotunda's finances led Carlile to offer it to the NUWC for its weekly meeting free of charge, with the proceeds of the entry charge (penny for members, twopence for non-members) going to him. And so from 27 July the NUWC held its main weekly meeting on Wednesday at the Rotunda, with an average attendance of 500. This led most of the Rotundanists and the Finsbury Spencean–Owenite group to join, especially as Gast and Osborne were already members. Moreover the BAPCK also finally ended and the NUWC absorbed some of its leading figures, such as Watson and Hibbert.

And so by July the new union had absorbed all the ultra-radical groups in London, and felt strong enough that month to hold a public open-air meeting with Wakley in the chair. Through the Lancashire delegates the NUWC felt it was participating in a national movement, a conviction heightened by the publication of its proceedings in the *Voice of the People*, the formation in August of a Manchester and Salford Union of the Working Classes, and by Hetherington's secret provincial tour in July to make arrangements to sell the *Guardian*, as a result of which and of press publicity its weekly sales were said to be 11,000.

The growth of the NUWC was reflected in the formation of branches. Two sections were formed in Bethnal Green at silk-weavers' houses of call under the leadership of Dean and Clements. A Westminster branch was formed by a group of Owenite radicals there who had combined in the Westminster Co-operative Society, educational activity and circulation of the unstamped.[37] The north-western branch covered Marylebone. The Finsbury branch centred on the group of Owenite co-operators and Spenceans led by Watson and Gast;[38] these were united not by residence, for Gast lived in Rotherhithe and Osborne in Southwark, but by ideology. Other branches made the London total up to sixteen by December, each with its own organisation, activities and meetings (the Rotunda ones were mainly for publicity).

In August another successful public meeting was held, to commemorate the July Revolution. Excitement in the NUWC was kept up by a number of issues—the unstamped struggle and imprisonments, Hunt's motions and speeches in Parliament, troop clashes with tithe rebels in Ireland, sympathy for the Poles. When in September Lovett refused to serve in the militia the union and *Guardian* took up his cause, and when his goods were seized for sale placards ensured that none of the chief brokers dared sell them. The enthusiasm and growth in the union were in marked contrast to the general decline in political interest and general weariness over the long debates over the second Reform Bill; one must not exaggerate the amount of excitement the Bill aroused before October. It had long been obvious that the Bill would pass the Commons, and the real question was 'What will the Lords do?' During the Bill's later stages in the Commons there had been few petitions in its favour from working people, and all the running seemed to be made by its opponents, Hunt and his supporters in the manufacturing districts, and Hetherington's papers.[39] The NUWC declared for the main radical points and for abolition of Corn Laws, Church of England and House of Lords, and called for a national convention. And in connection with such a convention Benbow began advocating a month's holiday, a general strike. The union was well poised to become of real significance in the next political crisis, in October—November.

In October the House of Lords rejected the Reform Bill. The reaction was staggering. Within two days there were more meetings in London than ever before. Hunt happened to be holding one at the Rotunda, and a crowd marched behind him to the City. The Marylebone radicals Savage, Potter, Warden and Webb held a very big meeting at Regent's Park, with Hume chairman, attended by working men from all over town. Burdett and Hobhouse had theirs at the Crown and Anchor. Thomas Bowyer and some others organised on 12 October a very successful procession in which 25,000 took part despite the wet morning, though it was followed by window-breaking. There were many other meetings, and placards appeared all over London singling out the bishops for particular attack and calling for their exclusion from the House of Lords and for confiscation of Church property, and urging refusals to pay tithes and church-rates.[40]

October was marked by tremendous excitement, and this opened the possibility of more extensive political reforms. Savage and his friends set the tone at their meeting with a clear message—if this Bill does not quickly pass we must get a better one; and to Hume's alarm he talked of a provisional government. Others, dismayed at the radical temper, desperately wanted the Bill passed to check something worse and feared that the ministers would back-track. All this intensified agitation, and there was the chance that the supporters of the Bill would split.

All this also benefited the NUWC, whose membership grew, and there now seemed to them to be a real chance of gaining universal suffrage. The fears of the replacement of the ministry by one under Wellington fanned excitement further. Speeches at the meetings of the union and at the separate Monday evening Rotunda political meetings grew more violent. They might soon, said Cleave, be called on to do their duty, and he urged a refusal of taxes should a Tory government return. A massive open-air meeting was planned for 7 November at White Conduit House under Wakley's chairmanship. John Doherty now came to London and associated with Benbow, and in his fury at the Lords' action dropped his support for the Bill and urged a campaign for universal suffrage through the device of simultaneous meetings. The committee approved, and a call went out to all provincial unions to hold meetings on 7 November.

Matters seemed to be reaching a crisis, especially with the news of destructive riots at Nottingham, Derby and Bristol and Benbow's savagely intemperate expressions of joy. And new bitterness was added when the NUWC, with its hopes that the widespread excitement would end in full radical reform, now saw the formation of a new union precisely to prevent this. Place persuaded a group of reformers to drop their suggestion of calling an illegal national conference of delegates in favour of the Bill, and instead to plan a union of workmen and employers on the Birmingham model. An inaugural open-air meeting was held at Lincoln's Inn Fields on 30 October under Burdett's chairmanship. It was preceded by a meeting at the Crown and Anchor at which the ultras Murphy and Wakley agreed to compromise over the full radical programme and to support the Bill, and at the open-air meeting Savage and Detrosier also appealed for a united front. It was a blow to the hopes of the NUWC, and Lovett came and made a brilliant speech to propose an amendment in favour of universal suffrage. But Cleave, seconding it, was shouted down and it was lost. Wakley then came forward to propose that half of the council be working men, and to Place's annoyance this was easily carried. But Place carefully contacted working men he trusted, got a large number to join and gained candidates for the council whom he considered suitable, including William Wallis and several of the old BAPCK such as Styles, Millard, Lawrence and M'Diarmid. These were all elected, but only Lovett, Savage and Wakley were successful from the NUWC, for few from that union or from the Rotunda had joined. Though many middle-class reformers had been frightened off by the Rotundanists, a large number of artisans joined.[41]

This rivalry and antagonism occurred in the middle of massive excitement. The ultra-radicals were aroused by the excitement and by clashes with the police on 12 October, the passage of a Bill legalising man-traps and spring-guns against poachers, the provincial riots and the rival union. Many other people were alarmed at the riots and the speeches at the Rotunda and there was a new panic over the imminence of a frightful convulsion and attacks on property. There was widespread advocacy of a householders' National Guard to protect property. In opposition Hibbert and Hetherington urged popular arming, and Carlile published a booklet by Macerone giving instructions on street-fighting against troops. The NUWC publicised it, while Benbow was selling staves to be taken to the 7 November meeting, on which all eyes were now turned. The Home Secretary, Melbourne, thereupon banned it. A special meeting of delegates of the branch unions decided to submit and called it off, and though a few hundred did meet on 7 November at the Rotunda with staves, and some even went to the meeting place, all the branches endorsed the decision to cancel, as did most speakers at the general meeting the following week.

Excitement nevertheless continued throughout November, the National Political Union (NPU) formed branches, Lovett and Hibbert called on the people to arm and Watson displayed his Macerone spear. In Manchester the Huntite leaders Curran, Broadhurst and Ashmore were planning simultaneous meetings and a national convention, in both of which they were supported by the Huddersfield Political Union. When on 21 November a royal proclamation forbade branch unions, the NPU's branches became separate unions, while the NUWC abolished its branches and merged them all into a single union, with weekly meetings at its main centres—Rotunda, Watson's chapel, and the Blind Beggars in Bethnal Green. But before this Benbow's suggestion of grouping the members into classes was adopted. Classes were to contain 25, and have a class-leader appointed by the general committee who was to hold fortnightly class discussions, collect the subscription (which had gone up to twopence) and each fortnight attend the committee meeting. These classes became the basis of the union and some, like Lovett's and Watson's, took the work of political education very seriously. Yet in December the NUWC was in decline. This was mainly because with the news that Parliament was called for 6 December instead of February and that the Bill would be reintroduced, the agitation subsided and political calm returned. Numbers at the NUWC's Rotunda meetings were back at 300–500 and it was in debt. The rival union was also a blow, for several members, such as Styles, seem to have gone over to it, and its members were mostly artisans. In December the Rotundanists Dias Santos, Augero and Grady failed dismally with a motion for universal suffrage, while in the elections to the new council in January,

Lovett, Augero, Watkins, Grady, Dias Santos, Carpenter, Cleave and Fall all stood, but only Carpenter was successful.

To make matters worse, the NUWC leadership was split by disagreements. Probably all of them were 'revolutionary' in the sense of wishing for the total overthrow of the political system, believing that the chance of doing this was near at hand, and being ready to use force if needed. But, as in the post-war period, most radicals thought in terms of a continual increase in activity until there was a mass movement confronting the authorities. The people would then be irresistible. They thought in terms of ultimate confrontation, but not of provoking violence. Any violence would come from the authorities and, in their intense suspicion of attack from them, they urged arming in self-defence, Watson, Cleave, Lovett and Hibbert doing so as much as anyone. But the essential thing was to mobilise and not provoke a clash before this occurred, and here disagreements arose. Cleave was reluctant in July to hold public meetings as he did not think public support was assured.[42] By October such doubts had gone, and the essential thing was to hold a large meeting and avoid its being banned. And so they issued a declaration on 10 October that all property acquired honestly or legally (however unjustly) was sacred, and disclaiming any intention of chaos. When Melbourne banned it all the same they tried to change his mind by offering to be sworn in as special constables. When this did not move him they were not prepared to ignore the ban and thus provoke a clash. As Place saw, they did not think the people were yet mobilised.[43] The main opponents of this group were the Irish Owenite Mansell, Dias Santos, the publisher George Edmonds, George Petrie, and above all William Benbow, whose praise of the Bristol riots had gained such notoriety. These men were more reckless, and the 10 October declaration was a manoeuvre against them. Mansell, Edmonds and Benbow all condemned the decision to postpone the 7 November meeting. All agreed on the class system (Benbow wanted ex-soldiers as class-leaders), but when on 23 November Benbow proposed to the committee his plan whereby everyone should accumulate provisions for a week, go on strike for a month, elect a national convention and requisition food, it was opposed by Hibbert, Cleave and Watson as a 'mad plan' and withdrawn.

Another issue dividing the leadership was Owenism, which again set Benbow against Lovett. With the decline of the NUWC at the end of 1831, Hibbert, Watson, Lovett and Cleave were trying to win more support for Owenism, and Watson particularly became a very prominent speaker at the Rotunda meetings as well as those at his chapel. But Benbow led a group who had nothing but contempt for Owenism, and this increased the tension.

Early in 1832 developments seemed to favour Benbow. There were very strong feelings indeed over the death sentences on the Bristol and Nottingham rioters, and Lovett himself became very violent. At one stormy meeting at the Rotunda, despite Hibbert's appeals from the chair for moderation, there were rows about the newly-released Carpenter's capitulation over publishing illegal unstamped papers and about the Bristol executions. Hibbert thereupon resigned both from the committee and as treasurer of the NUWC, and with James Savage and the Irish tailor Duffey formed a new group meeting at the Castle Street rooms. But while Cleave, Watson and Cooper were also considering resigning, Hibbert was replaced as treasurer by Benbow's henchman, the jeweller David Watkins. A memorial to the King was signed by 1,270 protesting against the executions, and a large number marched behind the deputation headed by Benbow which saw Melbourne about it. In January Benbow also published his plan for a 'grand national holiday' as a pamphlet, and interest was intense. He expounded the plan at two packed meetings at Watson's chapel, and though at the first 'Gast though admitting the "Soundness" of the plan thought it was at present Impractible', and at the second, 'Gast, Edwards, Merrick, Selby and Thompson spoke at length on his plan which was admitted and carried as a good one, but at present Impractable', the plan did arouse great enthusiasm, the pamphlet rapidly sold out and a second edition appeared.

In January Eliza Sharples, who had come to London as a disciple of Carlile's and was soon pregnant by him and became his common-law wife, began a new periodical, the *Isis*, on Carlile's and Taylor's behalf and took over the Rotunda for moral and religious meetings, Hibbert and Gale Jones still being constant attenders. The NUWC was no longer able to hold its meetings there, and for a while Watson's chapel was its chief meeting-place. In February Benbow's dishonesty caught up with him again, he went bankrupt and lost his coffee-shop. But secretly he managed to move his stock to premises in Theobalds Road taken by his friend Hutchinson. Here they opened an 'Institution of the Working Classes' which became the main meeting-place of the NUWC (and by drawing attendances away from Watson's chapel it increased tensions).[44] Benbow's importance was thereby intensified, and his group also began a new co-operative society there, anti-Owenite and therefore against the

Lovett group. Its storekeeper, Osborne, was also secretary of the NUWC.

The NUWC meanwhile tried to extend its activities. Weekly meetings were now held at Stepney, Shoreditch, Hampstead, Hammersmith and Camberwell. In 1831 Gast had occasionally spoken at Rotunda meetings, but his main activity was at Watson's chapel 'in his usual strain of abuse of Aristocracy'.[45] In February 1832 it was he and Watson who led the procession of Finsbury members to the general meeting at Saville House against the sentences at Bristol, Nottingham and Manchester. But he was also rallying his acquaintances in Bermondsey and Rotherhithe in support of the NUWC, and in February weekly meetings began there. But they finished in April, presumably through lack of support, and Gast then returned to Watson's chapel, with occasional appearances in Southwark.

By February cholera was spreading fast and the NUWC was thrown back into united activity by proposals for a day of fasting to appease the Almighty's wrath. Members were ready to hold public, open-air meetings on such a day. By March tension was clearly rising with the cholera, an intensification of the tithe war in Ireland and use of troops to coerce it, and the resultant inevitable fears of military rule at home. Many members had now got arms, and a group were doing sword exercises in the Minories. The general fast came at a critical time, and the union was able to hold the most sucessful of all its demonstrations when it was estimated that 100,000 marched behind Lovett and the newly released Hetherington. But though some had hoped for trouble the crowd remained peaceable, despite having their intended route repeatedly blocked by the police (though at one point a group led by Benbow did force their way through a police cordon). Afterwards they held a number of public dinners, taking advantage of the fact that meat was cheaper that day. Several were arrested, and Lovett, Watson and Benbow were charged, along with some people who had no connection with the NUWC, with conspiracy to cause disorder. Their acquittal in May completed the triumph.

But by now a new crisis had arrived, for the third Reform Bill was in the Lords. There was exultation when it passed the second reading, but fury when it was then held up, the ministry resigned and Wellington tried to take over. There was a flood of parish meetings, the membership of the NPU shot up, and Murphy, Rogers, Wakley and Carpenter were exceeded by none in their vehemence denouncing Whigs and King and talking of more radical Reform. There was unprecedented agitation, placards appeared all over London, and men began to refuse taxes, withdraw money from banks and savings banks, convert bank notes into gold, and hoard food. Place and his friends secured the rejection in the council of a plan for a monster meeting on Hampstead Heath, but the meetings of the NPU were huge, delegates came from Birmingham, legality was thrown to the winds, there were ideas of resisting the troops, and the union organised a run on gold. To many it seemed a revolution was very near.

The NUWC similarly had a great accession of members. There was an attendance of 2,000 at Theobalds Road, Hetherington had in April reprinted Macerone's pamphlet in his *Guardian*, speeches became very violent, and there were fears of military rule under Wellington, with rumours that Austrian and Prussian troops were coming and that the aristocracy were sending their possessions abroad. The Hibbert–Savage section now rejoined the main body, the union supported refusal of taxes, tithes and rents, while Cooper and Benbow kept pressing the committee to adopt a resolution in favour of a national convention. The bill now appeared totally irrelevant, especially as it seemed likely to be dropped, and the real issue was radical Reform. An armed clash was apparently inevitable, and Benbow, Cooper, Watson and Lovett led the arming, but the NUWC's policy was to avoid *provoking* a clash and instead wait on events, but at the same time to support the NPU's campaign of refusal of taxes, withdrawals from savings banks and the run on gold. Some of the more vehement members of the NPU, like Rogers and Carpenter, now took part at meetings at Theobalds Road, as there was something of a united campaign.

But when Wellington failed to form a government and the King sent for Grey, the vast meetings and the run on gold ceased, and when the Bill passed the Lords the crisis was over. For the members of the NUWC the outcome was a great disappointment, for they had been hoping for much more radical reform. Cleave expressed their feelings when he said that the Bill itself had not been their concern; it was 'the production and the idol of the enemies of the working classes', and the 'war between labour and property had commenced'.[46] This, of course, was because one of the declared aims of the Bill had always been to enfranchise the 'middle classes', men of a certain amount of property. These had now joined the ranks of 'privilege', leaving the excluded 'people' much more clearly the working men. Thus the 'people' became synonymous with workmen, while the greatest amount of radical bitterness was directed not so much at the aristocracy as those middle classes who had betrayed them and gone over to the other side. The lesson of this betrayal was that any movement to secure radical reform must be based primarily on the workmen. The post-Reform period was thus marked by radical attacks on the middle classes, or 'shopocrats', a word beautifully combining the odium attached to aristocracy with a criticism, not of the middle classes' economic interests, but of their political behaviour. Cleave had enunciated a war, not between labour and capital, but between labour and property.

In June the NUWC did adopt the resolution in favour of a national convention, and the excited discussions were a sign of how far members were aroused. But this was unrealistic, for with the Bill's passage political excitement and activity slumped. There were then in the following months efforts to elect radical MPs and make candidates agree to a list of pledges, but Savage and Murphy were not elected in Marylebone and Wakley failed in Finsbury. The parish unions ended, and the NPU shrank.[47] But Hobhouse's Vestry Act was immediately adopted in Marylebone and St Pancras, and the radical groups led by Savage and Murphy captured control, reduced corruption and expenditure, and conducted a running battle with the churches. Radical politics tended to concentrate on parishes rather than national issues, though in 1833 several ish groups united in a violent campaign against the assessed es.[48]

he NUWC was the exception in this general decline, for though crisis had gone, it extended its activities. In July Hunt chaired a ge meeting on military flogging, and in August the July Revolution was again celebrated. The number of weekly meetings grew to thirteen and in October the number of classes was still over 70. In March 1833 Gast again arranged meetings in Bermondsey. What happened was that as the other unions disappeared, it absorbed a few members from each of them to become again *the* radical union. Thus the surgeon Webb, Gale Jones and Edmund Stallwood became active members. In October, Hetherington, Cleave and Mee went to the Midlands and in alliance with Wade, Hunt and delegates from Lancashire, Yorkshire and Derby and in opposition to the Attwoodites formed unions in Birmingham, Walsall and Northampton. In July there were complaints from the Bethnal Green members that their meetings were never reported in the *Poor Man's Guardian* and they advocated local committees instead of a single central one at Theobalds Road. The result was a break-away Tower Hamlets Union of the Working Classes, but at the same time there was in London an active Irish Anti-Union Association which included many members or ex-members of the NUWC, like Lawless, Berthold and Duffey. Led by the Irishmen Cleave, Osborne and Mansell the NUWC now arranged a fusion and added Repeal to its aims, indeed for the whole of September Repeal was the topic for discussion. Though many members disliked this alliance and preoccupation, it did bring an important accession of strength. At the end of 1832 Cleave and Watson took over the *Republican* and turned it into the *Working Man's Friend* to report some of the other meetings of the NUWC and to campaign for Repeal. Then in April 1833 the Tower Hamlets Union rejoined.

But factions in the committee continued. The Benbow group, including Watkins, Petrie, Cooper and Hutchinson, were opposed by the group, mostly Owenites, led by Lovett, Watson, Cleave and Preston. Plans were made to defeat the Benbow group in the June 1832 quarterly elections to this committee (now to be fifty in number as the union had grown), and so Watson and Hetherington stood. But the plan failed, and Lovett and Watson soon quarrelled with Benbow over his dishonest claims for expenses at the late trial and resigned from the committee. Benbow now seemed supreme, with his Institution the headquarters of the NUWC, and a branch of his thriving co-operative society there opened at his 'Temple of Liberty' at King's Cross. In both places his wife led a fifty-strong radical female society. The Theobalds Road Institution also had regular lectures and discussions, often of a religious character. The officers of the union were Benbow's men; in July he began his own periodical, the monthly *Tribune of the People*, and he had Irish contacts through Duffey, the most vehement of all critics of Owenism.

But in October the *Tribune* ended when Benbow quarrelled with his young printer, Richard Lee.[49] That month the accounts of Osborne and Watkins were both found to be in a mess and in arrears, and both were eventually dismissed by the NUWC. Osborne was also in arrears at the co-operative society which broke up in December in quarrels, Benbow's leadership being overthrown by Lee, with whom Petrie was now allied. That month Duffey's attacks on the NUWC's committee had become so intransigent that Hetherington and Petrie secured his expulsion from the union. In March 1833 the union ceased meeting at Benbow's Institution and went back to the Rotunda. Benbow now founded a Republican Association and when Taylor was released from prison and quarrelled with Carlile he lectured at the Institution and Benbow became his publisher. James Smith was also drawn to this centre of religious radicalism. But in December 1833 Benbow quarrelled with his partner and lost the premises, and in 1834 was facing ruin.[50]

The new treasurer of the NUWC in January 1833 was Watson, but when he was imprisoned in March for selling the *Poor Man's Guardian* Neesom took over. With Hetherington again in prison and Lovett concentrating on his class and the Victim Fund which financed the unstamped campaign, the dominant figure in the union was Cleave, tireless in attendance at weekly meetings all over town as well as organiser of the actual payment of unstamped victims. In recognition of his dominance Carlile called the Union 'Cleave's club'.[51] The other chief figures were Spenceans or near-Spenceans —Neesom, Mee, Lee, Petrie and Bailey, all Finsbury men except Lee, whose area was south of the river.

In the early part of 1833, though there was a decline in the NUWC's membership, the large Irish contingent was very excited over the tithe war and attendant repression. Language became wilder, and the two meetings at Theobalds Road on 24 and 25 February were so violent and seditious that the government decided to prosecute.[52] The fury reached its height in March, with the government's Irish Coercion Bill and more fears of military rule and rumours of German troops. Meetings of the union were addressed by prominent Irish politicians like Murphy and several MPs, including Feargus O'Connor and O'Connell, whose denunciations of the 'base, bloody and brutal Whigs' knew no bounds. It was now that firebrands like the young Yearly brandished pistols, that one of the union's leaders south of the river, John Simpson, formed an armed group in Camberwell, and that a stormy open-air meeting advocated a run on gold and other tactics of 1832. Lee, Petrie, George, Yearly and Simpson secured the adoption of a resolution in favour of the traditional revolutionary expedient, a national convention. A public meeting was fixed for 13 May to 'take preparatory steps' for carrying this into effect. The sub-committee to organise it did not include Cleave, who disapproved, and consisted of Petrie, Lee, Mee, Bailey, Yearly, Preston and Plummer. The resolutions they prepared not surprisingly contained a condemnation of private ownership of land, but they did not include any mention of a convention. Petrie's proposal to attack the Bank and the Tower was opposed and Mee was chosen as chairman, whereupon Petrie withdrew, followed by Bailey. A few thousand did go to the meeting, despite placards banning it which, being unsigned, were regarded by many as a hoax. But the crowd was brutally dispersed by the police, in the course of which two policemen were killed. In the very great

bitterness that resulted, Bailey, Preston and Gast addressed an
angry meeting at the Borough Chapel and it was agreed that at any
future open-air meetings they should carry the tools of their trade
(this tactic was followed in the great trade union procession the
following year). The attack also raised a storm of liberal protest, the
jury returned a verdict of 'justifiable homicide' at the inquest on one
of the policemen, and the prosecution of a member of the NUWC
for the murder of the other one failed. This was followed by the
moral victory of Cobbett's brilliant exposure of the police *agent
provocateur* Popay.

Nevertheless the attack was a blow from which the NUWC never
recovered. By July apathy was obvious and unity was collapsing
with the appearance of separate unions in Wandsworth, Kensington, Hammersmith and Chiswick, and south of the river. In August
there was a sudden drop in membership and subscriptions, so that
they could barely pay the secretary's salary, and public meetings
were suspended for several consecutive weeks while a conference
discussed the state of the union. This blow to continuity was fatal,
and henceforth only one meeting was held each week. Membership
continued to fall, especially as many were preoccupied with trade
union activity. But several isolated classes continued, and the union
lingered on until November 1835, holding the occasional public
meeting, usually on the stamp duty.

The odd public meeting on a specific issue, and regular discussion
meetings—these were by now the chief elements in Gast's activity.
When Watson had lost his chapel in October 1832 the NUWC class
leaders who had used it, led by Neesom, found in December an old,
cold and wet cellar cow-shed near St Luke's burial ground. This they
opened as the 'Finsbury Forum' for NUWC meetings and anti-
Christian lectures. The leaders here were the same group of Spenceans, Owenites and freethinkers. But in April 1833 they left it for
the Bowling Square Chapel in Lower White Cross Street.[53] NUWC
meetings were also held at a 'Mechanics Forum' in Brighton Street.
But Gast had been speaking at both religious and NUWC meetings
at the Borough Chapel from June 1832 (except for the brief series
of Bermondsey meetings in March 1833) until the regular weekly
meetings of the union ended in August 1833. Thereafter although
he still spoke at occasional meetings at the Borough Chapel, he
went back to his original group now using the Bowling Square
Chapel. Here they also formed a Society for Scientific, Useful and
Literary Information, with lectures by Mee, Bailey, Neesom,
Davenport, Gast, the two Marylebone ex-Freethinking Christians

Savage and Potter, and others, on such subjects as the blessings of monarchy, Christianity, religion, machinery, astronomy, twilight, music, elocution and articulation:

> I myself belong to an institution in town Which give Lectures every Sunday Evening, and some times in the Week, and we have a good attendance, we are all Working men that Lecture, and it sometimes comes to my turn four or five times in the Quarter, and I can assure you that Drunkards and Drunkenness come in for a very great share of our Reproof.[54]

The occasional public meeting on a specific issue, and regular discussion meetings—these were also characteristic of London radicalism generally. With the end of political excitement and of hopes of immediate achievements, radicals confined themselves to trying to keep up some contacts and solidarity and to discussing political questions. One expedient was exclusive dealing, begun by Simpson's class, no. 91, in Camberwell, and Bailey's, no. 42, at the United Trades' Coffee Rooms in Bunhill Row.[55] This was presumably mainly an exchange of services, a form of co-operation and solidarity. A bricklayer, Peck, advertised that he would do bricklaying work for any members of the NUWC.[56] At the Bowling Square Chapel met a new hundred-strong co-operative society to establish exclusive dealing and a fund for sickness and old-age relief.[57] But far more numerous were discussion and educational groups, such as the one to which Gast belonged. This had always existed to some extent, even at the height of the Reform crisis, in the NUWC's classes or in the reading-room at the Halifax Arms in Mile End. But now they were relatively more important. The Borough Chapel had lectures on arts and sciences, at the Castle Street rooms a Society for the Acquisition of Useful Knowledge had political and religious discussions,[58] the Mechanics' Forum opened a Sunday School in August 1833,[59] while at his home in St George's in the East, Thomas Heins, member of the NUWC, had a library, newsroom and a Society for Promoting Free Enquiry for discussions and 'improvement in political, theological, and philosophical knowledge'.[60] In March 1833 the Westminster Owenite group—Farren, Hassell, Huggett and Glanville—began a Westminster Society for the Diffusion of *really* Useful Knowledge, at whose Rational School and General Scientific Institution lectured Smith, Carlile and, above all, Detrosier.[61] In 1834 Watson opened his Mechanics' Hall of Science in the City Road.[62] And there were several others.[63]

Educational activity was not just a second-best to political action. We have already seen the artisans' great interest in education, and how it was an integral part of radicalism to emphasise education as a means to reform. But the Westminster Society was an example of the growing sense that many forms of knowledge were inappropriate. It must be knowledge of men's rights and importance in society, and their title distinguished their knowledge from the kind offered in mechanics' institutions, the Society for the Diffusion of Useful Knowledge and its *Penny Magazine*; 'the *Penny Magazine*—', wrote O'Brien, 'what does it teach?—the nature of bats, beetles, butterflies, kangaroos, dromedaries'.[64] We also have seen in Gast, Lovett and Hetherington the tendency of men who had improved themselves to condemn their fellows' 'wasteful' and 'vicious' habits. Though at times they would blame such evils on poverty and injustice, there was certainly a tendency, most clearly in periods of a movement's decline, to blame the artisans for their shortcomings. In 1828 Gast ascribed

> all the woes of the country to that iniquitous system which prevails in election of members of Parliament, which will, he fears, go on so long as the labouring classes take more delight in boxing, bull-baiting, cockfighting and other descriptions of senseless and brutal amusement, than in the preservation of their own interests and the extension of the liberties of the country.[65]

The NUWC blamed its decline on the 'dissipated habits of the people'.[66] It was a common reaction to conclude that the people had not yet attained the moral and educational level to achieve reform and to concentrate on efforts to remedy this situation. Gast had expressed such an attitude in the failure of his attempts at general union in the late 1820s, and Lovett's relapse into educational activity after 1840 is the best-known example. But Lovett did the same in the 1830s. In 1832 on his withdrawal from the committee of the NUWC in response to Benbow's popularity, and with the final ending of the First London Co-operative Trading Association, Lovett took over its premises in Greville Street and for two years ran it as a coffee-house and discussion centre. It was a congenial activity and he later looked back on these years as among the happiest in his life. Here also was formed a society of 'Social Reformers', led by Lovett, Foskett and Styles. The new group was a reaction to the failure of both co-operative trading and radical agitation, in which all three had been involved. The Social Reformers were a purely educational body who had concluded that social change was a long way off and that the public must be prepared for it. They therefore sought to disseminate knowledge of general science, the powers of production, the resources of society and the laws of nature, and drew up a plan for a self-supporting school to help train the minds of the rising generation.[67] It was the trade union expansion of 1834 that brought some of them, notably Styles, out of purely intellectual activity.

The decline of the NUWC seems comparable to other periods of radical decline, confined as it was to isolated meetings, educational activity, journalism and some rather isolated underground activity (late in 1834 Cleave and Benbow went to Manchester, Macclesfield and Yorkshire for secret meetings to revive some sort of union).[68] But it was crucially distinctive that in this case journalism meant the unstamped, and an important part of the activity of the discussion groups was its circulation. The unstamped and its persecution certainly reinforced the belief in the role of education in effecting change, that knowledge was power, but it also provided a focus and coordinating element for the scattered groups. Most of the public meetings were on the stamp duty. Lovett's activities in the service of education included managing the Victim Fund which financed the illegal campaign, and writing superb articles in Hetherington's illegal *Twopenny Dispatch*.[68] The Westminster educationalists Hassell, Huggett and Hattersley distributed the unstamped, while Heins was imprisoned in 1835 for being the main agent in his area. Many radicals, like Neesom and Stallwood, became newsagents specifically to help the unstamped and so developed an interconnected network over London as the basis for any future radical movements. While political unions languished, Hetherington's and Cleaves' twopennies both had a weekly sale of over 20,000. The NUWC, said Cleave, might be said to have emanated from the unstamped.[70] But the unstamped outlived it. While the intensity of the Reform crisis was crucial in deepening and extending radicalism, and the NUWC made the reputation of many later London Chartists (Giles Lovett, Simpson, Stallwood, Thomas Wall, Henry Ross, Neesom, George Harney), the unstamped preserved and developed this radical opinion, nourished a groundwork of newsagents and coffee-house keepers, and maintained the contacts and sense of participation in a common movement which were essential to Chartism.

15
TRADE UNIONISM AND RADICALISM

Although the Reform Bill gave political reform priority at some times in the early 1830s, trade unionism was just as important, culminating in 1834 in the Consolidated Trades' Union (CTU). And many of the characteristics and preoccupations of that year persisted in those that followed.

The three London trades taking the lead in these trade union developments were, predictably, the carpenters, tailors and shoemakers, all suffering as they were in acute form from the familiar problems of competition between masters and between workers in a situation of labour surplus and developing capitalism, with the inevitable results of lower earnings, longer hours, and greater intensity of work. They saw chances of redress in the economic revival which began in 1833. Their remedies were the usual ones which Gast had enunciated, including projects of general unionism. But, faced with the mounting tide of unskilled labour, they went on to make efforts to unionise unskilled, non-society men and even women. The two general themes in this trade unionism were thus attempts at general union *and* efforts to extend unionisation.

In the months September to November the Grand Lodge of Operative Tailors of London was founded.[1] Their aims were clearly related to the problems of their trade. All tailors must be united in a single, unexclusive association; all work must be done on proper employers' premises, and homework should be abolished; hours must be limited so as to share work; piece-work, which led to overwork, must be ended; the day-rate must be fixed. In this way greater regularity of employment and earnings would be secured. A proper amount of work would be guaranteed by the traditional daily stint. Older and inferior hands would not be able to achieve this, and they could be paid at a lower rate, but only with the permission in every case of the union's 'board of controul'. It was essential that these demands be put to the masters at the start of the brisk season, when the men were at their strongest, and so, despite the committee's doubts, they were presented in April 1834.

> The present is just the season for a strike, because summer is near, and people will require new clothes to be in keeping with the gaiety of the season.
>   Masters as well as men knew if the strike had not taken place in May it could not be in June; therefore the trade would have been in suspense for a twelvemonth longer.[2]

But most masters refused, and one replied:

> SIR—I hope the Government will now interfere, and transport one-half of *you* blasted thieves, which I think will very shortly take place. If I was on the jury, I should wish it to be done, and promote the sentence.[3]

The tailors' strike was the largest and most dramatic of the considerable number that occurred in that year. But in fact their resources were not adequate to support it and despite recourse to the traditional expedient of co-operative production it was totally defeated amidst great suffering, bitterness and the employers' use of the 'document' (obliging employees to declare against union membership) to smash trade unionism.

The shoemakers had the same problems of the growth of chamber-masters and the surplus of labour. There seem also to have been some changes in style which meant more work per pair of shoes and therefore lower earnings. But we are much worse informed on the shoemakers than on the tailors. There were several shoemakers' societies in the United Trades' Association, and in October 1833 there were meetings of the whole trade to discuss labour exchanges. A Grand Lodge of Operative Cordwainers was formed in December 1833 with William Hoare as Grand Master.[4]

The building workers' grievances were common to many towns, and a general Builders' Union was formed in 1832 uniting the different trades and also organising the unskilled builders' labourers. It was joined by the General Union of Carpenters (FSOC), which grew rapidly in London in 1833 and took the lead in the London Builders' Committee. In May 1834 it issued its demands, the chief ones being the restoration of the day-rate to 5s.; the abolition of task-work; the abolition of sub-letting; and the ending of overtime. Thus competitive wage-cutting, overwork and unemployment would be reduced.[5]

Many trades tried to make good the losses of previous years. In 1833 there were strikes in individual firms by plasterers and bricklayers, the sawyers struck in 1833 and 1834, the hatters in 1834. In 1834 the coopers, in response to technical changes which meant that each barrel needed more labour, struck over hours and payment. There was activity among hitherto unorganised groups, with strikes by gasworkers, washerwomen and stove-makers, and new unions formed among gasworkers, bakers, and female groups like garment-dyers, straw-plaiters, sewers, bleachers and blockers, Tuscany and Leghorn bleachers, pressers and dyers, and bonnet-makers. Co-operative production in relation to unemployment and strikes spread. Several trade unions attended the London co-operative congress in October 1833 where Owen, fresh from his alliance with the Builders' Union and Fielden's Regeneration Society, launched his Grand National Moral Union. The Builders' Union, Leeds Clothiers' Union and the Bradford Order extended ideas of general union. Warden led the formation of a lodge of saddlers and harness-makers as part of a union with lodges in Birmingham and Walsall. The lock-out of the Derby silk-weavers in 1833–4 aroused sympathy and support equal to those given in 1818 to the cotton-spinners and in 1825 to the wool-combers. Committees collected money in several towns which went to help the Derby men set up their own business, some of whose products were sold at Owen's labour exchange. The Derby agitation gave an impetus to the moves towards unity.[6]

All these developments came together in the Consolidated Union (CTU). The London tailors, conscious of their weakness and knowing their effort must come at the start of the brisk season in April, took the lead in calling and managing the London conference of February 1834. The basis of this conference was the Derby committees; the delegates went through the Derby accounts and the new union ordered a shilling levy for the Derby and Worcester strikers. The United Trades' Association suspended its sittings during the conference, and some of its prominent members, like Hoare, Pryer the tailor, and Norman the chair-maker became leaders in the new union. The four chief aims of the CTU identified basic artisan preoccupations—mutual support in strikes; sick and superannuation benefits; employment of members on strike; employment of out-of-work members. It included twenty-nine London artisan trades, including the familiar distressed tailors, shoemakers, silk-weavers, silk-dyers, cabinet-makers, sawyers and ropemakers. It supported co-operative trading, which was intertwined with exclusive dealing, of which there were several attempts in 1833. The executive urged the use of funds to set up stores or to employ

butchers, bakers, cheesemongers and grocers as agents to buy in
bulk and sell, with a fair commission, at shops the unions would
use.[7] It sought to organise women workers and unorganised men,
and contained lodges of gardeners (formed by Stallwood), coal-
whippers, bakers, female shoebinders, two female lodges, and three
'miscellaneous lodges' of shopmen, grocers, porters and clerks.
Hostility to employers did not entail hostility to shopkeepers, dealers, professional men and others of the 'middle classes' nor did
exclusive dealing mean hostility to shopkeepers. Davenport wanted
an alliance:

> the middle and lower classes of shopkeepers are as much dissatisfied
> with the government as the working people are; and it is with these
> classes that the working classes would do well to form an alliance . . . The
> plan by which I propose to form alliance between the working classes
> and the lower class of shopkeepers or middlemen, is exclusive dealing.[8]

There were Owenite dealers, like Murphy and Savage, and the
former urged that:

> It was for the middle classes, as they were called, to feel that they were
> deeply interested, as they were, in the question; it was for them to feel
> that their interests were identified with those of the working classes; . . .
> but if they, with one honest and determined voice, united, the labourer
> and the middle man would assume his consequence in society, and the
> capitalist, in his turn, be lorded over by him.[9]

Large meetings of shopkeepers supported the builders in their
strike in August and September 1834.

The new union thus enveloped a host of familiar tendencies. It
was the most important development in the general atmosphere of
confrontation which permeated the early part of 1834, nourished by
a flurry of strikes in February and March, the near-universal press
condemnation of trades unionism, and the masters' use of the
document. The feeling was heightened by the conviction that government and employers were leagued against the trade unions,[10] a
belief amply confirmed by the events of the disputes of the Derby
weavers and London coopers. The Dorchester sentence on the
Tolpuddle labourers in March further solidified trade union solidarity and involved radicals in a joint campaign which culminated in the
great procession on 21 April when 40,000 unionists marched.
Excitement reached a peak, and men like Morrison and the coopers' leader Abraham wanted simultaneous meetings, a general
strike and a national convention. *The Times* was particularly violent
against trades unionism, rejoicing in the defeat of the Derby men
and urging the master tailors to defeat their strike by importing

German men and women. The unionists held several funerals of deceased members, attended by large numbers from many trades, sometimes to the extent of 20,000. They were very impressive demonstrations of moral solidarity, and evaded the law against demonstrations on Sundays. On 28 April the House of Lords debated this 'intimidation' and the Lord Chancellor, Brougham, took the opportunity to deliver a very strong attack on the unions.

> I am an enemy to them, my Lords, simply and only because I think they are the worst nuisances of the country, although not so bad for the country generally, as for the members of the trades' unions themselves.[11]

By now the master carpenters had decided to support the master tailors by not giving any orders for tailoring work until the strike was ended. In May the brewery firm of Coombe, Delafield and Co. discharged all trade unionists from their employment, and the unions thereupon boycotted their beer. Similar action by the coal firm of Pope Brothers produced the same response. There were now schemes for a masters' union to break trade unionism. The leaders in this were the building employers, planning to smash the Builders' Union, which they succeeded in doing in the autumn.[12] By then the CTU had been irreparably shaken by the disastrous tailors' strike and the split among the shoemakers. It was remodelled in August, but the silk-weavers left soon after. It held a conference in April 1835, and still had thirteen member trades plus three miscellaneous lodges. It still existed in July, but was no longer of much importance.[13]

With the builders' defeat in September, the union efforts of 1834 had ended in defeat, but just as the NUWC had established radical contacts and reputations and bequeathed in the unstamped a focus for the undoubted radical opinion, so the CTU bequeathed contacts, traditions and some organisational unity in the Dorchester Labourers' Committee.

It was fitting that Gast was so fully involved in most of the events of 1829–34. But surprisingly he seems not to have been involved in the general unionism of 1834, though there was in May an attempt to form a lodge of shipwrights, ship-joiners, caulkers and smiths.[14] Yet the CTU drew together the many activities of the 1820s in which he had played so prominent a part. But in the years that followed there was an important difference from the 1820s. A leading role in inter-trade activities was no longer taken by the shipwrights, who had provided the context within which Gast flourished and who had been his overriding concern. As the shipwrights overcame their difficulties they became exclusive and aloof and produced no more Gasts. This is to reiterate the point that we must not generalise on the activity and aims of 'the artisans'. They did share common social ideals, but their differing experiences led them into very different paths. In this sense the shipwrights were not betraying Gast's ideals.

The shipwrights diverged from the tailors and shoemakers because their union retained its control on the Thames.[15] Despite the 1825 strike and the distress that followed, the union survived, and even revived late in 1828. There was still rigorous enforcement of apprenticeship, the gang contract system remained in full force, the new day-rate of 6s. was maintained and prices for piece-work rose. The limitation on hours of work was maintained.[16] Largely because of the 1825 strike the builders accepted this situation, and labour relations remained very good. The union's price-book had been so well compiled that in time it was accepted by all the builders, and it regulated all Thames wooden old work.

The union's success in preserving the traditional system was made possible by the economic circumstances of shipbuilding, for the builders had little monetary incentive to reduce labour costs unless there were competition for work. In the 1830s the post-war situation of chronic depression in shipping and shipbuilding at last came to an end, and the steady rise in foreign and coastal trade began to arrest the fall in freights. In 1834 and 1835 there was a sharp rise in shipbuilding. Soon the volume of foreign trade was enough to justify a boom, intensified by the China War and the large corn imports due to bad harvests. Nationally the years 1837–42 were ones of depression and severe unemployment, but shipbuilding was the great exception, these being years of prosperity. In 1839 for the first time total tonnage exceeded that of 1816. World-wide depression and the end of the China War then checked trade and freights, but total national tonnage continued to grow and shipbuilding recovery began again in the later 1840s, though not up to the levels of 1838–41.

Difficulties for British shipbuilding continued, but the Thames gained particularly from two lines. First, there were the most expensive or experimental ships, in which price was less important and the superior Thames skill was an asset; these high-quality vessels were mainly for the East India Company, Royal Navy (which continued to order at least 60% of its outside building from Thames yards) and foreign governments, all of which could afford to pay well. The second was the great amount of repair work due to London's importance as a port.

And so the problems of country and overseas competition, with which Gast had been so concerned in the 1820s, were to some extent overcome on the Thames, and the shipwrights did not have his worries. They felt secure and had little interest in the ship-wrights' wider activities of the 1820s or Gast's views. It was especially important that they did well in those terrible depression years which were a formative influence for so many others. The Provident Union, in the absence of industrial troubles, became almost entirely a benefit society, with large funds. They had no need of wider unionism. As one of the Webbs' researchers noted of the Thames shipwrights at the end of the century, they 'Remained for 100 years the same good type of stationary unprogressive body', their ranks largely filled by hereditary succession. 'They have always completely shut themselves off from general labour Movement.'[17] It was not until the 1860s that the crisis came for Thames shipbuilding, and its yards soon disappeared. But even after that the volume of repair work continued and the Thames shipwrights could still persist in their traditional ways, though they were no longer of much economic importance.

The conservative, traditionalist, isolated Thames shipwrights of the late nineteenth century might seem poles apart from those led by Gast in the 1820s. This was because the very same aims and ideals could, with changes in circumstances, lead to widely different activities and conclusions, varying from co-operation with employers over apprenticeship and tariff policies to conflict with them over wage rates, or from strong unionism preventing a labour surplus by rigid apprenticeship and leading to general exclusiveness and aloofness, to general unionism, militant class terminology and a critique of the whole economic, social and political system. Those developments among the artisans which we have traced through Gast's career were found in the 1840s among trades other than the shipwrights.

But in the later 1830s the shipwrights were still leading members of the trades' Combination Committee and were very generous to the bookbinders during their long strike in 1838–9. They were also important members of the Dorchester Labourers' Committee, and Gast took part in this campaign.[18] This committee was formed in February 1835 with the twin aims of getting the six convicts pardoned and returned to England, and in the meantime to support their families, giving them a total of £7 each week. It was formed by the CTU, two of whose council sat on its committee alongside delegates from trades. The secretary, Robert Hartwell, had been in

Cleave's class in the NUWC and was leader of the Grand Lodge of Operative Letterpress Printers. The committee also included several men already prominent in London trade unionism or later to become so, and the trades represented had all been in the CTU or Builders' Union.[19] The response was so good that not only were the families supported but when the men were pardoned and finally returned there was a surplus to give to them. Another trade union procession took place in April 1838, and a penny subscription financed settling the men on farms, though the response was now far less than had been expected. But the support for the Dorchester subscription had never been solely from the trades but also from radical individuals and groups. In 1835 some district radical committees were formed, the Surrey one led by John Simpson.

The unstamped and the Dorchester agitations provided the foci for the multitude of groups, trades, booksellers and newsagents, coffee and public houses, discussion and educational groups that flourished in London. There was no lack of activity. There were strikes against reductions in 1836 by goldbeaters and in 1838 and 1839 by ropemakers, while in 1836 the engineers struck for a reduction of hours.[20] In every case support came from the other trades. The London carpenters united in 1836 and 1838 to support strikes by the Glasgow carpenters, continued their efforts to secure a reduction of hours to check the unemployment that became serious again in the 1836 slump, and began funds to erect almshouses for aged and infirm carpenters.[21] Radicals were active in discussion groups (some of which, until the end of 1835, were still classes of the NUWC), and in some parishes, notably St Marylebone, St Pancras and Lambeth, small tradesmen, chandler's shopkeepers and artisan democrats secured control of local government, resisted the assessed taxes and the new Poor Law (a blow to parochial self-government), and campaigned on the general radical programme, so that in the 1835 general election not one Conservative was elected in the whole of London.

Some organisational unity was provided for these groups by the radical associations of 1835–6. The first was, naturally, in Marylebone, at the public house now run by John Savage, the resort of the area's democrats. The dominant figure was soon Feargus O'Connor, now ejected from Parliament, who made his name in London radicalism in the campaigns against Irish coercion and later in support of the chief radical paper in London, the evening *True Sun*, which he even edited for a while. In September 1835 this group formed the Great Marylebone Radical Association, which absorbed the defunct NUWC. While O'Connor soon began the first of his tours of the manufacturing districts, the efforts of Wade and others secured the formation of district radical associations, based on existing groups and figures—Glanville and Hassell in Westminster, Simpson in Walworth, Preston and the secretary of the silk-dyers in Tower Hamlets, Henry Ross in Lambeth.[22] The two chief radical issues were the Dorchester labourers and the newspaper stamp. The latter soon predominated. In August 1835 seizures were made of Hetherington's and Cleave's presses and stock, which provoked a number of public protest meetings, Gast addressing two at the Borough Chapel alongside Davenport, Waddington and Preston.[23] But Cleave and Hetherington defiantly continued their papers.

Early in 1836 the government proposed, not to abolish the four-penny stamp, but to reduce it to a penny, and at the same time impose much more stringent provisions and severer penalties against evasion. This raised a storm of protest at the latest example of Whig duplicity for not only was the proposal an unacceptable half-measure like the Reform Act, but it put evasion out of the question. It would therefore cheapen the majority of newspapers but raise the price of the radical ones, and in fact kill off the cheap press. At the same time as Cleave was imprisoned and sentenced to a £600 fine, there was a campaign inside Parliament and a furious one outside against the government's bill. There were deputations, petitions, open-air meetings, and angry articles by George Edmonds and the rest, notably in the new stamped weekly *Radical* run by the newly-arrived Jamaican A. H. Beaumont. The agitation was led by the Marylebone Radical Association, of which Hetherington, Cleave, Bell and Edmonds were all members. The last months of the unstamped were thus marked by an increase of agitation, and the failure to achieve a total repeal left a residue of great bitterness not only against the Whigs but also the parliamentary radicals, all of whom, except Wakley and Col. Thompson, accepted the 'compromise' that destroyed the poor man's press.[24]

Yet after 1833 Gast had dropped out of importance. He was still secretary to the shipwrights' union but apart from this his main activity was educational. He seems still to have been a member of the Finsbury group of Owenites and co-operators who from 1834 met regularly at Watson's Hall of Science off the City Road. Here the familiar figures of Watson, Savage, Warden, Wigg, Bailey, Saull and Gast, as well as the coopers' leader Abraham, discussed education, poverty and freedom of the press, and advocated public works for the unemployed, a national system of relevant education, and 'the study of science and nature'. (Saull had his own geological museum open to the public.)[25] It was therefore appropriate that in the evening of his life Gast should be involved in founding the Working Men's Association.

16
THE WORKING MEN'S ASSOCIATION

The Working Men's Association (WMA), grew directly out of the campaign for a free press, but came to include a number of members of the Dorchester committee, prominent trade unionists and veteran politicians. It expressed many of the traditional artisan attitudes and was also characteristic in that it encompassed a variety of activities. It was a classic example of the tendency to concentrate on educational activity in a period of political calm after a storm, but it also expressed the deep sense of betrayal over the questions of Reform and stamp repeal. The trade union and political context made it impossible for it to remain purely educational, and it was eventually to be drawn into the Chartist movement.[1]

One of its prime movers was Dr Roberts Black of Kentucky, who came to England early in 1834 and was imbued with the common aim of forming associations of working men as the means of their emancipation. In his efforts to meet such men, he contacted the obvious figure, Detrosier, in June. But by now Detrosier had failed to establish any educational movement with a momentum of its own and was totally dependent on the Owenite institutions for employment. He was therefore lacking in enthusiasm, and in too straitened circumstances to help. But he gave Black some names to contact. The first was Lovett, running his own coffee-house but by now, in Place's words, soured by disappointments, and Black found him cold, guarded, suspicious and unwilling to help. The second was Styles, who had no time at all to help, having taken over as secretary to the London builders. They were facing the prospect of the general lock-out which in August crushed their union. By chance Black heard of Gast and contacted him, but Gast had seen too many of his own organisations fail to be hopeful. He did actually sound out a few of his friends on Black's behalf, but failed to interest them. The turning-point came when in August Black met Place. This was not only because Place encouraged him in his efforts towards what he had himself been preaching for years. More important, Place's home was still a rendezvous on Sundays for working men seeking advice on club, trade and personal affairs, and through regular attendance Black got to know many of them. They included a number of Spitalfields weavers, some of the coopers' leaders (in 1834 Place and Hume had helped them in their strike and prevented government intervention to break it), Styles (who had been Place's ally in the NPU) and probably Gast. Later, in 1835, Lovett became one of the group through making Place's acquaintance in the course of an early 'standard-of-living' controversy in Hetherington's *Dispatch*.[2] And through him Place got to know other frequenters of his coffee-house.

The outlook of most of these men resembled Gast's, and Place and Black disapproved of their 'extreme' views, which they attributed to Owenism, and of their great bitterness against the middle classes because of the Reform Act. On Place's suggestion he and Black decided to win their confidence by constitutional agitation in favour of repeal of the newspaper stamp duty. In April 1835 Black formed some of the artisans into a committee, opened an office in Leicester Square, and set to work to secure petitions for repeal from all over the kingdom. Place wrote fifty letters of introduction to MPs and other influential men, and put Black in touch with his provincial contacts.[3] Alongside this, in the winter of 1835-6, Black also began classes in subjects like grammar, mathematics and French, always with the additional aim of 'moderating' the artisans' views and winning them over to educational activity.

In 1836, in the midst of the final upsurge of furious activity over the sentences on Hetherington and Cleave and the government's proposals, some of Black's committee set up another committee to collect subscriptions to pay off the fines imposed on Hetherington and Cleave. The secretaries were Lovett and John Roberts (the corresponding secretary of the FSOC), and the treasurers Place and Birkbeck. The members included Gast, Hartwell, some of Lovett's coffee-house group, and the non-workmen Black, Beaumont, Murphy, Owen, George Rogers, Saull and Savage. In April Black also formed a society wholly of workmen to campaign against the government's bill, the Association of Working Men to Procure a Cheap and Honest Press. This consisted mainly of the same working men, including Gast.[4] The last months of the unstamped were marked by the increase in agitation, but in May the bill passed and the punishment on Cleave was remitted. Upon this defeat Black now proposed to the cheap press association an educational society. Meetings were held at his home, other men were drawn in, Lovett drew up a rough sketch which a provisional committee expanded, and in June began the Working Men's Association for benefiting politically, socially and morally the useful classes. Gast was a founder-member and was elected to the first committee.

Full membership was confined to working men, and new members had to be proposed and seconded by existing members and then voted on at a general meeting. Non-workmen, and working men in the provinces, could become honorary members and participate at meetings but not hold office or have any say in the management. When Black had to give up his premises they met at Lovett's in Greville Street, but with the failure of his coffee-house he also had to move and the association then rented the first floor of his new home at £30 per annum. Here a reading-room was open from 3 pm to 11 pm. On occasional Monday evenings lectures were given by members; every Tuesday was a general meeting; the committee met on Wednesdays, and a political discussion was held every Thursday. Friday was open night, and on Saturdays were readings and recitations. One of the new association's first actions was to set up committees to collect information on the weavers, tailors, shoemakers and printers. Some lectures in the autumn of 1836 by Col. Thompson on free trade aroused such interest that, on Place's suggestion, weekly discussions on political economy were held on Sunday mornings from 10 am to 1 pm.

The association grew slowly but steadily, and after a year there were a hundred ordinary members and 35 honorary ones. It was exclusive, but had a general London importance because of the prominence of many of its members. It included nearly all of the previous fines committee and cheap press association (though not Styles). As well as Hartwell it had several others of the Dorchester committee who were also leading men in their own trades or districts. It attracted men who had been prominent in the co-operative movement, the NUWC, and trades' unionism in 1834–5, and it included men later prominent in Chartism. The honorary members were those who had been on the fines committee, others active in the unstamped, some radical MPs, some leading Owenites and some other radical gentlemen.[5]

The association's importance was increased by the absence of radical organisations in London at that time. With the stamp duty reduction O'Connor's Radical Association disintegrated, as did most of the branches, though the Surrey branch, of which White was secretary, did survive. While the WMA was being formed there were quarrels over its low-level goals and gradualist, slow-moving approach. In the wake of the emotion of the campaign against the penny stamp and the 'betrayal', in which the cheap press association had shared, some now saw the new association as another betrayal and, in their impatience, seceded. They were led by the excitable Augustus Beaumont, who now condemned the new association and allied with O'Connor, who had by now made several successful provincial tours. The pair united to promote a rival Universal Suffrage Club, also to be run by working men, secured publicity in the *Weekly True Sun* and Hetherington's *London Dispatch* and gained support from some of the leading radicals. But Lovett, Hartwell and Black led resistance to their association's being taken over by it, and in the end it was the Universal Suffrage Club which failed. From November the WMA was joined by many of the abortive club's leaders.[6] Moreover, Beaumont now quarrelled with O'Connor and went over to the association again, and became with Black joint editor of the *London Dispatch*. When in November 1836 the association issued an address to the Belgian working classes, signed by Gast and the rest of the committee, it was Beaumont who translated it for them. But the affair of the club was the beginning of a hostility between O'Connor and the Lovett group.

The only other radical body of note in London was the East London Democratic Association (ELDA), formed in March 1837. Its basis was partly the Spencean–Owenite educational group to which Gast belonged. In January 1836 they formed a Mutual Instruction Society in Great Tower Street. Some of these people, such as Neesom, Davenport and Mee, had been leaders of some of the last classes of the old NUWC that had kept going into 1835, and the ELDA also included some other such leaders in East London, like Thomas Sherman in Spitalfields, John Harper in Stepney, and Edward Harvey.[7] Their main activity was in connection with the unstamped. Heins had his centre in Swan Street, near the Minories, and when he was imprisoned in July 1835 he was supported by Davenport and Sherman, while Harvey took over his premises.[8] When George Julian Harney, who had hawked the unstamped and been employed by Hetherington, was released from prison in 1835 he joined the group and became leader of a class in Southwark.[9] From this group Harney imbibed his republicanism and belief in common ownership of the land. It was these people who formed the new ELDA which was, equally with the WMA, heir to the NUWC. Being Spenceans they had links with Thomas Preston, John George in Southwark and Gast in Rotherhithe. But for some time this association remained small and localised.

The WMA thus derived importance from the general situation of London radicalism and the standing of many of its members. But it was not a homogeneous group. Despite its role in the origins of Chartism, it was intended primarily as an educational society, small, founded on existing personal contacts, welcoming a variety of opinions and taking a variety of periodicals. It did illustrate many of the points made in this book about the artisans. It was not a general workers' association, but one of skilled artisans: 'Most of us are members of trade societies.'[10] It expressed the familiar pride in the value of artisans: 'the arts and sciences have been raised to such a height, chiefly by the industry, skill and labours of the artisan'.[11] It was respectable in its social composition. But it was respectable also in the character of its members, who were not admitted indiscriminately. It prided itself on consisting of 'over a hundred picked men', men of ability who had attained a respectable position through effort and self-control. Inevitably it expressed disapproval of men who would not make such efforts and of traditional practices that hindered them, especially drinking. 'We felt further convinced that no healthful tone of political morality could be formed among us . . . so long as our fellow-workmen continued to croak over their grievances with maudlin brains, and to form and strengthen their appetites for drink amid the fumes of the tap-room.'[12] It sought to improve its members and the means was education rather than temperance. But they thought in terms of their order, not merely of individuals. Education would certainly reduce crime, pauperism, drunkenness and prostitution. Yet they defended working people against accusations of immorality, laying the blame on oppressive institutions, great extremes of wealth and the enslavement of their class. They sought, by the spread of information, to secure a collective respectability, both by impressing their superiors and so dispelling the indifference and contempt these felt for the working millions, and also by ending the divisions and dissensions among working people themselves and the indoctrination whereby they were led to believe it was natural that some should toil and others not. They even saw this as a universal campaign, and had meetings and sent addresses for the working classes of Belgium, Europe, Canada and America, and had links with the Polish Democratic Society in London.

But, in contrast to the mechanics' institutions, the educational aspect was not vocational. Its aims were 'social' and it must be 'useful', contributing towards social and political emancipation. White's lectures on ancient history were seen in this light, and most subjects were political. When Hoare emigrated to America he was presented with the works of Paine. They all shared the universal radical belief that political change would come about through enlightenment, when the people would no longer tolerate the exclusive power of wealth and privilege.

The association also rejected paternalism. The conflicts in the mechanics' institutions were to be avoided by totally excluding non-workmen from a say in the running. It condemned charity as diminishing the energies of self-dependence and leading to hypocrisy and servility. It demanded education 'not as a charity, but as a right'. It was the duty of government to provide it, but the association totally rejected any governmental control on Prussian lines as a new form of tyranny; each locality should have a school committee elected on universal suffrage. There was a conscious rejection of political leadership, for working men

> were always looking up *to leadership* of one description or another; were being swayed to and fro in opinion and action by the *idol* of their choice, and were rent and divided when some popular breath had blown that *idol* from its pedestal. In fact the masses, in their political organizations, were taught to look up to '*great men*' (or to men *professing greatness*) rather than to great principles.[13]

At discussions members could only speak once and had to remain seated, to avoid declamation. At their first public meeting the chair was taken by a working man, Hartwell.

The association contained a remarkable body of men, and in this sense was not at all typical of London artisans generally. But it certainly did express and encourage attitudes and tendencies that were widespread. There was the sense of constant betrayal.

> The working man had been so often betrayed, deceived, and deluded by leaders, that his spirits were cast down, and that indisputable fact would, in great measure, account for his apathy.[14]

Even the rival Universal Suffrage Club had very similar aims, being formed 'to elevate the moral, intellectual, and political character of the Working Classes', to re-establish their self-respect and prove their fitness to manage their own affairs. Its prospectus was drawn up by the artisans Goldspink, White and Cameron, it had a high subscription, and it planned a library, a newspaper and a periodical room as well as a dining room. There was precisely the same objection to any non-workman's having a say in the management, an issue that was one of the reasons for its failure.

The WMA's educational activity included propaganda as well as discussion, with addresses, petitions, public meetings, tracts and missionary tours. These all stressed the specific interests of working men (or artisans), the need to achieve emancipation, and support for radical reform as both result and *means* of full development of political responsibility. But this all allowed a wide variety of opinions on specific issues.

There was general agreement on trade union rights, and the association was drawn into this field of activity. With the long depression which began in 1836, the trades were in a weak position. There were strikes against reductions and efforts to lessen unemployment by reducing hours. Of the leading trades of 1834, the tailors had been so crushed that, although there were still some houses of call, it was not until the economic recovery of 1843-4 that they repeated their attempts to abolish homework, reduce hours and unite the skilled and less skilled. Meanwhile, like the carpenters, they supported schemes for relieving old and infirm workers.[15] The shoemakers were experiencing increasing problems from underworking masters and some technical changes, and in 1838 the City men's shoemakers struck in favour of increasing the pay of the lowest-paid workers, in the interests of equalisation. Despite some concessions, the strike was quickly beaten in the situation of labour surplus, so that in both City and West End the men's shoemakers ended the exclusive character of their societies, and tried to strengthen their organisation and set up their own business to alleviate unemployment.[16] A general consciousness of weakness inclined the trades against strikes and in favour of other courses. It also strengthened support for closer union, and it was fitting that Gast had a hand in this. In 1836 the Staffordshire potters, the last of the great unions of 1834, struck and appealed for help. There was a strong response in London, with a trades' committee to collect money and a spirited public meeting in November. The chairman was Gast, who now made one of his last public speeches, but one that was also one of his most outstanding.

> He wanted to see, not merely isolated unions in the several trades, but a general union made up out of the whole . . . He would never be satisfied until he had seen that project realized; for then, and then only, should he feel assured of the complete emancipation of the working classes. By means of such union the labouring classes of these kingdoms might, by very small contributions, lay up six months' provisions in store, and having done that, they would be in a condition to dictate terms to their oppressors, who now deprived them of the fruit of their labour, and then provided them with the blessings of the starving Poor-law.—He would

tell them what would be the effect of it. They would have the wealthy classes, who now rolled in luxury, petitioning them to take compassion on them, and return to their labour.—It was upon the working classes that they were dependent for the food they ate, the clothes they wore, the houses they lived in, the luxuries they enjoyed—in a word, for everything they possessed; and let the working classes but once put themselves in a condition by the means he had suggested, to take a six month's holiday, and those who now held them in contempt and trampled upon them would be brought to their senses . . . Men's minds were now enlightened, and he hoped, before he closed his days, to see the desire of his heart satisfied.[17]

O'Brien later recalled his plea for unity,[18] and his message was emphasised when in February 1837, after twenty weeks, the Staffordshire men were beaten. The immediate outcome was a Central Association of London Trades. This expressed the general outlook of the trades in strongly deprecating strikes and hoping to be able to arbitrate in disputes but at the same time trying to strengthen their bargaining power by formalising the machinery for strike aid, though the committee could only *recommend* help for a strike. In the eyes of many members, this help would be more effective if used for co-operative production as the cork-cutters had recently done successfully. This Central Association of London Trades remained the chief trade union organisation until 1845.[19]

In June 1837 the type-founders struck against an Edinburgh firm which had a foundry in London at which it paid below London rates. They appealed for help both to the Central Association of London Trades and to the Working Men's Association of which their leader, Isaacs, was a prominent member. The WMA responded by launching a subscription and holding a successful public meeting at which Gast made his last public speech and repeated his call for a general strike.[20]

Several of the Dorchester committee were members of the WMA, which helped organise the annual anniversary dinner in April 1837 and the procession in April 1838.[21] Later that year the arrest of the Glasgow spinners' committee on charges of conspiracy, unlawful oaths and secret transactions, a violent press campaign against trade unions and calls for new legislation, all aroused a storm of protest and fears of persecution among trade unions all over the country. In London the Dorchester committee at first organised support, but soon a specific Glasgow trades' committee was formed; the WMA nominated three members and took part in the campaign. In the ensuing bitterness at the sentence and the hostility of the press some of the trades, echoing Gast's sentiments of 1825, established a newspaper in November 1838.[22] The *Operative*, edited by O'Brien, naturally devoted most attention to the new Chartist movement, but had a regular trades' section.

The Glasgow case had aroused an outcry against the tyranny of combinations, and O'Connell secured the appointment of a Commons' select committee. The threat of new legislation was a repetition of 1825, and Place wrote to his contacts and urged the WMA to take the lead and to make White again their parliamentary agent. But Place was not prepared to do as much as in 1825, and a committee of London trades had immediately been formed independently under the engineers' leader, John Hawkins, at their headquarters, the Bell, Old Bailey. Somehow Lovett then became secretary of this Combination Committee, which collected money from town and country and conducted a very economical campaign. This included a very able address and pamphlet by Lovett which expressed the familiar artisan rejection of the view that wages should be determined by 'natural' forces and the familiar argument that high wages were beneficial as they stimulated consumption.[23] In 1839 the Combination Committee and the Central Association of London Trades agreed to a fusion, but in the meantime William Carpenter, at a loose end, persuaded the former to set up a newspaper. It was a repetition of 1825, and Lovett became secretary of a committee of management of societies holding shares in the *Charter*. It began in January 1839, edited by Carpenter and published by Hartwell.[24]

In 1839 London seemed to have realised Gast's consistent hopes of trade union unity, even to the extent of two newspapers (though these became rivals). In the late 1830s, in London and the provinces, there was growing trade union exasperation at reductions, unemployment, unsuccessful strikes, legal prosecutions and an anti-trade union feeling that seemed strong in public opinion, Parliament and government. At meetings on potters, type-founders or Glasgow, speakers always took a wider viewpoint and stressed the common interests of all working men, the antagonism between capital and labour, the power of middlemen. In his last speeches Gast always linked trade union aims with universal suffrage, and in London, Lancashire and elsewhere, trades were regularly expressing their support for radicalism.

17
INTO CHARTISM

Although the Working Men's Association's involvement in trade union and political matters clearly illustrated that it was an umbrella organisation, the rise of political excitement and pressing specific issues was fatal to it, and the educational body's variety of opinions now became a liability and source of disunion.

The problems arose from its leading place in London radicalism, from the anti-Poor Law movement, and from the rise of Chartism. The first was due to the reputation of many of its members, its trade union contacts, and publicity in the *London Dispatch*, which had a national circulation. But it arose equally from the absence of rivals. In 1837, to be sure, an attempt was made to unite London radicalism in a Central National Association (CNA). But this failed because of the withdrawal of the WMA, and the hostility of Hetherington and his *London Dispatch*.[1]

The leading East London democrats Harney, Neesom, Thomas Ireland and Davenport now tried to join the WMA, but only Harney and Ireland were elected. The opposition to Neesom seems to have been due to his anti-Christian views, for the association sought to avoid religious controversy as divisive. Some, like Lovett, had experienced this divisive controversy in the co-operative movement, while in September 1831 the *Poor Man's Guardian* had complained that the spread of the NUWC was hampered by 'Deistical Ranters'.[2] Hetherington and Cleave had always opposed Petrie's anti-Christian outbursts.[3] In September 1837 the association did agree to hold Sunday meetings again but to exclude theological discussion, though in October the day was changed to Thursdays and theology was allowed. Saull's application to become an honorary member was also rejected. The secularist Watson resisted the exclusion of his old friends Neesom and Saull, and finally the former was admitted.

At the same time the East London democrats and Ross and George had begun subscriptions for the aged Gale Jones and Thomas Preston. This activity became formalised as the Metropolitan Society for the Relief of Distressed Patriots. The old links with Gast remained, and in November he was collecting contributions in Rotherhithe.[4] But on 5 November he died of a rupture of a blood vessel in the head, leaving a widow, Elizabeth. His death was unnoticed in the press.[5]

With the failure of the CNA the WMA was left alone in the field as leader of London radicalism, a role it began to relish but for which such an exclusive body was unsuited. It had achieved attention by a series of addresses written by Lovett and printed in the *London Dispatch*. It made its name nationally with the excellent pamphlet, the *Rotten House of Commons*. And in February 1837 it held a very successful public meeting at the Crown and Anchor to adopt a petition in favour of universal (including female) suffrage, annual parliaments, ballot, equal electoral districts and no property qualifications for MPs. The next month it held another successful public meeting on Canada. Exultant, it decided in April to hold a joint meeting composed of thirty members, Place and any interested radical MPs, to agree on a parliamentary bill on the lines of the petition. In June, thirteen MPs attended meetings with some of the WMA and eleven agreed to support bills for universal suffrage, the other 'five points' (including payment of MPs) and reform of the House of Lords. In July the first provincial working men's associations were formed on the London model. In the autumn, Cleave, Vincent and Hetherington went on speaking tours in Yorkshire, the Midlands and the West Country and many such associations were formed. In April 1838 Lovett, with Place's help, finished the draft of a bill for the six points. This was approved by the joint committee with MPs and by the association, as the 'People's Charter'. Late in 1837 the Birmingham Political Union had revived and been welcomed by the association. By May 1838 the Birmingham National Petition and the People's Charter were the twin documents of the new movement, and a convention of delegates to present the petition was soon agreed to.

But the manufacturing districts had already been aroused by movements in which London took no part, like the factory movement, and above all, the anti-Poor Law movement. The WMA supported the ten hours movement and made Oastler and Douthwaite honorary members, and most of them opposed the new Poor Law. Cleave's and Hetherington's unstamped papers had furiously condemned the new law, while Lovett was moved by it to regard the middle classes as the worst enemies of the working people.[6] But despite such reactions, as well as parochial opposition and general antagonism to the new workhouses, there was nothing in London to match the widespread, excited and violent campaign in the north, encouraged as it was by middle-class opposition to the new law. Most members of the WMA were not directly threatened with the workhouse, and could not identify with the sporadic violence of the small industrial communities of Yorkshire or the wild language and 'coarse abuse' of Oastler, Stephens and O'Connor. Moreover the association's policy of emphasising general political questions and including a wide variety of opinions meant that their honorary members included some strong supporters of the new Poor Law like Place, Black and Roebuck. Though this in no way reflected the attitude of most members, it inevitably increased suspicion of the association. The matter was more serious when in the manufacturing districts the anti-Poor Law movement rapidly switched into the Chartist movement, which could not but alarm Lovett and his friends. They had seen working men's associations formed all over the country, agreement on a radical reform bill which several MPs were pledged to support, and a growing, organised, peaceable agitation, punctuated by huge, orderly mass meetings. They now saw this movement invaded by groups who seemed irresponsibly intransigent and, in many cases, not really radicals at all.

A further problem arose from the fact that the WMA was ready to work with any MP who would support the six points. This included Daniel O'Connell, increasingly distrusted by English radicals because of his alliance with the Whigs and his opposition to factory legislation and trade unionism. The rupture between O'Connell and Chartism was of crucial importance in London as elsewhere, for though some hitherto constant Irish supporters like Cleave and Murphy now reluctantly concluded he was their enemy, most Irish politicians stayed with O'Connell and, like Grady, supported the anti-Corn Law agitation, and Chartism was inevitably weakened. The leaders of the WMA shared the suspicion of O'Connell, but could not reject the help of so influential and popular a figure. This intensified suspicions of the WMA, even in London. Already in January 1837 the Lambeth Radical Association, led by White and Ross, had clashed with O'Connell, and by the end of the year White had left the WMA, and the Surrey (i.e. Lambeth) Radical Association was denouncing the WMA as allies of O'Connell and 'Malthusian' enemies of the working people.[7] Matters came to a head with O'Connell's attacks on trade unions, resulting early in 1838 in the resignation of Harney, Neesom and Ireland from the WMA, and a furious quarrel between it and O'Connor, the most influential radical in the country. The Harney group re-formed a London Democratic Association in opposition to the WMA, and O'Connor was forced to ally with them as a source of support in London, a move made easier by their hostility to his enemy O'Connell and their strong support for Stephens and the anti-Poor Law movement.

The final problem for the WMA was the question of violence, though the matter has probably received exaggerated attention from historians. The association's addresses do teem with praise of reason and moderation; 'whatever springs from knowledge and justice will sustain itself'.[8] But these were all written by Lovett, and it is an elementary mistake to equate his views with those of a society characterised by differences of opinion. It would be easy to amass a number of statements by Watson, Hetherington or even Lovett on the right to resist despotism. The association's members were at one with radicals generally on the rights to bear arms and resist attacks on liberty, in their intense suspicion of the political system and expectation of violence from the authorities, in their strategy of mobilising and uniting the people. It was a generalised attitude quite compatible with a fervent belief in education, temperance or moral reform, as O'Brien, Neesom or Vincent all showed. It was a concept in contrast to the local, sporadic violence of Luddism or the anti-Poor Law movement, which heightened London antipathy to the latter. But this general consensus masked disagreement in detail, for though unity could be built up by ever bigger demonstrations, it was essential to avoid provoking the authorities into violence before this unity was achieved and attacks could be repelled. This was what Lovett disapproved of in Benbow in 1831–2, and Benbow was now one of those in the north who, in the eyes of the group around Lovett and Cleave, were irresponsibly provoking arrests and repression which would crush the fledgling movement. The more immediate the problem became, the more there were disagreements.

The WMA's leadership tried to resist developments which they thought would ruin the movement. They managed the election of the eight metropolitan delegates to the forthcoming general convention quite unscrupulously through a meeting in the Westminster Palace Yard. The Democrats' proposal to share the representation was rebuffed, no one was allowed to speak from the floor, and the attempt by Henry Ross to criticise this procedure was thwarted. The WMA then nominated, entirely from among its members, a London committee to collect the national rent to finance the convention. But not all members agreed with the leadership's stance, and there were secessions. One was Henry Ross. Another was the chemist J. C. Coombe, who had lectured to the members on electro-magnetism and believed as fervently as Lovett that working-class knowledge of science would lead to harmony and remove that love of drink that was the only obstacle to their emancipation. But at the end of 1838, disagreeing with the leadership's attitude to violence when the problem was now a pressing one, he resigned and joined the Democratic Association.[9]

What lay behind the disagreements on violence was not so much principle as differing assessments of the situation, and to a large extent this stemmed from the lack of excitement in London contrasted with the high pitch elsewhere. Though in May 1836 the WMA had decided to hold district meetings in London, it had not done so and in fact its missionary activities were concentrated on the provinces. This, together with the fact that London had not been aroused by the anti-Poor Law movement meant that before 1839 London Chartism was virtually non-existent. Despite the association's role in producing the Charter, London Chartism really began in response to provincial Chartism, mainly with the arrival early in 1839 of the delegates to the convention, who were appalled by the apathy of London. It was therefore difficult before 1839 for Londoners to see the people as united and mobilised enough to resist the authorities, and provocative talk of violence seemed very misguided. The WMA's insufficient comprehension of the emotion and grievances aroused by the new Poor Law was part of a general ignorance of provincial conditions and developments. Place noted that the provincial newspapers in the association's reading room were unread.[10] They therefore failed to realise the extent to which people *were* united and mobilised in many areas.

But as members became aware of the depth of feeling in the country, their attitudes changed. The first was Beaumont who, as a result of tours of north-east England and southern Scotland, condemned the lack of energy and courage of the 'rotten' WMA that was trying to hold the movement back.[11] Several of the association's missionaries came to feel the same, notably Hartwell, Vincent and, to some extent, Hetherington. The first two secured in December 1838 the formation of a 'committee of agitation' for the metropolis, while Hartwell pressed for enlarging the association's membership to make it 'more useful', and in January 1839 some changes were made.[12] With other members, it was participation in the convention itself that brought home to them the state of the country and modified their attitudes, and this included Lovett himself.

The WMA was never typical of London Chartism. Its importance was chiefly due to the lack of rivals, and when in 1839 a number of Chartist societies appeared it sank into insignificance. The same is also largely true of the LDA, which sought to recreate a mass organisation like the NUWC, as large as possible, including the poor of the East End, and so condemned the exclusive 'respect-ables' of the WMA. Its base was in the poorer areas of the East End among unorganised groups and it did have an outlook different from Lovett's. It supported the factory movement and Stephens, Oastler and O'Connor, and saw any emphasis on the need for moral reform, temperance or education and any decrying of violence as 'passive obedience'. Harney unrealistically wanted a rising on the day the convention met, 4 February. He saw the LDA as a Jacobin club which should purge the convention of traitors, and constantly issued rhetorical appeals to begin fighting.[13]

The rhetoric was extreme, but the fairly rapid spread of the LDA in the winter of 1838–9 in the City, Shoreditch, Stepney and Southwark did not reflect acceptance of Harney's position, merely the absence of any alternative radical activity. The spread of the association was local, not ideological, capturing the awakening political interest in certain areas. But with the awakening of London Chartism generally, Harney and Coombe aroused great unpopular-ity by their constant attacks on the convention, while in Bethnal Green itself an opposition society was formed. The latter did not rule out force, or talk of it, but merely Harney's peculiar brand. Even within the LDA Harvey aroused opposition and the branches soon became separate societies leaving the parent body small. There were plans for a great demonstration on 5 May, the day the national petition was to be presented. Harney and his friends seem to have hoped this would lead to a clash, probably in concert with provincial groups. But it passed quietly, and with Harney's departure from London a reconciliation was effected with the Bethnal Green Working Men's Association and the Democrats ceased to be out on a limb.[14] This is all to say that the particular *organisational* situation in London in the winter of 1838–9 should not be used as evidence of a distinctive London *ideological* view-point.

The successful Chartist societies were confined to local areas. The

Chartism of 1839 was in fact based on existing groups whose leaders were already experienced radicals—Hunter and Harper in Stepney; Dr Webb, Wall, Lee, Jordan and Cardo in St Pancras and Marylebone; Hassell and his group in Westminster; Blandford, his son, and Washington in the City; George in Wandsworth; Stallwood and Mee in Hammersmith; Ridley in Chelsea; Sherman in Queenhithe; George Rogers in Bloomsbury; some of the Savage brothers in Bethnal Green. It involved, as had the Reform Bill agitation, a mass of groups and aims, attracting those who saw the Charter as the means of changes in the landed system and the Church, reductions in taxation and government expenditure, achieving a system of national education, legal reforms or improvements in social conditions, or, as in the case of the Boot and Shoemakers' Charter Association, the end of a system of 'one-sided free trade' which admitted foreign manufactured goods but not cheap corn and timber.[15] Under the impetus of the convention London Chartism grew steadily in numbers and intensity, reaching a climax in July and August 1839 at the time of the riots in Birmingham and arrests of leading Chartists. There were big protests, loyal support for the 'ulterior measures' and excitement at the proposed national holiday.

> We have obeyed your request, We are dealing exclusively to the utmost of our Power—we are abstaining from all luxuries—we drink neither Gin, Rum or Brandy—nor more beer than is absolutely necessary—we are also carrying out your recommendations as regards the Banks—and likewise as respects the rights of freeman [sic].[16]

There were plans, not for a rising in London, but, as in 1832, for mass agitation there to keep police and soldiers occupied and unable to deal with provincial disturbances. The Democrats were organising arming and drilling, and there were plans to resist any attack on the large Kennington Common meeting on 12 August (the day of national protest). But the calling-off of the holiday, arrests, the collapse of the convention and general failure led to a clear decline, with the familiar features of, on one hand, emphases on educational, 'moral' and other legal activities and, on the other, a small conspiratorial wing hampered by lack of co-ordination, distrust and fear of spies. By November there were secret societies and arming, Neeson went on a tour of his native Yorkshire to concert plans and Hetherington was one of those who knew of plans for a rising in Bradford. These reactions were encouraged by the emotion at the death sentences on Frost and the Newport rebels, and there were plans for a rising on the day of the executions. But this was checked by arrests in London of Neesom, Joseph Williams and the other leaders, by a concentration of troops and mounted police, and by the commutation of the death sentence.[17] But meantime most Chartists had returned to long-standing interests that had been set aside in the hopes of immediately achieving political reform. There were political tract societies, courses of lectures, Chartist Church attendance, the tea-parties of the East London Female Patriotic Association, Chartist temperance groups, a Lambeth Joint Stock Co-operative Society and Cameron's lectures in favour of co-operative production. By July 1840 London Chartism was in serious decline, but much of what remained was gathered together in a Metropolitan Charter Union that organised public meetings, lectures and discussions, and planned co-operative provision stores, a co-operative building fund, radical coffee-houses with reading rooms, and a weekly periodical.[18]

The Chartist upsurge and decline of 1839–40 seemed to repeat the pattern of earlier periods of political excitement. But there were differences. In July 1840 a Manchester conference established a National Charter Association to which most remaining London societies soon adhered and which for the rest of the decade united Chartism in an organised national structure. Though Chartism in 1839 had been something of an umbrella movement, it does seem that its violence did alienate many of the more propertied and shopkeeping radicals so that by the second half of the year it consisted mainly of manual workers. And most of those who came to prominence in the course of 1839 and were to be the leading figures in the 1840s were working men, like the tailors John Parker and William Cuffay and the shoemaker William Robson. Non-working-class radicals tended to go into anti-Corn Law agitation, like Fall, Grady, Foskett and Gast's old ally the wire-worker West.[19] Chartism was henceforth, in London as in the manufacturing districts, a movement of working men. Trade societies had become involved in Chartism in 1839 through subscriptions, support for Lovett on his arrest, or even the formation of Chartist societies: these included shoemakers, type-founders, carpenters, silk-weavers, stonemasons, carvers and gilders, and Morocco leather-finishers. Moreover, with the passing of the feeling of crisis and the recognition that it would take a long time to gain the Charter (one result of which was the foundation of the permanent National Charter Association), Chartist propaganda in London, Manchester and elsewhere began to concentrate specifically on involving the trade unions and making its programme more clearly relevant to their needs.[20] This was a momentous development, and London Chartism was especially characterised by its involvement with the trades.

CONCLUSION

Gast the Respectable Artisan

We have now finished tracing the development of Gast's outlook and, through him, of the outlook of his fellow artisans. The bedrock was the respectable mechanic. As a shipwright Gast belonged to one of the oldest, most skilled and most prestigious crafts in England, whose value could not be questioned. His and the other mechanics' respectability derived from occupations that were honourable, honourable because they were of value to the community, because they demanded the possession of skills acquired through training, and because they enabled men to maintain themselves and their families by their labour at a decent social level, above subsistence and with sufficient leisure to engage in respectable activities. This situation supported a level of independence, both at work and in running their own clubs without interference from above. Such a position was achieved without recourse to unrespectable means, such as thieving or prostitution, or to charity, whether in working life or old age. Many of these artisans aspired to the positions of master, foreman or dealer, as did Gast himself, but all were clearly distinguished from the mass of the poor, who did not maintain themselves at a respectable level by honourable labour. Gast and his fellows never forgot this distinction or ceased to regard the mechanics as a much more useful part of the population. And since many of the means of maintaining this respectability lay in individual ability, effort, skill, thrift, foresight and control of drinking, a critical attitude to those who failed to do so was natural.

But this respectability was to be secured by corporate as well as individual action, by common efforts to guard against the hazards of sickness, accident and old age, to help find work for those in need of it in London or the country, to ensure a proper training through apprenticeship. The institutions developed to do this centred on the

two foci of artisan life, the trade and the public house. The trade was
a centre of pride, whose traditions and customs must be preserved.
When in 1827 the brassfounders gave up their annual procession
because of lack of support and funds, the *Trades' Newspaper* criticised 'this departure from established usage' as 'tending to lower the
trade in the estimation of their brother mechanics'.[1] The trade
should be kept respectable by keeping members off the parish, even
aged ones, and by preserving considerate and fair working conditions and level of reward to 'give the honest and industrious
mechanic the means of appearing with that respectability which his
professional avocations give him a just right to'.[2] This focus on the
trade often led to exclusiveness and particularism, especially as each
trade had its own status position.

But the skilled artisans were also aware of themselves as an order,
and Gast's concern was with the mechanics as a whole, not just the
shipwrights. He drew on established traditions and practices of
mutual support between the trades. And though the outlook of the
trade societies might be traditionalist and backward-looking, concerned not with improvement but the maintenance of an established
position, it became abundantly clear in Gast's lifetime that there
were many threats to the artisans' aspiration to a secure and
respected place in society. These threats included wartime inflation,
currency fluctuations, rising food prices, higher taxation, cyclical
unemployment, undercutting masters, and competition from cheap
labour in London, the provinces and abroad. Gast and his associates
never made the mistake of regarding these as inevitable facts of life,
and never stopped seeking remedies for them. Rapidly rising prices
during the war necessitated substantial increases in money earnings,
which were only achieved in a period of wartime demand for labour
and a growing number of disputes with employers. In the past
unprincipled masters had often been checked by general disapprobation in the trade, recourse to the law, or by guilds, companies or
journeymen's clubs, but such control was becoming much more
difficult in a period of industrial change, very rapid expansion of
numbers and the growth of new, larger employers. The remedy
therefore lay in strong trade union organisation and the securing of
legislation that was in itself new but sought to defend practices
sanctioned by immemorial custom. Many of the dishonourable
masters were ignorant of or ignored the traditional practices, and
tried to use cheaper, unskilled labour. Disputes were over privileges
and autonomy as well as money. Even when masters were well
disposed, they might feel forced by competition and absence of

orders to 'innovate'. And they were enabled to do so by the steady growth of a labour force in excess of demand, competing for work, ready to accept inroads on practices and earnings, working longer hours and so increasing the competition for work. In trades like tailoring or shoemaking, journeymen became small working masters and hastened this process.

Artisans sought remedies through preserving traditional stints, rates, privileges and hours, insisting that masters and men should have served a regular apprenticeship, banning female labour and enforcing a closed shop. They saw high food prices and taxation as not only reducing artisans' earnings but also, by increasing the cost of living, as making foreign competition more dangerous. They sought remedies in co-operative trading, repeal of the Corn Laws and tax reform. They recognised that in many trades the undercutting masters were connected with production for export rather than the home market, and saw free trade and the emphases on overseas markets as a basic threat, leading to wage cuts and the use by British industry of cheap labour, whether in the provinces or from immigrants to London. Whereas recourses like tramping and unemployment relief had been developed to deal with seasonal and sporadic unemployment, the appearance of nation-wide prolonged cyclical depression and unemployment made these inadequate. The 'crises of overproduction' were seen as resulting from a lack of spending power at home which was due to a misguided policy of wage-cutting, itself due to competition, free trade and concentration on sales abroad. The use of machinery was a clear result of this misguided policy and though its potentiality for good was clear, in practice it increased unemployment. These problems of unemployment should be remedied by reducing hours to share out work; by controlling the use of machinery so that it led to shorter hours for all, not to loss of work; by reducing the burden of taxation on the poor and replacing it by one on the rich, the wartime property tax being a model; by raising real wages to allow working people to live comfortably and honourably and so increase home consumption and provide employment for industry; and by ending tariff reductions that exposed them to unfair foreign competition.

The means of effecting these aims varied, sometimes in industrial action over wages, laws, apprenticeship, conditions and rights, sometimes in co-operative production to support this action, to employ men out of work or to exchange goods and so increase home consumption, sometimes through legal or parliamentary action to enforce apprenticeship, fix hours and secure uniform wage rates.

Gast was aware of all these problems, sought all these remedies, and adopted all these means. He was distinctive in his constant advocacy of a general union of mechanics to achieve common action and purpose and to augment their power. Ideally such a union should embrace not only the London trades but the whole country and so end the provincial threat to London industry. He constantly railed at the workers' failure to achieve this union, blaming drink, selfishness and a lack of education for their failure to understand. 'We are told that the march of intellect is making rapid advances among the labouring classes. If, by this assertion, be meant that its progress is general, I must pronounce it a gross libel.'[3] But he also recognised that purely industrial action alone would not suffice, and saw the need for legislative help. Many of his aims—tax reform, repeal of the Corn Laws, tariff policies—demanded political action. Inevitably, whether they wished it or not, the artisans, in their attempts to defend their way of life, had to become involved in politics.

Gast, like other educated men, was interested in politics and shared the national belief in representative institutions. He saw a man's labour as his property and so entitled to as much protection as any other form. Parliament should represent all the chief interests of the nation, especially the mechanics, perhaps the most useful of all. But this interest was not represented and Parliament as at present constituted did not recognise the vital importance of 'that valuable member of the community, a working mechanic'.[4] Appeals were unheeded, other interests had their way and the State even interfered in the artisans' own trade, benefit, educational, religious and discussion clubs. And so Gast and his associates wanted parliamentary Reform to give their order its due weight; 'they do not recognise the right of Parliament to interfere in the regulation of the working classes, as Parliament does not represent them, but, on the contrary, the opulent classes only.'[5]

Although their ideal of independence through labour might lead to contempt for the destitute, it could provide a basis for criticising those landowners, financiers, merchants or speculators who did not labour. These men were parasitic, living off the rest of the community, and the key to their position was political power. Radical reform would sweep this system away and destroy the aristocracy by removing their power and, probably, their estates. Manhood suffrage would basically fulfil a negative function, serving as a barrier against corruption and tyranny. And the change would probably come about unconstitutionally, through mobilising the people.

It is not surprising that Gast shared in the radical culture that cherished 'the immortal memory of Thomas Paine'.[6] Painite radical-ism drew on the artisans' political awareness and independence, and expressed their negative view of politics, their analysis of taxation and debt and their sense of rights under attack. And Paine's specific proposals over a graduated property tax, old age pensions, funeral grants and public funds for workshops for the unemployed related to some of their chief preoccupations.

Gast was one of the great number whose path to radicalism lay through religious Dissent and very radical rational religion. In Painite radicalism and Deism he also assimilated some of the ideas of the Enlightenment—rationalism, belief in progress, and confi-dence that society could be changed. But his ideal was always the respectable, independent artisan. This ideal should be attained by self-help in morality, drinking, education, work and skill. It should be achieved by unity; 'let all the useful and valuable members of every trade, who wish to appear respectable, unite with each other, and be in friendship with all other trades, and you will render yourselves worthy members of society, at once respectable and respected.'[7] They must resist attempts by 'the employers to enrich themselves by a grinding and oppressive system in reference to their labourers'.[8] But increasingly social, political and economic developments were threatening this ideal. As such, society, economics and politics were at fault. In defence of a traditional ideal, Gast would advocate far-reaching changes and condemn the system.

Artisans in Perspective

But this was not equally the case with all artisans. For although skilled artisans were a distinct social group with distinctive common attitudes and ideals, experiences between trades varied widely. They encountered to very contrasting degrees problems arising from expansion, flooding of the labour market, dilution, capitalism and competition, developments which were all related. Some trades prospered and were able successfully to maintain both their position and the ideal that they shared with less fortunate artisans. Coach-makers, compositors, bookbinders, and engineers took little part in supra-trade activity, although each one of these trades at different times experienced enough problems to become involved in inter-trade committees. And so within the generally-shared ideals a wide variety of attitudes could appear, and this lack of uniformity in experience meant that artisan activities varied from aloof, exclusive conservatism to efforts in favour of equalisation, organising women and promoting militant general unionism. This thesis is most clearly demonstrated by the case of the Thames shipwrights and the great contrast between their activities of the earlier and the later nineteenth century. In general the tailors, shoemakers, cabinet-makers, carpenters and some other building trades experienced the problems most acutely and played the most consistent roles in radicalism, trades unionism and co-operation. At times, spasmodically, other trades, including very superior ones, experiencing more particular (but related) problems, acted with them, like shipwrights and sawyers in the 1820s. All could be as militant as any other workers and could fully participate in the tendency of any dissatisfied group of workers to adopt militant class terminology. The language of class polarisation was as prevalent in London as elsewhere.

All the views and aims that Gast advocated had been fully developed by the end of the 1820s, and did not change much in the following decades. But the years 1829–34 were particularly dramatic. There was the co-operative movement, in its many aspects. The Reform crisis deepened and extended artisan radicalism, seemed to detach the middle classes from the people, and provided a precedent for political change. There were exciting developments in trade unionism that culminated in the Consolidated Trades' Union of 1834–5.

It is difficult to deny the special character of these years. They witnessed new levels of activity, and these forms of activity were not separate but overlapped to a great degree. A major role in uniting them was played by the radical press, most of it illegal. By 1833–4 these papers were full of class feeling, appealing to a specific, working section of the community, bitterly assailing the 'shopocrats' in 1833 in the rapid disillusion at the results of the Reform Act, and stressing the issues of factory reform and trade unionism. Some of the most militant trades, especially the tailors, had been led into new forms of activity, seeking to group men and even women of very varying skills in a single trade association that was to be part of a national organisation embracing all kinds of workers, many of them hitherto unionised. This was a dramatic departure. The leading journalists, notably O'Brien (in *Poor Man's Guardian* and *Destructive*) and Morrison (whose *Pioneer* had a weekly sale in excess of 20,000) brilliantly articulated the conflict between capital and labour. But despite these changes, the ideology remained one appropriate to the artisans. The lower middle classes were not seen as having economic interests necessarily opposed to the workers', nor small masters necessarily as exploiters:

> almost every individual when he is kept out of employment by machinery or any other contrivance, turns his attention towards merchandize, and becomes a trader or a little middleman; others again, finding their income or wages too small to provide for an increasing family, take a shop for their wives to manage, while they follow their regular employment.[9]

As O'Brien expressed it:

> Remember we do not blame them for being middlemen—for this may be the mere result of accident or necessity—but we do blame them for the disposition they have shown to monopolize the Government to themselves.
> We quarrel with no man for being a middleman, or for wishing to become one; but we do quarrel with all middlemen, and with all other descriptions of men, who employ their power to prevent the enfranchisement of the working classes.[10]

The same emphasis on political, rather than economic roles is found. When factory owners were attacked, it was not as masters in a new system of industrial capitalism, but as 'tyrants' enslaving their workforce, 'millocrats' who were linked with the political establishment. O'Brien did, of course, denounce the economic role of middlemen, but we should be careful here over contrasting 'old' and 'new' analyses. The capitalists he attacked were not small masters but were mercantile middlemen, as were found in some of the handicraft trades, and much of their power was attributed to *political* connections and the political structure generally. It is continuity that is the most important feature in these intellectual developments.

Such developments, fed through the 1830s by a series of issues and threats, led on naturally to Chartism as the culmination, particularly in the 1840s. For in that decade the shoemakers, tailors and carpenters resumed their efforts to check the cheapening of labour by underworking masters and reached out towards wider, national organisation. The Central Association of London Trades, which Gast had helped inspire, took the lead in 1845 in calling the two national conferences of trades' delegates that set up the National Association of United Trades. In these, and in a National Association for the Organisation of Trades formed in London in 1849, we see all the grievances, analyses and remedies that Gast had propounded. The overriding aim was to secure a proper position and reward for the workman, a fair day's wage for a fair day's work. The failure of strikes to achieve this end meant that the power of trade unions must be increased by general union and co-operative production, by a machinery for the arbitration in disputes, by convincing employers and public of the good effects of good wages, and, to prevent the situation whereby reductions by a few masters forced the rest to follow, by making wage agreements legally binding. The pressure to reduce wages that followed from concentration on exports should be checked by protective duties and by augmenting the home market. The unjust currency and taxation systems should be reformed, the latter by replacing all taxes by a property tax. There should be a national system of education.

Many of the statements of the later 1840s could have been by Gast. The problem of unemployment was as acute then as in the 1820s, intensifying competition for work and leading to wage reductions. There was now much clearer recognition of Gast's message that traditional forms of unemployment relief were no use in a situation of cyclical and technological unemployment, and the basic reason for the unemployment, competition for work and weakness of the working classes was the 'surplus of labour'. The remedies lay in reducing hours, home colonisation, public works and checks to foreign competition. The rejection of political economy and the Manchester School was quite explicit.

Just as before, hostile press opinion and intervention by the authorities during strikes reinforced the need for working men to take part in politics through such means as campaigns, their own press and political representation. Like Gast they combined trade unionism with political radicalism and supported the Chartist demands. Trade localities of the National Charter Association were formed and Chartism was consciously allied with trade unionism. Under O'Connor's leadership it moderated its negative view of politics and sought to form a working men's political party which should participate permanently in the political system, viewing, as had Gast, labour as an interest. And the Chartist Land Plan was launched specifically as a remedy for the overriding problem of the surplus of labour.[11]

London Chartism was not peculiar or incidental. Apart from the strikes of 1842 in the provinces, Chartism was in the 1840s as strong in London as anywhere else, and in 1848 popular radical feeling was particularly marked there. The Working Men's Association must not lead us into supposing that London was unusual. I have tried to give specific reasons for the stance of the WMA in 1837–8, and to argue that it was not typical of London Chartism as a whole. London Chartism was part of the common pattern in the 1840s because of the prevalence of artisans in it everywhere. The artisans were the most numerous and most important of all the organised groups of workers in the first half of the nineteenth century, though this fact is only beginning to be recognised. For this reason, though this study has been confined to London, its conclusions are valid for artisans over the whole of England and have indeed a more general importance.

The artisans' experience and preoccupations set the tone for movements elsewhere. Their outlook and problems were shared by domestic outworkers like handloom weavers, degraded artisans with the same values of independence and status though with a much greater communal solidarity and social egalitarianism. They were shared by degraded skilled workers in the textile industry, like wool-combers. They were shared by the cotton-spinners. For the mule-spinners were not downtrodden proletarians, but an elite among the factory workers, aristocratic, organised from the start in friendly societies and trade clubs like those of skilled handicraftsmen. Men of skill and ability, they saw their occupation as a 'trade' and organised to limit entry to it and impose wage levels comparable to those of artisans. They experienced the same problems of labour surplus, growing labour intensity, wage cuts and technological innovation, and like skilled artisans they turned in periods of difficulties to general unionism (that is the federation of *existing* unions), political radicalism, and class militancy.[12] But the anti-capitalist ideas which evolved in this period were those appropriate to artisans, not opposing all masters but condemning 'merchant capitalism', the monopolist middlemen.[13] It was a theory, not of exploitation within production, but of unequal exchange. And for most of those who held it, this was no 'false consciousness' but an accurate analysis of the situation.

And so, in recognising the strength of the language of class polarisation and the undoubted intensity of working-class feeling in Chartism, we must nevertheless recognise that it was not shared by all workers equally and that the fundamental task is analysis of different occupations, to explain why some groups went into such class movements more than did others. We must also recognise, as Mr Thompson has shown, that political factors were just as important as economic changes in provoking working-class consciousness, so that class antagonisms and definitions could be as much in political as economic terms. Further, we must not assume that once

a militant standpoint or class attitude was adopted, it was necessarily a permanent acquisition; different economic or political circumstances might displace them. Finally, we must not misunderstand the title of Mr Thompson's outstanding book. Anyone looking in it for the origins of the modern working class will be disappointed; it has much more about stockingers than factory-workers.
The years 1829-34 did not see the formation of a working class that
has persisted ever since. That book is mainly about artisans, with
whom it deals so sensitively. It is true for England as elsewhere in
Europe that 'much of what historians mean when they speak of the
"rise of the working class" ' is artisans becoming politically active.[14]

A study of London has therefore a much wider significance. For
the artisans of Western Europe as a whole demonstrated the same
characteristics. They had the same concerns with status distinctions
and the honour of their trade,[15] similar values of respectability[16] and
aversion to charity,[17] emphases on traditional privileges,[18] the tendency to envisage their appropriate reward in traditional terms,[19]
the same guild-like ideals of regulation.[20] They were similarly concerned with problem like sickness and accident,[21] old age,[22] seasonal
fluctuations[23] and rises in the prices of provisions.[24] They were
similarly concerned with funds for unemployed[25] and for loans,[26]
labour exchanges,[27] benefit societies,[28] apprenticeship[29] and wage-
scales.[30] They had the same types of trade societies.[31] The tavern
was as important in their life as was the pub to their English
equivalents.[32] To varying extents they experienced crises of expansion and labour surplus,[33] the cheapening of labour through sub-
contracting and sweating,[34] the swelling of the ready-made and
dishonourable side, and machines.[35] In response they sought the
same variety of remedies, including public works,[36] banning of
piece-work, limitation of hours,[37] wage-fixing and 'boards of
trade'.[38] They tried industrial action, co-operative trading,[39] producers' co-operatives,[40] supra-trade activity. Again and again the
tailors, shoemakers, cabinet-makers and carpenters were the enduring backbone of supra-trade movements, joined from time to time
by groups with special problems. In similar ways they saw small
masters at times as the worst employers,[41] blamed wage reductions
and mechanisation on a drive for exports, and stressed how higher
wages would stimulate consumption.[42] They saw the basic evil in
competition,[43] and developed similar forms of anti-capitalism and
stress on labour value.[44] Drawing often on rational religious sects,
there was a similar type of political radicalism, seeing political
privileges as the source of distress,[45] expressing a negative view of

politics,[46] and, especially in times of defeat, placing the chief hopes of effecting change in the spread of enlightenment and education,[47] to which drink was a major obstacle, but in which the press became the chief agent. There was the same tendency for the 'people' and 'useful' to become the working classes.[48]

The importance of the artisans was not confined to the first half of the century, for after mid-century even the English artisans retained their importance in society and proportion of total population. There was in the third quarter of the century no great extension of factories in England, and there were still very few outside textiles. There were few important technological changes apart from in woollen-weaving and combing and in carpet-weaving. Much of the increase in steam-powered factory production was due to a fall in capital–output ratios. This was clearest in cotton, which saw no real technological changes after the power-loom, only more intensive use of existing methods. Engineering remained on the whole the preserve of small firms and skilled workers. Outside these areas, the numbers of artisans rose, including shoemakers, tailors and, especially, building workers[49] (even though, as we have seen, labour surplus and sweating meant for many of them a decline in their position). The importance continued of the 'immemorial crafts of old Europe' and the traditional town life of 'the cobbler, the tailor and the (probably related) corner-shop grocer'.[50]

The absence of technological change may have meant a slowing-down of pressure on the artisans. Though we now know better than to talk glibly about 'mid-Victorian prosperity', and there was undoubtedly very extensive casual employment, there was cyclical recovery from 1848 and then gains during the Crimean War which was not financed by taxation and occurred in a situation of full employment. From the mid-1860s there was a clear upward trend in real wages, with skilled workers gaining the most and the differential from the unskilled probably widening. The artisans may then have found it easier to maintain their position through organisation and so been less concerned with the unskilled workers than in earlier times. No doubt, also, the development of the capitalist commercial and manufacturing system was so firmly established that practical politics demanded reconciliation with it, and they learned 'the rules of the game'. There can be no doubt that they also felt less excluded from political recognition and that they had more effective outlets, for there had been a decline in paternalistic efforts to interfere in their societies and activities. But on the whole there was no great change in their attitudes or concerns.[51]

The most striking change was certainly political, for Chartism as a national movement was broken, and radical artisan clubs supported liberal candidates at elections. But we must never exaggerate the uniformity of liberalism, nor assume that the artisans had modified their social ideals. Nor, on the other hand, should we conclude that they had really been liberals all along and that only very unusual circumstances could lead them into militancy (it is also a mistake to equate 'moral force' with liberalism). They were never Smilesian liberals. Radical artisans did after 1850 find accommodation possible with certain sections of the Liberal party who moved closer to their own aims.[52] Independence and respectability were essential elements of liberalism. The artisans' opposition to bureaucracy and taxation, their desire to be left alone to run their own affairs, their support for parliamentary Reform, were compatible with elements in the Liberal Party. So also were specific aims like property tax, co-operative production, arbitration, legislation to reduce hours, national education, trade union freedom, home colonisation, admission of artisans to full political citizenship, and even land nationalisation. This reflected changes in liberalism rather than artisans' capitulation to a new ideology, and future research on artisan liberalism will probably reveal the persistence of artisan resistance to political economy and free trade alongside the persistence of artisan secularism. For there were always limits to the accommodation with liberalism, most especially in the continuance of the trade union basis to their attitudes. The change had been only a political one. The artisans maintained their autonomous ideals into the last two decades of the century.

Though Gast would have recognised much as familiar in the later nineteenth century, he had lived through a special age in the English artisans' history. He had seen the repercussions of the Enlightenment, French Revolution, the growth of machinery and steam-power, political repression, population growth. He had most directly experienced the pressures of the great war and the sufferings of post-war depression. He had participated in and helped to forward the advances in literacy and adult education, the dramatic expansion of the political nation and the development of techniques of mobilising public opinion. He had associated with Hunt, with Thistlewood, with Spenceans, with Owen. He had been interviewed by MPs, kissed a Queen's hand, helped draw up an act and managed a newspaper. But he had never been a shifting, rootless agitator. His feet had always been firmly planted on the ground, in his own trade.

Though he had disapproved of some of their traditional practices, particularly drinking, he had retained the shipwrights' unshaken confidence for over thirty-five years. He had led their societies, unions and strikes, he had been their spokesman before shipbuilders and politicians, and in the press. Yet alongside these deep, steady roots in his superior, traditionalist trade he had engaged in the most violent and extreme political activities, in Owenite communitarianism, and in the wildest religious speculations. The contrast is only apparent. There is no paradox. These attitudes were compatible with, grew out of, the artisans' basic outlook. The circumstances of the time led into those paths many another who was, as Gast pre-eminently was, 'that valuable member of the community, a working mechanic'.

APPENDIX: THE LARGEST TRADES

The population of London grew rapidly during the period covered by this book. In 1750 it is estimated to have been about 670,000. From 1801 the ten-yearly censuses give the following figures, to the nearest thousand:

1801	959, 000
1811	1, 139, 000
1821	1, 379, 000
1831	1, 655, 000
1841	1, 948, 000

It would be very valuable to know the numbers of people engaged in the different trades, but unfortunately the 1831 Census is the first to give an occupational analysis. We cannot therefore know the numbers before that date or be accurate about the expansion of the labour force in any trade.

The 1831 Census gives the occupations of 180,755 males of 20 years or over engaged in Retail Trade, or Handicrafts, as Masters or Workmen. It does not distinguish between employers and journeymen, and its figures are not always very reliable. It gives, for instance, only 2 braziers and 10 tin-plate workers. The 1841 Census seems much more accurate, and the differences it shows from the 1831 list are not all due to the growth of population and the fact that 1841 used a slightly larger metropolitan district. The 1831 enumerators were given a list already drawn up of trades or callings into which men had to be entered. In 1841 people gave their own description of their occupation, and the returns were afterwards combined to give a list that contains many trades that do not appear in 1831. In addition to males of 20 years and over (numbering in London 448,845), 1841 also gives the occupations of males under

	1831	1841	
Shoe and boot maker or mender	16,500	22,500	Boot and shoemaker
Tailor, breeches-maker	14,500	18,500	Tailor and breeches-maker
Carpenter and joiner	13,000	17,000	Carpenter and joiner
House painter	5,000	10,500	Painter, plumber
Glazier and plumber	2,500		and glazier
Baker, gingerbread, fancy	5,500	8,000	Baker
		3,500	Silk manufacture*
		3,500	Weaver
Cabinet-maker	5,500	6,500	Cabinet-maker and
Upholsterer	1,000		upholsterer
Chair-maker	0	1,500	Chairmaker
Bricklayer	5,000	6,500	Bricklayer
Blacksmith, horse-shoes	3,500	6,000	Blacksmith
Printer	3,500	5,500	Printer
Engineer	6,500	3,500	Engineer and engine worker
Jeweller	3,000	3,500	Jeweller, goldsmith
Goldsmith ⎱ Silversmith ⎰	500		and silversmith
Clock and watchmaker	2,500	3,500	Clock and watchmaker
Hatter and hosier	2,500	2,500	Hatter and hat manufacturer
Sawyer	2,000	3,000	Sawyer
Coach-maker	2,000	4,000	Coach-maker
Cooper	2,000	3,000	Cooper
Whitesmith	2,000	500	Whitesmith
Plasterer	2,000	2,500	Plasterer
Mason or waller	2,000	3,000	Mason, paviour and stonecutter
Brass-worker, tinker	2,000	1,000	Brass-finisher and worker
		500	Brazier and tinker
Bookbinder	1,500	3,500	Bookseller, bookbinder
(Bookseller and vendor	1,000)		and publisher
Carver and gilder	1,500	1,500	Carver and gilder
Saddler	1,000	2,000	Saddler, harness and
Harness and collar maker	500		collar-maker
Turner	1,500	1,500	Turner
Boat-builder, shipwright	1,500	2,000	Shipbuilder, carpenter and wright
		500	Boat and barge-builder
Dyer	1,500	1,500	Dyer, calenderer and scourer
Tinman	1,000	1,500	Tinplate worker and tinman
Currier	1,000	2,000	Currier and leather seller
Wheelwright	1,000	2,000	Wheelwright
Copper-plate printer, engraver	1,000	1,500	Engraver
		500	Copper-plate printer
Pianoforte maker	0	1,000	Pianoforte maker and tuner

* In the 1820s it was estimated that there were 13,500 silk-weaving looms in Spitalfields and Bethnal Green.
The 1841 Census also returned 1,500 builders.

20 years of age, females of 20 and over, and females under 20, respectively 53,411, 187,005 and 44,299.

Accuracy over the number of journeymen in the various London trades in the period of this book is therefore not possible. But the 1831 and 1841 lists do on the whole tally over the *order* of size of the trades, and so we can have a clear idea as to which were the chief trades. The list gives all the trades returned in one or both censuses as having over a thousand males of 20 years or over, with such figures, to the nearest 500.

Calculations from the two censuses of the total number of artisans in the metropolis of 20 years and over give figures of roughly 130,000 for 1831 and 200,000 for 1841. Of these, the trades listed opposite would amount to 85% and 75% respectively.

NOTES

Introduction

1.   J. H. Clapham, *An Economic History of Modern Britain. The Early Railway Age 1820–1850* (Cambridge, 1930), esp. chaps. 2, 5; D. S. Landes, *The Unbound Prometheus. Technological Change and Industrial Development in Western Europe from 1750 to the Present* (Cambridge, 1969), pp. 118–21; E. J. Hobsbawm, *Industry and Empire. An Economic History of Britain since 1750* (1968), pp. 53–4; A. E. Musson, 'Industrial Motive Power in the United Kingdom, 1800–70', *Economic History Review* 29 (1976); R. Samuel, 'Workshop of the World: Steam Power and Hand Technology in mid-Victorian Britain', *History Workshop* 3 (1977).

2.   E.g. for France: H. Sée, 'Quelques aperçus sur la condition de la classe ouvrière et sur le mouvement ouvrier en France de 1815 à 1848', *Revue d'histoire économique et sociale* 12 (1924); G. Duveau, 'Comment étudier la vie ouvrière', *ibid.*, 26 (1940–7); E. Coornaert, 'La pensée ouvrière et la conscience de classe en France de 1830 à 1848', *Studi in Onore di Gino Luzzatto* (Milan, 1950), vol. 3; J.-P. Aguet, *Les grèves sous la Monarchie de Juillet* (Geneva, 1954); P. N. Stearns, 'Patterns of industrial strike activity in France during the July Monarchy', *American Historical Review* 70 (1965).

3.   E. P. Thompson, *The Making of the English Working Class* (1963), p. 193; A. Briggs (ed.), *Chartist Studies* (1965), pp. 4–10.

4.   C. H. Johnson, *Utopian Communism in France. Cabet and the Icarians, 1839–1851* (1974), p. 159.

5.   R. J. Bezucha, 'The "Preindustrial" Worker Movement: the *canuts* of Lyon', in Bezucha (ed.), *Modern European Social History* (1972), p. 93.

6.   W. H. Sewell, 'Social change and the rise of working-class politics in 19th century Marseille', *Past and Present* 65 (1974), 106.

7.   E.g. R. Gossez, *Les Ouvrier de Paris*, I, *L'Organisation, 1848–1851* (Paris, 1967); M. Agulhon, *Une Ville Ouvrière au Temps du Socialisme Utopique. Toulon de 1815 à 1851* (Paris, 1970); J. W. Scott, *The Glassworkers of Carmaux. French Craftsmen and Political Action in a Nineteenth-Century City* (Cambridge, Mass., 1974); C. H. Johnson, 'Economic Change and Artisan Discontent: the tailors' history, 1800–48', in R. Price (ed.), *Revolution and Reaction. 1848 and the Second French Republic* (1975).

8.   Hobsbawm, *Industry and Empire*, p. 71.

346   Notes to pages 3–14

9.   G. Stedman Jones, 'Society and politics at the beginning of the world economy', *Cambridge Journal of Economics* 1 (1977), 87.
10.   Thompson, *Making of the English Working Class*, p. 193.
11.   *Ibid*., esp. pp. 24, 194–9; *idem*., 'The Moral Economy of the English Crowd in the Eighteenth Century', *Past and Present* 50 (1971), 136; *idem*., 'Patrician Society, Plebeian Culture', *Journal of Social History* 7 (1974).
12.   Cf. P. Hollis, *The Pauper Press, A Study in Working Class Radicalism of the 1830s* (1970), p. 300; G. Stedman Jones, 'England's First Proletariat', *New Left Review* 90 (1975), 57.
13.   'Chartism in London', *Past and Present* 44 (1969); 'London Chartism and the Trades', *Econ. Hist. Rev.* 24 (1971).
14.   See below, pp. 42, 213, 337. Cf. R. S. Neale, *Class and Ideology in the Nineteenth Century* (1972), p. 67.
15.   The phrase is used by Sewell, *art. cit*., pp. 89 foll.
16.   S. and B. Webb, *The History of Trade Unionism* (1920), pp. 84–5 n. 2.
17.   Thompson, *Making of the English Working Class*, p. 774.
18.   *Select Committee on Combination Laws*, Parl. Papers, 1825, IV (hereafter *SC* 1825), p. 299.

Part One: Artisans in War and Peace

Chapter 1. The Man from Deptford

1.   Public Record Office, H[ome] O[ffice] 42/179, Watson to Thistlewood, 24 July 1818.
2.   PRO HO 42/177, Thistlewood, 29 June 1818; Thistlewood to Julian Thistlewood, 11 June 1818.
3.   HO 42/190, report by C, 18 May 1818.
4.   For these informers, see especially: HO 40/7 (1); 40/9 (4), fo. 218; 42/189, I.S. (J. Shegog) to Conant, 15 July 1819.
5.   HO 42/180, C, 4 Sept. 1818; 42/179, Hanley to Maule, 31 Aug. 1818.
6.   Bristol Archives Office, Bristol Apprentices Book, fo. 371 (14 June 1786). For William, see: *Matthew's Bristol Directory*, vols. 1807–20; *SC* 1825, p. 302 (Gast). The other brother is mentioned in HO 40/25, 8 Nov. 1830.
7.   For shipbuilding, see: C. Wilson, *England's Apprenticeship 1603–1763* (1967), pp. 171, 280; R. Davis, *The Rise of the English Shipping Industry in the Seventeenth and Eighteenth Centuries* (1962), pp. 44–77, 139–40, 374–82; T. S. Ashton, *An Economic History of England: The 18th Century* (1955), pp. 97, 140–1; R. G. Albion, *Forests and Sea Power. The Timber problem of the Royal Navy 1652–1862* (Cambridge, Mass., 1926); Sir W. Abell, *The Shipwright's Trade* (Cambridge, 1948); J. G. B. Hutchins, *The American Maritime Industries and Public Policy, 1789–1914* (Cambridge, Mass., 1941), esp. pp. 74–198; Clapham, *Economic History of Modern Britain*, pp. 177–8, 212–13; L. Jones, *Shipbuilding in Britain mainly between the two World Wars* (Cardiff, 1957), pp. 7–25; S. Pollard, '*Laissez-faire* and Shipbuilding', *Econ. Hist. Rev.* 5 (1952); A. J. Holland, *Ships of British Oak. The rise and decline of wooden shipbuilding in Hampshire* (Newton Abbot, 1971), Part I; D. Wilson, 'Government Dock-Yard Workers in Portsmouth 1793–1815' (unpublished Ph.D. thesis, Warwick,

1976); *The Shipwright's Vade-Mecum: a clear and familiar introduction to the Principles and Practice of Ship-Building* (1805); *The Book of English Trades, and Library of the Useful Arts* (1821), pp. 284–90; A. Rees, *The Cyclopaedia; or, Universal Dictionary of Arts, Sciences, and Literature* (1819), XXXII; C. Thomson, *The Autobiography of an Artisan* (1847), pp. 27, 32, 47–50, 55–6, 60, 67–8, 72–6, 116, 117, 159; *Morning Chronicle*, 5 Sept. 1850, p. 5 (reprinted in E. P. Thompson and E. Yeo (eds.), *The Unknown Mayhew. Selections from the Morning Chronicle 1849–1850* (1971), pp. 394–410).

8.   *Ibid.*, pp. 403–4.
9.   *SC* 1825, pp. 172–3 (Taylor), 302 (Gast). For the Liverpool shipwrights, see: Webb, *History of Trade Unionism*, pp. 39–40; Clapham, *Economic History of Modern Britain*, pp. 39–40.
10.   *Trades' Newspaper* (hereafter *TN*), 3 Sept. 1826, p. 59.
11.   PRO, Portsmouth Extraordinary Pay Books, Adm. 42/1316(1), fo. 43. For the royal dockyards, see: Albion, *op. cit.*, pp. 68–88; C. Wilson, *England's Apprenticeship*, p. 171; Pollard, *art. cit.*; D. Wilson, 'Government Dock-Yard Workers'; H. E. Richardson, 'Wages of Shipwrights in H.M. Dockyards, 1496–1788', *Mariner's Mirror* 33 (1947).
12.   *The Times*, 1 July 1794, p. 3; H. Hunt, *Memoirs of Henry Hunt, Esq. written by himself* (reprint Bath, 1967), I, 147–54.
13.   For this dispute, see: Adm. 106/1868, 24 and 27 April 1797; Adm. 106/2660, 28 April and 9 June 1797.
14.   *SC* 1825, p. 298 (Gast).
15.   Adm 106/2660, 28 April, 2 and 5 May 1797; 106/1868, 23 May; 106/1881, 4 May; 42/1316 (2), fo. 22.
16.   *SC* 1825, p. 299 (Gast).
17.   *TN*, 1 Jan. 1826, p. 387.
18.   *Independent Whig* (hereafter *IW*), 18 Sept. 1808, p. 725.
19.   *SC* 1825, p. 300 (Gast); Kent County Record Office, 'A Register or Calender of all the Recognizances taken by the Justices of the Peace for the County of Kent', years 1810–12; 'Ale-house Recognizances', parish of St Paul, Deptford, years 1810–12; *Bristol Mirror*, 29 Feb. 1812, p. 3; HO 42/180, I.S. to Conant, 8 Sept. 1818.
20.   Gast to Place, 1 March 1827, British Library, Place Collection (hereafter Place Coll.), set 57, fo. 24.
21.   British Library, Additional Manuscripts (hereafter Add. MSS.), 27,798, fo. 31; 27,819, fo. 23.
22.   *Morning Chronicle*, 8 Sept. 1818, p. 3.
23.   Thompson, *Making of the English Working Class*, p. 20.

Chapter 2. The London Artisan

1.   D. MacPherson, *Annals of Commerce, Manufacturers, Fisheries and Navigation* (London, 1805), IV, 535; Davis, *Rise of the English Shipping Industry*, pp. 34–5; Clapham, *Economic History of Modern Britain*, p. 16; C. N. Parkinson, *Trade in the Eastern Seas 1793–1813* (Cambridge, 1937), p. 226; E. P. Thompson and E. Yeo (eds.), *The Unknown Mayhew. Selections from the Morning Chronicle 1849–1850* (1971), pp. 409–10.
2.   HO 42/43, Lord Romney, 8 July 1798; 42/139, Police Committee to Greenwich and its Environs, 23 May 1814.

3. For discussion of London's economic and industrial structure, see: E. A. Wrigley, 'A Simple Model of London's Importance', *Past and Present*, 37 (1967); M. D. George, *London Life in the Eighteenth Century* (1930); Clapham, *Economic History of Modern Britain*, esp. pp. 67–72, and chap. 5; F. Sheppard, *London, 1808–1870: The Infernal Wen* (1976), chap. 5; G. Stedman Jones, *Outcast London. A study in the relationship between classes in Victorian society* (Oxford, 1971), chaps. 1–2; H. A. Shearring, 'The Social Structure and Development of London, c 1800–1830' (unpublished Oxford D.Phil. thesis, 1955); T. R. Mandrell, 'The structure and organization of London trades, wages and prices, and the organization of labour 1793–1815' (unpublished Cambridge M.Litt. thesis, 1972); S. Alexander, 'Women's Work in Nineteenth-Century London: a study of the years 1820–1850', in J. Mitchell and A. Oakley (eds.), *The Rights and Wrongs of Women* (1976); E. J. Hobsbawm, 'The London labour market', in R. Glass (ed.), *London : aspects of change* (1964).

4. *Select Committee on Artizans and Machinery*, Parl. Papers, 1824, IV, 96 (Lang); *Gorgon*, 26 Sept. 1818, p. 150; Webb Coll., A, XLV, fo. 223; *Select Committee on the Apprentice Laws*, Parl. Papers, 1812–13, IV, pp. 53, 56; G. Pattison, 'Nineteenth Century Dock Labour in the Port of London', *Mariner's Mirror* 52 (1966); *idem.*, 'The Coopers' Strike at the West India Docks, 1821', *ibid.* 55 (1969), 177.

5. *TN*, 19 Nov. 1826, p. 146. For the general points, see E. J. Hobsbawm, *Labouring Men. Studies in the History of Labour* (1965), chap. 17.

6. *Select Committee on East-India-built shipping*, Parl. Papers, 1813–14, VIII, pp. 7, 9 (Hillman), 341 (Noakes); *SC* 1825, pp. 187, 188, 192–4 (Fletcher), 216 (Young), 241 (Castles), 246 (Snook), 254 (Lomax), 291 (P. Hardy), 313, 315 (Gast), 353 (Balltiss), 361–2 (Greeve), 370 (Purdy); *Select Committee on Navigation Laws*, Parl. Papers, 1847, X, 5th report, p. 139 (Grieve); *Morning Chronicle*, 5 Sept. 1850, p. 5; *Royal Commission on Trades Unions*, 9th report, Parl. Papers, 1867–8, XXXIX, pp. 28–9 (Divers), 61 (Bayley); S. Pollard, 'The decline of Shipbuilding on the Thames', *Econ. Hist. Rev.* 3 (1950–1), 72–4.

7. Carlile in *Republican*, 16 Dec. 1825, p. 768; R. D. Owen in *Crisis*, 26 Jan. 1833, pp. 18–19.

8. *Select Committee on East-India-built shipping*, p. 367. For this ideal of independence through labour, see W. Kiddier, *The Old Trade Unions, from unprinted records of the brushmakers* (1931), p. 191.

9. *TN*, 8 Jan. 1826. p. 783; *Northern Star (NS)*, 20 Feb. 1847, p. 7; Shearring, op. cit., p. 461. Cf. sawyers, *TN*, 7 Jan. 1827, p. 205.

10. Thompson, *Making of the English Working Class*, pp. 526, 534, 543–4; *idem.*, 'English trade unionism and other labour movements before 1790', *Bulletin of the Society for the Study of Labour History*, 17 (1968).

11. The main sources for this analysis of benefit societies are: George, *London Life in the 18th Century*, pp. 301–3; *Monthly Magazine and British Register*, July 1797, pp. 4–5; Aug., p.88; Sept., pp. 200–1; P. Colquhoun, *A Treatise on the Police of the Metropolis* (1797), p. 381; *Select Committee on the Poor Laws*, Parl. Papers, 1817, VI, pp. 135–8 (Morgan); Place to Mill, 7 Sept. 1815, and 9 and 20 Aug. 1816, Add. MS. 35,152, fos. 166–7, 201–4; *Mechanic's Weekly Journal; or, Artisan's Miscellany*, 29 Nov. 1823, pp. 42–4; 13 Dec., pp. 74–5; 20 Dec., pp. 92–3; 10 Jan. 1824, pp. 130–1; 17

Jan., pp. 154–5; 24 Jan., p. 171; 21 Feb., pp. 227–8; 28 Feb., pp. 244–5; J. T. Becher, *The Constitution of Friendly Societies upon legal and scientific principles* (1824); *Felix Farley's Bristol Journal*, 19 Feb. 1825, p. 3; *People's Journal*, III, 250, 327–8; IV, 41; Thomson, *Autobiography of an Artisan*, pp. 320–7; *Articles of Agreement, to be observed by the Union Society of Carpenters* (Bristol, 1795). The rules of many benefit societies are in the Friendly Society files at the Public Record Office. The only general study of this crucially important workers' institution is P. H. J. H. Gosden, *The Friendly Societies in England 1815–1875* (Manchester, 1961).

12.   *SC on Poor Laws*, 1817, p. 136 (Morgan); 'The Plumber, Painter and Glazier', in (T. Carter and others), *The Guide to Trade* (1838–9), p. 83; British Library, Place Coll., set 53, E, fo. 62.

13.   *Gorgon*, 3 Oct. 1818, p. 158; *Crisis*, 30 Nov. 1833, p. 109; George, *London Life in the 18th Century*, pp. 293–4.

14.   For tramping, see: Kiddier, *Old Trade Unions*, pp. 13–27, 50–1, 159–70; (G. White and G. Henson), *A Few Remarks on The State of the Laws, at present in existence, for regulating Masters and Workpeople* (1823), pp. 84–5; Webbs, *History of Trade Unionism*, pp. 451–2; *Rules and Regulations of the Friendly Society of Operative House Carpenters and Joiners of Great Britain and Ireland* (1836), p. 9 (in Webb Coll., C); Hobsbawm, *Labouring Men*, chap. 4.

15.   A. Perdiguier, *Mémoires d'un Compagnon* (Paris, 1914), pp. 67–349; E. Coornaert, *Les Compagnonnages en France du moyen age à nos jours* (Paris, 1966), *passim*; *NS*, 16 May 1846, p. 5.

16.   For discussion of apprenticeship, see: G. Unwin, *Industrial Organisation in the Sixteenth and Seventeenth Centuries* (Oxford, 1904), pp. 117, 181, 401, 467; George, *London Life in the 18th Century*, pp. 223–41, 275–84; Ashton, *Economic History of England: The 18th Century*, pp. 223–4; P. Mantoux, *The Industrial Revolution in the Eighteenth Century* (1948), pp. 462–7; Thomson, *Autobiography of an Artisan*, p. 60; Mandrell, 'Structure and organization of London trades', pp. 303–25; Add. MSS. 35,142, fos, 133–4.

17.   J. Latimer, *Annals of Bristol in the Eighteenth Century* (Bristol, 1893), p. 21. There are several apprenticeship certificates from the period in the Bristol Archives Office, including some belonging to Toombes' apprentices.

18.   Bristol Archives Office, Bristol Apprentices Book, vol. 1777–1787.

19.   *Ibid.*, no. 100; Bristol Burgesses Book XVIII (1812–18), p. 85.

20.   PRO, FS 1/702A. 212/Surrey (I owe this reference to Mr Mandrell); Webb Coll., A, XXII, fos. 4, 124–7; *Morning Herald*, 24 Aug. 1802, p. 3; *SC* 1825, pp. 300, 301, 316, 317 (Gast). For accounts of some of the London trade societies, see : Kiddier, *Old Trade Unions*; E. Howe and J. Child, *The Society of London Bookbinders 1780–1951* (1952); E. Howe (ed.), *The London Compositor. Documents relating to Wages, Working Conditions and Customs of the London Printing Trade 1785–1900* (1947); E. Howe and H. E. Waite, *The London Society of Compositors* (1948); (J. D. Burn), *A Glimpse at the Social Condition of the Working Classes during the early part of the present century* (n.d.), pp. 38–9.

21.   *Loc. cit.*; *MM*, 8 Nov. 1823, p. 175; George, *London Life in the 18th century*, pp. 290, 292; Add. MS. 27, 803, fos. 213–14; (C. M. Smith), *The*

Working Man's Way in the World: being the Autobiography of a Journeyman Printer (n.d.), pp. 252–8.

22. W. Lovett, *The Life and Struggles of William Lovett in his pursuit of Bread, Knowledge, and Freedom* (1967), p. 25; *Poor Man's Guardian* (hereafter *PMG*), 23 Feb. 1833, p. 63; *Working Man's Friend* (hereafter *WMF*), 13 April 1833, p. 131; 18 May, p. 176.

23. *MM*, 20 Dec. 1823, pp. 270–2.

24. Kiddier, *op. cit.*, pp. 149–50.

25. *SC* 1825, p. 257 (Lomax). See also *A Cooper to Sir James Graham* (1834), Add. MS. 27, 835, fo. 65; Place in Add. MS. 27,800, fos. 134, 181; *MM*, 29 Nov. 1823, p. 220.

26. Webb Coll., A, xlv, fo. 213.

27. *Gentleman's Magazine*, Jan. 1801, p. 80.

28. *The Times*, 10 July 1819, p. 3.

29. Unwin, *Industrial Organisation in the 16th and 17th Centuries*, pp. 117, 196–226; B. Manning, *The English People and the English Revolution 1640–1649* (1976), pp. 148–52.

30. Unwin, *op. cit.*, pp. 212–13.

31. HO 48/8, Petition of Daniel Swallow and others, Feb. 1799.

32. Thompson, 'English trade unionism and other labour movements before 1790', p. 22.

33. J. Gast, *Calumny Defeated: or, A Compleat Vindication of the Conduct of the Working Shipwrights, during the late Disputes with their Employers* (Deptford, 1802), p.16.

34. Webb Coll., A, xiii, fo. 39; xxxii, fo. 127.

35. E.g. *Gorgon*, 3 Oct. 1818, pp. 157–60. For a useful summary of a 'pre–industrial' trade society, see R. N. Price, 'The Other Face of Respectability: violence in the Manchester brickmaking trade 1859–1870', *Past and Present* 66 (1975), 111–19.

36. Kiddier, *op. cit.* p. 61; *SC on Artizans and Machinery*, 1824, p. 98 (Lang); *Gorgon*, 3 Oct. 1818, p. 158. For the hatters, see: (Burn), *op. cit.*; *SC on Artizans and Machinery*, 1824, evidence of Lang and Watkins; *TN*, 28 Aug. 1825, p. 192.

37. G. Rudé, *The Crowd in History, 1730–1848* (1964), chap. 4. Cf. E. J. Hobsbawm and G. Rudé, *Captain Swing* (1969), pp. 293, 294.

38. Mandrell, 'The structure and organization of London trades, wages and prices, and the organization of labour 1793–1815', pp. 180–1, 206–7, 210, 213.

39. *Statesman*, 28 Nov. 1812, p. 4.

40. Gast, *op. cit.*, p. 34.

41. P. Colquhoun, *A Treatise on the Police of the Metropolis* (1800), p. 575; *Monthly Magazine*, July 1797, p. 5.

42. *Select Committee on the State of Mendicity in the Metropolis*, Parl. Papers, 1814–15, iii, p. 58 (Colquhoun); Place to Mill, 7 Sept. 1815, Add. MS. 35,152, fo. 167.

43. George, *London Life in the 18th Century*, p. 163; G. Rudé, *Wilkes and Liberty. A social study of 1763 to 1774* (Oxford, 1962), p. 13.

44. For the importance of seasonal fluctuations, see: F. Place, 'Trades Unions Condemned Trades Clubs Justified', Add. MS. 27, 834, fos. 64–6; Place in Place Coll., set 16, i, fo. 214; Place to Doherty, 7 April 1829, ii, fo.

92; *SC on Apprentice Laws*, 1814, pp. 53 (Nottage), 56 (Winson); Mandrell, 'Structure and organization', pp. 220, 240–1. For economic fluctuations, see A. D. Gayer, W. W. Rostow and A. J. Schwartz, *The Growth and Fluctuations of the British Economy 1790–1850* (Oxford, 1953), i. The relationship between prices and wages is also seen in *Gorgon*, 26 Sept. 1818, p. 149; Add. MS. 27,799. See also extract from Davenport's autobiography in *National Co-operative Leader*, 1 March 1861, p. 196; Pattison, 'The Coopers' Strike', p. 181 (on timing of nineteenth-century coopers' strikes); Thomson, *Autobiography of an Artisan*, pp. 108, 307 (on Hull), and, especially, Mandrell, 'Structure and organisation of London trades, wages and prices', pp. 103–220. (I am very grateful to Mr Mandrell for allowing me to read his dissertation before its final presentation.)

45. Place's excellent and well-informed account is in *Gorgon*, 26 Sept. 1818, pp. 148–51; 3 Oct., pp. 157–60; 10 Oct., pp. 161–5. See also: *The Book of English Trades, and Library of the Useful Arts* (1818), pp. 394–7; (T. Carter), *Memoirs of a Working Man* (1845), pp. 122–8, 136, 151–4); F. W. Galton, *Select Documents illustrating the History of Trade Unionism*. I. *The Tailoring Trade* (1896), esp. pp. xli–xlv, lvii–lxxvi, 86–163; George, *London Life in the 18th Century*, pp. 206, 210–11, 270; *SC on Artizans and Machinery*, 1824, pp. 44–6 (Place); Add. MS. 27.799.

46. Ibid., fos. 10–23; HO 42/65, *c.* March 1802; Galton, *op. cit.*, pp. lx–lxix, 88–131.

47. Thos. Large to Thos. Roper, 24 April 1812, *Records of the Borough of Nottingham, being a series of extracts from the Archives of the Corporation of Nottingham, VIII: 1800–1835* (Nottingham, 1952), p. 143; quoted also in Thompson, *Making of the English Working Class*, p. 238. For a similar development of a 'trade union consciousness' in Lancashire in response to the persistently rising prices, see J. Foster, *Class Struggle and the Industrial Revolution. Early industrial capitalism in three English towns* (1974), p. 38. For the type-founders, see A. E. Musson, 'The London Society of Master Letter-Founders, 1793–1820' *The Library* (1955).

48. Gast, *Calumny Defeated*, p. 25.

49. Howe and Child, *Society of London Bookbinders*, p. 84.

50. Webb Coll., A, xx, fos. 10–11.

51. *A Full and Accurate Report of the Proceedings of the Petitioners against a bill instituted 'A Bill to Prevent Unlawful Combinations of Workmen'* (1800). For the passing of the Combination Laws, see A. Aspinall, *The Early English Trade Unions. Documents from the Home Office Papers in the Public Record Office* (1949), pp. ix–xviii.

52. *House of Commons Journals*, lv (1800), 645, 646, 648, 665, 672, 706, 712, 770.

53. (Carter), *Memoirs of a Working Man*, pp. 123–4. For the tailors' experience, see *ibid.*, pp. 152–3, 161, 163, 169; *Gorgon* references given above, n. 45; *Labourer's Friend and Handicraft's Chronicle*, Oct. 1821, p. 311; Place Coll., set 41, fo. 17; *Pioneer*, 19 April 1834, p. 309.

54. *IW*, 1 June 1806, p. 4; *Morning Post*, 6 Aug. 1806, p. 3; *NS*, 16 May 1846, p. 5. For the shoemakers, see: *Book of Trades, or Library of the Useful Arts* (1804), ii, 86–92; J. Devlin, 'The Shoemaker', in (T. Carter and others), *The Guide to Trade* (1838); *SC on Artizans and Machinery*, 1824,

evidence of Alexander, Ablett, Burn and Thompson; Place in Add. MS. 27,800, fos. 158–62, 164–6; George, *London Life in the 18th Century*, pp. 195–202; Clapham, *Economic History of Modern Britain*, pp. 167, 169–70, 181, 209; Thompson and Yeo, *Unknown Mayhew*, pp. 228–79; R. A. Church, 'Labour Supply and Innovation 1800–1860: The Boot and Shoe Industry', *Business History* 12 (1970).

55.   S. Pollard, *The Genesis of Modern Management* (1965), pp. 85–6; Sheppard, *London, 1808–1870*, pp. 96–100.

56.   Gast to Place, 3 July 1834, Add. MS. 27,829, fo. 19.

57.   Protheroe in House of Commons, *Felix Farley's Bristol Journal*, 21 May 1814, p. 4. Cf. Bristol tailors' warning in *Bristol Mirror*, 13 June 1812, p. 2.

58.   For Thames shipbuilding, the chief source is the exhaustive detailed survey of *SC on East-India-built shipping*, 1814. See also: *Quarterly Review*, Oct. 1813, pp. 1–27; Jan. 1814, pp. 467–76; April, pp. 235–47; *Remarks on the Calumnies in the Quarterly Review, on the English Ship-Builders* (1814); H. Green and R. Wigram, *Chronicles of Blackwall Yard* (1881); Davis, *Rise of the English Shipping Industry*, pp. 55-6, 62, 68–71, 374–5, 382; Hutchins, *American Maritime Industries*, pp. 144–54, 170–5, 203–4; D. Wilson, 'Government Dock-Yard Workers in Portsmouth', pp. 275-86; S. Pollard, 'The decline of Shipbuilding on the Thames', *Econ. Hist. Rev.* 3 (1950–1); Parkinson, *Trade in the Eastern Seas*, pp. 121–3.

59.   Mayhew in *Morning Chronicle*, 5 Sept. 1850, p. 5.

60.   For East Indiamen, see Parkinson, *op. cit.*, chap. 5.

61.   *Ibid.*, p. 124; HO 42/176, Wigram to Sidmouth, 29 April 1818; Wigram to Hobhouse, 30 April 1818.

62.   *SC on E.I.-built shipping*, 1814, pp. 78, 346–53.

63.   Gast, *Calumny Defeated*, p. 5; Webb Coll., A, xxxiii, fo. 315; *SC on E.I.-built shipping,* p. 145 (Chapman).

64.   For the 1802 strike, see: Gast, *Calumny Defeated*; PRO Adm. 106/2665, Navy Board Minutes, 15 June, 16 and 23 July, 3 Aug. 1802; 106/1819, Chatham Officers' reports, 14 and 28 Aug., 28 Sept. 1802; 106/1809, Chatham Commissioner's reports, 29 and 30 July, 3, 22, 23, 25, 28 and 31 Aug. 1802; 106/3006, Dismissals of Artificers, Aug.–Sept. 1802; HO 42/65, Harriott to King, 28 July 1802; 42/66, Aug–Nov. 1802; 65/1, 2 Aug.–21 Sept. 1802; *The Times*, 2, 4, 5, 10 and 24 Aug. 1802; *Morning Chronicle*, 4, 23, 25, 26 and 29 Aug.; *Morning Herald*, 24 Aug., p. 3; *Morning Post*, 23 and 25 Aug.; *Bell's Weekly Messenger*, 29 Aug., 5 and 12 Sept.; *SC on E.I.-built shipping*, pp. 8 (Hillman), 340–1 (Noakes), 422 (Johnson); *SC* 1825, pp. 184 (Fletcher), 300, 316 (Gast); Parkinson, *Trade in the Eastern Seas*, p. 103.

65.   Gast, *Calumny Defeated*, p. 34.

66.   Albion, *Forests and Sea Power*, pp. 319–24, 370, 381–9; R. Glover, 'The French Fleets 1807–1814. British Problems and Madison's Opportunity', *Journal of Modern History* 39 (1967); Gayer, Rostow and Schwartz, *Growth and Fluctuation of the British Economy*, i, 95, 122; ii, 695; Society of Shipowners of Great Britain, *An Account of the Present State of Shipbuilding for the Merchants Service within the Port of London* (1806); *Reports and Papers on the impolicy of employing Indian Built Ships in the Trade of the East-India Company, and of admitting them to British Registry*

(1809), pp. x–xii; Parl. Papers, *Estimates and Accounts*, 1813–14, XI, 359; *SC on E.I.-built shipping*, 1814, *passim*.

67.   *Ibid*., pp. 6, 9 (Hillman), 28 (Hughes), 145 (Chapman); HO 48/8, petition of Daniel Swallow and others, Feb. 1799; *Resolutions of the Master Manufacturers and Tradesmen of the Cities of London and Westminster and the vicinity, on the Statute of 5 Eliz. Cap. 4, for the Regulation and Protection of the Arts, Manufactures, and Trade of this Kingdom* (1814), resoln. 13 (these were inserted in the main daily newspapers as an advertisement during January 1814, e.g. *Morning Chronicle*, 21 Jan. 1814, p. 1); *SC on Apprentice Laws*, 1813, pp. 41–3 (Clarke).

68.   Albion, *op. cit.*, pp. 389–91; Gayer, Rostow and Schwartz, *op. cit.*, II, 695; *SC on E.I.-built shipping*, 1814, pp. 336–7 (Noakes).

69.   *Ibid.*, p. 142 (Chapman). The first such ship built in India was in 1735.

70.   *Morning Chronicle*, 1 Feb. 1825, p. 3.

71.   *SC* 1825, pp. 300–2 (Gast); *House of Commons Journals*, LXXXIII, 1828, 328.

72.   *SC* 1825, p. 317 (Gast).

73.   For the issues and campaign, see: *Reports and Papers on the impolicy of employing Indian built ships*; *SC on E.I.-built shipping*, 1814; *Quarterly Review*, Oct. 1813, pp. 1–21; Jan. 1814, pp. 467–76; April, pp. 235–47; *Remarks on the Calumnies published in the Quarterly Review*; *Substance of the Speech of William Harrison, Esq. before the Select Committee of the House of Commons, on East-India-built shipping* (1814); *Substance of the Reply of William Harrison, Esq. before the Select Committee of the House of Commons, on East-India-built shipping* (1814); *Hansard*, XXVII, cols. 341 (23 March 1814), 394–5 (31 March); *House of Commons Journals*, LXVIII, 1813, pp. 192, 249, 277; LXX, 1814, pp. 130, 148, 154, 158, 277, 301, etc.

Chapter 3. The Apprenticeship Campaign

1.   *National Co-operative Leader*, 1 March 1861, p. 196.

2.   T. K. Derry, 'The repeal of the apprenticeship clauses of the Statute of Artificers', *Econ. Hist. Rev.* 3 (1931), 67–9; HO 42/138, Messrs. Swainson to Sidmouth, 31 March 1814.

3.   E. E. Ebblewhite, *The Worshipful Company of Shipwrights. Its History and Work* (1925), p. 8; Derry, *op. cit.* pp. 69–71.

4.   The sources for this account of the campaign are: Guildhall Library, Broadsides 20.31 and 20.32; Guildhall Library, Minute Book of Clockmakers' Committee of Malpractices, 1808–13, vol. 1, 10, 15, 18 and 22 Nov. 1813; vol. 2, 14 Dec. 1813, 10 Jan. and 25 Feb. 1814; Add. MS. 38,256, fo. 318; Place to Wakefield, 2 and 16 Jan. and 11 Feb. 1814, and Wakefield to Place, 20 Dec. 1813 and 27 Jan. 1814, Add. MS. 35,152, fos. 22–5, 29, 35–7; HO 42/138, Wilson and Preston to Beckett, 11 April 1814; Webb Coll., A, XX, fos. 4–6; *The Tradesman; or, Commercial Magazine*, Sept. 1813, pp. 201–6; Oct., pp. 271–5; *Statesman*, 4 Nov. 1812, p. 1; 2 April 1814, p. 1; 7 April, p. 1; 27 April, p. 1; 28 April, p. 2; 14 May, p. 2; 18 May, p. 2; 24 May, p. 3; 8 June, p. 2; 10 June, p. 1; 15 June, p. 2; 16 June, p. 1; *Felix Farley's Bristol Journal*, 23 Jan. 1813, p. 3; 8 May, p. 4; 6 Nov., p. 3; 13 Nov., p. 4; 20 Nov., p. 2; 5 March 1814, pp. 1, 3; 19 March, p. 4; 2 April, p. 3; 9 April, p. 3; 30 April, p. 3; 21 May, p. 4; *Public Ledger*, 14 May 1814,

p. 2; *Liverpool Mercury*, 20 May 1814, p. 373; *Resolutions of the Master Manufacturers and Tradesmen of the Cities of London and Westminster and the vicinity, on the Statute of 5 Eliz. Cap. 4, for the Regulation and Protection of the Arts, Manufacturers, and Trades of this Kingdom* (1814); J. Chitty, *A Practical Treatise on the Law relative to Apprentices and Journeymen, and to Exercising Trades* (1812); (G. White and G. Henson), *A Few Remarks on the State of the Laws at present in existence, for regulating Masters and Workpeople* (1823), pp. 59–60; S. Romilly, *Memoirs of the Life of Sir Samuel Romilly* (1840), III, 134; *SC on Apprentice Laws*, 1813; *House of Commons Journals*, LXVIII, 426, 444, 455, 488, 531, 556; LXIX, *passim*; *Hansard* XXV, cols. 1129–31 (3 May 1813). There is an account of the course of events in Derry, *op. cit.*

5. GL Broadside 20.32; *Statesman*, 4 Nov. 1812, p. 1.

6. *Felix Farley's Bristol Journal*, 23 Jan. 1813, p. 3; 6 Nov., p. 3; 20 Nov., p. 2; 2 April 1814, p. 3; 30 April, p. 3; Romilly, *Memoirs*, III, 135. See also the Bristol tailors' warning in *Bristol Mirror*, 13 June 1812, p. 2.

7. *Commons Journal* LXVIII, 28 April 1813, 426.

8. 'Condition de la classe ouvrière en Angleterre (1828). Notes prises par Gustave d'Eichthal', *Revue historique* 79 (1902), 82.

9. Thompson, *Making of the English Working Class*, pp. 278, 280–1, 527–52.

10. GL Broadside 20.32.

11. *TN*, 9 July 1826, p. 827. The date of the *Beacon* is given in the *Gorgon*, 17 Oct. 1818, p. 176.

12. Thompson, *Making of the English Working Class*, p. 253.

13. *Statesman*, 25 July 1812, p. 1.

14. *Resolutions of the Master Manufacturers and Tradesmen*, no. 11.

15. HO 42/132, Hay to Sidmouth, 4 Feb. 1813; 42/195, Sweet to Sidmouth, 30 Sept. 1819. Cf. *Felix Farley's Bristol Journal*, 23 April 1814, p. 3; HO 42/138, March 1814.

16. HO 42/133, 27 May 1813. The memorial was also inserted in the *Public Guardian*, 23 June 1813 (in Add. MS, 27, 802, fo. 2). It is reprinted in Aspinall, *Early English Trade Unions*, pp. 161–3.

17. *SC on Apprentice Laws*, 1813, pp. 53–4 (Nottage).

18. Chitty, *Practical Treatise*, pp. 19–20. Cf. *Tradesman*, 1 Dec. 1808, pp. 506–10.

19. J. B. Jefferys, *The Story of the Engineers* (1970), pp. 9–16; A. E. Musson and E. Robinson, *Science and Technology in the Industrial Revolution* (Manchester, 1969), pp. 474–7; Thompson, *Making of the English Working Class*, pp. 244–6; *SC on Artizans and Machinery*, 1824, pp. 27–8 (Galloway).

20. 'The Origin, Object and Operation of the Apprentice Laws; with their application to times past, present and to come', *Pamphleteer*, vol. 3, no. v, March 1814.

21. Romilly, *Memoirs*, III, 13 May 1814, 134–5.

22. *Felix Farley's Bristol Journal*, 21 May 1814, p. 3.

23. W. Playfair, *A Letter to the Right Honourable and Honourable the Lords and Commons of Great Britain, on the advantages of apprenticeships* (1814). Playfair had already in 1805 inserted a defence of apprenticeship into an annotated edition of the *Wealth of Nations*.

24.   *Resolutions of the Master Manufacturers and Tradesmen*, no. 13.

Chapter 4. The End of the Wars

1.   *SC on E.I.-built shipping*, 1814, pp. 19–20 (Hughes), 343, 441.
2.   *Ibid.*, p. 19 (Hughes).
3.   *Ibid.*, pp. 426–8, 431 (Jordan); 406; *SC* 1825, p. 306 (Gast).
4.   Kent County Record Office, 'A Register or Calender of all the Recognizances taken by the Justices of the Peace for the County of Kent', years 1810, 1811, 1812; 'Ale-house Recognizances', parish of St Paul, Deptford, years 1810, 1811, 1812; *Bristol Mirror*, 29 Feb. 1812, p. 3; HO 42/180, I.S. to Conant, 8 Sept. 1818; *The Times*, 10 Sept. 1818, p. 3.
5.   *Quarterly Review*, April 1814, p. 247.
6.   Gayer, Rostow and Schwartz, *Growth and Fluctuation of the British Economy*, I, 149, 285; II, 709, 801; R. C. O. Matthews, *A Study in Trade-Cycle History. Economic Fluctuations in Great Britain 1833–1842* (Cambridge, 1954), p. 119; *IW*, 12 Jan. 1817, pp. 13–14; *Morning Chronicle*, 6 June 1820, p. 2; 1 Feb. 1825, p. 3; *The Times*, 7 June 1823, p. 2; *MM*, 11 Oct. 1823, p. 107; *TN*, 15 Oct. 1826, p. 106.
7.   *Public Ledger*, 2 May 1823, p. 3.
8.   *Loc. cit.*
9.   Gayer, Rostow and Schwartz, *op. cit.*, I, 108–12, 135–7.
10.   Add. MS. 27, 799, passim; Webb Coll., A, xx, fo. 3; G. Pattison, 'The Coopers' Strike at the West India Dock, 1821', *Mariner's Mirror* 55 (1969), 165.
11.   For the silk industry, see: George, *London Life in the 18th Century*, pp. 181–95; *MM*, 6 Sept. 1823, pp. 20–3; Place Coll., set 16, vol. 2, part ii; Add. MS. 27,819, fo. 287; *TN*, 9 July 1826, p. 827 (Place); *IW*, 18 Aug. 1816, p. 263; 1 Dec., p. 386.
12.   Gast to Place, 3 July 1834, Add. MS. 27,829, fo. 19.
13.   Thompson, *Making of the English Working Class*, p. 252. Cf. Thomson, *Autobiography of an Artisan*, pp. 55–6, 73, 108, 307; Foskett in *Magazine of Useful Knowledge and Co-operative Miscellany*, 30 Oct. 1830, p. 39.
14.   M. W. Flinn, 'Trends in Real Wages, 1750–1850', *Econ. Hist. Rev.*, 27 (1974).
15.   A. J. Taylor, 'Progress and Poverty in Britain, 1780–1850: A Reappraisal', *History* 45 (1960), 27; M. I. Thomis, *The Town Labourer and the Industrial Revolution* (1974), pp. 85, 142, 153–4.
16.   Thompson, *op. cit.*, p. 243.
17.   Add. MS. 27, 799, passim; HO 42/176, Hopkinson, 30 April 1818; Webb Coll., A, xx, fo. 4; *SC on Artizans and Machinery*, 1824, pp. 173–4 (Seabrook); 176 (Crowhurst); Pattison, 'The Coopers' Strike', p. 165.
18.   The articles of the Philanthropic Hercules are in Add. MS. 27,799, fo. 143. The quotations are from this, from the address on fo. 144, and from the 'Address to Mechanics' in HO 42/182, Nov. 1818, most of which was reprinted in *Gorgon*, 5 Dec. 1818, p. 232.
19.   HO 42/139, May 1814, petition of debtors in Newgate prison, Bristol.
20.   HO 40/4 (4), Thomas to Conant, 9 and 27 Nov., 14 Dec. 1816; 5, 17 and 20 Jan. 1817; HO 40/8, B, 2 Oct. 1817, fo. 205.

21. *The Times*, 1 Feb. 1817, p. 3.
22. *Courier*, 13 Nov. 1816, p. 3.
23. HO 40/8, E, 2 Oct. 1817, fo. 51.

Part 2: Post-War Radicals

Prologue

1. For the enduring idea of a national convention, see: T. M. Parssinen, 'Association, Convention and Anti-Parliament in British Radical Politics, 1771–1848', *EHR* 87 (1973); I. Prothero, 'William Benbow and the Concept of the "General Strike" ', *Past and Present* 63 (1974), 135–41.

Chapter 5. Gast the Radical

1. See above, p. 39.
2. *IW*, 18 Sept. 1808, p. 725.
3. Hardy to Richardson, 1807, Add. MS. 27,818, fo. 64.
4. *Felix Farley's Bristol Journal*, 29 Feb. 1812, p. 3.
5. The sources for the Bristol elections of 1812 are: *ibid.*, Feb. 1812–April 1813; *Bristol Mirror*, Dec. 1811–March 1813; *Bristol Gazette, and Public Advertiser*, 1812; *Statesman,* 9 April 1812, p. 4; 30 June, p. 4; 2 July, p. 4; 3 Dec., p. 1; 13 March 1813, p. 4; *Bristol Poll Book* (1812); *An Authentic Report of the Evidence and Proceedings before the Committee of the Hon. House of Commons, appointed to try the merits of the Bristol Election of October 1812* (Bristol, 1813); Stedfast Society, 'Election Proceedings 1806–1812' (in Bristol Archives Office); H. Hunt, *Memoirs of Henry Hunt* (1820–1), II, 495–568; III, 1–136; Romilly, *Memoirs*, III, 1–3, 21, 28–9, 54–60; J. Latimer, *Annals of Bristol in the Nineteenth Century* (Bristol, 1887), pp. 50–3.
6. *Felix Farley's*, 29 Feb. 1812, p. 3.
7. J. Latimer, *Annals of Bristol in the Eighteenth Century* (Bristol, 1893), pp. 410–11. Cf., for Hull, Thomson, *Autobiography of an Artisan*, pp. 58–9.
8. *Bristol Mirror*, 29 Feb. 1812, p. 3; *Felix Farley's*, 29 Feb. 1812, p. 3.
9. H. Hunt, *Address to the Public of the City of Bristol* (Bristol, 1807), p. 7.
10. *Bristol Mirror*, 21 April 1810, p. 3; *Felix Farley's*, 21 April 1810, p. 3; *IW*, 22 April 1810, p. 1405; *Statesman*, 18 April 1810, p. 4; 19 April, p. 3; HO 42/106, Cole to Freeling, 12 April 1810; Add. MS. 27,817, fo. 97.
11. Stedfast Soc., 'Election Proceedings', 28 June 1812, fo. 87.
12. Bristol Archives Office, Burgesses Book 1812–1818; *Authentic Report of the Evidence*, pp. 17–18, 21–2, 37–8 (Harris).
13. The result was: Davis—2,895; Protheroe—2,435; Romilly—1,683; Hunt—523. But Davis and Protheroe had 349 and 194 plumpers respectively and shared 2,141, while Romilly and Hunt had 767 and 11 plumpers, and shared 422.
14. Hunt, *Memoirs*, III, 110.
15. *Statesman*, 3 Dec. 1812, p. 1.
16. *IW*, scattered references; *Sun*, 2 Nov. 1808, p. 4; 24 Nov. 1809, p. 4; Add. MS. 27,850, fos. 156–64; (Carter), *Memoirs of a Working Man*, p. 118.

17. HO 42/182, A to Maule, 7 Dec. 1818.

18. *Morning Chronicle*, 22 July 1819, p. 2.

19. For a different assessment of this rule, see Thompson, *Making of the English Working Class*, pp. 21–2.

20. W. H. Reid, *The Rise and Dissolution of the Infidel Societies in this Metropolis* (1800), p. 20.

21. C. Hill, *Society and Puritanism in Pre-Revolutionary England* (1969), pp. 127–40; B. Manning, *The English People and the English Revolution 1640—1649* (1976), chap. 6 and pp. 196–227, 237–61, 295–7.

22. Thompson, *Making of the English Working Class*, p. 757 (referring to Cobbett).

23. Hill, *Society and Puritanism*, p. 459; *idem.*, 'The Many-Headed Monster in Late Tudor and Early Stuart Political Thinking', in C. H. Carter (ed.), *From the Renaissance to the Counter-Reformation* (1966); K. Thomas, 'The Levellers and the Franchise', in G. E. Aylmer (ed.), *The Interregnum: Quest for Settlement 1646–1660* (1972); Manning, *op. cit.*, pp. 307–17.

24. *Gorgon*, 8 Aug. 1818, pp. 89–92.

25. HO 42/181, Stafford to Clive, 22 Oct. 1818. Cf. the brushmaker, William Kiddier, later: 'When I think of the male population of England I see two groups. The one is the skilled workmen: the other mostly adventurers. Skilled workmen may be defined as men that came to their trade as boys. The adventurers are the rest. These include endless sorts of men from the Prime Minister to the common beggar.' (*The Old Trade Unions*, p. 149).

26. Gast, *Calumny Defeated*, p. 9.

27. *IW*, 27 Aug. 1815, p. 277; 17 Sept., pp. 301–2; 22 Oct., p. 340; 14 April 1816, p. 117; 30 June, p. 212; T. Evans, *Christian Policy, the Salvation of the Empire* (1816). For Spence and the Spenceans, see: Add. MS. 27,808; *Quarterly Review*, Oct. 1816, pp. 263–71; O. D. Rudkin, *Thomas Spence and his connections* (1927); T. M. Parssinen, 'Spence on the English Land Question', *Journal of the History of Ideas* 34 (1973); *idem.*, 'The Revolutionary Party in London, 1816–1820', *BIHR* 45 (1972); T. R. Knox, 'Thomas Spence: The Trumpet of Jubilee', *Past and Present* 76 (1977). I cannot agree with the last that Spence's attitude to violence and revolution was different from most ultra-radicals'; it seems to me identical with what I regard as the usual view; see my 'William Benbow and the Concept of the "General Strike" ', *Past and Present* 63 (1974).

28. These included John 'Jew' King and the Irishmen Davenport Sedley and Patrick William Duffin (a United Irishman in the 1790s).

29. For Thistlewood see: G. T. Wilkinson, *An Authentic History of the Cato-Street Conspiracy* (n.d.), pp. 70–1, 395–7; Add. MS. 35,152, fo. 60; Hardy to O'Connor, 24 Dec. 1814, Add. MS. 27,818, fo. 184; HO 42/136; 44/4, Castles, fo. 366.

30. HO 42/136, reports by Kidder and Smith (Feb. 1813); 42/130, 8 Dec. 1812. For Margarot, see M. Roe, 'Maurice Margarot: A Radical in Two Hemispheres', *BIHR* 31 (1958).

31. HO 42/141, Evans to 'Captain' (Julian) Thistlewood, 4 Nov. 1814; 44/5.

32. Wilkinson, *op. cit.*, p. 22.

33. HO 42/136, Smith, Feb. 1813.

34.   For the Spa Fields meetings and aftermath, see, in addition to the daily press, reports of trials and the familiar works, also: HO 40/4 (3); 40/8, E, 2 Oct. 1817, fo. 51, and W—r, 31 Jan. 1818, fo. 167; 40/9 (2), Oliver's narrative, and (5), Hanley to Lichfield, 13 Feb. 1818, fo. 356; 42/182, Moggridge, 26 Dec. 1818; 44/4, fos. 78, 80; *British Press*, 5 May 1818, p. 3; *Sherwin's Political Register*, 26 Sept. 1818, pp. 327/35; H. B. Fearon, *Sketches of America* (1818), pp. 211–13.

35.   HO 40/7 (1); 40/8, fos. 205 foll.; 40/15, 3 May 1820, fo. 19; *IW*, 7 Sept. 1817, p. 156; 14 Sept., p. 167.

36.   HO 40/9 (5), C, 11 Feb. 1818, fo. 363.

37.   HO 42/180, Hanley to Maule, 21 Sept. 1818.

38.   HO 40/9 (5), B, fo. 297; C, 11 Feb. 1818, fo. 361.

39.   E.g. HO 42/180, Hanley to Maule, 21 Sept. 1818; 42/181, C, 12 Oct.

40.   For the radical scene at the end of the wars, see: *IW*; *Statesman*; *Alfred*; *British Press*; G. D. H. Cole, *The Life of William Cobbett* (1925); N. C. Miller, 'John Cartwright and radical Parliamentary reform, 1808–1819', *EHR* 83 (1968); *idem.*, 'Major John Cartwright and the Founding of the Hampden Club', *Historical Journal* 17 (1974); J. R. Dinwiddy, ' "The Patriotic Linen Draper", Robert Waithman and the Revival of Radicalism in the City of London, 1795–1818', *BIHR* 46 (1973); J. M. Main, 'Radical Westminster, 1807–1820', *Historical Studies* (Australia and New Zealand) 13 (1966); W. Thomas, 'Whigs and Radicals in Westminster. The election of 1819', *Guildhall Miscellany* 3 (1970); A. Prochaska, 'The Practice of Radicalism: Educational Reform in Westminster', in J. Stevenson (ed.), *London in the Age of Reform* (Oxford, 1977).

41.   Hunt, *Memoirs*, III, 498–500, 501–7, 526–48; *IW*, 2 March 1817, p. 69; 29 March 1818, pp. 202–4; 24 May, p. 347; *Sherwin's Political Register*, 23 May 1818, pp. 17–18; 30 May, pp. 35–40; *Westminster Election* (n.d. = 1818); *Manchester Observer*, 20 June 1818, p. 193; Thomas, 'Whigs and Radicals'. For the Westminster election, see the press generally; (Carter), *Memoirs of a Working Man*, pp. 201–2; Cleary in *IW*, 11 July 1819, pp. 1317–20; 18 July, pp. 1335–6; 25 July, pp. 1349–51.

42.   *Sherwins' Political Register*, 6 June 1818, p. 56.

43.   HO 42/177 and 178.

44.   *Morning Post*, 21 Aug. 1819, p. 3.

45.   *British Press*, 5 May 1818, p. 3; *IW*, 10 May 1818, p. 301; *Shamrock, Thistle and Rose*, 29 Aug. 1818, pp. 4–11 (in HO 42/182).

46.   HO 42/175, 176 and 177; 179, Fletcher, 5 Aug. 1818; Boroughreeve to Sidmouth, 9 July; *Manchester Observer*; S. Bamford, *Passages in the Life of a Radical* (1844), pp. 167–8.

47.   *Medusa*, 3 July 1819, p. 154.

48.   *British Press*, 8 Sept. 1818, p. 2.

49.   E.g. HO 42/197, 8 Aug. 1819.

50.   *Morning Chronicle*, 8 Sept. 1818, p. 3.

Chapter 6. From Palace Yard to Cato Street

1.   *Gorgon*, 12 Sept. 1818, p. 129.

2.   HO 42/179, C, 17 Aug. (1818).

3.   HO 42/182, Hooley to Hobhouse, 19 Dec. 1818.

4. HO 42/177, A, 29 June (1818); 42/179, A, 20 July; 42/180, Norris to Sidmouth, 22 Sept. 1818.
5. HO 42/179, 21 Aug. 1818; A, 17, 21 and 25 Aug.; C, 17 Aug.
6. HO 42/179, C, 24 Aug.; A, 25 Aug. For the trades' meetings and the Philanthropic Hercules, see also: 42/179, Hanley to Maule, 31 Aug. 1818; 42/180, 26 Sept.; Hanley to Maule, 8 and 21 Sept.; Perry, 6 Sept.; 42/181, placard enclosed; C, 12 Oct.; 42/182, address enclosed; 42/187, Poole to Sidmouth, n.d.; 42/190, I.S. to Conant, 5 Jan. 1819 and 28 Dec. (1818); Add. MS. 27,799, fos. 143–5; *Gorgon*, 5 Dec. 1818, p. 232; 23 Jan. 1819, p. 286; *Medusa*, 3 July 1819, pp. 153–5.
7. *Constitutional*, 25 Nov. 1836, p. 3.
8. HO 42/182, A, 7 Dec. and 2 Nov. 1818. The following account of the Watson–Thistlewood group up to Cato Street is mainly based on an exhaustive use of the Home Office papers, 42/178–203, and 44/1–6. Detailed references for each statement seem unnecessary.
9. HO 42/178, A, 7 July 1818; 42/179, July–Aug.
10. Ibid., C, 13 July 1818; anon., 21 Aug.; A, 17 Aug.; Hanley to Maule, 8 Aug.
11. HO 42/178, A, 7 July 1818; *The Rights of the People, Unity or Slavery* (in HO 42/180). In June Preston had gone to Birmingham for information on their penny weekly subscriptions (HO 42/177, Fairbrother to Thistlewood, 1 June 1818).
12. For the meeting, see: issues for 8 Sept. 1818 of *New Times, Morning Advertiser, Morning Post, British Press, Morning Chronicle,* and *The Times*; *IW,* 6 Sept. 1818, p. 574; 13 Sept., p. 588; *Sherwin's Political Register,* 12 Sept. 1818, p. 3; HO 42/180, Hanley to Maule, 8 Sept.; anon., 4 Sept.
13. Ibid., 16 Sept. 1818. For the speech, see above pp. 19, 98.
14. Ibid., 42/181, Stafford to Clive, 19 Oct. 1818; 42/182, 2 Nov.; Stafford to Clive, 16 Nov.; C, 14 Dec.; 42/190, C, 4 Jan. 1819.
15. HO 42/181, Stafford to Clive, 26 Oct. 1818; 42/182; 42/190, 28 Dec. 1818; C, 18 Jan. 1819. Wolseley, brother-in-law of Henry Clifford, had just issued a letter to the country gentlemen (*Sherwin's Political Register,* 10 Oct. 1818, pp. 360–2), and Northmore, founder of the original Hampden Club, had just stood as a reformer for both Exeter and Barnstaple.
16. HO 42/182, A, 7 Dec. 1818; 42/190, C, 4, 11 and 18 Jan. 1819.
17. HO 42/180, 28 Sept. 1818; 42/181, Stafford to Clive, 26 and 5 Oct.; Hanley to Maule, 12 Oct.; C, 16 and 12 Oct.; 42/182, C, 9 Nov.; W—r, 11 Nov.; Stafford to Clive, 16 Nov.; C, 16 and 23 Nov.; 42/190, C, 13 July 1819.
18. HO 42/190, C, 11 and 18 Jan. 1819; *Black Dwarf*, 6 Jan. 1819, p. 6 (I owe this reference to Mr A. J. Newcombe, to whom I am also grateful in several places in this chapter for information arising out of his researches into Lancashire radicalism 1818–19).
19. HO 42/181, Hanley to Maule, 12 Oct. 1818; C, 12 Oct.; Stafford to Clive, n.d.; 42/182, Fletcher to Sidmouth, 26 Dec.; 42/184, Fletcher to Sidmouth, 27 Feb. 1819.
20. HO 42/181, Stafford to Clive, 26 Oct. 1818; Hanley to Maule, 12 Oct.; 42/190, C, 4 and 11 Jan. 1819.
21. Loc. cit.

22.   *IW*, 8 Feb. 1818, pp. 91–4; 22 Feb., p. 123; 5 April, p. 216; *Manchester Observer*, 7 Feb. 1818, p. 44; *Black Dwarf*, 4 Feb. 1818, p. 76; HO 42/176, Cleary to Thistlewood, 14 April 1818; 42/180, 26 Sept. 1818; *Sherwin's Political Register*, 26 Sept. 1818, pp. 327–35.

23.   For the 1819 Westminster election, see: the press generally; Thomas, 'Whigs and Radicals in Westminster'; Main, 'Radical Westminster'; Major Cartwright, *Address to the Electors of Westminster* (1819); HO 42/182, 17 Nov. 1818; 42/190.

24.   Wolseley in *IW*, 18 April 1819, p. 1127; HO 42/190, C, 15 Feb. and 23 March 1819.

25.   *Cobbett's Weekly Political Register*, 22 Aug. 1818, pp. 15–31; *Morning Post*, 9 Sept. 1818, p. 3; HO 42/190, C, 3, 8 and 29 March, 13 and 20 April 1819.

26.   HO 42/190, A, 15 April 1819. Wedderburn, a jobbing tailor, mulatto son of a West Indian slave, had taken over the leadership of Evans' group when he and his son were imprisoned in 1817 (see *The 'Forlorn Hope'*, and *The Axe laid to the Root*). After this rupture, he soon opened his own chapel and as 'Rev. R. Wedderburn' gave most violent harangues. For Davenport, see: HO 42/197, 27 and 18 Oct.; his articles and verse in *Sherwin's, Medusa, Theological Comet, Diligent Observer, Radical Reformer, or People's Advocate*; his verse pamphlet *The Kings* (in HO 42/207); and entry in J. O. Baylen and N. J. Gossman (eds.), *Biographical Dictionary of Modern British Radicals since 1770*, vol. I (Brighton, 1977).

27.   HO 42/189, W—r, 4 July 1819; 42/190, 29 April.

28.   Ibid., C, 15 June.

29.   HO 42/175, Cleary to Sidmouth, 2 March 1818; 42/188, Hunt to Pendrill, 17 June; 42/190, C, 18 May; BC, 24 July; 44/11, Mitchell to Sidmouth, 5 Feb. 1822, fo. 76; *Statesman*, 29 June 1819, p. 2; *Medusa*, 3 July 1819, pp. 155–9; 10 July, p. 168; 17 July, p. 176; 21 Aug., p. 216; H. Hunt, *The Green Bag Plot* (1819); T. Cleary, *A Reply to the Falsehoods of Mr. Hunt* (1819). I have not traced a copy of Watson's threepenny pamphlet.

30.   HO 42/180, Hanley to Maule, 8 Sept. 1818.

31.   For an analysis of this radical attitude, see my 'William Benbow and the concept of the "General Strike" ', *Past and Present* 63 (1974), 147–54, 163–6.

32.   Thompson, *Making of the English Working Class*, p. 682.

33.   HO 44/4, fo. 69; 42/188, I.S. to Conant, 30 June 1819.

34.   Ibid., G. Parker, 20 June 1819; anon., 30 June.

35.   HO 42/189, W—r, 4 July 1819; Burton to Sidmouth, 3 July. John George was a veteran from the LCS and had been a member of Spence's group.

36.   HO 42/190, Watson to Harrison, 30 June 1819.

37.   HO 42/188, 29 June 1819; W—r, 14 July; 42/189, W—r, 14 July; 42/190, W—r, n.d.

38.   HO 42/189, W. Parker, 17 July 1819; 42/190, Humphreys to Stafford, n.d.

39.   HO 42/190, C, 29 March and 15 June 1819.

40.   HO 42/188, 29 June 1819; 42/190, C, 29 June and 13 July; W—r, 4 July; A, 5 July.

41. Ibid., C, 29 June and 20 July 1819. For the preparations for the meeting, see: HO 42/188–90; *IW*, 11 July 1819, p. 1329; 18 July, p. 1341; *Morning Post*, 17 July 1819, p. 3.

42. For the meeting, see: issues for 22 July 1819 of *The Times, Morning Advertiser, Morning Chronicle, Morning Herald, Morning Post, Courier, New Times, British Press, Statesman; IW*, 25 July 1819, pp. 1351–4; *Medusa*, 24 July 1819, pp. 179–80; *A Report of the Meeting held in Smithfield onWednesday July 21 1819* (n.d.); HO 42/190.

43. Ibid., C, 29 July 1819; W—r, 20 July; BC, 29 July; 42/191, BC, 2 Aug.; A, 9 Aug.; 42/192, 15 Aug.

44. *Smithfield Meeting* (1819).

45. HO 42/190, BC, 29 July 1819; 42/191, BC, 1, 2 and 4 Aug.; A, 2 Aug.; 44/5, B, fo. 7.

46. *Black Dwarf,* 21 July 1819, pp. 474–82; HO 42/190, BC, 29 July (1819); 42/192, Chambers, 14 Aug.

47. Ibid., C, 18 Aug. (1819).

48. HO 42/191, C, 4 and 10 Aug.; BC, 6 and 11 Aug.; A, 9 and 12 Aug.; anon., 7 and 8 Aug.; W—r, 6 Aug.; 42/192. Cf. Carlile in *Scourge*, 21 Feb. 1835, p. 134.

49. HO 42/192, Allen, 19 Aug. 1819; 42/197, 18 Aug.

50. HO 42/192, anon., 21 Aug. 1819; Thomas, 20 Aug. For the preparations for the Smithfield meeting, see: HO 42/192; *IW*, 22 Aug. 1819, p. 1400.

51. *Statesman,* 20 Aug. 1819, p. 3; *IW*, 22 Aug. 1819, p. 1400; *Courier*, 23 Aug. 1819, p. 4; Place to Hodgskin, 8 Sept. 1819, Add. MS. 35,153, fo. 69; HO 42/192.

52. For the Smithfield meeting, see: *Morning Advertiser*, 26 Aug. 1819, p. 2; *Morning Chronicle*, 26 Aug. 1819, p. 3; *IW*, 29 Aug. 1819, p. 1405; *London Alfred; or People's Recorder*, 1 Sept. 1819, pp. 9–14; 8 Sept., p. 18; HO 42/193; 42/194, C, 2 Sept.

53. Ibid., C, 2 Sept. 1819; BC, 1 Sept., 44/5, B, fo. 8; *IW*, 5 Sept. 1819, pp. 1412–13; Place to Hodgskin, 8 Sept. 1819, Add. MS. 35,153, fo. 69.

54. HO 42/192, P—r, 22 and 24 Aug. 1819; 42/194, C, 2 Sept.

55. HO 42/192, 22 Aug.; 42/194, BC, 5 Sept.

56. *IW*, 12 Sept. 1819, pp. 1423–4, 1426; Place Coll., set 40; HO 42/193, 30 Aug.; 42/194, reports 1–10 Sept.

57. *IW*, 19 Sept. 1819, pp.1431–3, 1434; HO 42/194, BC, 15 Sept.; 42/195, Preston to Hunt, 17 Sept., Hanley, 20 Sept.

58. Ibid., BC, 26, 21 and 17 Sept.; 42/197, 10 Oct.

59. HO 42/192, A, 16 Aug.; anon., 15 Aug.; 42/195, BC, 17, 21 and 26 Sept.; Hanley, 20 Sept.; 42/196, BC, 8 Oct.; 42/197, BC, 10 and 16 Oct.; anon., 26 Sept.; 44/4, fo. 243.

60. HO 44/5, B, fo. 12.

61. Ibid., fo. 9; 42/197, BC, 14 Oct. (1819).

62. HO 42/196, Jones to Clive, 12 Oct. (1819); 42/197, BC, 22 and 10 Oct.; anon., 28 Oct.; 44/6, 12 April 1820, fo. 35.

63. HO 42/197, BC, 18 and 24 Oct.; 42/198, BC, 14 Nov.; 42/199, 21 Nov.

64. *Democratic Recorder*, 9 Oct. 1819, p. 26; HO 42/196, BC, 7 and 8 Oct.; C, 4 Oct.; 42/197, BC, 16 Oct.

65.   HO 42/196, BC, 7 Oct.; anon., 8 Oct.; C, 13 Oct.; 42/197, anon., 10 Oct.; BC, 10 Oct.; Hanley, 25 Oct.

66.   HO 42/196, 8 Oct.; C, 13 Oct.; 42/197, BC, 24 Oct.; Hanley, 25 Oct.; C, 20 Oct.

67.   *Manchester Observer*, 23 Oct. 1819, p. 787; 30 Oct., pp. 796, 798; 6 Nov., p. 799; *Courier*, 25 Oct. 1819, p. 4; 30 Oct., p. 4; *Black Dwarf*, 27 Oct. 1819, pp. 701–2; *Cap of Liberty*, 29 Sept. 1819, p. 59; 13 Oct., pp. 93–5; *White Hat*, 30 Oct. 1819, p. 39; *Radical Reformer, or People's Advocate*, 27 Oct. 1819, pp. 49–56; Place Coll., set 40; HO 42/197, C, 29 Oct.; Hanley, 25 Oct.; Thompson, *Making of the English Working Class*, pp. 697–8.

68.   HO 42/196, BC, 7 Oct. (1819); 42/197, BC, 25 Oct. For the preparations for the Finsbury meeting, see: HO 42/197; *IW*, 31 Oct. 1819, p. 1471; *Briton*, 23 Oct. 1819, p. 39.

69.   For the meeting, see: issues for 2 Nov. 1819 of *Courier, Morning Chronicle, Morning Herald*; *IW*, 7 Nov. 1819, p. 1489; *Manchester Observer*, 6 Nov. 1819, p. 803; *Cap of Liberty*, 3 Nov. 1819, pp. 129–40; *Briton*, 6 Nov. 1819, pp. 51–5; *London Alfred*, 10 Nov. 1819, pp. 83–6; 17 Nov., pp. 88–96; HO 42/198; 44/5, B, fos. 9–10.

70.   HO 42/197, C, 29 Oct.; 42/198, BC, 1 Nov.

71.   HO 42/197, 5 Nov.; 42/198, BC, 7 Nov.

72.   Ibid., BC, 9 Nov.; C, 10 Nov.; *Briton*, 13 Nov. 1819, p. 60.

73.   HO 42/197, 9 Nov.; 42/199, BC, 18 Nov.

74.   *London Alfred*, 10 Nov. 1819, p. 87; HO 42/192, Chambers, 14 Aug. (1819); 42/195, I.S., 18 Sept.

75.   HO 42/197, 12 Nov.; 42/198, C, 10 Nov.; *Medusa*, 13 Nov. 1819, p. 308.

76.   *IW*, 14 Nov. 1819, p. 1493; HO 42/198, BC, 3 and 9 Nov. They later, on 31 January 1820, went again to hoot Atkins (HO 42/203, 25 Jan. (1820); 44/5, B, fo. 14).

77.   For preparations for the last Smithfield meeting, see: HO 42/198, BC, 14 Nov. (1819); 42/199; Place Coll., set 40, fo. 194.

78.   HO 42/198, 14 Nov. 1819; 42/199, BC, 22 Oct.; Taylor to Sidmouth, 22 Nov.

79.   Ibid., Hanley, 22 Nov.; cf. Norris to Sidmouth, 20 Nov.

80.   Ibid., Norris to Sidmouth, 24 and 25 Nov.; C, 29 Nov.; Sharp, 24 Nov.

81.   HO 42/197, 12 Nov.; 42/198, anon. and BC, 14 Nov.; 42/199, BC, 22 Nov.; *Republican*, 12 Nov. 1819, p. 178.

82.   For the meeting, see: *Morning Advertiser*, 25 Nov. 1819, p. 3; *IW*, 28 Nov. 1819, p. 1513; HO 42/197, 24 Nov,; 42/199, Stafford's reports, 24 Nov.

83.   Ibid., W—r, 1 Dec.; BC, 28 Nov.; Norris, 29 and 30 Nov.

84.   HO 42/197, 24 Nov.; 42/199, BC, 28 Nov.

85.   Ibid., Nov. 1819; Hanley, 22 Nov.

86.   Ibid., BC, 30 Nov.; 42/200, BC, 1 Dec.; Bevin, 1 Dec.; *Cap of Liberty*, 8 Dec. 1819, p. 216.

87.   HO 42/199, anon., 7 Dec. (1819).

88.   Ibid., 7 Dec.; 42/200, BC, 6 and 7 Dec.; C, 6 Dec.; Lord Mayor, 8 Dec.; I.S., 9 Dec.; 44/5, Edwards' deposition, fos. 1–2; *British Press*, 1 Dec.

1819, pp. 4–5; *The Times*, 9 Dec. 1819, p. 3.; *IW*, 12 Dec. 1819, p. 1529.

89. HO 42/200; 44/5, Edwards, fo. 2; 44/6, fo. 339; *IW*, 12 Dec. 1819, pp. 1525–9.

90. HO 44/5, Hayward, 7 March 1820, fo. 100; Edwards, fos. 2–4.

91. HO 42/199, 9 Dec. 1819; 10 Feb. 1820; 44/5, Edwards, fos. 5–8.

92. Ibid., fos. 10–19; 42/199, 13 and 16 Dec.; W—r, 15 and 20 Dec.; 42/206, BPC, 23 Dec. 1819; 44/4, fos. 70, 71.

93. HO 40/9 (5), C, 11 Feb. 1818, fo. 363; 42/191, BC, 7 Aug. 1819; 42/199, W—r, 15 and 20 Dec.; 44/5, Edwards, fos. 14, 21.

94. HO 42/197, 12 Dec.; 42/199, 25 and 12 Dec.; 42/200 and 201; 42/203, Sharp to Sidmouth, 1 Jan 1820; Norris to Sidmouth, 2 Jan.; *Courier*, 13 Dec. 1819, p. 3; 16 Dec., p. 3; 17 Dec., p. 3.

95. HO 42/197, 14 Dec.; 42/199, 22 Dec.; W—r, 1 Dec. 1819, and 23 Jan. 1820; 42/201, BC, 20 Dec.; 44/2, JB, 24 July 1820; 44/4, BPC, 27 Jan. 1820; 44/5, B, fos. 10–11, 13; Hanley, fo. 42.

96. HO 42/199, 23 Dec. (1819); 44/5, Edwards, fos. 23–6.

97. HO 42/199, 25 and 28 Dec. 1819; W—r, 16 Jan. 1820; 44/4, BPC, 10 Jan. 1820.

98. Wilkinson, *Authentic History of the Cato-Street Conspiracy*, p. 22.

99. HO 42/199, 25, 27, 28 and 29 Jan. 1820; 44/4, fos. 10, 14, 16; 44/5, Edwards, fo. 113.

100. Ibid., fo. 99.

101. Ibid., fos. 99, 102–5; 42/199, W—r, 29, 28 and 30 Jan.

102. Ibid., 9 Feb. 1820; 44/1, BPC, 13 Feb.; 44/4, BPC, 25 Jan. 1820; 44/5, Adams, fo. 21; B, fo. 14.

103. Ibid., Adams, fos. 16, 28–9.

104. HO 42/199, W—r, 22 Feb. 1820; anon., 25 Jan., 20 Feb.; 44/5, Adams, fos. 30–40, 53–69.

105. Ibid., Francis, fos. 32–4.

106. Apart from HO 42 and HO 44, see also: TS 11/206, No. 879; Place Coll., set 40; Wilkinson, *op. cit.*; J. Stanhope, *The Cato Street Conspiracy* (1962); D. Johnson, *Regency Revolution* (Salisbury, 1974); Thompson, *Making of the English Working Class*, pp. 700–8.

107. HO 44/2, JB, 27 April 1820; 44/5, BC, fo. 114; fos. 373, 382, 504; I.S., 24 March; 44/6, fos. 38, 51, 76, 101, 115, 208; *IW*, 12 March 1820, p. 85; *Traveller*, 23–5 May 1820; Place Coll., set 40, fos. 267, 323, 325.

108. HO 44/2, 10 May 1820.

Chapter 7. Queen Caroline

1. HO 40/15, I.S., 4 Feb. 1820, fo. 9; 44/1, anon to Sidmouth, 2 March 1820; 44/2, Brittan, Oct. 1820; J.B., 27 April, undated and 17 May 1820; 44/6, fo. 208; *Black Dwarf*, 22 Nov. 1820, p. 727.

2. *Ibid.*, 17 May 1820–5 Feb. 1823; *IW*, 14 May 1820, p. 164; HO 40/14, Alpha, 21 Aug. 1820, fo. 851; 40/15, *passim*; 40/17, fo. 444; 44/5, March 1820, fo. 504; 52/1, Lord Mayor to Sidmouth, 22 and 19 May (1820), fos. 42, 65.

3. HO 40/14, Norris to Sidmouth, 26 Oct. 1820, fo. 865.

4. HO 44/2, Brittan, 14 Feb. 1820; *Black Dwarf*, 26 July 1820, pp. 129–32.

5. For general accounts of the Queen Caroline affair, see: E. Halévy, *History of the English People in the Nineteenth Century*, II, *The Liberal Awakening (1815–1830)* (1961), 80–106; Cole, *Life of William Cobbett*, chap. 16; S. Maccoby, *English Radicalism 1786–1832. From Paine to Cobbett* (1955), pp. 283, 291–302, 366–82; C. New, *The Life of Henry Brougham to 1830* (Oxford, 1961), pp. 79–118, 228–62; J. Stevenson, 'The Queen Caroline Affair', in Stevenson (ed.), *London in the Age of Reform*. The last is the only one that really analyses the agitation, but it does not concentrate on the aspects considered here, and does not make much use of the press, my main source. The sources for the following account are the contemporary press, especially *Black Dwarf, British Press, Courier, IW, Independent Observer, Morning Advertiser, Morning Post, New Times, Statesman, The Times* and *Traveller*; HO 40/15–16; 44/2, 44/8–10; 52/1; Place Coll., sets 18, 71.

6. HO 42/203, 25 Jan. 1820; 44/5, Edwards' deposition, fo. 224.

7. HO 40/15, 14 Feb. 1820, fo. 11; 6 June, fo. 43; 44/5, March 1820, fo. 504.

8. *IW*, 11 June 1820, p. 192.

9. Place to Parr, 7 June 1820, Place Coll., set 18, I.

10. *IW*, 25 June 1820, p. 205; HO 40/15, 12 June 1820, fo. 47; 44/2, Brittan, July.

11. *IW*, 18 June 1820, pp. 196, 198–9; 2 July , pp. 214–15; 9 July, p. 233; HO 40/15, 1 July (1820), fo. 57; Place to Parr, 7 June 1820, Place Coll., set 18, I.

12. Add. MS. 35,146, fo. 95 (19 Jan. 1828).

13. *Republican*, 19 May 1826, p. 613; *Black Dwarf*, 5 July 1820, p. 27; 12 July, p. 63; HO 40/13, Lloyd to Hobhouse, 8 May 1820, fo. 251; 40/14; 44/2; 44/8; Place Coll., set 18; set 19, fo. 310; set 71, II.

14. HO 40/15, 10 July 1820, fo. 65; 44/8; *News*, 21 May 1821, p. 157. There are many specimens of these bills, placards and tracts in the BL.

15. *Black Dwarf*, 2 Aug. 1820, p. 172.

16. *Morning Herald*, 1 Aug. 1820.

17. *Statesman*, 1 Aug. 1820, p. 2; 4 Aug., p. 4; *Morning Post*, 2 Aug. 1820, pp. 2, 3; *New Times*, 1 Aug. 1820, p. 2; 16 Aug., p. 3; *Traveller*, 15 Aug. 1820, p. 3; HO 52/1, Lord Mayor to Hobhouse, 4 Aug. 1820, fos. 18–18a; Place Coll., set 18, I.

18. *The Times*, 18 Sept. 1820, p. 3; *New Times*, 16 Aug. 1820, p. 3; *IW*, 24 Sept. 1820, p. 310.

19. *The Times*, 10 Aug. 1820, p. 2; 16 Aug., p. 3; *New Times*, 16 Aug. 1820, p. 3; *Morning Post*, 16 Aug. 1820, p. 3; *Traveller*, 16 Aug. 1820, p. 3; *Morning Advertiser*, 16 Aug. 1820, p. 3; *British Press*, 16 Aug. 1820.

20. *Courier*, 13 Nov. 1820, p. 3; 15 Nov., p. 2; *Morning Post*, 15 Nov. 1820, p. 2; *IW*, 12 Nov. 1820, pp. 366, 367; 19 Nov., p. 374; Anne Cobbett to James P. Cobbett, 15 Nov. 1820, in L. Melville (ed.), *The Life and Letters of William Cobbett in England and America* (1913), II, 174–5.

21. Cole, *Life of Cobbett*, p. 251; Thompson, *Making of the English Working Class*, p. 709.

22. Cole, *op. cit.*, p. 248.

23. *IW*, 1 Oct. 1820, pp. 314–15; Wood to Place, 27 Sept. 1820, Place Coll., set 18, II, fo. 169.

24.   *Courier*, 3 Oct. 1820, p. 2; 4 Oct., p. 2; *Statesman*, 3 Oct. 1820, p. 2; *New Times*, 3 Oct. 1820, p. 3; *Traveller*, 2 Oct. 1820, p. 2; 3 Oct., p. 3; *Morning Advertiser*, 3 Oct. 1820, p. 2; *IW*, 8 Oct. 1820, p. 322.

25.   HO 40/15, 16 Oct. (1820), fo. 69; 44/3, 21 Sept. (1820); Place Coll., set 18, II–III; *Courier*, 17 Aug. 1820, p. 3; *Traveller*, 16 Aug. 1820, p. 3; 11 Oct., p. 3; 12 Oct., p. 4; *IW*, 17 Sept. 1820, p. 305; 8 Oct., p. 328; *Morning Advertiser*, 12 Oct. 1820, p. 3. The deputations and processions are reported in the press generally.

26.   *Courier*, 29 Nov. 1820, p. 1; 30 Nov., p. 2; *Statesman*, 29 Nov. 1820, p. 2; *New Times*, 30 Nov. 1820, p. 2; *Morning Post*, 30 Nov. 1820, p. 3; *IW*, 3 Dec. 1820, pp. 377–8.

27.   HO 52/1, Lord Mayor to Hobhouse, 23 Oct. (1820), fo. 67; to Sidmouth, 25 Oct., fo. 77; Add. MS. 27,799, fo. 145; Place Coll., set 71, II; *British Press*, 23 Jan. 1821, p. 3.

28.   *IW*, 10 Sept. 1820, pp. 294–5; Place Coll., set 18, I–II; *Report of a Committee appointed by a public meeting held at the Crown and Anchor Tavern . . . 28 Aug. 1820* (1820).

29.   *IW*, 15 Oct. 1820, p. 336; 5 Nov., p. 360; *Black Dwarf*, 11 Oct. 1820, pp. 507–9; 18 Oct., p. 561; 29 Nov., pp. 779–800; 18 April 1821, p. 550; HO 40/14; Place Coll., set 18, II–III; set 71, I.

30.   HO 40/15, 5 Dec. 1820, fo. 87; 40/16, I.S., 17 Feb. 1821, fo. 49; 42/192, 15 Aug. 1819; BC, 15 Aug.; *Black Dwarf*, 11 Oct. 1820, p. 527; 29 Nov., p. 779; 25 April 1821, p. 667; *Statesman*, 19 April 1821, p. 3; Place Coll., set 18, I; Ensor to Place, n.d., Add. MS. 35,153, fo. 196.

31.   HO 40/14, Alpha, 21 Aug. 1820, fo. 851; 40/15, 30 Nov., fos. 509, 505; Norris to Sidmouth, 7 Dec., fo. 531; Chippendale, 9 Dec., fo. 563; fos. 609, 701; 40/16, Byng, 28 March 1821, fo. 395; Norris to Sidmouth, 31 July, fo. 891; 44/3, 18 Dec. 1820; *Black Dwarf*, 13 Sept. 1820, p. 378; 20 Sept., p. 447.

32.   See above, p. 141. Wood to Place, 27 Sept. 1820, Place Coll., set 18, II, fo. 169.

33.   *IW*, 29 Oct. 1820, pp. 346, 351; HO 40/15, 6 Nov., fo. 77.

34.   *Traveller*, 14 Aug. 1821.

35.   *British Press*, 16 Nov. 1820, p. 1; Place Coll., set 18, III, fo. 12.

36.   *Courier*, 16 Nov. 1820, p. 3; *Statesman*, 18 Nov. 1820, p. 3; *New Times*, 18 Nov. 1820, p. 3; *British Press*, 16 Nov. 1820, p. 1 (from which the quotations are drawn); HO 40/15, 18 Nov., fo. 81.

37.   *IW*, 10 Dec. 1820, pp. 394–5; *Courier*, 7 Dec. 1820, p. 2; *Cobbett's Weekly Political Pamphlet*, 16 Dec. 1820, pp. 1529–30.

38.   *Black Dwarf*, 4 Oct. 1820, p. 480; 1 Nov., p. 624; 15 Nov., pp. 703–5; 28 March 1821, p. 454; HO 44/9, Stoddart to Hobhouse, 27 Aug. 1821, fo. 74; 40/16, fo. 40; *Morning Advertiser*, 12 Dec. 1820, p. 2; *British Press*, 12 Dec. 1820, p. 3; 23 Jan. 1821, p. 3; *Courier*, 22 Jan. 1821, p. 3; *Statesman*, 22 Jan. 1821, p. 3; *IW*, 28 Jan. 1821, p. 29.

39.   *Ibid.*, 24 Dec. 1820, p. 418; *Statesman*, 19 Dec. 1820, p. 4; *Courier*, 18 Dec. 1820, p. 3; *Morning Advertiser*, 19 Dec. 1820, p. 2.

40.   Wood to Place, 11 Jan. 1821, Place Coll., set 18, III. The deputations and processions are reported in the press; for some of the preparations and specific points, see: *The Times*, 29 Dec. 1820, p. 2; 23 Jan. 1821, p. 2; 27 Feb., p. 3; *Traveller*, 28 Dec. 1820, p. 3; *British Press*, 28 Dec. 1820, p. 2;

Statesman, 23 Jan. 1821, p. 2; 26 Feb., p. 3; 17 July, p. 2; *IW*, 10 Dec. 1820, p. 395; 28 Jan. 1821, p. 29; *Independent Observer*, 22 July 1821, p. 131; Place Coll., set 18, III.

41.   *IW*, 11 Feb. 1821, p. 50; 40/16, I.S., 17 March 1821, fo. 53.

42.   *Statesman*, 27 Feb. 1821, p. 3; *Black Dwarf*, 11 April 1821, pp. 530–1; HO 40/16, fos. 299, 301; 44/7, Blandford to Sidmouth, 8 Jan. 1821, fos. 28–28a; 64/11, 20 Nov. 1830; Place Coll., set 39, fo. 41.

43.   HO 44/7, Blandford to Sidmouth, 9 March (1821), fo. 66; 40/16, 6 April, fo. 59; 64/11, 20 Nov. 1830.

44.   Place Coll., set 19, fo. 1; HO 40/16, I.S., 2 May 1821, fo. 67.

45.   HO 40/16, 12, 13 and 16 July 1821, fos. 71, 75, 79; *Statesman*, 2 June 1821, p. 3; 17 July, p. 2; *Independent Observer*, 20 May 1821, p. 63; 27 May, p. 69.

46.   *Statesman*, 16 July 1821, p. 3; 18 July, p. 3.

47.   Burdett to Hobhouse, 9 Aug. 1821, Add. MS. 36,459, fo. 90.

48.   Memorandum in HO 44/9.

49.   HO 44/9, fos. 163, 76.

50.   HO 44/9, Sharp to Hobhouse, 25 Aug. 1821, fo. 85.

51.   *Traveller*, 14 Aug. 1821.

52.   For the events of 14 August, see: *The Times*; *Traveller*, 14 Aug.; *Statesman*, 15 Aug., pp. 1–3; *John Bull*, 19 Aug. 1821; *Independent Observer*, 19 Aug. 1821, pp. 162–4; HO 44/9, esp. Baker's report 16 Aug., White's report 18 Aug., and Baker's letter 19 Aug.; 44/10; Place Coll., set 71, II.

53.   HO 44/9, Stafford, fo. 174; 44/10, Stafford, 11 Sept. (1821), fo. 202; Galloway to Mrs Francis, 17 and 20 Aug., fos. 202b, 202d.

54.   *Statesman*, 22 Aug. 1821, p. 3; *Courier*, 25 Aug. 1821, p. 4; 27 Aug., p. 3; *Observer*, 26 Aug. 1821, p. 4; HO 44/9, Stoddart to Hobhouse, 22 Aug. (1821), fo. 74; Rev. Wood, 23 Aug., fo. 78; Sharp to Hobhouse, 25 Aug., fo. 85; Place Coll., set 71, II.

55.   *Courier*, 27 Aug. 1821, p. 3; *Observer*, 27 Aug. 1821, p. 4.

56.   For the events of 26 August, see: *The Times*, 27 Aug, 1821, p. 2; *Courier*, 27 Aug., p. 3; *Statesman*, 27 Aug., pp. 1–2; 28 Aug., p. 2; 29 Aug., p. 3; 31 Aug., p. 3; *Observer*, 27 Aug., p. 4; HO 44/9, esp. reports by Coulter, Dowly, Baker, Conant, Macneil, Glossop, Freck, Calvert and Birnie; City of London Common Council, *Report of the Committee for General Purposes; with Minutes of Evidence Relative to the Disturbances at Knightsbridge on Sunday the 26th Day of August 1821* (1821).

57.   *Statesman*, 19 Sept. 1821, p. 4; 25 Sept., p. 2; *The Times*, 25 Sept., p. 3.

58.   HO 40/17, Hervey to Sidmouth, 16 Jan. 1822, fo. 5; Fletcher to Peel, 6 Feb., fo. 71.

59.   HO 64/11, 20 Nov. 1830.

60.   *New Times*, 12 Nov. 1822, p. 3; *British Press*, 12 Nov. 1822, p. 3; *Englishman*, 17 Nov. 1822, p. 1.

61.   *The Times*, 9 Dec. 1819, p. 3; HO 42/200, Lord Mayor, 8 Dec. 1819.

62.   HO 40/17, fos. 845, 851.

63.   For the preparations for Hunt's reception and the events on his arrival, see: *Statesman*, 5 Nov. 1822, p. 1; 11 Nov., pp. 1, 2; 12 Nov., p. 2; *British Press*, 4 Nov. 1822, p. 3; 11 Nov., p. 3; 12 Nov., p. 2; *Observer*, 3

Nov. 1822, p. 2; 10 Nov., p. 3; 11 Nov., p. 4; *The Times*, 12 Nov. 1822, p. 2; *New Times*, 12 Nov. 1822, p. 3; *Englishman*, 17 Nov. 1822, p. 1; *Public Ledger*, 12 Nov. 1822, p. 3; *Black Dwarf*, 23 Oct. 1822, p. 596; 30 Oct., p. 637; 6 Nov. 1822, p. 664; 13 Nov., pp. 685, 689–91; HO 52/3, Collins to Peel, 24 Oct. 1822; 40/17, fos. 845, 849, 859, 866, 870.

Part 3: Artisans in Boom and Depression

Prologue

1. Gayer, Rostow and Schwartz, *Growth and Fluctuation of the British Economy*, I, 171–3, 208–10.
2. Information on London trade union activity is in the daily press, Place papers and *TN*. For the carpenters' strike, see: *New Times*, 4 June 1825, p. 3; Add. MS. 27,805, fos. 365–9; *TN*, 24 July 1825, p. 20; 31 July, p. 35; *Artizans' London and Provincial Chronicle*, 12 June 1825, pp. 1, 5; 19 June, p. 10; HO 40/18, fo. 514.
3. *The Times*, 21 Sept. 1825, p. 2.
4. For the sawyers, see: *SC* 1825, p. 197 (Fletcher); HO 40/18, fos. 520, 529; *TN*, 23 Oct. 1825, p. 228; 13 Nov., pp. 276–7.
5. *Ibid.*, 11 Sept. 1825, p. 137; 21 Aug., pp. 83–4, 85; *New Times*, 19 Aug. 1825, p. 1. Lists of subscriptions are in *TN*, 19 Aug. 1825–22 Jan. 1826.
6. *The Times*, 21 Sept. 1825, p. 2. Cf. *European Magazine*, Sept. 1825, pp. 89–90.
7. *Felix Farley's Bristol Journal*, 29 Oct. 1825, p. 3.
8. *The Times*, 23 Sept. 1825, p. 3.
9. Frettman to Solicitor-General, June 1825, Add. MS. 40,379, fo. 131. For the cabinet-makers' strike, see *New Times*, 7 April 1825, p. 4; and, for an earlier dispute, *Independent Observer*, 22 July 1821, p. 136.

Chapter 8. The Thames Shipwrights' Provident Union

1. Gayer, Rostow and Schwartz, *Growth and Fluctuation of the British Economy*, I, 285–6; II, 709, 801; R. C. O. Matthews, *A Study in Trade-Cycle History* (Cambridge, 1954), p. 119; *New Times*, 6 June 1820, p. 2; 25 July 1825, p. 2; *Morning Chronicle*, 6 June 1820, p. 2; 1 Feb. 1825, p. 3; 22 Aug., p. 3; *Public Ledger, passim*, e.g. 5 Dec. 1822, p. 1; 1 Jan. 1823, p. 3; 15 March, p. 3; 22 March, p. 3; 29 March, p. 3; 10 April, p. 3, 21 April, p. 1; 2 May, p. 3; 18 May, p. 2; 17 June, p. 3; 27 June, p. 1; *The Times*, 7 June 1823, p. 2; *Statesman*, 2 June 1821, p. 3; *MM*, 11 Oct. 1823, p. 107; 25 June 1825, p. 179; 2 July, p. 206; 9 July, p. 220; 13 Aug., p. 299.
2. Webb Coll., A, XXXIII, fos. 309, 315.
3. For all the grievances, see esp. evidence in *SC* 1825; also: *MM* 9 July 1825, p. 219; *Public Ledger*, 28 April 1825, p. 1.
4. For Gast's analysis, see *ibid.*, 18 Dec. 1822, p. 3; 1 Jan. 1823, p. 3; 2 May, p. 3; 27 June, p. 3.
5. *Ibid.*, 28 June 1823, p. 1; *House of Commons Journals* LXXVIII (1823), 442; *SC* 1825, p. 317 (Gast); *TFP*, 1 April 1827, p. 299. Cf. Foster, *Class Struggle and the Industrial Revolution*, p. 121.

6. *House of Commons Journals* LXXVIII (1823), 361; *Public Ledger*, 4 June 1823, p. 2.

7. *Morning Chronicle*, 1 Feb. 1825, p. 3; *New Times*, 1 July 1825, p. 3.

8. *SC* 1825, App. 12, rules 11 and 12, pp. 44, 45; pp. 251, 255, 257 (Lomax), 302 (Gast).

9. *SC* 1825, pp. 250–2 (Lomax); HO 40/18, April 1824, fo. 132. Add. MSS. 27,801, fo. 204; 27,803, fo. 154; *Morning Chronicle*, 1 Feb. 1825, p. 3; D. J. Rowe, 'A Trade Union of the North-East Seamen in 1825', *Econ. Hist. Rev.* 25 (1972), p. 81. In Sunderland was printed an address to the shipbuilders *identical* to one written by Gast in 1802 (Gast, *Calumny Defeated*, pp. 36–8; Add. MS. 27,799, fo. 56).

10. These aims were set out at its first two general meetings and early committee meetings; see: Webb Coll., A, XXXII, fos. 131–7; *SC* 1825, Apps. 12, pp. 42–8; 13, pp. 48–9; 20, pp. 61–3; also pp. 252–3 (Lomax).

11. *Ibid.*, App. 12, p. 43.

12. *Ibid.*, pp. 222 (Green), 242–3 (King), 244 (Evans). Cf., for Green, Webb Coll., A, XXXII, fo. 144 (28 Feb. 1825).

13. *SC* 1825, App. 12, no. 11, p. 44.

14. *Ibid.*, p. 291 (P. Hardy).

15. *Ibid.*, pp. 178, 191 (Fletcher).

16. *Ibid.*, pp. 266 (Lomax), 305, 306–7 (Gast).

17. *Ibid.*, p. 307 (Gast).

18. *Ibid.*, p. 373 (Purdy).

19. *Ibid.*, p. 172 (Taylor).

20. *Ibid.*, pp. 221 (Green), 311 (Gast); *Public Ledger*, 2 May 1825, p. 3.

21. For the history of the union and the disputes in 1824–5, see: *SC* 1825; Webb Coll., A, XXXII, esp. extracts from minute-book; *Morning Chronicle*, 1 Feb. 1825, p. 3; 23 Feb., p. 3; *Public Ledger*, 27 April 1825, p. 1; 28 April, p. 1; 2 May, p. 3; 10 Aug., p. 2; 15 Aug., p. 3; 22 Aug., p. 2; 16 Sept., p. 1; 19 Sept., p. 3; *New Times*, 25 July–15 Oct.; *The Times*, 10 Aug., p. 3; 17 Sept.–11 Oct.; *TN*, 31 July–23 Oct.; 12 March 1826, p. 559; 21 May, p. 721; *Hampshire Telegraph and Sussex Chronicle*, 8–22 Aug.; N. G. Clark, *A Scale of Prices for Job Work* (1825); Add. MS. 27,802; Wigram to Peel, 30 July (1825), Add. MS. 40,380, fos. 305–7; HO 40/18, fos. 370, 372, 428, 466, 708; *Hansard* XII, 598 (21 Feb. 1825).

22. *Morning Chronicle*, 1 Feb. 1825, p. 3; Webb Coll., A, XXXII, fo. 141 (10 Feb. 1825); Gast to Place, 19 March 1825, Add. MS. 27,802, fo. 180; J. McKenzie, *An Appeal to the Public on the Subject of the 'Shipwright's Provident Union'* (1825).

23. Add. MSS. 27,798, fos. 26–9; Gast to Place, 19 March 1825, 27,802, fo. 180; Place to Hume, 10 March 1825, 27,803, fo. 175.

24. Add. MSS, 27,798, fos. 31, 32–5; Place to Burdett, 20 June 1825, 27,802, fos. 34–5.

25. HO 40/18, J. Fletcher to Peel, 11 May (1825), fo. 440; Wigram to Peel, 30 May, fo. 460.

26. *New Times*, 26 July 1825, p. 3.

27. *SC* 1825, pp. 6–7.

28. Add. MSS. 27,798, fo. 38; 27,803, fo. 212; *Hansard* XII, col. 1347 (24 June 1825); *MM*, 13 Aug. 1825, p. 298.

29. *Royal Commission on Trades Unions*, 9th report, 1867–8, p. 7 (Wig-

ram); H. Green and R. Wigram, *Chronicles of Blackwall Yard* (1881), p. 58 (where the strike is wrongly dated 1830).

Chapter 9. The Combination Laws

1. Place's account is in Add. MS. 27,798, with accompanying papers in Add. MSS. 27,799–27,804. It is followed in S. and B. Webb, *History of Trade Unionism*, pp. 96–109, but treated critically by Thompson, *Making of the English Working Class*, pp. 516–21. The most recent account is in R. G. Kirby and A. E. Musson, *The Voice of the People. John Doherty, 1798–1854. Trade unionist, radical and factory reformer* (Manchester, 1975), pp. 34–9. On Place himself, see also W. E. S. Thomas, 'Francis Place and Working Class History', *Historical Journal* 5 (1962).
2. Add. MSS. 27,823, B, fos. 101–11; 35, 152, fos. 54–64.
3. Place to Mill, 15 Jan. 1815, Add. MS. 35,142, fo. 128; Place to Lovett, 6 Nov. 1835, Add. MS. 35,150, fo. 91; Place to Ensor, 18 Jan. 1818, Add. MS. 35, 153, fo. 40.
4. Add. MS. 27,800, fo. 3; Place to Hodgskin, 8 Sept. 1819, and Hodgskin to Place, 28 Nov. 1820, Add. MS. 35,153, fos. 68, 183; *House of Commons Journals* LXXIV (1819), 560–1; *Hansard* XL, cols. 1290–1 (22 June 1819).
5. *Ibid.*, x, col. 141 (12 Feb. 1824); *The Times*, 13 Feb. 1824, p. 2; Add. MS. 27,798, fos. 14–15.
6. Add. MS. 27,800, fo. 6; *House of Commons Journals*, March–July 1823; *Hansard* VIII, 366–7 (3 and 27 March 1823); IX, 540–50 (27 May); *The Times*, 4 March 1823, p. 3; 22 April, p. 2; 26 May, p. 2.
7. Kirby and Musson, *op. cit.*, p. 35; Add. MS. 27,800, fo. 46.
8. *Ibid.*, fos. 57, 189; Place to Hume, 6 Jan. 1824, Add. MS. 27,804, fo. 117; circular, fo. 150; *Black Dwarf*, 14 Jan 1824, pp. 57–9; 11 Feb., p. 189; *Hansard* x, 141-50 (12 Feb. 1824); *House of Commons Journals* LXXIX (1824), 29; *The Times*, 13 Feb. 1824, p. 2.
9. HO 40/18, Eckersley to Byng, 25 Feb. (1824), fo. 100.
10. For the petitions, see *House of Commons Journals* LXXIX (1824).
11. *Select Committee on Artizans and Machinery*, Parl. Papers, 1824, v. The other Londoners examined were Ravenhill, Alexander, Ablett, Burn, Thompson, Watkins, Martin and Seabrook.
12. HO 44/13, 10 April 1824; Hunt, 18 March; Smith, 26 May; 44/15, Brown to Peel, 25 March 1825. John Brown was an active factory reformer who around 1823 wrote down the celebrated memoirs of Robert Blincoe: see Brown to Peel, 2 Feb. and 23 May 1823, Add. MSS. 40,354 and 356; A. E. Musson, 'Robert Blincoe and the Early Factory System', in his *Trade Union and Social History* (1974).
13. *House of Commons Journals* LXXIX (1824); *The Times*, 4 June 1824, pp. 2, 3; 5 June, pp. 2, 3.
14. *MM*, 17 July 1824, p. 290.
15. Place to McDougal and Smith, n.d., Add. MS. 27,801, fo. 237.
16. HO 40/18, Eckersley to Byng, 27 Jan. 1825, fo. 318. Combinations in 1824–5 are reported generally in the press and HO 40/18.
17. For the events of 1825 concerning legislation, see: Place papers, esp. Add. MS. 27,802; *Hansard* XII–XIII; *House of Commons Journals* LXXX; the

daily press; *Felix Farley's Bristol Journal*, 7 May 1825, pp. 2, 4; 18 June, p. 3; 2 July, p. 3; *SC* 1825, pp. 392–3 (Woodruffe); *Journeyman, and Artizans' London and Provincial Chronicle* (hereafter *Artizans' Chronicle*); Kirby and Musson, *op. cit.*, pp. 36–9.

18. *Public Ledger*, 1 Jan. 1823, p. 3; *TN*, 16 April 1826, p. 635.
19. Gast to Place, 2 and 8 April 1825, Add. MS. 27,803, fos. 184–6; *New Times*, 21 April 1825, p. 4.
20. *SC* 1825, evidence of Chippendale, Chappell, Raven, Richards; Add. MS. 27,799, fos. 138–40; Webb Coll., A, xliv, fos. 10–13.
21. *SC* 1825, Report; *House of Commons Journals* lxxx; *New Times*, 17 June 1825, p. 2; 20 June, p. 2; 27 June, p. 2; 28 June, p. 2.
22. *Loc. cit.*; Place to Burdett, 25 June 1825, Add. MS. 27,802, fo. 37; *Hansard* xiii, col. 1404 (27 June 1825); Parl. Papers, 1825, i, 309; *Artizans' Chronicle*, 26 June 1825, p. 17.
23. *Hansard* xiii, col. 1406 (27 June 1825); *The Times*, 28 June 1825, p. 2; 30 June, p. 2.
24. *Loc. cit.*; *Morning Chronicle*, 30 June 1825, p. 1; *New Times*, 30 June 1825, p. 1.
25. *Loc. cit.*; *The Times*, 30 June 1825, p. 2; Place to Burdett, 25 June 1825, Add. MS. 27,802, fo. 37.
26. Loc. cit.
27. Add. MS. 27,798, fos. 39–40; *Hansard* xiii, cols. 1400–7 (27 June 1825); *The Times*, 28 June 1825, p. 2; 30 June, p. 2; *New Times*, 28 June 1825, p. 2; 30 June, p. 1; *Morning Chronicle*, 30 June 1825, p. 1; *House of Commons Journals* lxxx (1825), 29 June; *TN*, 17 July 1825, p. 6; *Artizans' Chronicle*, 3 July 1825, pp. 25, 27–30.
28. *House of Commons Journals* lxxx, 30 June; *Hansard* xiii, col. 1422 (30 June); *The Times*, 1 July, p. 2.
29. Place to Hobhouse, 2 July 1825, Add. MS. 36,461, fo. 141; Add. MS. 27,802, fo. 40; *House of Commons Journals*, 5 July.
30. *The Times*, 5 July 1825, p. 2; Add. MS. 27,803, fo. 1; *Artizans' Chronicle*, 10 July 1825, pp. 33, 35.
31. *TN*, 31 July 1825, p. 38.
32. Longson to Place, 1 June 1825, Add. MS. 27,803, fo. 286; Kirby and Musson, *op. cit.*, pp. 37–41.
33. *Op. cit.*, p. 38; HO 40/18, Sunderland magistrates to Peel, 16 Sept., fo. 768; Gray, 26 Sept., fo. 774; D. J. Rowe, 'A Trade Union of the North-East Coast Seamen in 1825', *Econ. Hist. Rev.* 25 (1972), p. 95.
34. *Felix Farley's Bristol Journal*, 13 Aug. 1825, p. 3; *TN*, 7 Aug. 1825, p. 51. For the Staffordshire union, see HO 44/13, Dec. 1825.

Chapter 10. The Trades' Newspaper and Francis Place

1. Place Coll., set 16, i, fo. 13; set 61, fo. 47; *Artizans' Chronicle*, 26 June 1825, p. 18.
2. See above, p. 54.
3. Shipwrights' resolution, *TN*, 29 Oct. 1826, p. 122.
4. Gast's letters in favour of General Union are in *TN*, 1 Jan. 1826, p. 387; 16 April, pp. 635–6; *Trades' Free Press* (hereafter *TFP*), 12 July 1828, p. 406; *Weekly Free Press* (hereafter *WFP*), 4 Oct. 1828, p. 499; 22 Nov., p.

554. His ideas can also be studied in: the many reports of his speeches in these three newspapers; *Public Ledger*, 18 Dec. 1822, p. 3; 13 Jan. 1823, p. 3; 27 June, p. 3; Gast to Place, 15 Feb. 1827, Place Coll., set 57, fos. 17–20.

5.   *TN*, 1 Jan. 1826, p. 387; 19 March, p. 566; *WFP*, 4 Oct. 1828, p. 499.

6.   *TN*, 16 April 1826, p. 636.

7.   Gast to Place, 15 Feb. 1827, Place Coll., set 57, fo. 20.

8.   Gast to Place, 3 July 1834, Add. MS. 27,829, fo. 20.

9.   *TN*, 16 Oct. 1825, p. 218; 13 Nov., p. 282; 11 Dec., p. 346; 18 Dec., p. 363.

10.   See below, chap. 14.

11.   Gast to Place, 15 Feb. 1827, fo. 18.

12.   Add. MS. 27,803, fo. 403; *Laws and Regulations of the Trades' Newspaper Association* (n.d. = 1825), p. 3; *TN*, 17 July 1825, p. 1. Cf. Gast: 'it had long been an object with him to induce the working classes to give up their sensual indulgences—to inform their heads as well as their bellies—and to procure for themselves an organ of defence in which the public might see the truth reflected as from a polished mirror, and the falsehoods of their enemies exposed fully and fearlessly' (*TN*, 5 Nov. 1826, p. 133). See also *TN*, 16 July 1826, p. 2.

13.   Thompson, *Making of the English Working Class*, p. 775.

14.   Wooler to Place, 21 Feb. 1824, Add. MS. 37,949, fo. 140; *Black Dwarf*, 28 Jan. 1824, p. 107; *Public Ledger*, 6 Dec. 1825, p. 3. The *New Times* carried reports on workers' activities from 15 April to 19 Aug. For popular periodical literature generally, see: A. E. Dobbs, *Education and Social Movements 1700–1850* (1919); R. K. Webb, *The British Working Class Reader 1790–1848. Literacy and social tension* (1955), pp. 28–34, 49–52, 58–63; R. D. Altick, *The English Common Reader* (Chicago, 1957), chap. 14.

15.   For the origins of the *Trades' Newspaper*, see Add. MSS. 27,802 and 27,803; *TN*, 17 July 1825, p. 1; *Artizans' Chronicle*, 12 June 1825, p. 4; *Laws and Regulations*; Phillips to Place, 5 March (1826), Add. MS. 37,949, fo. 150.

16.   *Laws and Regulations*, p. 12; *TN*, 9 July 1826, p. 827.

17.   *MM*, 16 July 1825, p. 239; Place to Hobhouse, 5 Dec. 1830, Add. MS. 35,148, fo. 74.

18.   Woodruffe to Place, 27 July 1825, and Knowles to Place, 18 Sept., Add. MS. 27,803, fos. 85, 252.

19.   Letters to Place in Add. MS. 27,803 from: Woodruffe, 9 July and 17 Aug. 1825; Adams, 15 June; Hodgson, 10 July; McDougall, 8 July; Tester, 10 July; Clarke, 16 July; Foster, 25 July; Longson, 6 Aug.; Knowles, 18 Sept.; fos. 79, 81, 100, 249, 252, 314, 321, 344, 386, 470; also fos. 399, 401; *Artizans' Chronicle*, 12 June 1825, p. 4.

20.   Tester to Committee of the Trades' Societies, Add. MS. 27,803, fos. 556–7. Cf. *TN*, 23 July 1826, p. 13.

21.   *Ibid.*, 11 Dec. 1825, p. 344; 8 Jan. 1826, p. 404; 22 Jan., p. 437; Tester to Place, 19 Feb. 1826, Add. MS. 27,803, fo. 410.

22.   Carlile in *Lion*, 19 Jan. 1829, p. 42.

23.   *TN*, 19 March 1826, p. 569; 9 July, p. 827.

24.   *Ibid.*, 8 Jan. 1826, p. 404; 22 Jan., p. 437; 19 March, p. 569; 26 March, p. 592.

25. *Ibid.*, 9 Oct. 1825, pp. 198–9; 8 Jan. 1826, p. 404; 26 March, p. 587; 2 July, p. 819; Anderson to Place, n.d., Add. MS. 27,803, fo. 421.

26. Loc. cit., and fo. 422; *TN*, 4 June 1826, p. 749; 23 July, p. 13.

27. *Ibid.*, 6 Aug. 1826, p. 29; 20 Aug., p. 43; 8 Oct., p. 101; 22 Oct., p. 116; 10 Dec., p. 172; 17 Dec., p. 180; 24 Dec., p. 188; 29 April 1827, p. 330.

28. *Ibid.*, 8 Oct. 1826, p. 99; 5 Nov., p. 133; 26 Nov., p. 158; 17 Dec., p. 182; 24 Dec., p. 187.

29. *Ibid.*, 7 Jan., 1827, p. 205; 28 Jan., p. 228; 4 Feb., p. 236; *TFP*, 21 Oct. 1827, p. 100; Add. MS. 35,146, fo. 16 (30 April 1826).

30. Place to Worsley, 16 May 1825, Add. MS. 27,803, fo. 396.

31. *MM*, 14 Feb. 1824, p. 400; 6 March, p. 444; 24 July, p. 316.

32. Add. MS. 27,803, fos. 400, 402, 403.

33. Woodruffe to Place, 9 and 20 July and 7 Oct. 1825, and Hume to Place, 23 and 30 July, Add. MS. 27,803, fos. 79, 114, 404, 406, 408.

34. T. Kelly, *George Birkbeck, Pioneer of Adult Education* (Liverpool, 1957), chaps. 4–7. I have drawn mainly on Place's account and accompanying papers in Add. MSS. 27,823–4, and *MM* from 11 Oct. 1823 to 16 July 1825; also: Add. MS. 35,146, fo. 48 (23 Sept. 1826); *TN*; J.F. in *Republican*, 4 Aug. 1826, pp. 107–9. See also: Robertson to Peel, 22 April 1825, Add. MS. 40,377, fo. 71, and in *The Times*, 7 June 1828. For the general context, see also: Kelly, 'The Origins of Mechanics' Institutes', *British Journal of Educational Studies* 1 (1953), 17–27; Webb, 'Working Class Readers in Early Victorian England', *EHR* 65 (1950), 333–57; *idem.*, *British Working Class Reader*, esp. chaps. 1–2 and pp. 62–6; Dobbs, *Education and Social Movements*; Altick, *English Common Reader*, chap. 9; Thompson, *Making of the English Working Class*, pp. 711–46. For the earlier West London Lancasterian Association, see Prochaska, 'The Practice of Radicalism: Educational Reform in Westminster', in Stevenson, *London in the Age of Reform*.

35. *MM*, 26 March 1824, p. 427; 16 April, p. 30; 30 April, pp. 50–2; 21 May, p. 108; 18 Feb. 1826, p. 272; 25 Feb., p. 302; 25 March, p. 354. See also S. Pollard, '*Laissez-faire* and Shipbuilding', *Econ. Hist. Rev.* 5 (1952).

36. Place to Mill, 9 Aug. 1816, Add. MS. 35,152, fo. 202; Place to Burdett, 6 Dec. 1833, and to Coates, 22 Dec., Add. MS. 35,149, fos. 241, 257.

37. *The Times*, 29 Nov. 1825, p. 2; *Morning Chronicle*, 29 Nov. 1825, p. 3; *Public Ledger*, 30 Nov., p. 2; *New Times*, 29 Nov., p. 3; *TN*, 4 Dec., p. 327; 29 April 1827, p. 330.

38. *Ibid.*, 23 July 1826, p. 10.

39. Lovett to Place, 16 Jan. 1837, Add. MS. 35,150, fo. 225.

40. *Republican*, 2 Dec. 1825, p. 681.

41. *The Times*, 29 Nov. 1825, p. 2.

42. Thompson, *Making of the English Working Class*, p. 766.

43. Place to Burdett, 6 Dec. 1833, and to Coates, 22 Dec., Add. MS. 35,149, fos. 241, 257; Cray to Place, 4 Nov. 1835 and n.d., Place Coll., set 52, fos. 102–3, 107–9.

44. *MM*, 24 July 1824, pp. 308–9; 31 July, pp. 323–5; 11 Sept., p. 429; 11 Dec., pp. 187–92.

45. *Mechanic's Weekly Journal; or, Artisan's Miscellany*, 6 Dec. 1823, p. 60; 13 Dec., p. 75; 10 Jan. 1824, p. 141; 21 Feb., p. 236.

46. *MM*, 18 Sept. 1824, pp. 436–42.

47. *Ibid.*, 6 Dec. 1823, pp. 234–8.

48. *Lion*, 10 April 1829, p. 477; Lovett, *Life and Struggles*, p. 29.

49. *NS* , 15 Aug. 1846, p. 5 (M'Grath).

50. *Republican*, 27 May 1825, pp. 668–9; 29 Dec. 1826, pp. 791–2; Lovett, *op. cit.*, pp. 28–9.

51. *Republican*, 13 Jan. 1826, p. 41.

52. *Gauntlet*, 17 Feb. 1833, p. 17.

53. *TN*, 4 Dec. 1825, p. 323; 28 May 1826, p. 731; *Republican*, 8 Sept. 1826, p. 269; 6 Oct., pp. 413–15; *Lion*, 4 Jan. 1828, p. 1.

54. *Republican*, 27 Jan. 1826, p. 104; *New Times*, 30 March 1825, p. 3; *TN*, 16 July 1826, p. 1; 14 Jan. 1827, p. 201.

55. Johnson, *MM*, 29 Nov. 1823, p. 220.

56. J.F. in *Republican*, 8 Sept. 1826, p. 269.

57. E. Royle, 'Mechanics' Institutes and the Working Classes, 1840–1860', *Historical Journal* 14 (1971), 308.

58. E.g. the printer, Richard Taylor, the engineers Galloway, Martineau, Maudslay and Donkin, and Place himself.

59. Add. MS. 27,804, fo. 150.

60. 'A *combination* to obtain a certain price for labour is but a species of intimidation' (*MM*, 13 March 1824, p. 10). The attacks on Place's evidence are in 13 March, p. 10, and 27 March, p. 42. There are comments on the Combination Laws from 24 Jan. to, esp., 12 June, p. 212.

61. *TN*, 17 July 1825, p. 7; 31 July, p. 34; 4 Dec., p. 329.

62. *Ibid.*, 30 Oct. 1825, p. 248; 13 Nov., p. 284; 27 Nov., pp. 297, 309.

63. E.g. Single in *ibid.*, 9 July 1826, p. 828.

64. *Ibid.*, 3 Sept. 1826, p. 59; 17 Sept., p. 74; TFP, 19 Sept. 1827, p. 49; 21 Feb. 1828, p. 223; *MM*, 13 Oct. 1827, p. 208; 22 Dec., p. 368; 22 March 1828, p. 142; Kelly, *George Birkbeck*, pp. 109–10.

65. *MM*, 31 March 1827, p. 200; 7 April, p. 215; 21 April, pp. 244–7; 12 May, pp. 295–6; vii, p. 450; *TN*, 29 April 1827, p. 330.

66. *TFP*, 2 Sept. 1827, p. 44; 9 Sept., p. 49; 30 Sept., p. 73; Add. MSS. 27,824, fo. 127; 35,146, fo. 10 (14 April 1826).

67. Place's views were given frequently in *TN* (1825–6, 1827), *Bolton Chronicle* (1825–6), and in his letters. See also: *Morning Chronicle*, 1 Sept. 1825, p. 3; *Republican*, 11 Aug. 1826, pp. 145–8; 18 Aug., pp. 162–70; 13 Oct., pp. 426–7; *Lion*, 20 June 1828, pp. 774–80; 27 June, pp. 815–20; Place Coll., set 61, fo. 29; Place to Ensor, 18 Jan. 1818, Add. MS. 35,153, fo. 40; Place to Burdett, 1 May 1824, Add. MS. 27,823, fo. 337. For a summary of his outlook, see Thomas, 'Francis Place and Working Class History'; and for the 'Malthusian' issue: Thompson, *Making of the English Working Class*, pp. 742 n. 2, 777; A. McLaren, 'Contraception and the Working Classes; the Social Ideology of the English Birth Control Movement in its early years', *Comparative Studies in Society and History* 18 (1976).

68. *TN*, 9 Oct. 1825, p. 193.

69. Place Coll., set 16, i, fo. 214; ii, fo. 92.

70. W. J. Linton, *Memories* (1895), p. 158.

71.   *Black Dwarf*, 25 Feb. 1824, pp. 238–44; *TN*, 11 Sept. 1825, p. 129; *Artizans' Chronicle*, 4 Sept. 1825, p. 100; *New Times*, 1 Aug. 1825, p. 2.
72.   Letters to Place from Rippon, 5 Dec. 1825; Longson, 6 Aug.; Tester, 13 Aug.; Mowatson, 19 July, Add. MS. 27,803, fos. 119, 321, 347, 478; Add. MS. 27,805, fo. 357; Place Coll., set 16, fo. 43.
73.   G. J. Holyoake, *The Life and Character of Richard Carlile* (1870), p. 20. See Carlile's praise of Place in *Operative*, 17 Feb. 1839, p. 6.
74.   *Republican*, 6 May 1825, pp. 548–69; 17 Feb. 1826, p. 200; HO 64/11, 29 Nov. (1831); Smith to Place, 18 March 1826, and Tait to Northouse, 23 Jan. 1827, Place Coll., set 61, fos. 60, 93.
75.   *MM*, 7 March 1824, p. 42; 12 June, p. 211; *TN*, 17 July 1825, pp. 1–2; 24 July, p. 17; 31 July, p. 33; 11 Sept., pp. 129–30.
76.   Gast in *Public Ledger*, 18 Dec. 1822, p. 3.
77.   *TN*, 20 May 1827, p. 357.
78.   Place to Doherty, 7 April 1829, Place Coll., set 16, II, fo. 92.
79.   Place Coll., set 16, I, fo. 211. Cf. *Manchester Gazette*, quoted in *TN*, 24 July 1825, p. 17. Place and Longson engaged in a controversy in the *Bolton Chronicle* in 1826.
80.   *TN*, 21 May 1826, p. 717; 10 Sept., p. 65.
81.   J.F. in *Republican*, 22 Sept. 1826, p. 333.
82.   *TN*, 4 Dec. 1825, p. 323.
83.   Single in *ibid.*, 13 Nov. 1825, p. 273.
84.   *TN*, 21 Aug.–23 Oct. 1825, and Hodgskin's letters 30 Oct. 1825, p. 242; 29 Jan. 1826, p. 452; *Artizans' Chronicle*, 14 Aug. 1825, p. 73.
85.   Add. MSS. 27,791, fos. 269–70; 35,146, fo. 48 (23 Sept. 1826).
86.   J.G. (Gast) in *Public Ledger*, 1 Jan. 1823, p. 3. Cf. G. Stedman Jones, 'England's First Proletariat', *New Left Review* 90 (1975), 58.
87.   Lacey and Knight, preface to *MM*, v; Add. MS. 35,146, fo. 10 (13 April 1826); *TN*, 5 March 1826, p. 537; 19 March, p. 569.
88.   Farrar to Place, 13 March 1826, Add. MS. 27,803, fos. 556–9. Another man seeking the editorship was Sir Richard Phillips, who found himself without an income (Phillips to Place, 5 and 7 March (1826), Add. MS. 37,949, fos. 150, 152).
89.   See Place's diary, Add. MS. 35,146, fos. 11, 16, 24, 25, 26, 28, 44, 63, 88.
90.   Ibid., fo. 34 (25 July 1826). See above, n. 000.
91.   Ibid., fos. 75 (19 March 1827), 78 (4 April), 101–2 (4 May 1829); Woodruffe to Place, 8 March 1827, Add. MS. 37,949, fo. 194; Place Coll., set 16, II, fo. 151.

Chapter 11. The Trades in Depression

1.   Gayer, Rostow and Schwartz, *Growth and Fluctuation of the British Economy*, I, 171, 173–4, 210, 238–40.
2.   Place to Hume, 9 Feb. 1824, Add. MS. 27,804, fo. 178. For the position of the silk industry, see: *TN*, 29 Jan. 1826, p. 456; Place Coll., set 16, II, 'Silk'; Thompson and Yeo, *The Unknown Mayhew*, pp. 104–15.
3.   Add. MSS. 27,799, fos. 163–71; 27,800, fo. 49; 27,805; HO 40/18, fo. 48; *New Times*, 15 April 1825, p. 3; *TN*, 14 Aug. 1825, p. 69; Wallis and Bolter to Peel, 27 June 1825, Add. MS. 40,379, fo. 358.

4.   *TN*, 18 Dec. 1825, pp. 361, 368; 25 Dec., p. 375; 8 Jan. 1826, p. 403; 22 Jan., pp. 435–6, 440–1; 29 Jan., pp. 455–6, 457; 5 Feb., p. 473; *MM*, 11 Feb. 1826, pp. 262–3; *New Times*, 4 Oct. 1825, p. 3; HO 40/18, Maddick to Peel, 14 Nov. (1825), fo. 872; 40/19, Hale to Peel, 9 Jan. 1826, fos. 1–8; 40/20, fo. 292; 40/21, fos. 146, 162, 226, 227, 230, 279, 286, 309; 40/22, fos. 70, 73, 75, 77, 83; 40/23, fos. 53, 166, 167, 207, 310; 40/24, fos. 31, 98; Add. MS. 34,243, B, fos. 5–20; Cray to Place, n.d., Place Coll., set 52, fos. 99–100; Place Coll., set 21, fo. 45; set 16, II, 'Silk'. The distress of the Spitalfields weavers needs no further references.
5.   For the activities of the weavers 1826–31, see: *TN, TFP, WFP passim*; HO 40; and also: *London Free Press*, 15 July 1827; *Carpenter's Political Letters*, 23 Dec. 1830, p. 14; 28 Jan. 1831, pp. 14–15; Add. MS. 35,146, fo. 28 (18 June 1826); Place Coll., set 16, II, 'Silk'; set 41, fo. 12; *PMG*, 7 Jan. 1832, p. 238; *London Dispatch*, 14 May 1837, p. 274; *Spitalfields Weavers' Journal*, Dec. 1837, pp. 34–5.
6.   For the shoemakers in the 1820s, in addition to the references above, p. 351, note 54, see: *TN*, 11 Dec. 1825, p. 340; 25 Dec., pp. 372–3; *PMG*, 17 May 1834, p. 119; Lovett in *Hetherington's Dispatch*, in Place Coll., set 56, 1836, fo. 10; Foster, *Class Struggle and the Industrial Revolution*, pp. 85–7. For the 1825 City men's shoemakers strike, see: *Courier*, 23 Aug. 1825; *New Times*, 5 May 1825, p. 3; 25 June, p. 3.
7.   *TN*, 25 Dec. 1825, p. 373. Cf. Davenport in *ibid.*, 4 Dec. 1825, p. 323.
8.   *Ibid.*, 21 Aug. 1825, p. 85; 28 Aug., p. 100; 6 Aug. 1826, p. 27; 13 Aug., p. 38; 20 Aug., p. 43.
9.   For the tailors, in addition to references above, p. 351, n. 53, see: *The Times*, 27 March 1830, p. 7; *WFP*, 3 July 1830; *Man*, 24 Nov. 1833, p. 159; 1 Dec., p. 161; 8 Dec., p. 173; *Crisis*, 30 Nov. 1833, pp. 109–10; *Pioneer*, 15 March 1834, pp. 253–4; 3 May, pp. 329–30, 334, 335; 10 May, pp. 338, 343; *True Sun*, 29 April 1834, p. 1; 6 May, p. 2: 9 May, p. 1; Place Coll., set 51, fos. 246–7; set 52, fos. 87–9; Lovett in *Hetheringtons' Dispatch*, 6 July 1836, in set 56, fo. 10; Place to Longson, 28 May 1834, Add. MS. 35,149, fo. 293; Webb Coll., A, XIV, fos. 44–66; *Red Republican*, 16 Nov. 1850, pp. 169–70; 23 Nov., pp. 177–9.
10.   For the carpenters, see below, p. 385, n. 2. For cabinet-makers, Lovett, art. cit.; Thompson and Yeo, *The Unknown Mayhew*, pp. 358–99, esp. 388–91.
11.   *SC on Artizans and Machinery*, 1824, p. 154 (Watkins); Add. MS. 35,146, fo. 10 (14 April 1826).
12.   *New Times*, 2 May 1825, p. 3; *TN*, 11 Dec. 1825, p. 339; 2 April 1826, p. 595.
13.   *Morning Chronicle*, 17 Aug. 1825, p. 2 (quoting an evening paper).
14.   *New Times*, 1 Aug. 1825, p. 2.
15.   *TN*, 4 March 1827, p. 269; *WFP*, 14 Aug. 1830.
16.   *TN*, 17 July 1825, p. 3; *PMG*, 1 March 1834, p. 1; *People's Conservative*, 15 March 1834, pp. 43–4; Add. MSS. 27,835, fos. 64–6; Place to Parkes, 21 April 1834, 35,154, fos. 198–200; Place to Hume, 6 March 1834, Place Coll., set 51, fo. 213; (Burn), *Glimpse at the Social Condition of the Working Classes*, p. 41.
17.   *IW*, 18 Feb. 1821, p. 50; J.F. in *Republican*, 4 Aug. 1826, p. 106.
18.   HO 40/16, I.S., 13 July (1821). fo. 79; *TN*, 17 Sept. 1826, p. 74; 7

Jan. 1827, p. 206; 23 July, p. 11; HO 40/25, 4 Nov. (1830), fo. 84; *Crisis*, 6 July 1833, p. 204; *Pioneer*, 21 Sept. 1833, p. 20; Thompson and Yeo, *The Unknown Mayhew*, pp. 323–35. Cf. Thompson, *Autobiography of an Artisan*, pp. 165–7, 171, 173–4, 176.

19.   *New Times*, 2 May 1825, p. 3; *TN*, 24 Dec. 1826, p. 190; 14 Jan. 1827, p. 213; 18 March 1827, p. 281; *Morning Chronicle*, 15 Sept. 1830; HO 40/25, 4 Nov. (1830), fo. 79; Howe, *London Compositor*, pp. 293–5; Howe and Waite, *London Society of Compositors*, pp. 151–4.

20.   *TN*, 16 April 1826, p. 636.

21.   *TFP*, 12 July 1828, p. 406.

22.   *TN*, 1 Jan. 1826, p. 387.

23.   *Ibid.*, 19 March 1826, p. 566. Cf. 'If all the working Classes of Society could see & feel as I do, I would never trouble either "King or Parliament,—but, notwithstanding this opinion of mine, I still think were the working classes is to weak of themselves & not united enough to protect themselves from any Chance of Circumstance which might occur, The Legislature ought to step in between and prevent the overwhelming distress that now deluge the Country' (Gast to Place, 15 Feb. 1827, Place Coll., set 57, fo. 19).

24.   *Ibid.*, fo. 20.

25.   HO 40/22, Wigram to Peel, 25 Sept. 1828, fo. 384.

26.   *TN*, 15 Oct. 1826, p. 106; *Select Committee on British Shipping*, Parl. Papers, 1844, VIII, 24–5, 37 (Somes).

27.   *TN*, 5 Feb. 1826, pp. 476–7.

28.   *TFP*, 1 April 1827, p. 299.

29.   *Republican*, 14 April 1826, p. 459; HO 44/16, fos. 19–21.

30.   *TN*, 19 March 1826, p. 566.

31.   *Republican*, 23 Dec. 1825, p. 771.

32.   Purdy, *TN*, 5 Feb. 1826, p. 476. Cf. Watkins, 19 Feb. 1826, p. 503.

33.   See above, p. 160. *TN*, 5 Feb. 1826, p. 476; 26 Feb., p. 518.

34.   *Ibid.*, 5 Feb. 1826, pp. 476, 480; 19 Feb., pp. 502, 503, 512; 26 Feb., pp. 519–20; 12 March, p. 560.

35.   *Ibid.*, 29 Jan. 1826, pp. 450–1; 19 Feb., p. 501; HO 44/16, Fletcher to Hobhouse, 5 March 1826; 40/19, Fletcher, 21 March (1826), fo. 197; 9 April, fo. 217.

36.   *TN*, 8 Jan. 1826, p. 401; 29 Jan., p. 449; 5 March, p. 529; 12 March, p. 545; 23 April, p. 641; 15 Oct., p. 107; 29 Oct., p. 126; 12 Nov., p. 139; *Republican*, 27 Oct. 1826, p. 481; Add. MS. 35,146, fos. 44–59 (30 Sept–21 Nov. 1826); Place Coll., set 13; HO 40/22, fos. 3, 49, 57, 64 (27 Nov.), 76 (26 March).

37.   *TN*, 4 March 1827, p. 269; *TFP*, 28 Oct. 1827, p. 106; 4 Nov., p. 117; 2 Dec., p. 147; *WFP*, 1 Nov. 1828, p. 534; 13 Dec., p. 580; 7 Feb. 1829; 21 Feb.; 28 Feb.; Place Coll., set 13. Cleary helped found the Westminster one.

38.   *TN*, 9 April 1826, p. 612.

39.   *Ibid.*, 12 March 1826, p. 547.

40.   *Ibid.*, 26 Feb. 1826, p. 521.

41.   *Public Ledger*, 18 Dec. 1822, p. 3.

42.   Gast's letters on the Corn Laws are in *TN*, 19 March 1826, p. 566; 16 April, pp. 635–6.

43.   *Ibid.*, 24 Dec. 1826, p. 190; 7 Jan. 1827, p. 205; 28 Jan., p. 226; 18 March, p. 281; *Carpenter's Political Letters*, 21 Oct. 1831, p. 16.

44.   For the Golden Lion meetings, see *TN*, 7 Jan.–25 Feb. 1827. Also, Gast to Place,15 Feb. 1827, Place Coll., set 57, fo. 17; and the case against machinery in *TN*, 16 July 1826, p. 3. The bookbinders were worried about the introduction of rolling machines (Howe and Child, *Society of London Bookbinders*, chap. 12).

45.   *Plain and Practical Observations on the Use and Application of Machinery, in a Series of Letters, drawn up at the request of the Frome Committee* (Bath, 1827); *TN*, 11 Feb. 1827, p. 245; 29 April, p. 331.

46.   HO 40/18, Longson to Peel, March 1823, fo. 21; 40/19–20; 44/16; *The Times*, 31 May 1823, p. 2; Place Coll., set 16, I, fo. 211, and B; Thompson, *Making of the English Working Class*, pp. 276–80; Kirby and Musson, *Voice of the People*, pp. 41–2.

47.   Place Coll., set 16, I, fos. 185, 187, 195, 211, 214, 219, 222, 228, 237, 244, 263, 267, 275, 280; HO 44/17, Ramsay to Peel, 16 March (1826).

48.   W. Longson, *An Appeal to Master, Workmen and the Public, shewing the Cause of the Distress of the Labouring Classes* (Manchester, 1827), pp. iii, 14, 15.

49.   *TN*, 21 May 1826, pp. 715–16; Add. MS. 35,146, fos. 76–7 (21–7 March 1827), 83 (30 April); Place Coll., set 16, I, fos. 244, 267, 275; II, fos. 17–19; *TFP*, 1 April 1827, p. 298.

50.   *TN*, 25 Feb. 1827, p. 259.

51.   See above, p. 39.

52.   *TN*, 11 Sept. 1825, p. 135; 2 Oct., p. 180; 6 Nov., p. 263; 13 Nov., p. 280; 4 Dec., pp. 322–3; 11 Dec., pp. 338–9; 1 Jan. 1826, p. 389.

53.   *Ibid.*, 16 April 1826, p. 635.

54.   J. Powell, *An Analytical Exposition of the Erroneous Principles and Ruinous Consequences of the Financial and Commercial Systems of Great Britain* (1826), p. 485. For Powell's ideas, see also his: *A Letter addressed to Edward Ellice, Esq. M.P.* (1819); *A Letter addressed to Weavers, Shopkeepers and Publicans on the great value of the principle of the Spitalfields Act* (1824); *TN*, 5 Feb. 1826, p. 475; 6 Aug., p. 25; 27 Aug., p. 49; 3 Sept., p. 57; 17 Dec., p. 182.

55.   For this society, see: *Morning Post*, 23 Aug. 1819, p. 4; 19 Dec. 1820, p. 2; *Morning Chronicle*, 23 Aug. 1819, p. 3; HO 42/189, Wills to Sidmouth, 6 July 1819; *MM*, 15 May 1824, p. 154; *TN*, 24 Dec. 1826, p. 187; *WFP*, 26 Sept. 1829.

56.   For the General Association, see: *TN*, 8 April 1827, p. 308; 15 April, p. 317; 29 April, p. 330; 23 Feb. 1828, p. 247.

57.   *Public Ledger*, 18 Dec. 1822, p. 3.

58.   *TN*, 19 March 1826, p. 566.

59.   Webb, *British Working Class Reader*, p. 99.

60.   *MM*, 22 May 1824, p. 168; Add. MS. 27,798, fos. 63–4.

61.   *TN*, 13 Nov. 1825, p. 273; 8 Oct. 1826, p. 97.

62.   *Ibid.*, 4 Dec. 1825, p. 324.

63.   *Ibid.*, 13 Nov. 1825, p. 273; 12 Feb. 1826, p. 487.

64.   Add. MSS. 27,824, fos. 205–7, 210, 213–19, 231, 237; Burdett to Place, 3 Dec. 1833, and Place to Burdett, 6 Dec., and to Coates, 22 Dec., 35,149, fos. 240, 241, 257–9.

65.   *TN*, 7 Jan. 1827, p. 206.
66.   *Ibid.*, 22 July 1827, p. 425; *TFP*, 9 Aug. 1828, p. 437; *WFP*, 27 March 1830.
67.   Add. MS. 35,146, fo. 45 (8 Oct. 1826).
68.   Ibid., fos. 44–7 (3–17 Oct. 1826), 68–71 (5–16 Dec.); Hume to Place, 30 Sept. 1826, Add. MS. 37,949, fo. 168; Place Coll., set 61, fo. 57; *New Times*, 18 Jan. 1828, p. 3.
69.   Add. MS. 35,146, fos. 69 (9 Dec. 1826), 76 (21 March 1827), 89, 91 (14 and 21 June); *TN*, 22 July 1827, p. 425; *London Free Press*, 22 July 1827.
70.   *TN*, 22 July 1827, p. 425; *TFP*, 12 July 1828, p. 401.
71.   *Ibid.*, 25 Nov. 1827, p. 140; 13 Jan. 1828, p. 193; 3 May, p. 322; 12 July, p. 401; *Lion*, 23 Jan. 1829, pp. 125–6; Add. MS. 35,146, fo. 107 (7 Jan. 1830).
72.   *WFP*, 7 March 1829; 18 Sept. 1830; *Carpenter's Monthly Political Magazine*, Sept. 1831, p. 11; *DNB*.
73.   *TN*, 3 June 1827, p. 373.
74.   For the Kidderminster meetings, see: *TFP*, 24 May–20 Sept. 1828; *The Times*, 5 June 1828; 18 July, p. 1; 19 July, p. 4; *Morning Advertiser*, 21, 24 and 31 July, 19 and 21 Aug. 1828; *Morning Chronicle*, 14 Aug. 1828, p. 1; 20 Aug., p. 3. See also: *TFP*, 9 Aug. 1828, p. 437; 23 Aug., p. 454; *WFP*, 6 Sept. 1828, p. 466; 4 Oct., p. 499; *Sunday Herald*, 17 Aug. 1828, p. 3.

Chapter 12. The Benefit Societies' Campaign

1.   J. Wade, *The Black Book* (1823), II, 148; *Black Dwarf*, 2 April 1823, p. 487.
2.   *Public Ledger*, 21 Aug. 1812, p. 3. For criticisms of benefit societies, see: *MM*, 1 Nov. 1823, p. 147; *Felix Farley's Bristol Journal*, 19 Feb. 1825, p. 3; *Public Ledger*, 16 Oct. 1824, p. 4; *The Times*, 3 July 1827; 20 Jan. 1828, p. 4; 30 June 1829, p. 3; Becher, *Constitution of Friendly Societies*, pp. 49–63. For the 1819 Act and the enquiries, see: *New Times*, 10 Sept. 1825, p. 1; 18 Oct., p. 4; *The Times*, 29 Oct. 1827, p. 2; Gosden, *The Friendly Societies in England*, pp. 173–6.
3.   *Select Committee on Laws respecting Friendly Societies*, Parl. Papers, 1825, IV; do., 1826–7, III.
4.   *TFP*, 29 July 1827, p. 3; 19 July 1828, p. 414.
5.   *Ibid.*, 7 Oct. 1827, p. 83.
6.   For the early meetings, under Gast's chairmanship, see: *TN*, 22 April 1827, p. 321; *TFP*, 29 July, p. 3; 9 Sept., p. 5; 7 Oct., p. 83; 9 Dec., p. 157; 16 Dec., p. 164.
7.   Add. MSS. 35,146, fos. 87 (24 May 1827), 88 (3 June); Place to Hobhouse, 23 Dec. 1827, 35,148, fo. 9.
8.   *TPF*, 9 Dec. 1827, p. 157; 16 Dec., p. 164; 13 Jan. 1828, p. 196. From Jan. 1828 the chairman was G. R. Cotter.
9.   *A Bill to consolidate and amend the Laws relating to Friendly Societies*, Parl. Papers, 1828, *Bills, Public* (1), p. 501.
10.   For the campaign against the bill, see: *TFP*, 22 March–2 Aug. 1828; Place Coll., set 61, fo. 151; set 62, fo. 147; *House of Commons Journals* LXXXIII (1828); *Hansard* XVIII, cols. 601–2 (21 Feb. 1828); XIX, cols. 13–14

(22 April); *The Times*, 22 Feb. 1828, p. 2; 23 April, p. 1; 25 April, p. 1; 29 April, p. 3; 30 April, p. 1; 17 May, p. 1.
11.   *Ibid.*, 22 Feb. 1828, p. 2; 23 April, p. 1; 16 May 1829, p. 3.
12.   *TN*, 22 April 1827, p. 321; *TFP*, 16 Dec. 1827, p. 164; 22 March 1828, p. 273; 24 May, p. 346; 19 July, p. 413. There was some worry at Courtenay's bill of 1819 at the time (HO 42/188, Trenfield to Sidmouth, 30 June 1819).
13.   *TFP*, 24 May 1828, p. 347; 19 July, pp. 413–14; *The Times*, 16 July 1828, p. 3.
14.   *WFP*, 20 Dec. 1828, p. 588; 17 and 24 Jan. 1829; 14 Feb.; 25 April; 18 July; 1 Aug; 12 Sept.; 3 and 24 Oct.; *The Times*, 7 May 1829, p. 4; 16 May, p. 3; 15 July, p. 3. Lovett, *Life and Struggles*, gives the date wrongly as 1836. In 1834–5 there were renewed fears among the benefit societies over adverse legislation, and a new delegate committee was formed.
15.   Gosden, *op. cit.*, p. 177.
16.   *TFP*, 16 Aug. 1828, p. 446; *WFP*, 30 Aug. 1828, p. 457; 22 Nov., p. 554; 25 April 1829; 8 Aug.; *Morning Advertiser*, 18 Aug. 1829.
17.   See above, pp. 27–8, 36, 37.
18.   *House of Commons Journals* LXXXIII (1828), 328; *TN*, 4 Sept. 1825, p. 117; *TFP*, 28 June 1828, p. 388; *WFP*, 22 May 1830, p. 41.
19.   *WFP*, 22 Nov. 1828, p. 554.
20.   *TFP*, 22 March 1828, p. 273; 12 April, pp. 298–9; 24 May, p. 346. Cf. *TFP*, 30 Sept. 1827, p. 77; 7 Oct., p. 82; 4 Nov., p. 113; 11 Nov., p. 122.
21.   *WFP*, 22 Nov. 1828, p. 554.

Chapter 13. Co-operation

1.   For Owen and Owenism, see: J. F. C. Harrison, *Robert Owen and the Owenites in Britain and America: Quest for the New Moral World* (1969); S. Pollard and J. Salt (eds.). *Robert Owen: Prophet of the Poor* (1971).
2.   For the London Owenites, see: *Co-operative Magazine and Monthly Herald*; *Public Ledger*, 2 April 1825, p. 7; *TN*, 2 Oct. 1825, p. 181; *Lion*, 22 Feb. 1828, pp. 228–32.
3.   *Articles of Agreement for the formation of a Community on principles of Mutual Co-operation, within fifty miles of London* (1825); *First Community of Mutual Co-operation* (1825); *Artizans' Chronicle*, 12 June 1825, p. 1; 19 June, p. 16; *TN*, 2 Oct. 1825, p. 192.
4.   *Co-operative Magazine*, Feb. 1826, pp. 55, 57.
5.   *TN*, 25 Sept. 1825, p. 175; Longson to Place, 6 Aug. 1825, and Tester to Place, 27 Aug. 1825, Add. MS. 27,803, fos. 321, 349.
6.   *TN*, 5 Nov. 1826, p. 133; 20 May 1827, p. 358.
7.   *Co-operative Magazine*, July 1826, p. 224; Oct., pp. 308–14; *TFP*, 16 Sept. 1827, p. 57; *Associate*, 1 Feb. 1829, pp. 8, 11.
8.   Lovett in Add. MS. 27,822, fo. 17; *Lion*, 16 Oct. 1829, p. 481; *WFP*, 1 May 1830, p. 20; Lovett, *Life and Struggles*, p. 33; W. Carpenter, *Proceedings of the Third Co-operative Congress* (1832)—table of societies. By 1829 the chief figures in this association were James Watson (printer), William Millard (trunk-maker), William Lovett (cabinet-maker), Thomas Powell (ironmonger—later a leading Welsh Chartist), and James Tucker (coal-merchant).

9.   *TFP*, 23 Dec. 1827, p. 174; *Lion*, 28 March 1828, p. 416; *WFP*, 24 Jan. 1829.
10.   *Lion*, 9 Jan. 1829, p. 41. Cf. *Associate*, 1 Jan. 1830, pp. 49–50.
11.   *WFP*, 18 Oct. 1828, p. 516; 25 Oct., p. 528; 8 Nov., p. 544; 24 Jan. 1829; 7 and 14 March; 11 and 25 April; 20 June; 22 Aug.; 17 Oct.; 9 Jan. 1830; 13 Feb.; 6 March; 1 May; G. R. Skene to Owen, 19 Jan. 1830, Owen Collection, Co-operative Union Library, No. 184.
12.   *WFP*, 6 June 1829; 17 Oct.–24 July 1830, *passim*; *British Co-operator*, Aug. 1830, p. 101; *London Co-operative Magazine*, 16 March 1830, p. 48; *Lion*, 15 May 1829, pp. 611–12; *Associate*, 1 Oct. 1829, pp. 37, 40; 1 Nov., p. 44; *Magazine of Useful Knowledge, passim*; *Carpenter's Political Letters*, 21 Oct. 1830, p. 16; 31 Dec., p. 16; 13 Jan. 1831, p. 11; *Penny Papers for the People*, 8 Nov. 1830; 8 Jan.–24 April 1831, *passim*; *PMG*, 30 July 1831, pp. 30–1; *Report of the Committee, and Proceedings at the Fourth Quarterly Meeting, of the British Association for Promoting Co-operative Knowledge* (1830); Lovett in Add. MS. 27,822, fos. 17–19; Lovett, *Life and Struggles*, pp. 34–5. The figures for societies in which the BAPCK was in contact were: 63 in May 1829, 172 in Jan. 1830, 266 in April, 312 in July, over 400 in Oct.
13.   *WFP*, 1 May 1830, p. 20; 15 May, p. 38; *British Co-operator*, May 1830, p. 44; Aug., p. 103; *Associate*, 1 Nov. 1829, pp. 43–4; *Carpenter's Political Letters*, 15 Oct. 1830, p. 16; 7 Jan. 1831, p. 15; HO 64/16, 7 Jan. 1831.
14.   *Union*, 2 Jan. 1832, p. 256; 3 March, p. 301; *Crisis*, 14 April 1832, p. 2; 3 Nov., pp. 137–8; 12 Jan. 1833, p. 4; 4 May, p. 133; Lovett, *Life and Struggles*, p. 39. For Gast's attendance at the Institution, see e.g. *Crisis*, 17 Nov. 1832, p. 146.
15.   *Ibid.*, June–July 1832; Lovett, *loc. cit.*
16.   *Crisis*, 22 Sept. 1832, p. 113; 29 Sept., p. 117; 20 Oct., p. 130; 5 Jan. 1833, p. 176; 12 Jan., pp. 4–6; 26 Jan., p. 18; 7 June 1834, p. 70.
17.   *Ibid.*, 11 May 1833, p. 143.
18.   *Ibid.*, 1 June 1833, p. 163; 6 July, pp. 201–3; 19 Oct., pp. 60–1.
19.   *Ibid.*, 19 Oct. 1833, pp. 63–4; *Man*, 13 Oct. 1833, pp. 108–10; *Destructive*, 26 Oct. 1833, p. 308.
20.   *TFP*, 23 Dec. 1827, p. 174; *WFP*, 6 June 1829; 16 and 30 Jan. 1830; 20 March; 7, 21 and 28 Aug.; *Carpenter's Political Letters*, 12 Feb. 1831, p. 16; 24 April, p. 16; *Report of 4th Quarterly Meeting of BAPCK*, p. 7; *PMG*, 7 Jan. 1832, p. 239; 17 March, p. 320; 7 April, p. 341; 11 Aug., p. 496; 1 Sept., p. 520; 20 Oct., p. 576; 10 Aug. 1833, p. 259; Lovett, *Life and Struggles*, pp. 38–9; *Crisis*, 5 May 1832, suppt., p. 24; 29 Sept., p. 119; 21 Sept. 1833, p. 19; *Isis*, 8 Sept. 1832, p. 476. There was also, later, a 'First Union Exchange' in Spitalfields (*PMG*, 2 March 1833, p. 72; *Man*, July 1833). For the Central Co-operative Society, see also: R. E. Lee, *Victimization, or Benbowism Unmasked* (1832), pp. 7–8; Carpenter, *Proceedings*, p. 62; HO 64/12, March, April, 18 and 20 Sept. 1832.
21.   *Crisis*, 29 Sept. 1832, p. 119.
22.   *WFP*, 6 March 1830.
23.   HO 64/12, 23 April, 12 June 1832; Lee, *op. cit.*, p. 6; *Trial of William Benbow, and Others* (1832). p. 7; *Crisis*, 12 Jan. 1833, p. 6; *Agitator*, Dec. 1833, p. 11 (in Place Coll., set 51).

24.   Cf. *Co-operator*, Aug. 1829, p. 3.
25.   *TFP*, 19 Jan. 1828, p. 204; 23 Aug., p. 449; *WFP*, 11 Oct. 1828, p. 508; 7 Nov.; 30 Dec.; 31 Jan. 1829, p. 180; *Lion*, 23 Jan. 1829, p. 125.
26.   *TFP*, 16 Feb. 1828, p. 237; *WFP*, 21 Nov. 1829; *Magazine of Useful Knowledge*, 30 Oct. 1830, p. 34.
27.   *Loc. cit.*; *WFP*, 25 Oct. 1828, p. 528; 21 Nov. 1829; *London Co-operative Magazine*, 1 Jan. 1830, p. 7; Lovett, *Life and Struggles*, p. 33.
28.   Place in Add. MS. 27,791, fos. 258–60; Wilson, 'Government Dock-Yard Workers in Portsmouth', p. 388; G. D. H. Cole, *A Century of Co-operation* (Manchester, 1944), pp. 13–15; Thompson, *Making of the English Working Class*, p. 795; *idem.*, 'The Moral Economy of the English Crowd in the Eighteenth Century', *Past and Present* 50 (1971), 136. For retail co-operation, see *Economist*, 7 April–20 Oct. 1821, *passim*.
29.   *WFP*, 11 April 1829; 20 June.
30.   Lovett, *Life and Struggles*, p. 37.
31.   *Cosmopolite*, 28 July 1832.
32.   *WFP*, 12 Sept. 1829; 6 Feb. 1830; 24 April, p. 14; *Penny Papers*, 4 June 1831, p. 5; Lovett in Add. MS. 27,822, fo. 18; Lovett, *op. cit.*, p. 35. Cf. *London Co-operative Magazine*, 1 March 1830, p. 35.
33.   The introduction of credit ruined the Westminster society in 1832 (Styles, in Carpenter, *Proceedings*, p. 83).
34.   *WFP*, 13 March 1830; July–Aug., *passim; British Co-operator, passim*; *Carpenter's Political Letters*, 21 Jan. 1831, p. 16; *Prompter*, 19 March 1831, pp. 311–12; *Penny Papers*, 11 June 1831, p. 8; Carpenter, *Proceedings*, table; HO 64/11, 19 Jan. 1831, April and 27 July.
35.   *British Co-operator*, April 1830, p. 24; *WFP*, 15 Aug. 1829; 20 Feb. 1830; *Carpenter's Political Letters*, 26 Feb. 1831, p. 16; Carpenter, *loc. cit.*; Lovett, *op. cit.*, p. 33; *PMG*, 7 Jan. 1832, p. 239.
36.   Add. MS. 35,142, fos. 207–8; Howe and Child, *Society of London Bookbinders*, pp. 53–4; *Gorgon*, 6 Feb. 1819, p. 303; Gast, *Calumny Defeated*, pp. 16–17; *SC* 1825, p. 365 (Huxtable); App. 20, 6 April 1825, p. 63. Cf. *Man*, 11 Aug. 1833, p. 46.
37.   *TN*, 13 Aug. 1826, p. 34. In 1826 the Dundee shipwrights, in the course of a strike, set up a company which lasted for several years (D. Chapman, 'The New Shipwright Building Company of Dundee, 1826 to 1831', *Econ. Hist. Rev.* 10 (1940)). At Liverpool the master shipbuilders were men of such small means and the journeymen so powerfully organised, that the latter did repairs direct for the shipowners (*SC on Artizans and Machinery*, 1824, 4th report, p. 192).
38.   *WFP*, 22 Aug. 1829.
39.   *TFP*, 2 Aug. 1828, p. 429; *WFP*, 11 April 1829; 28 Aug. 1830; *Lion*, 9 Jan. 1829, p. 39; Lovett, *Life and Struggles*, pp. 33–4.
40.   *Ibid.*, pp. 35–6.
41.   *TN*, 3 Dec. 1826, p. 166; *WFP*, 25 April 1829; 22 Aug.; 24 Oct.; 7 Nov.
42.   *PMG*, 7 Jan. 1832, p. 239; Carpenter, *Proceedings*, table.
43.   Lovett in Add. MS. 27,822, fo. 19; *Crisis*, 29 Dec. 1832, p. 169; 4 May 1833, p. 134; 11 May, p. 138; 8 June, p. 176; 19 Oct., pp. 53, 59.
44.   *Ibid.*. 6 July 1833, p. 205; 13 July, p. 216.

45.   *Ibid.*, 20 Oct. 1832, p. 130; 29 Dec., p. 169; March–June 1833; 19 Oct., pp. 59–63; 14 Dec., p. 122; 11 Jan. 1834, p. 160; 22 March, p. 248. By the summer of 1833, the United Trades' Association contained 3 societies of carpenters, 2 of tailors, 3 of shoemakers, 2 of cabinet-makers, 2 of female needle-workers, and one each of carvers and gilders, brass-cock founders, painters, sawyers, copperplate printers, turners, hatters, brushmakers, and straw-bonnet-makers.

46.   *Ibid.*, 15 June 1833, p. 179; 22 June, p. 191; 24 Aug., p. 271; 4 Jan. 1834, p. 152.

47.   *Ibid.*, 19 Oct. 1833, p. 59; 26 Oct., p. 77; *Man*, 3 Nov. 1833, p. 134.

48.   *Crisis*, 20 April 1833, p. 114; June–July; 31 Aug., p. 283; 5 Oct., p. 39; 26 Oct., p. 71; 30 Nov., pp. 107, 109; 8 Feb. 1834, p. 197.

49.   *Ibid.*, Aug. 1833—Feb. 1834; *Destructive*, 23 Nov. 1833, p. 336.

50.   *WFP*, 25 Sept. 1830.

51.   *Ibid.*, 25 April 1829, p. 4.

52.   *Carpenter's Political Letters*, 5 March 1831, p. 24.

53.   Loan societies among artisans were common, e.g. Vialls' society (see above, p. 229). In 1821 a group of 'operative artisans and mechanics' in Clerkenwell set up an association to make loans to members at low interest (Place Coll., set 19, fo. 307).

54.   *WFP*, 18 Oct. 1828, p. 516; 11 April 1829; 8 Aug.; *Associate*, 1 April 1829, p. 22; *Carpenter's Political Letters*, 24 April 1831, p. 16; *Crisis*, 9 Nov. 1833, p. 85.

55.   *WFP*, 25 April 1829; 26 Dec.; 13 Feb. 1830; May–June; 3 July; 4 Sept.; *British Co-operator*, April 1830, p. 20; Carpenter, *Proceedings*, table, and p. 41; *Carpenter's Political Letters*, 5 March 1831, p. 24; *Crisis*, Dec. 1832–Jan. 1833; 24 Aug. 1833, p. 272; 4 Jan. 1834, p. 152; 1 March, p. 224; 12 April, p. 5; 24 May, p. 56; *PMG*, 22 Dec. 1832, p. 656; G. J. Holyoake, *Sixty Years of an Agitator's Life* (1893), p. 187.

56.   *Crisis*, 7 Dec. 1833, p. 119; 21 Dec., p. 131.

57.   *Magazine of Useful Knowledge*, 30 Oct. 1830, p. 34; *WFP*, 1 May 1830, p. 20; *Carpenter's Political Letters*, 21 Jan. 1831, p. 16; 5 March, p. 24; 8 April, p. 16; HO 64/11, n.d.; *Penny Papers*, 21 Jan. 1831, p. 7; 12 March, p. 8; 18 March, p. 7; 11 June, p. 8; *PMG*, 7 May 1831, p. 8; 10 Nov. 1832, p. 608; 6 April 1833, p. 112.

58.   *Gauntlet*, 15 Sept. 1833, pp. 497, 498.

59.   Add. MS. 27,822, fos. 17–18; Lovett, *Life and Struggles*, pp. 39–41; Carpenter, *Proceedings*, pp. 47–8, 93.

60.   *WFP*, 24 April 1830, p. 14; *Report of 4th Quarterly Meeting of BAPCK*, pp. 12–15.

61.   *The Magazine of Useful Knowledge and Co-operative Miscellany.*

62.   *Penny Papers*, 8 Nov. 1830. For the origins of the unstamped war, see below, pp. 279–80.

63.   *Carpenter's Political Letters*, 26 March 1831, p. 16; *PMG*, 30 July 1831, pp. 30–1; *Destructive*, 30 March 1833, p. 70.

64.   *Crisis*, 21 July 1832, pp. 76–7; 22 Sept., p. 113; 29 Sept., p. 117; 27 Oct., p. 136; *PMG*, 21 July 1832, pp. 470–1; 22 Sept., pp. 541–2; 29 Sept., pp. 548–9; Carpenter, *Proceedings*, pp. 53–4, 71, 72.

65.   *PMG*, 28 Jan. 1832–16 March 1833.

66.   *Report of 4th Quarterly Meeting of BAPCK*, pp. 12–14.

67. *TN*, 21 Aug. 1825, p. 85; *WFP*, 16 Jan. 1830; 24 July; 7 Aug.; *British Co-operator*, Aug. 1830, p. 100; *Crisis*, 4 May 1833, p. 134.
68. *TN*, 6 May 1827, p. 342; *WFP*, 19 Dec. 1829; 24 July 1830; Carpenter, *Proceedings; Crisis*, 22 Sept. 1832, p. 113; 27 April 1833, p. 124; 27 Oct., p. 135; Styles to Owen, 1 March 1832, Owen Coll., no. 520.
69. *TN*, 20 Aug. 1826, p. 43; *WFP*, 24 July 1830; *Carpenter's Political Letters*, 24 April 1831, p. 16.
70. Thompson, *Making of the English Working Class*, p. 806.
71. Petrie in *Carpenter's Political Letters*, 5 March 1831, p. 24.
72. *WFP*, 17 Oct. 1829.
73. Davenport was a friend of Spence, and later his biographer; he was a prolific writer of radical verse in 1819, and a fiery lecturer at Wedderburn's chapel (HO 42/197, 27 Oct. 1819; 42/198, JS, 1 Nov.; 42/207, 'The Kings'; *Sherwin's Political Register*; *Medusa*; *Theological Comet*; *Radical Reformer, or People's Advocate*; *Diligent Observer*; *Republican*; *TN*; Davenport, *Queen of the Isles* (1820)). For Jennison in 1819, see HO 42/188, W—r, 30 June 1819; 42/190, A, 15 April; and for this period: *WFP*, 17 Oct. 1829; *Penny Papers*, 8 Jan. 1831, p. 8; Carpenter, *Proceedings*, table; *Crisis*, 27 July 1833, p. 228; 19 Oct., p. 61; *New Moral World*, 19 Sept. 1835, p. 373; *Cleave's Weekly Police Gazette (WPG)*, 30 July 1836; 3 Sept. For Mee: 42/182, CHY to Sidmouth, 3 Nov. 1818; Stafford to Clive, 5 Nov.; 42/188, W—r, 30 June 1819. Hunter, an ex-Dissenting minister and associate of Thistlewood, was secretary to the benefit societies' delegates' committee in 1828–9, and was later a Chartist; see HO 40/25, Mon. (8 Nov. 1830); 64/12, 14 Aug. (1832); Hunter to General Convention, 13 and 18 Feb. (1839), Add. MS. 34,245, fos. 45, 46; Hunter to Owen, 30 Jan. 1840, Owen Coll., no. 1239.
74. *PMG*, 22 Nov. 1834, p. 336; *NS*, 18 Jan. 1845, pp. 2, 3; 27 June 1846, p. 3; 29 Aug., p. 3; 8 June 1850, p. 1; 15 June, p. 4.
75. *Carpenter's Political Letters*, 5 March 1831, p. 24. In 1833–4 Petrie and Richard Lee ran the *Man*, one of the chief unstamped papers.
76. Thomasson in *Lion*, 31 Oct. 1828, pp. 551–5.
77. *WFP*, 24 April 1830, p. 14; 8 May, p. 31; 15 May, p. 38; 16 Oct.; *Carpenter's Political Letters*, 31 Dec. 1830, p. 16; 26 March 1831, p. 16; HO 64/11, n.d.; Lovett in Add. MS. 27,822, fos. 17–18; Lovett, *Life and Struggles*, p. 35.
78. A. E. Musson, 'The Ideology of early Co-operation in Lancashire and Cheshire', *Transactions of the Lancashire and Cheshire Antiquarian Society* 68 (1958); *Crisis*, 14 Dec. 1833, p. 125. As Owen put it: 'The founder of the Christian religion was a poor man, a carpenter's son; he was a Reformer, and his great object was to benefit the poor and working classes. From some causes this effort had not yet produced that effect, and the poor were poor and miserable still . . . Something to remove the causes of this misery must now be done; and they were met to bring the moral principles of Jesus Christ into every-day practice' (*Union*, 7 Jan. 1832, p. 99).
79. For the Freethinking Christians, see: 'Samuel Thompson', *DNB*; Add. MS. 35,152, fo. 3; *Medusa*, 17 April 1819, p. 66; *Courier*, 16 July 1819, p. 3; *Statesman*, 29 Sept. 1819; *Republican*, 15 March 1822, p. 331–2; *Lion*, 17 April 1829, p. 491; HO 42/195, I.S., 25 Sept. 1819; 40/15, 18 Dec. 1820, fo. 95; Kelly, *George Birkbeck*, pp. 121–2; H. Hetherington,

Principles and Practice Contrasted; or, a peep into 'The only true Church of God upon earth', commonly called Freethinking Christians (1828). For Savage, see *Crisis*, 29 Sept. 1832, p. 119.

80.   *Republican*, 15 April 1825, p. 477–1 Dec. 1826, p. 669; *Scourge*, 4 Oct. 1834, p. 2; *Reasoner*, 16 Aug. 1848, p. 188–90; *Spitalfields Weavers' Journal*, 19 Oct. 1837; *TFP*, 28 Oct. 1827, p. 110; *Lion*, 15 Feb. 1828, pp. 212–13; HO 64/11, 20 Sept. (1827).

81.   Ibid., 13 Aug. 1827; 15 Sept.; *Lion*, 4 Jan. 1828, pp. 12–13, 32; *Isis*, 7 July 1832, p. 344. For the activities of Carlile and Taylor, see: E. Royle, *Victorian Infidels* (Manchester, 1974), pp. 31–43.

82.   *Isis*, 4 Oct. 1834, p. 2; *Lion*. Jan.–Feb. 1828; HO 64/11, 13 Aug. 1827; 1 and 20 Sept.; 17 Dec.; Feb. 1828; Add. MS. 35,146, fo. 86 (15 May 1827); Place Coll., set 61, fos. 121–3. Place helped Taylor prepare his defence.

83.   The group was led by Saull, Pummell (a radical fishmonger in Walworth), Brooks (radical bookseller and publisher), Freeman, Aungier, Brushfield (silk-weaver) and Henman (performer at radical debating clubs). See: *Lion*, 29 Feb. 1828, p. 273; 14 March, p. 349; 21 March, p. 361; 28 March, p. 385; HO 64/11, reports March–May 1828. In addition to his own school, Carlile also supported a chapel set up by 'Rev. R. Wedderburn'. Miss Macaulay later preached at the Rotunda (*Isis*, 14 July 1832, p. 357) and lectured for the St Simonian mission (*PMG*, 11 Jan. 1834, p. 436); at the end of the 1830s she returned to the stage. In 1820 Fitch was running a British Lyceum in Stepney, and was a director of the Liberal Alliance (HO 40/15, 30 May 1820, fo. 39).

84.   *Lion*, Jan.–May 1829; *Scourge*, 18 Oct. 1834, p. 22. For Baume, see also: *Lion*, 9 Oct. 1829, p. 459; 23 Oct., pp. 534–5, 581; *British Co-operator*, Aug. 1830, pp. 113–14; *Carpenter's Political Letters*, 15 Oct. 1830, p. 7; HO 64/16, 10 Oct. 1830; *Crisis*, 8 June 1833, p. 175; 31 Aug., p. 284; *Man*, 29 Sept. 1833, p. 101; G. J. Holyoake, *History of Co-operation in England* (1875–9), I, 349–51; II, 404–5; *DNB*. For Medler, see: HO 42/189, I.S. to Conant, n.d., and 15 July 1819; 42/190, Hanley's deposition; 44/5, Hanley, 2 March, fo. 42; 40/33; Place Coll., set 61, fo. 16; he died at the end of 1835. For the Optimist Chapel and Gast's activity, see: HO 64/11, 22 Nov. 1830–early 1831, and 27 July; 40/25, Nov. 1830.

85.   *British Co-operator*, May 1830, p. 44; Aug., p. 101; *Crisis*, 22 Sept. 1832, p. 113.

86.   HO 64/11, n.d.; 40/25, fo. 171.

87.   HO 64/11, 1831; *WFP*, 17 Oct. 1829; 1 May 1830.

88.   The leading figures in this group were: Watson; Gast; the Spenceans Davenport, Hunter, Mee, Jennison, Preston, Neesom and Harris (in whose home Thistlewood had been captured in 1820); and the Owenites Saull, Medler, Lowe, Wigg, Osborne, Bull and Bailey. The main source is 64/11 and 12; see also *PMG* and *Ballot* for 1831. The carpenter William Bailey, though holding Owenite views, had no time for Owen's 'fanaticisms' (*PMG*, 7 July 1832, p. 452). For the surveyor, Thomas Bull, see also *Prompter*, 13 Aug. 1831, p. 718.

89.   The topics included: the Spencean system, hereditary legislation, popular remedies for public distress, union among the useful classes, new era of society, individual competition, Benbow's plan for a general strike,

aristocratical domination, general fast, scriptural education, common law, labour exchanges, morality and Christianity contrasted, election pledges, existence of God, machinery, rights of the working classes. For Gast, see 64/11 and 12.

90. HO 64/12, Oct.–Nov. 1832; 64/15, 22 April 1833. For Ward, see: HO 40/15, I.S., 8 Jan. 1820; 44/15, I.S., 6 March 1820; *Isis*, 29 Sept.–15 Dec. 1832; Thompson, *Making of the English Working Class*, pp. 799–800.

91. HO 64/12, Oct.–Nov. 1832; *PMG*, 22 Sept. 1832, p. 544; 29 Sept., p. 552; *Crisis*, 12 May 1832, p. 26; May–June 1833; 23 Aug. 1834, pp. 154–5; *Isis*, March and Sept.–Dec. 1832; *Ballot*, 29 April 1831, p. 3.

92. See above, p. 63.

93. Colquhoun, *Treatise on the Police of the Metropolis* (1800), pp. 128–31; *Society for the Suppression of Vice* (1825), pp. 5, 44–5.

94. *PMG*, 25 Aug. 1832, p. 512.

95. HO 64/12, 12 Nov. 1832. There were contributions by a 'J.G.' in Carlile's *Republican* and Smith's later periodical, the *Shepherd*.

96. Thompson, *Making of the English Working Class*, p. 727.

97. *Lion*, 14 Nov. 1828, pp. 614–19; 20 Feb. 1829, pp. 250–6; 23 Oct., p. 534.

98. One example was phrenology. See T. M. Parssinen, 'Popular Science and Society: the phrenology movement in early Victorian Britain', *Journal of Social History* 8 (1974).

Part Four: From Reform Crisis to Chartism

Chapter 14. Reform

1. *WFP*, 6 Sept. 1828, p. 466.

2. For the situation among the carpenters, and the building trades generally, see: *WFP*, 20 Nov. 1830; *PMG*, 13 Aug. 1831, p. 45; 2 Aug. 1834, p. 207; *Man*, 7 Nov. 1833, p. 147; *Weekly True Sun*, 14 Sept. 1834, pp. 434, 437; 'The Plumber, Painter, and Glazier', in *Guide to Trade*, pp. 5–8; Thompson and Yeo, *The Unknown Mayhew*, pp. 335–58. For the activities of the carpenters in the late 1820s, see *TN*, *TFP*, *WFP*.

3. *TFP*, 2 Dec. 1827; 3 May 1828, p. 326.

4. *TN*, July 1825; *Artizans' Chronicle*, 12 June 1825, p. 20; Add. MS. 27,805, fos. 365–9.

5. *TN*, 6 May 1827, p. 342; 3 June, p. 371; 22 July, p. 428; *TFP*, 5 Aug. 1827, p. 16; 2 Aug. 1828, p. 432; Webb Coll., A, xi.

6. *PMG*, 13 Aug. 1831, pp. 45–6; 17 Sept., p. 83; HO 64/11, 9 Aug. (1831).

7. See above, p. 251.

8. For the origins of this new union, see: *Penny Papers*, 12 March–27 May 1831; Lovett in Add. MS. 27,822, fos. 19 foll.; *Carpenter's Monthly Political Magazine*, Jan. 1832, pp. 178–80; *Ballot*, from 3 April 1831; *Carpenter's Political Letters*, 8 April 1831, pp. 12–13; Add. MS. 27,835, fo. 251. One of the early members was the veteran Spencean, John George. For Higginbottom, see *WFP*, 22 May 1830, p. 41; 19 March 1831. For Rogers, *Crisis*, 27 April 1833, p. 128, and foll. nos.

9. *TN*, 20 May 1827, pp. 357–8.

10. In his *Lancet* Wakley conducted a running war against the Royal

College of Surgeons and its nepotism; his group saw medical reform as coming through legislation in a reformed Parliament. Cobbett's followers, mainly tradesmen and farmers, were fervent admirers of his attacks on the current commercial and monetary policies, and felt vindicated by the depression. The most radical ward in the City was Farringdon Without, where the leading reformers were Galloway, Richard Taylor, Wooler, Hunt and the Freethinking Christians Thompson and Fearon. In 1829, after the Clare election, crowds of Irish and radicals gathered at the opening of Parliament to see O'Connell try to claim his seat. Once an MP, O'Connell demanded Irish reforms, Repeal of the Union, and radical reform, while many London Irish were also excited by peasant tithe resistance and the coercive use of troops.

11.   For the parish reform movements, see: the daily press; *Select Committee on Laws and Usages under which Select and other Vestries are constituted in England and Wales*, Parl. Papers, 1830, IV; *Ballot* (especially for Bloomsbury); J. W. Brooke, *The Democrats of Marylebone* (1839); F. H. W. Sheppard, *Local Government in St. Marylebone 1688–1835. A study of the Vestry and the Turnpike Trust* (1958), chaps. 16–17. The Lambeth reformers were led by William Carpenter, John Grady (an Irish attorney's clerk), Jasper Judges, George Fall (accountant), and Augero (teacher).

12.   Simpson at Surrey Radical Association, *LD*, 20 Nov. 1836, p. 75.

13.   *TFP* 12 July 1828, p. 406. Cf. very similar sentiments in *Penny Papers*, 27 May 1831, p. 5.

14.   *Morning Journal*, Feb.–March 1830; *WFP*, 12 March 1831; HO 40/25, 14 Nov. (1830), fos. 517, 519; 64/11, Dec. 1831.

15.   Ibid., Feb. and 10 June (1828), 21 June (1829), Aug.–Sept. 1830.

16.   Ibid., 17 Dec. (1828), 25 Sept. 1830; 64/16, Nov. 1830; Lovett, *Life and Struggles*, p. 29; (Carter), *Memoirs of a Working Man*, pp. 186, 191; *Crisis*, 9 Aug. 1833, pp. 142–3.

17.   *TFP*, Sept. 1827; 26 July 1828, p. 418; *WFP*, Oct. 1828; 28 March 1829; 18 July; 8 Aug. 1829–14 Sept. 1830; *Lion*, 9 Oct. 1829, pp. 449–51; 23 Oct., pp. 514–17; 25 Dec., pp. 801–2; *Carpenter's Political Letters*, Nov. 1830–Jan. 1831; *Republican*, 28 May 1831, p. 3; *Prompter*, 3 Sept. 1831, p. 754; *Gauntlet*, 4 Aug. 1833, p. 403; *PMG*, 1 Nov. 1834, p. 310; Add. MS. 27,789, fo. 137. The early leaders were: W. E. Andrews, associated with Hunt and Watson in 1819; Grady, the Lambeth radical, who also became president of a Metropolitan Catholic Tract Society; and Dias Santos, leading member of a north-east London Catholic Free Schools Association and treasurer of a Catholic charity school in Spitalfields which in 1827 was attacked by an anti-Catholic mob. The East End group and Carlile's associates both held aloof from the RRA, preserving their distrust of Hunt, and disliking the religious reformers.

18.   For the formation of the MPU, see: *WFP*, 21 Feb.–7 Aug. 1830; *The Times*, 10 March 1830, p. 4; *Weekly Dispatch*, 14 March 1830, p. 1; *Morning Journal*, 25 Feb.–8 April 1830; *Authorised Copy of the Resolutions adopted at the Great Public Meeting . . . for forming a Metropolitan Political Union, for the recovery and protection of public rights* (1830); *Carpenter's Political Letters*, 15 Oct. 1830, pp. 3–6; *Scourge*, 8 Nov. 1834, p. 45; Add. MS. 27,789, fo. 145. The council included: the MPs O'Connell, Wood, Hume and Cave; members of the RRA, both Irish (Grady, Dias

Santos, Andrews, Cleave, French, Cavanagh) and English (Hunt, Augero, Waylen, Hetherington, Warden, Lovett, Watson, Carpenter, Hand); Sir Richard Phillips, Charles Pearson, James Walker (a Spitalfields leader), James Mee. Other members were George Rogers, Wakley, Baume, Brooks (the publisher), Cleary, Saull and Millard.

19. *Morning Journal*, 19 Jan. 1830, pp. 2, 3; *WFP*, 23 Jan. 1830.

20. *Prompter*, 13 Nov. 1831, pp. 7–9; HO 64/11, 29 Nov. (1831).

21. For the failure of the MPU, see *WFP*, 14 and 21 Aug. 1830; *The Times*, 12 Nov. 1830, p. 4; HO 64/11; Add. MS. 27,789, fos. 145–6; *Prompter*, 4 June 1831, p. 481; 3 Sept., p. 754; *Gauntlet*, 4 Aug. 1833, p. 403; *Scourge*, 18 Oct. 1834, p. 23; *PMG*, 1 Nov. 1834, p. 310; Lovett, *Life and Struggles*, p. 46.

22. Add. MS. 35,146, fos. 122–4 (1830); Place to Hobhouse, 8 Nov. 1830, Add. MS. 35,148, fos. 69–70; HO 41/26, Nov. 1830.

23. For the crisis in November, see: HO 40/25; 64/11; *The Times*, Nov. 1830; *Carpenter's Political Letters*, Nov. 1830; H. Vizetelly, *Glances back through Seventy Years* (1893), pp. 57–65. There are also comments on the London situation and organisations in the period covered by this chapter in D. Large, 'William Lovett', in P. Hollis (ed.), *Pressure from Without in early Victorian England* (1974); D. J. Rowe, 'London Radicalism in the Era of the Great Reform Bill', in Stevenson, *London in the Age of Reform*.

24. For these origins of the unstamped war, see: *Carpenter's Political Letters*, esp. 29 Oct. 1830, p. 3; 18 Dec., p. 16; *WFP*, 11 Dec. 1830; HO 64/11, Nov. 1830; 64/16, Nov. 1830; *Cosmopolite*, 14 July 1832; *Carpenter's Monthly Political Magazine*, Oct. 1831, p. 42; *London Dispatch*, 11 Dec. 1836, pp. 98–9; Add. MS. 27,791, fos. 271–3; Lovett, *Life and Struggles*, p. 48.

25. For the end of the RRA, see: *WFP*, 2 Oct. 1830; *Carpenter's Political Letters*, 25 Nov. 1830, pp. 4–5; *Prompter*, 20 Nov. 1830, pp. 22–3; 4 Dec., p. 51; *The Times*, 12 Nov. 1830, p. 4; HO 40/25, fos. 523, 928; 64/11, 13 Nov. 1830.

26. *Penny Papers*, 8 Jan. 1831, pp. 1–2; 15 Jan., pp. 1–2; *Carpenter's Political Letters*, 13 Jan. 1831, p. 11; *WFP*, 15 Jan. 1831; HO 64/11, n.d.

27. The chief sources for the Rotunda meetings are the *Prompter* and *Republican*. The leading figures at the political meetings were Hibbert (the regular chairman), Hetherington, Watson, James Osborne (journeyman currier), Cooper, Millard and Palin. For Carlile's exultation at his sentence, see Add. MS. 35,146, fo. 130. For Ward and Twort, see above, p. 262. On their release they resumed lectures at the Borough Chapel, and later at the Castle Street Assembly Rooms (*Gauntlet*, 30 March 1834, p. 953).

28. The account of the NUWC in this chapter is based on a thorough use of the following sources: *Penny Papers* and *PMG* (1831–5); *WMF* (1833); *Destructive* (1833); *Union* (1831–2); *Ballot* (1831–2); *Gauntlet* (March–Oct. 1833); *Man* (1833); HO 64/11–15; 79/4; Lovett in Add. MS. 27,822, fos. 19 foll.; Lovett, *Life and Struggles*, pp. 55–70; Add. MSS. 27,822, fos. 19 foll.; 27,791, fos. 241–386; 27,796, fos. 302–39; 27,797. Other sources used are: *Republican, Radical, Cosmopolite, True Sun, Agitator; The Trial of William Benbow, and Others* (1832); *A Correct Report of the Trial of Messrs. Benbow, Lovett, & Watson, as the leaders of*

the farce day procession (1832); *Select Committee on the petition of Frederick Young, and others*, Parl. Papers, 1833, XIII; Place Coll., set 62.

29.   *Prompter*, 5 March 1831, p. 273; 12 March, p. 303; 16 April, p. 369; *Republican*, 30 April 1831, p. 24; *Penny Papers*, 26 March 1831, pp. 7–8; *Carpenter's Political Letters*, 5 March 1831, pp. 1–5; *Carpenter's Monthly Political Magazine*, Sept. 1831, pp. 1–2.

30.   *WFP*, 12 March 1831; 19 March; 2 April.

31.   *Penny Papers*, March–April 1831; HO 64/11, 5 July (1831).

32.   Carpenter, introduction to *Carpenter's Political Letters*, pp. 1–12; *Penny Papers*, 21 May 1831, pp. 1–4; 24 June, pp. 1–6; *Republican*, 21 May 1831, pp. 2–4; *PMG*, 30 July 1831, pp. 30–1; *Prompter*, 25 June 1831, p. 531; Add. MS. 27,791, fo. 290; Lovett, *Life and Struggles*, pp. 48–9. For the unstamped campaign, see: J. H. Wiener, *The War of the Unstamped. The movement to repeal the British Newspaper Tax, 1830–1836* (1969); P. Hollis, *The Pauper Press, A Study in Working Class Radicalism of the 1830s* (1970).

33.   *Voice of the People*, May–July 1831; *PMG*, July 1831; Add. MS. 27,822, fo. 334; HO 64/11, 4 and 5 July (1831). I am grateful to Mr R. A. Sykes for information on Lancashire radicalism. Hunt's friend, O'Brien, was now in Birmingham as editor of the *Midland Representative*, in which he also opposed the Bill.

34.   HO 64/11, 6 Aug. (1831).

35.   *PMG*, 16 July 1831, p. 16; Add. MS. 27,791, fo. 294.

36.   *Prompter*, 4 June 1831, pp. 481–9; 16 July, p. 608; 20 Aug., p. 734; *PMG*, 16 July 1831, p. 15; HO 64/11, 4 July (1831), 20 Aug. Carlile had been hostile to Hetherington and Cleave since 1828, when they had clashed over religion and Carlile's population views; Cleave was at that time a Baptist, and his wife was very religious.

37.   This group was led by Styles, the deformed clerk William Hassell, George Huggett (undertaker), and William Farren (lithographer). For the group, see: *WFP*, 14 Aug. 1830; *Carpenter's Political Letters*, 25 Nov. 1830, p. 16; *PMG*, 4 Aug. 1832, p. 488; *Gauntlet*, 6 Oct. 1833, p. 550; 27 Oct., p. 603; *Crisis*, 16 Nov. 1833, p. 93. At the end of the 1830s and the early 1840s, Farren led the efforts to establish a 'Trades Hall'.

38.   It included Medler, Lowe, Osborne, Bull, Aungier, Mee, Davenport, Jennison, Neesom, Preston and Abel Hall (a spy).

39.   *Prompter*, 3 Sept. 1831, p. 767; Bowyer, in Add. MS. 35,149, fo. 343.

40.   Loc. cit.; Add. MSS. 27,789, fo. 411; 27,790, fos. 5–29; 27,791, fos. 18–20, 47–9; *Prompter*, 15 Oct. 1831; *Carpenter's Monthly Political Magazine*, Nov. 1831, pp. 110–11; and the daily press. Thomas Bowyer was a member of the Spencean-republican group; in 1827 he was also involved in Gast's attempt at a general union, and ran a political educational group, the Soho Association for Bettering the Condition of the Working Classes.

41.   The sources for the NPU are: *The Times*, 1 Nov. 1831, pp. 3–4; Add. MSS. 27,791– 27,796; Place Coll., set 63, I–II; set 17; *Union*, Nov. 1831–Jan. 1832; *PMG*, 9 March 1832, pp. 76–7; *Gauntlet*, March–April 1833; *Destructive*, Feb.–June 1833; *WMF*, March–June 1833; *Man*, July 1833; *English Chartist Circular*, p. 189. The initial small group that planned the union included Murphy and the veteran John Thelwall. At the second public meeting, at which the membership of the council was approved,

Osborne's attempt to add Warden, Cooper and Hunt was defeated. Place's papers are also very valuable for the Reform crisis generally.

42.   *Penny Papers*, 2 July 1831, p. 8.

43.   Add. MS. 27,791, fo. 317. Cf. HO 40/25, fo. 172.

44.   The leaders of the Theobalds Road group were Benbow, Hutchinson, Watkins, Petrie and Dray.

45.   HO 64/12, 2 April (1832).

46.   *PMG*, 2 June 1832, p. 410; 23 June, p. 435.

47.   It lingered on until July 1833, when the Place group seceded to form a Radical Club, and the rump founded a very short-lived Metropolitan Political Union.

48.   Brooke, *Democrats of Marylebone*; *True Sun*; *Weekly True Sun*; *Gauntlet*, 5 May 1833–16 Feb. 1834; *Man*. Aug.–Sept. 1833.

49.   Lee, *Victimization, or, Benbowism Unmasked*; *PMG*, 21 July 1832, p. 472; 28 July, p. 479. For Lee, see *ibid.*, 7 April 1832, p. 344. For the co-operative society, see above, p. 246.

50.   *Destructive*, July–Aug. 1833; *PMG*, July–Aug. 1833, Jan. 1834; *The Times*, 23 Sept. 1833, p. 4; 13 Dec., p. 4; HO 64/15, Feb. 1834.

51.   *Gauntlet*, 4 Aug. 1833, p. 401; *Scourge*, 25 Oct. 1834, p. 26.

52.   HO 79/4, Phillips to Maule, 4 March 1833, fo. 219.

53.   The class-leaders at all three places were Neesom, Bailey, Kingsmill, Mee, Dove, Mills, Newton, Watson, Preston, Davenport, Aungier and Jennison.

54.   Gast to Place, 3 July 1834, Add. MS. 27,829, fo. 20; *Man*, 24 Nov. 1833, p. 259; *PMG*, 14 Dec. 1833, p. 404; *People's Conservative*, 28 Dec. 1833, p. 376; *Gauntlet*, 29 Dec. 1833–26 Jan. 1834. The society's original name was the Society for Dissemination of Useful Knowledge.

55.   *PMG*, 3 Nov. 1832, p. 600; 20 July 1833, pp. 230–1.

56.   *WMF*, 3 Aug. 1833, p. 264.

57.   *Man*, 8 Sept. 1833, p. 77; *PMG*, 12 Oct. 1833, p. 332.

58.   *Ibid.*, 30 May 1835, p. 550; *Shepherd*, 4 July 1835, p. 355.

59.   *Destructive*, 10 Aug. 1833, p. 220.

60.   *Ibid.*, 27 July 1833, p. 204; *Man*, 28 July–24 Sept. 1833.

61.   *Gauntlet*, 31 March 1833–23 March 1834; *Man*, July–Dec. 1833; *WMF*, 18 May 1833, pp. 173–4; *Crisis*, Jan.–April 1834; *Operative*, 16 June 1839, p. 33. A new member of the group, Charles Southwell, was later a leading Owenite missionary.

62.   *People's Conservative*, 12 April 1834, p. 77; Holyoake, *Sixty Years of an Agitator's Life*, p. 187. See above, p. 253.

63.   In Southwark, Sherman ran a Surrey Tract Society for the Diffusion of really Useful Knowledge (*PMG*, 16 Jan. 1834, p. 443). The old Western Union labour exchange bazaar in Poland Street was now used by the Friends of Free Discussion. There were discussions at Theobalds Road institution, and the Nag's Head in Hammersmith. See *Man* and *WMF*.

64.   *PMG*, 26 Jan. 1833, p. 25.

65.   *TFP*, 22 Nov. 1828, p. 554.

66.   *PMG*, 19 Oct. 1833, p. 337.

67.   Lovett, *Life and Struggles*, pp. 71–2; *Man*, 29 Sept. 1833, p. 101; *Crisis*, 28 Sept. 1833, pp. 26–7, 32; 19 Oct., pp. 59–60; *WPG*, 23 April 1836, p. 17. Styles had been in the Westminster Co-operative Society,

which collapsed in mid-1832, and was in 1833 secretary of the NPU until it folded in June. He was now also on the Owenite Social Missionary Council.
68.   HO 64/15, 31 Oct. 1834.
69.   Place Coll., set 56, 1836; *Hetherington's Twopenny Dispatch*, 10 Sept. 1836.
70.   *PMG*, 29 Sept. 1832, p. 547.

Chapter 15. Trade Unionism and Radicalism

1.   For a fuller analysis of the great tailors' strike, see T. M. Parssinen and I. J. Prothero, 'The London Tailors' Strike of 1834 and the collapse of the Grand National Consolidated Trades' Union: a police spy's report', *Int. Rev. Soc. Hist.* 22 (1977). See also Galton, *The Tailoring Trade*, pp. lxxxi–xcii, 179–210.
2.   *PMG*, 10 May 1834, p. 107; *Pioneer*, 31 May 1834, p. 384.
3.   *PMG*, 3 May 1834, p. 101.
4.   For the shoemakers, see: *Crisis*, 26 Oct. 1833, p. 79; 8 March 1834, p. 232; 15 March, p. 240; 28 June, p. 93; 2 Aug., p. 136; *Agitator*, Dec. 1833, p. 11; *Pioneer*, 26 June 1834, p. 420; *PMG*, 12 July 1834, p. 182; 26 July, p. 197; *Weekly True Sun*, 6 July 1834, p. 354; *NS*, 25 Jan. 1845, p. 8.
5.   *Man*, 17 Nov. 1833, p. 147; *Gauntlet*, March 1834; *PMG*, March, Aug.–Oct. 1834; *Weekly True Sun*, May–Sept. 1834. For the stonemasons, see *WMF*, 23 March 1833, p. 112.
6.   For these union developments, see: *True Sun*, *Weekly True Sun*, *Pioneer*, *Crisis*, *Gauntlet* (March); Place Coll., set 51; W. H. Oliver, 'Organisations and ideas behind the efforts to achieve a general union of the working classes in the early 1830's' (unpublished Oxford D.Phil. thesis, 1954); *idem.*, 'The Consolidated Trades' Union of 1834', *Econ. Hist. Rev.* I (1964). For the strikes: *Man*, 29 Sept. 1833, p. 99 (plasterers); *Gauntlet*, 1 Dec. 1833, p. 688 (bricklayers); *Crisis*, 6 July 1833, pp. 204, 205; *Pioneer*, 21 Sept. 1833, p. 20; Thompson and Yeo, *The Unknown Mayhew*, pp. 324, 326 (sawyers); *Pioneer*, 8 March 1834, p. 239; 29 March, p. 276; 31 May, p. 382; *Gauntlet*, 2 March 1834, p. 895; *People's Conservative*, 15 March 1834, pp. 43–4; Place to Parkes, 21 April 1834, Add. MS. 35,154, fos. 198–200 (coopers).
7.   *Pioneer*, 19 April 1834, p. 307; 24 May, p. 369.
8.   *PMG*, 7 Sept. 1833, p. 292. Cf. *Weekly True Sun*, 15 June 1834, p. 330; 29 June, p. 346.
9.   *Ibid.*, 10 Aug. 1834, p. 397.
10.   E.g. *Pioneer*, 22 March 1834, p. 257: 12 April, p. 290; 26 April, p. 314; *PMG*, 2 Aug. 1834, p. 207.
11.   *Mirror of Parliament*, 1834, II, 1314–16 (28 April).
12.   *True Sun*, 2 May 1834; *PMG*, 10 May 1834, pp. 108–9; 24 May, pp. 125, 130; 31 May, p. 130; *Crisis*, 26 July 1834, p. 125; HO 64/15, 5 June 1834; *Statement of the Master Builders of the Metropolis, in explanation of the differences between them and the workmen respecting the Trades' Unions* (1834).
13.   For the later history of the CTU, see: *Weekly True Sun*, 24 Aug. 1834, pp. 411, 413–14; 26 April 1835, p. 691; *Crisis*, 23 Aug. 1834, p. 153; HO 64/15, Roe to Duncannon, 8 Aug. (1834); *New Moral World*, 24 Oct.

1835; *PMG*, 7 Feb. 1835, p. 423; 21 Feb., p. 439; 14 March, p. 461; Place Coll., set 51, fo. 134; *Working Man's Advocate*, 4 July 1835, p. 10.

14.   *Crisis*, 3 May 1834, p. 32.

15.   For the later history of Thames shipbuilding and the shipwrights, see: *SC on British Shipping*, Parl. Papers, 1844, VIII, G. F. Young, J. Somes; *SC on Navigation Laws*, Parl. Papers, 1847, X, First Report, S. Browning; Fourth Report, G. F. Young; Fifth Report, J. P. Grieve; *SC of House of Lords on Navigation Laws,* Parl. Papers, 1847–8, XX, II, M. Wigram, G. F. Young; *RC on Trades Unions*, Ninth Report, Parl. Papers, 1867–8, XXXIX, C. Wigram, Samuda, F. J. Divers, P. J. Robson, G. Bayley; Webb Coll., A, XXXII; Webbs, *History of Trade Unionism*, pp. 247, 353, 429–30, 490–1, 551; Albion, *Forests and Sea Power*, pp. 398–409; Matthews, *A Study in Trade-Cycle History*, pp. 118–20, 204, 210; Hutchins, *American Maritime Industries*, pp. 198 foll.; Jones, *Shipbuilding in Britain*; Pollard, 'Decline of Shipbuilding on the Thames', *Econ. Hist. Rev.* 3 (1950–1); *idem*., 'British and World Shipbuilding, 1890–1914: a study in comparative costs', *Journal of Economic History* 17 (1957); G. S. Graham, 'The Ascendancy of the Sailing Ship, 1850–85', *Econ. Hist. Rev.* 9 (1956–7).

16.   *WFP*, 6 Sept. 1828, p. 466.

17.   Webb Coll., A, XXXII, fo. 33.

18.   *PMG*, 5 Sept. 1835, p. 662.

19.   The committee included delegates from carpenters, shoemakers, ropemakers, type-founders, whitesmiths, bricklayers, East End cabinet-makers, coppersmiths and braziers, bakers, sawyers, shipwrights, tin-plate workers and three miscellaneous lodges.

20.   Place Coll., set 51, fos. 297–303; *WPG*, Aug. 1836; *London Dispatch* (hereafter *LD*), Oct.–Dec. 1836; *London Mercury*, Oct.–Dec. 1836; *Operative*, 17 Feb. 1839, p. 16; *Charter*, 8 Dec. 1839, p. 733.

21.   *Weekly True Sun*, 27 March 1836, p. 1075; *New Weekly True Sun*, 2 April 1836; *LD*, 14 Jan. 1838, p. 555; *NS*, 5 June 1841, p. 8; Place Coll., set 52, fo. 285; J. A. Forsyth, *A Vindication of the Principles, Objects, and Tendencies of Trade Unions, or Associations of the Working Classes* (1838).

22.   *Weekly True Sun*, 4 Oct. 1835–18 Sept. 1836; *WPG*, 1835–6; *Hetherington's Twopenny Dispatch*, 1836; *LD*, 1836–7; *London Mercury*, 6 Nov. 1836–5 Feb. 1837; *New Moral World*, 10 Oct. 1835, p. 396; *NS*, 27 Jan. 1838, p. 5; 16 Jan. 1841, p. 7; Place Coll., set 51, fos. 151, 153; set 70; fos. 335–7, 408. The leaders of the Marylebone Association were Savage, Macconnell, Wade, Cleary, Murphy, Dr Webb, Goldspink, Thomas Wall (prominent in NUWC) and Jordan (carpenter, in United Trades' Association 1833).

23.   *Weekly True Sun*, 16 Aug. 1835, p. 821; Place Coll., set 51, fo. 151; set 70, fo. 261.

24.   For the end of the unstamped war, see; *Weekly True Sun*, 1836; *PMG*, 8 Aug. 1835, pp. 625, 628–30; 5 Sept., p. 662; *WPG*, 1836; Place Coll., set 70; Wiener, *War of the Unstamped*.

25.   Place Coll., set 70, fo. 335; *WPG*, 26 Dec. 1835; 9 July 1836. For Saull's museum, see also *NS*, 31 Oct. 1846, p. 3.

Chapter 16. The Working Men's Association

1.   The sources for the following account of the WMA are: *WPG*, 13 Aug.

1836, p. 33; *LD*, 16 Oct. 1836–24 March 1839; *London Mercury*, 5 March–6Aug. 1837; *Operative*, 2 Dec. 1838–26 May 1839; *Charter*, 27 Jan.–22 Dec. 1839; *NS*, 27 Jan.–29 Dec. 1838; Add. MSS. 27,819; 27,820; 27,835, fos. 131–2; 37,773; 37,950, fos. 208–21; Place Coll., set 56, 1836; Lovett, *Life and Struggles*, chaps. 5–10.

2. *Ibid.*, p. 136; Place Coll., set 56, fo. 10.

3. Add. MS. 35,146, fo. 132 (1835); *NS*, 27 Jan. 1838, p. 4; Hollis, *Pauper Press*, pp. 77–8.

4. *Weekly True Sun*, 21 Feb. 1836, p. 1038; *WPG*, 2 and 23 April 1836; Place Coll., set 56, 1836, fo. 1; set 70, fos. 407, 425. The fines committee included men from Lovett's coffee-house (Styles; Richard Moore, carver; George Glashan, chronometer-maker) and weavers (Cray, Claisse, Duce, Owen, Charles Cole, the last a poet and secretary of the weavers' union). The free press association also included the coopers' leaders Ainsworth and Raven.

5. Dorchester men: Simpson; Tomey and Jones (whitesmiths); Burkinyoung (brazier); Isaacs (type-founder). Co-operators: Foskett, Wigg, William Cameron. NUWC men: Hunter; Goldspink; Heins; Sherman; Benjamin Tilly; Thomas White (hatter). Trades' unionists 1834: Jordan, Hoare, Norman, Ridley (dyer). Later Chartists: Dyson (compositor), Henry Mitchell (turner), M'Frederick (bootmaker), Boggis. The honorary members included: from the fines committee, Black, Place, Beaumont, Murphy, Owen, George Rogers; from the unstamped, O'Brien, Carpenter, Bell; MPs Wakley, Col. Thompson, Whittle Harvey, Fielden, Roebuck, Molesworth, Leader; Owenites, J. and G. Dempsey, E. T. Craig, Tucker, Rosser, Alexander Campbell; others, Wade, W. J. Fox, Dr John Epps.

6. *Weekly True Sun*, 10 July–16 Oct. 1836; *WPG*, July–Aug. 1836; *Hetherington's Twopenny Dispatch*, July–Aug. 1836; *LD*, 17 Sept. 1836, p. 3; 7 May 1837, p. 267; Add. MS. 27,819, fos. 32–5; Place Coll., set 56, 1836, fos. 2–3. The chief figures in the club were Hetherington, Cleave, Wade, Bell, Murphy, Stallwood, White, John Russell, Goldspink, Henry Vincent, Richard Cameron (bracemaker).

7. For Harper, Sherman and Harvey in the NUWC, see *PMG*, 1835. For the East London Democratic Association, see: *London Mercury*, 12 March 1837, p. 204; June–Aug.; *LD*, 26 March 1837, p. 220; 4 June, p. 300; 11 Feb. 1838, p. 591; 1 July, p. 746; Add. MSS. 27,819, fo. 217; 27,820, fo. 145; 27,821, fo. 5; 37,773, fo. 44 (28 March 1837).

8. *PMG*, 6 July 1835, p. 558; 1 Aug., p. 622.

9. *Ibid.*, 30 Jan. 1835, pp. 413–14; 13 June, p. 566; 20 June, p. 574; Add. MS. 27,821, fo. 5; A. R. Schoyen, *The Chartist Challenge. A portrait of George Julian Harney* (1958), pp. 1–14.

10. *LD*, 25 Feb. 1838, p. 604.

11. Hartwell, *True Sun*, 1 March 1837, p. 4. Cf. Hoare, *London Mercury*, 12 March 1837, p. 201; and Lovett, p. 77.

12. *Ibid.*, pp. 75–6.

13. *Ibid.*, p. 75. Cf. Hartwell, *LD*, 5 March 1837, p. 198.

14. Williams, *ibid.*, 17 Sept. 1836, p. 3.

15. Place Coll., set 51, fo. 263; *Operative*, 24 Feb. 1839, p. 12. For the tailors' union in the 1840s, see: *NS*, 25 Nov. 1843–26 June 1847; Place Coll., set 53, fos. 89–149.

16. *Operative*, Nov.–Dec. 1838.
17. *Constitutional*, 25 Nov. 1836, p. 3; *True Sun*, 25 Nov. 1836, p. 1. For the Staffordshire Committee, see: *London Mercury*, 27 Nov. 1836, pp. 82, 84; *LD*, 27 Nov. 1836, p. 85; 22 Jan. 1837, p. 152.
18. *Operative*, 31 March 1839, p. 8.
19. *Ibid.*, March 1839; *LD*, Sept. 1839; *Charter*, 4 April 1839, p. 470; 15 Sept., p. 542; 22 Sept., p. 551; 8 Dec., p. 726; 5 Jan. 1840, p. 790; *NS*, 5 Oct. 1839, p. 7; 23 May 1840, p. 5; 4 May 1844, p. 1; 29 June, p. 6; 19 Oct., p. 1; 9 Nov., p. 8; 21 March 1846, p. 1.
20. *LD*, 23 April 1837, p. 253; June–July; *London Mercury*, 18 June 1837, p. 317; Add. MS. 37,773, fo. 53 (6 June 1837).
21. Ibid., fos. 43 (22 March 1837), 103 (9 April 1838); *LD*, 30 April 1837, p. 262; 15 April 1838, p. 667; Place Coll., set 51, fos. 170, 172.
22. *LD*, 15 Oct. 1837, p. 453; 5 Nov., p. 477; 10 Dec., p. 518; 4 Feb. 1838, p. 577; 11 Feb., p. 590; *Operative*, 4 Nov. 1838, p. 1; 2 Dec., p. 67; 28 April 1839, p. 8; *Charter*, 31 March 1839, p. 145; 7 April, p. 168; 29 Sept., p. 568; 10 Nov., p. 661; 1 Dec., p. 720; Add. MS. 37,773, fos. 68 (26 Sept. 1837), 81 (28 Nov.); Place Coll., set 52, fo. 257.
23. *Ibid.*, fos. 339 foll.; Add. MSS. 27,835, fo. 102; 37,773, fos. 98 (6 March 1838), 100 (13 March); *LD*, 25 March 1838, p. 634; *Charter*, 17 March 1839, p. 128; 1 Dec., pp. 715, 720; *Operative*, 19 May 1839, p. 8; Lovett, *Life and Struggles*, pp. 131–5; W. Lovett, *Combinations Defended* (1838).
24. *Charter,* 31 March 1839, p. 145; Add. MSS. 27,820, fo. 381; 27,821, fos. 22–3; Place Coll., set 56, Jan.–April 1841.

Chapter 17. Into Chartism

1. For the CNA, see: *London Mercury*, 19 March–10 Sept. 1837; *LD*, 2 April–20 Aug. 1837; Add. MS. 27,819, fos. 50–4, 217. The leading figures were James Bernard, O'Brien, Bell, O'Connor, Murphy, Rogers, Wade, Stallwood, George, Jennison, Ross and the East London Democrats.
2. *PMG*, 17 Sept. 1831, p. 85.
3. E.g. *ibid.*, 29 Sept. 1832, p. 548.
4. *London Mercury*, 20 Aug. 1837, p. 685; *LD*, Sept.–Nov. 1837; *NS*, 20 Sept. 1845, p. 1.
5. Death Certificate, Rotherhithe, 1837, No. 174.
6. *Hetherington's Twopenny Dispatch*, 10 Sept. 1836.
7. *London Mercury*, 15 Jan. 1837, p. 138; *LD*, 15 Jan. 1837, p. 143; 19 Feb., p. 182; 17 Dec., p. 527.
8. Lovett, *Life and Struggles*, p. 158.
9. *LD*, 6 Aug. 1837, p. 374; 17 Dec., p. 528; *Operative*, 13 Jan. 1839, p. 3. For London Chartism in 1838–9, the main sources are: *LD*; *Operative*; *Charter*; *NS*; *London Democrat*; Place Coll., sets 55, 56; Add. MSS. 27,820; 27,821; HO 40/44; 44/52; 43/57; 44/33; 61/21–4; 79/4. See also my 'Chartism in London', *Past and Present* 44 (1969); D. J. Rowe, 'The Failure of London Chartism', *Historical Journal* 11 (1968).
10. Add. MS. 27,820, fo. 137.
11. *LD*, 4 March 1838, p. 612; Add. MSS. 27,819, fo. 61; 27,820, fos. 11–13, 24. For Beaumont, see also: *Black Dwarf*, 24 March 1824, p. 368;

Gauntlet, 8 Dec. 1833, p. 690; *Northern Liberator*, 21 April 1838; W. H. Maehl, 'Augustus Hardin Beaumont, Anglo-American Radical', *Int. Rev. Soc. Hist.* 14 (1969).

12. *LD*, 23 Dec. 1838, p. 121; 30 Dec., p. 132; *NS*, 29 Dec. 1838, p. 3; *Charter*, 3 March 1839, p. 88; Add. MSS. 27,820, fos. 355–6; 37,773, fos. 135 (18 Dec. 1838), 137–8 (22 and 29 Jan. 1839).

13. For ELDA, see: *NS*, 24 March 1838–26 Jan. 1839; *Operative*, 4 Nov. 1838–16 June 1839; *London Democrat*; Add. MS. 27,820, fo. 145; HO 40/44; 44/52.

14. *Operative*, 20 Jan. 1839, p. 7; 28 April, p. 7; 12 May, p. 16; *Charter*, 28 April, p. 222; 5 May, pp. 229, 236–7; *London Democrat*, 4 May 1839, p. 32; Add. MS. 34,245, A, fo. 384; HO 40/44, fos. 548, 613–19, 794.

15. *Operative*, 28 April 1839, p. 262.

16. Dolling to General Convention, 21 July (1839), Add. MS. 34,245, B, fo. 55.

17. *NS*, 14 Dec. 1839, p. 3; 25 Jan. 1840, p. 2; *Charter*, 19 Jan. 1840, pp. 3, 4, 5; *National Reformer*, 20 July 1861, p. 7; Place Coll., set 56, Dec. 1839–Jan. 1840; HO 40/44, fos. 655, 667, and Nov. 1839; 61/24, 24 Dec. (1839); D. Thompson, *The Early Chartists* (1971), p. 27; A. J. Peacock, 'Bradford Chartism, 1838–40', *Borthwick Papers* 36 (1969).

18. *Southern Star*, 3 May–12 July 1840; *NS*, 30 May–29 Aug. 1840.

19. *Charter*, 3 Feb. 1839, p. 21; 10 Feb., pp. 40, 43.

20. E.g. *ibid.*, 5 Jan. 1840, p. 787; *Southern Star*, 21 June 1840.

Conclusion

1. *TN*, 22 April 1827, p. 322.

2. Gast in *MM*, 9 July 1825, p. 220.

3. *WFP*, 4 Oct. 1828, p. 499.

4. *Loc. cit.*

5. *LD*, 11 Feb. 1838, p. 590 (Norman).

6. *Ibid.*, 5 Feb. 1837, p. 163.

7. *TN*, 16 April 1826, p. 636.

8. *TFP*, 12 July 1828, p. 406.

9. Davenport in *PMG*, 7 Sept. 1833, p. 292.

10. *Ibid.*, 17 Aug. 1833, p. 262; 24 Aug., p. 270.

11. See also my 'London Chartism and the Trades', *Econ. Hist. Rev.* 24 (1971); *Address of the London Trades' Delegates to the Trades of Great Britain and Ireland* (1849); *Address of the Metropolitan Trades' Delegates* (1850); *Address of the London Trades' Delegates to the Trades of Great Britain and Ireland, on the industrial, social, & political Emancipation of Labour* (n.d.).

12. For the cotton-spinners see Kirby and Musson, *Voice of the People*.

13. Cf. G. Stedman Jones, 'England's First Proletariat', *New Left Review*, 90 (1975), 58.

14. Sewell, 'Social change and the rise of working-class politics in 19th century Marseille', p. 106.

15. *Dictionnaire Politique. Encyclopédie du Langage et de la Science Politiques* (Paris, 1842), 'Salaire', p. 862; Ministère du Commerce, de l'Industrie, des Postes et des Télégraphes. Office du Travail, *Les Associa-*

tions Professionelles Ouvrières, II (Paris, 1901), 604; L. J. Lyon, *La Lyre du Devoir* (Paris, 1846), pp. 2–3; M. Berryer, *Affaire des Charpentiers* (Paris, 1845), p. 11; T. Guillamou, *Les Confessions d'un Compagnon* (Paris, 1864), p. 16; *Fédération de tous les ouvriers de France. Règlement de la corporation des ouvriers cordonniers* (Paris, n.d.), p. 1; Archives Nationales (A.N.), F 7 6783 (6), report Paris Gendarmerie, 10 May 1836; 6784 (14), Sens Gendarmerie, 26 Oct. 1833. The following examples are all drawn from France, but on the basis of other secondary reading I feel these characteristics were general among Western European artisans.

16.   *Fédération de tous les ouvriers de France*, p. 2; *Adresse de l'Union du Parfait Accord des ouvriers Cordonniers et Bottiers de la ville de Montpellier et de ces Faubourgs, à leurs Maîtres* (Montpellier, n.d.), p. 2; *Règlement de la Société de l'Union des Doreurs* (Paris, n.d.), p. 1; G. Duchêne, *Actualités. Livrets et Prud'hommes* (Paris, 1847), p. 22; A. Boyer, *De l'État des Ouvriers et de son Amélioration par l'Organisation du Travail* (Paris, 1841), p. 7; *Écho des Ouvriers*, Oct. 1844, p. 146; M. Nadaud, *Mémoires de Léonard ancien garçon maçon* (Paris, 1976), p. 54 and n.

17.   Grignon, *Réflexions d'un ouvrier tailleur sur la misère des ouvriers en général, la durée des journées de travail, le taux des salaires* (Paris, n.d.), p. 2; Boyer, *op. cit.*, p. 90.

18.   A.N., BB 18 1218 9562, Préf. Pol. to Min. of Int., 13 Sept. 1832.

19.   *Règlement pour les Ouvriers Imprimeurs en Taille-Douce* (Paris, n.d.), p. 3.

20.   Efrahem, *De l'Association des Ouvriers de tous les corps d'état* (Paris, n.d.), p. 1; J. Leroux, *Aux Ouvriers Typographes. De la nécessité de fonder une association ayant pour but de rendre les ouvriers propriétaires des instrumens de travail* (Paris, 1833), pp. 13–14.

21.   Grignon, *op. cit.*, p. 2.

22.   *Adresse de l'Union du Parfait Accord*, p. 2; C. Noiret, *Mémoires d'un Ouvrier Rouennais* (Rouen, 1836), p. 54.

23.   Grignon, *op. cit.*, pp. 1, 3; J. Lion, *Plus de Patrons! Association des ouvriers cordonniers-bottiers de toute la France sous le concours du Gouvernement* (Paris, 1848), p. 4; *Lettres adressées au journal La Tribune par les ouvriers tailleurs, boulangers, cordonniers, concernant leurs demandes en augmentation de salaire* (Paris, n.d.), p. 5; *Écho des Ouvriers*, June 1844, p. 11.

24.   Grignon, *op cit.*, p. 1.

25.   A.N. F 7 6783 (3), 10 Nov. 1833.

26.   *Almanach des Associations Ouvrières pour 1850 publié sous les auspices de l'Union Essénienne* (Paris, n.d.), pp. 80–2.

27.   *Journal des Ouvriers*, 11 Sept. 1830, p. 2; A.N. C 934 (1) 2691, Carlier, 2 July.

28.   *Avenir de l'Ouvrier, par l'Association Philanthropique* (Paris, 1843); Noiret, *Mémoires*, pp. 48–9.

29.   *Artisan*, 10 Oct. 1830, pp. 1–2; Duchêne, *Actualités*, p. 48.

30.   *Ibid.*, p. 55; *Écho des Travailleurs*, 6 Nov. 1833, p. 4; A.N. BB 18 1239 3612, Nîmes, 29 May 1836.

31.   *Règlement pour les Ouvries Imprimeurs en Taille-Douce*; *Règlement de la Société de l'Union des Doreurs*; *Règlement de la Société Philanthropique des Ouvriers Tailleurs* (Nantes, 1836); *Gazette des Tribunaux*, 30

Nov. 1833, p. 2; A. A. Giraud, *Aux Compagnons et Ouvriers de tous les états et professions* (Lyon, n.d.), p. 6; A.N. BB 18 1366 4838, Poitiers, 26 Feb. 1837, 3 enclosures; *Les Associations Professionnelles Ouvrières*, *passim*, e.g. II, 16, 44.

32.   *Artisan*, 2 Oct. 1842, p. 2.

33.   Leroux, *Aux Ouvriers Typographes*, p. 11; *Lettres adressées au journal La Tribune*, p. 7; *Artisan*, 10 Oct. 1830, p. 1; Duchêne, *Actualités*, p. 48; Johnson, 'Economic Change and Artisan Discontent'; Sewell, 'Social change and the rise of working-class politics'.

34.   Johnson, *op. cit.*; Berryer, *Affair des Charpentiers*, p. 12; *Écho des Ouvriers*, Aug. 1844, p. 84; A.N. F 13 522, letters to Min. de Trav. Publics, 2 Aug. and 1 Sept.; *Associations Professionnelles Ouvrières*, II, 604.

35.   M.J., *Patriotisme du Constitutionnel, suivi de quelques réflexions sur l'introduction des Presses mécaniques dans l'imprimerie* (Paris, n.d.); H. Jador, *Procès de la Commission des Ouvriers Typographes* (Paris, 1830), p. 4.

36.   *Artisan*, 10 Oct. 1830, p. 3.

37.   *Réglement de la Société de l'Union des Doreurs*, p. 3.

38.   Noiret, *Mémoires*, p. 21; Duchêne, *Actualités*, p. 58.

39.   E. Flotard, *Le Mouvement Coopératif à Lyon et dans le Midi de la France* (Paris, 1867), pp. 4–40, 83–6.

40.   Efrahem, *De l'Association*, p. 2; Lion, *Plus de Patrons!*; *Fédération de tous les ouvriers*, p. 1; Leroux, *Aux Typographes*, pp. 13–14; *Lettres adressées au journal La Tribune*, p. 6; *Association Laborieuse et Fraternelle des Ouvriers Cordonniers-Bottiers* (several undated bills, Paris); *Association Fraternelle des Ouvriers Cordonniers* (Limoges, 1850); *Association Fraternelle des Ouvriers Cordonniers de Bar-sur-Ornain* (Bar, n.d.); E. Cabet, *Moyen d'Améliorer l'État Déplorable des Ouvriers* (Paris, n.d.), p. 8; Boyer, *De l'État des Ouvriers*, p. 131; A.N. BB 18 1339 9788, Carpentier to Min. de T., 28 Nov. 1833; BB 30 306 6245, Théodorat.

41.   *Règlement de la Société de l'Union des Doreurs*, p. 3; A. Boyer, *Les Conseils de Prud'hommes au point de uve de l'intérêt des Ouvriers* (Paris, n.d.), p. 4; *idem.*, *De l'État des Ouvriers*, p. 61.

42.   *Ibid.*, pp. 19–20; *Artisan*, 10 Oct. 1830; C. Noiret, *Aux Travailleurs* (Rouen, 1840), p. 5.

43.   Boyer, *Les Conseils de Prud'hommes*, p. 1.

44.   Grignon, *Réflexions*, p. 1; J. Leroux, *Le Prolétaire et le Bourgeois* (Paris, 1840), p. 16; *Artisan*, 22 Sept. 1830, p. 1; Duchêne, *Actualités*, pp. 43–4.

45.   *Projet de Pétition des Petits Commerçants, des Chefs d'Ateliers, et des Ouvriers de Nantes* (Nantes, n.d.).

46.   *Almanach des Associations Ouvrières*, pp. 10–11.

47.   *Les Justes Alarmes de la Classe Ouvrière au sujet Des Mécaniques* (Paris, 1830), p. 4; T.-M., *Aux Travailleurs, Paix et Courage* (Paris, 1845), p. 19; *La Ruche Populaire*, Dec. 1839, p. 5; *Journal des Ouvriers*, 2 Dec. 1830, p. 2; A.N. BB 18 1219 9800, Rouen, 13 Nov. 1832.

48.   *Artisan*, 10 Oct. 1830, p. 3; *Ruche Populaire*, Dec. 1839, p. 1; *Le Travail*, Sept. 1841, p. 22.

49.   On these points, see: R. A. Church, *The Great Victorian Boom 1850–1873* (1975); M. Blaug, 'The Productivity of Capital in the Lanca-

shire Cotton Industry during the Nineteenth Century', *Econ. Hist. Rev.* 13 (1961); Samuel, 'Workshop of the World'.

50.   J. R. Vincent, *The Formation of the Liberal Party 1857–1868* (1966), pp. 81, 82.

51.   See G. Crossick, 'The Labour Aristocracy and Its Values', *Victorian Studies* 20 (1976).

52.   Cf. T. R. Tholfsen, *Working-Class Radicalism in Mid-Victorian England* (1976), chap. 4.

BIBLIOGRAPHICAL NOTE

There seems little point in listing here all the sources and works I have drawn on, as it would be very long and I have already indicated them in the notes, which consist almost entirely of references. In particular, detailed lists of references will be found for the following: British shipbuilding (p.346 n.7); Thames shipbuilding (p.352 n.58, and p.391 n.15); benefit societies (p.348 n.11); apprentice-ship campaign (p.353 n.4); tailors (p.351 n.53, and p.375 n.9); shoemakers (p.351 n.54, and p.375 n.6); carpenters (p.385 n.2); Queen Caroline affair (p.364 n.5); repeal of Combination Laws (p.369 n.1, and n.17); origins of mechanics' institutes (p.372 n.34); National Union of the Working Classes (p.385 n.8, p.387 n.28); trades unionism 1833–4 (p.390 n.6); Working Men's Association (p.391 n.1); London Chartism (p.393 n.9). It may, however, be useful to note and comment on some of the main sources.

For the London trades, there are useful accounts of their work in *The Book of (English) Trades, or Library of the Useful Arts* (several editions from 1804); and (T. Carter and others), *The Guide to Trade* (1838). Valuable information on the artisans' work and way of life comes from a number of autobiographies: F. Place, breeches-maker, in Add. MSS. 35,142–4 (reprinted as M. Thale (ed.), *The Autobiography of Francis Place (1771–1854)* (Cambridge, 1972); (T. Carter, tailor), *Memoirs of a Working Man* (1845); (J. D. Burn, hatter), *A Glimpse at the Social Condition of the Working Classes during the early part of the present century* (n.d.); A. Davenport (shoemaker), in *National Co-operative Leader*, 1 March 1861, p.196; W. Lovett (cabinet-maker), *The Life and Struggles of William Lovett in his pursuit of Bread, Knowledge and Freedom* (1967 reprint); (C. M. Smith, compositor), *The Working Man's Way in the World: being the Autobiography of a Journey-*

man Printer (n.d.). These are all very revealing on workshop conditions, practices and attitudes, and Lovett's is valuable for a variety
of movements. Some information also appears in periodicals aimed
specifically at artisans, like the *Labourer's Friend and Handicraft's
Chronicle* (1821), *Mechanic's Weekly Journal; or Artisan's Miscellany* (1823), and *Mechanics' Magazine* (from 1823), but such
information is rather scattered since these periodicals are mainly
concerned with science and new technology. A crucial source is the
reports by Henry Mayhew for the *Morning Chronicle* in 1849–50.
These outline enduring attitudes among the artisans, the nature of
their societies, and their experiences over the previous three or four
decades (with possible exaggeration of good old times). The most
useful parts are reproduced in E. P. Thompson and E. Yeo (eds.),
*The Unknown Mayhew. Selections from the Morning Chronicle,
1849–50* (1971). The outstanding secondary work on the London
trades is M. D. George, *London Life in the Eighteenth Century*
(1930). An important dissertation is T. R. Mandrell, 'The structure
and organization of London trades, wages and prices, and the
organization of labour 1793–1815' (M. Litt., Cambridge, 1972).

The rules of many benefit societies are in the Friendly Society
files at the Public Record Office. But in general sources for the trade
societies are very patchy. There were over 150 handicraft trades in
London, and considerably more trade societies, many of them very
small and local. The majority of these are unknown. Very few trade
union records have survived. The few exceptions have been drawn
on in such works as: W. Kiddier, *The Old Trade Unions, from
unprinted records of the brushmakers* (1931); R. W. Postgate, *The
Builders' History* (1923); E. Howe (ed.), *The London Compositor.
Documents relating to Wages, Working Conditions and Customs of
the London Printing Trade 1785–1900* (1947); E. Howe and H. E.
Waite, *The London Society of Compositors* (1948); E. Howe and J.
Child, *The Society of London Bookbinders 1780–1951* (1952). F.
W. Galton, *Select Documents illustrating the History of Trade
Unionism. I. The Tailoring Trade* (1896), consists of reproduced
printed documents, with a long introduction.

Trade journals do not on the whole date from before the 1840s;
an exception is the *Spitalfields Weavers' Journal* (1837). The
printed rules of some societies have survived, and some pamphlets
and bills, usually putting their side of a dispute; many of them are in
the Home Office Papers and the Webb and Place Collections.

The Webb Collection of Trade Union Manuscripts at the Library
of Political Science, L.S.E., was the basis for the standard work by S.

and B. Webb, *The History of Trade Unionism* (1920). The collection consists of many volumes of manuscript notes, grouped by trade. Although they have much more on the latter part of the century, these notes are an invaluable source.

The Place Papers at the British Library consist of nearly 100 volumes in the Manuscript Room and the Place Collection, 180 volumes, in the Reading Room. They both cover a wide range of topics. The former contains several narrative histories by Place and his voluminous correspondence, including copies of many of his outgoing letters. In Add. MS. 35,146 there is a diary covering April 1826–July 1827. The latter largely consists of newspaper cuttings, tracts and bills (many of them unique), but does have some manuscript material (including the minutes of the National Political Union); several of the volumes are companions to accounts in the manuscript collection. Both collections contain scattered information on the London trades, especially in Add. MSS. 27,798–27,804; the information on the tailors is from personal knowledge, and the rest was built up from about 1815 when Place tried to gather information on any industrial dispute that came to his notice and made contact with several leading trade unionists, including Gast and Lang. But from the late 1820s his information came mainly from printed sources, which are in Place Coll., sets 13, 16, 51, 57, 61, 62.

The Home Office papers have some information, mainly in connection with a strike or disorders, or when political involvement was suspected. There is nothing after 1834. Most of the information for the early period is reproduced in A. Aspinall, *The Early English Trade Unions. Documents from the Home Office Papers in the Public Record Office* (1949). There is a little in HO 44 on disputes in the 1820s, mainly 1824–5, and something on general unionism in 1834 in HO 64/15. There is a selection from the full reports by Abel Hall on the tailors' strike in *International Review of Social History* 22 (1977).

There is useful information in Parliamentary Enquiries, particularly the Select Committee reports on *Apprentice Laws*, Parl. Papers, 1812–13, IV; *Artizans and Machinery*, 1824, V; *Combination Laws*, 1825, IV.

There is much other information in scattered and often unlikely places, which is very easy to miss. The chief source on trade unionism is therefore the newspaper press. To a large extent this consists of reports of trials and strikes and so, like the Home Office papers, mainly gives information on conflicts. Such information can, of course, be very revealing, but it does not provide continuous coverage or concern trades not involved in important disputes. The radical press itself has little on the trades before the 1830s, except for the *Gorgon* (1818–19), especially Place's account of the tailors. The situation changes with the appearance of the *Trades' Newspaper* (1825) which to an unprecedented extent had full reports on the activities of several of the London trades, but usually only those with shares in the paper. This content continues after the transformation into the *Trades' Free Press*, but when it becomes the *Weekly Free Press* trade union news drops out (but the paper is an essential source for co-operation and radicalism). From the 1830s the radical press has much on trade unionism, and there are more trade union newspapers. For the early 1830s there is most information in the *Man* (1833), *Crisis* (1833–4), and *Pioneer* (1834), the last being the organ of first the Operative Builders' Union and then the Consolidated Trades' Union, but all three remained very much also the platform for the views of their conductors. Equally important are the *True Sun* and *Weekly True Sun* in 1834, and there are also reports by the spies Hall and Ball in HO 64/15, 64/19 and 52/24. Hetherington's *Twopenny Dispatch* (later *London Dispatch*) was a real newspaper that from the latter part of 1836 provides excellent coverage for a year or so of all activities, including trade unionism. At the end of the 1830s were two new trade union papers, the *Operative* (1838–9), edited by O'Brien, and *Charter* (1839–40), edited by Carpenter, but both concentrated mainly on the Chartist movement. In the 1840s the excellent *Northern Star*, the great workman's paper, was always ready to insert trade union news, but most of the information is on strikes and attempts at wider unionism.

The sources for radicalism are much more easily located. For reform movements in London during the war period there are reform papers, the weekly *Independent Whig* and the dailies *Statesman*, *Alfred* and *British Press*, but unfortunately the last three do not cover 1815–17. Later the *Day* and *Traveller* are useful. Cobbett's *Political Register* and Wooler's *Black Dwarf* have useful information, but are chiefly vehicles for the views of their owners. From 1817 there were a number of ultra-radical journals in London, often short-lived, especially *Sherwin's Political Register* (at first called the *Republican*, a name resumed after Peterloo when Carlile had taken it over), *Shamrock, Thistle and Rose* (1818—in HO 42/182), *Medusa* (1818–19) and, in 1819: *Theological Comet, Briton, White Hat, Diligent Observer, London Alfred, Radical*

Reformer, *Cap of Liberty*, *Democratic Recorder* (in Place Coll., set 40). These were not newspapers and so recourse is essential to the well-informed established London dailies. Their political orientation does not determine their value: sometimes the ministerialist *Morning Post* and *Courier* and ultra-Tory *New Times* are more informative than the reforming *Morning Chronicle* or *The Times*. But all, of course, mainly deal with public events, and with meetings and trials. For the revolutionary group around Watson and Thistlewood there is much information, especially in HO 42, and also later in 40, 44 and 52. The reports of C (Williamson, 1817–19), A (Hanley, 1817–19), and BC (Banks, 1819) are accurate and well-informed, though Hanley's are less continuous. The reports of I.S., later B (J. Shegog) are usually not based on first-hand information and are often rather incidental, with excessive concentration on freethinking groups. But the reports of C, A and BC end late in 1819 and information is thereafter inferior, dependent on W——r (G. Edwards) until the Cato Street arrests, and thereafter on Shegog and miscellaneous information. The Place Papers mainly concern Westminster politics, and also have Thomas Hardy's correspondence in Add. MS. 27,818; they have little on ultra-radical movements, but Place Coll. sets 18 and 71 are essential for the Queen Caroline affair. H. Hunt, *Memoirs of Henry Hunt* (1820–1) are often very unreliable.

For radicalism in the 1820s, the chief periodicals were Carlile's *Republican* (ended 1826) and *Lion* (1828–9), but they were not newspapers and mainly expound the views of Carlile and Taylor. The *Trades' Newspaper* and its successors give excellent coverage of the variety of workers' movements of the later 1820s. Also useful is the short-lived *Journeyman, and Artizans' London and Provincial Chronicle* (1825). The daily papers are sometimes useful, such as the *Morning Chronicle* at various times, *The Times* and *New Times* for the shipwrights in 1825, and *The Times* for the benefit societies' agitation of 1828. The Place Papers are particularly valuable for the Combination Laws campaigns and the founding and management of the *Trades' Newspaper*. *Hansard* and the *Commons Journals* have information on the campaigns of 1824, 1825 and 1828–9.

For co-operation, the chief source is the press: the *Co-operative Magazine* (1826–30, run by Owenites and not very useful), *Weekly Free Press* (run by Carpenter and Cleave, the chief source for 1828–30), *Associate* (short-lived, not very informative, launched late in 1829 by London Co-operative Society), *British Co-operator* (begun 1830 by G. R. Skene as organ of his Manufacturing Community), *Magazine of Useful Knowledge* (launched late in 1830 by Carpenter after he left *Weekly Free Press*, only lasted four weeks), *Carpenter's Political Letter* (replaced preceding as organ of co-operative news, but its content was mainly political), *Crisis* (chief source 1832–3 for Owenism, Owen's Labour Exchange and the United Trades' Association). There is also information at times in *Union* (1831–2), *Poor Man's Guardian*, *Cosmopolite*, *Destructive* and *Man*. Other sources are the Owen Papers, Co-operative Union Library; W. Carpenter, *Proceedings of the Third Co-operative Congress* (London, 1832; includes a table of the societies represented—but there are dangers in generalising on a movement from a congress), and Lovett's remarks in Add. MS. 27,822 and in his autobiography.

The *Weekly Free Press* is the chief source for the Radical Reform Association, and the *Morning Journal* is useful for the Metropolitan Political Union. There is a mass of sources for the Reform crisis, including the daily press and the many unstamped papers. For guidance over the latter, see J. H. Wiener, *A Descriptive Finding List of Unstamped British periodicals, 1830–1836* (1970); idem., *The War of the Unstamped. The movement to repeal the British Newspaper Tax, 1830–1836* (1969); P. Hollis, *The Pauper Press, A Study in Working Class Radicalism of the 1830s* (1970). Place's papers, in Add. MSS. 27,789–97, and sets 17 and 63 have been microfilmed by Micro-Methods. They are mainly concerned with the National Political Union; the sections on the National Union of the Working Classes are based mainly on press reports and not on direct knowledge. The account of the NUWC by Lovett in 27,791, the version usually used by historians, is in fact Place's own modified copy of the original in 27,822. But Lovett was only a prominent member of the NUWC from late 1831 to June 1832, and so his account is not very reliable. There is a long series of very well-informed reports from 1830 to 1834 by Abel Hall on the Rotunda and, especially, the NUWC, in HO 40/25 and 64/11–16.

For activities in the mid-1830s the chief sources are the *True Sun, Weekly True Sun, Hetherington's Twopenny Dispatch* (later *London Dispatch*) and *Cleave's Weekly Police Gazette*. The last two do not survive for 1834 – early part of 1836, but there are cuttings in Place Coll., esp. set 51; see also set 70. The minute-book of the Working Men's Association is in Add. MS. 37,773, but is a pretty formal record.

The main sources for London Chartism are the newspapers *Operative* (1838–9), *Charter* (1839–40), *Southern Star* (1840) and

Northern Star (from 1838). There are also some reports on 1839 in HO 40/44 and 44/52, but they are largely reports of public meetings, and do not provide such good inside information as the reports of earlier years. The materials in the Place papers, except for sections on the WMA, Lovett's imprisonment and the *Charter* paper, are almost entirely drawn from newspaper reports.

INDEX